Praise for *Simply Human*

"*Simply Human* doesn't just explain the dynamics of hate – it equips us to confront them with clarity and care. Rooted in lived experience and interdisciplinary insight, this book challenges us to think more critically and lead more responsibly. In a time of confusion and division, it reminds us that some things are still up to us."
Eric K. Ward, Executive Vice President, Race Forward

"*Simply Human* takes on the complex topic of hate with insight, urgency, and compassion. Building on decades of expertise, editor Kenneth S. Stern curates a powerful collection of evidence-based perspectives, drawing from diverse fields such as law, neuroscience, sociology, and psychology. *Simply Human* offers a deeper understanding of hate, with informed strategies for individuals and communities working to replace fear and division with empathy, resilience, and meaningful connection. This is a timely and indispensable guide for anyone striving to build a more just and humane society."
Kristine F. Hoover, Professor and Chair of Organizational Leadership, Gonzaga University

"The hatred surrounding us readily creates bludgeoned helplessness. *Simply Human* counters this, analyzing who hates in different contexts, organizational versus individual approaches to lessen hate and how to tell if they work, and how different outgroups victimized by hate can become allies rather than competing for the legitimacy of their pains. This is a rare, important book, filled with dispassionate, fact-based thought that actually makes one *feel* hopeful."
Robert Sapolsky, John A. and Cynthia Fry Gunn Professor of Biology, Neurology, Neurological Sciences, and Neurosurgery, Stanford University, and author of *Determined: A Science of Life without Free Will*

"With so much hate unleashed in our country and world, understanding its history and its forms is crucially important. This book is critically timely and consequential for all of us working to identify and combat hatred in the variety of ways it rears its ugly head. As the former Special Envoy to Monitor and Combat Antisemitism in the US State Department, I saw firsthand how essential a better and more comprehensive understanding of hate is, and this book helps us navigate the challenge."

Hannah Rosenthal, Former Special Envoy to Monitor and Combat Antisemitism, US State Department

Simply Human

A Guide to Understanding and Combating Hate

EDITED BY KENNETH S. STERN

UNIVERSITY OF TORONTO PRESS
Toronto Buffalo London

Toronto Buffalo London
utppublishing.com
Printed in Canada

ISBN 978-1-4875-5183-4 (paper)   ISBN 978-1-4875-5184-1 (EPUB)
                                  ISBN 978-1-4875-5187-2 (PDF)

Library and Archives Canada Cataloguing in Publication

Title: Simply human : a guide to understanding and combating hate / edited
   by Kenneth S. Stern.
Other titles: Simply human (Toronto, Ont.)
Names: Stern, Kenneth S. (Kenneth Saul), 1953– editor
Description: Includes bibliographical references and index.
Identifiers: Canadiana (print) 20250197219 | Canadiana (ebook) 20250197227 |
   ISBN 9781487551834 (paper) | ISBN 9781487551841 (EPUB) |
   ISBN 9781487551872 (PDF)
Subjects: LCSH: Hate. | LCSH: Hate – Prevention.
Classification: LCC BF575.H3 S56 2025 | DDC 152.4 – dc23

Cover design: Will Brown

We wish to acknowledge the land on which the University of Toronto Press
operates. This land is the traditional territory of the Wendat, the Anishnaabeg,
the Haudenosaunee, the Métis, and the Mississaugas of the Credit First
Nation.

University of Toronto Press acknowledges the financial support of the
Government of Canada, the Canada Council for the Arts, and the Ontario Arts
Council, an agency of the Government of Ontario, for its publishing activities.

Canada Council   Conseil des Arts   ONTARIO ARTS COUNCIL
for the Arts   du Canada   CONSEIL DES ARTS DE L'ONTARIO
                                            an Ontario government agency
                                            un organisme du gouvernement de l'Ontario

Funded by the   Financé par le   **Canadä**
Government   gouvernement
of Canada   du Canada

MIX
Paper | Supporting
responsible forestry
FSC   FSC® C103567
www.fsc.org

To the late Bill Wassmuth, a courageous and smart leader against hate

Contents

Foreword

What is hate? What is bigotry? What is bias? Are there differences? How should they be distinguished? How should each be addressed? Not my job. Read the book!

I was born in 1943 and raised in Montgomery, Alabama, during the height of the post–World War II Jim Crow era. All I ever experienced during the late 1940s and 1950s was racial and religious separation. Neither bothered me. As a grammar school kid, one of my favorite games was Marbles, which involved drawing a circle in the dirt, placing a number of marbles within the circle, holding another marble in your hand and, finally, using your thumb to shoot that marble at the ones in the circle. The goal was to knock more out as each of your competitors took turns. Of course, someone had to go first. We recited a rhyme to determine who that would be. We started by pointing to one of the players, moving from that one to the next with each word until the last was said. That person got the first marble shot. Here's the rhyme: "Eeny, meeny, miny, moe. Catch a nigger by the toe. If he hollers, make him pay fifty dollars every day. My momma told me to pick this one."

Just in case you think we were unique in our use of this racist trope, different versions of the rhyme itself were used commonly among whites during the Jim Crow era. I have no idea where I learned it but have a visual imprint in my brain of the game and the rhyme. And, if you're offended by my use of the "N-word," I want all readers to fully appreciate its effect when read or heard.[1]

Did I hate? Was I a racist? Were my friends racist? As I grew older, I thought that could only be true if we understood the significance of what we were saying as kids. I kept that defensive posture until my late undergraduate years. We may not have appreciated the depth of hate and bias against Black people, but we fully believed that Black people were lesser than white people. As I moved into the early 1950s and

was able to ride the bus downtown to my father's law office, I understood that Blacks rode in the back of the bus and I rode in the front.
My father's office was located kitty-corner to the county courthouse. I
frequently crossed the street, went up the stairs and through the front
door to drink out of the water fountain in the lobby. Of course, I knew
which one to use. It was not the one labeled "Colored."

This book and its in-depth analysis of hate, bias, and bigotry across
the world would have brought me to an entirely different conclusion
much earlier in life.

My parents' histories were extreme opposites. My father, Joseph J.
Levin Sr., was Jewish, a native of Newport News, Virginia. In 1882, my
paternal great-grandparents, Isaac and Annie Lipman, ages sixteen and
fifteen, respectively, and married, walked from Odessa, Russia, to Bre-
men, Germany, and shortly thereafter immigrated to the United States.
They were escaping the "ethnic cleansing" instituted by Alexander III.
Alexander III succeeded his father, and like many of the Romanovs had
a global vision for Russia. He was committed to making Russia great
again through intense nationalistic and isolationist policies. Sound
familiar?

My dad had an easier trip. He migrated to college at the University
of Alabama and graduated from its law school in 1934. He moved to
Montgomery to practice law with a classmate, and eventually established his own commercial practice.

My mother, Anne Hutto, was born in Walker County, Alabama, a
descendant of generations of farmers, the youngest of fourteen siblings. She moved to Montgomery, met my father, and they married.
My mother was raised Christian but converted to Judaism. On her side,
the "Ottos," as they were known when they emigrated from Germany
to South Carolina around 1735, likely left Germany because of the religious persecution of Lutherans.

My maternal great-grandfather, John C. Hutto, was a major in the
Confederate Army. There's a Sons of Confederate Veterans camp
named for him in Walker County. As a kid, I was very proud of his
recognition. Given my civil rights history as a lawyer, I'm now occasionally asked what I think of my great-grandfather and his service.
Despite my later condemnation of the Confederacy, I can relate to the
environment in which John Hutto grew up and the imprint it made
upon him. How might my life and my childhood friends' lives have
been different if we had better understood the elements of hate, bigotry,
and bias as analyzed in this book?

And, just in case you might think that growing up Jewish made a
difference, it didn't. Jews as a group were just as racist as anyone else.

Those who weren't, a couple of "Yankee" rabbis, were run out of town by their congregations. Assimilation was the name of the game.

The Jewish community itself was sharply divided. There were Reform Jews, Conservative Jews, and Sephardic Jews, each carrying lots of attitude about the other. Before World War II and well into the 1940s and early 1950s, there was a country club for Reform Jews and one for "the others." Oh, and there was of course the Montgomery Country Club, all-white and all-Christian. Racial bias was just part of the package on both fronts.

In 1955, the bus boycott occurred. I was twelve years old, and until then rode the bus all the time. The day the boycott began was the last day I ever rode public transportation in Montgomery. The city proceeded to close down the public parks and cemented the public pools in order to avoid court-ordered desegregation. The atmosphere in Montgomery was poisonous.

There was little justice, and some of the lawyers and judges were the worst offenders. Judge Walter B. Jones, a Montgomery Circuit Court judge, was a vicious racist. As a judge, he banned the NAACP from operating in Alabama. In 1957, six years before his death, Jones published his most infamous editorial in the *Montgomery Advertiser*, where he was a frequent commentator. It was entitled "I Speak for the White Race" and, sadly, for his time, he did. He concluded his racist diatribe with the following words:

> We have all kindly feelings for the world's other races, but we will maintain at any and all sacrifices the purity of our blood strain and race. We shall never submit to the demands of integrationists. The white race shall remain forever white.[2]

If this sounds familiar it's because it is the voice of White Christian Nationalism and the alt-right of today. Not 1957, today! And these people were and are representative of a larger community. It's like what a wise commentator once said about the Texas legislature – "If you think these folks are bad, you ought to see their constituents."

I had at that time never experienced direct antisemitism. My first such contact with it was when I was signing up for the Army Reserve Officers' Training Corps (ROTC) at my all-white high school. I gave the Army Sergeant doing the enrollment my name, and he said, "What business does your daddy own?" I immediately felt the antisemitism associated with that remark. While I describe that as "direct," perhaps that was only because it was spoken to me personally.

More graphically, a retired and revered World War II admiral by the name of John Crommelin had grown up in Alabama and later made Montgomery his home. He was a strong supporter of antisemitic US Senator Joseph McCarthy and himself ran for the US Senate and for governor in Alabama in the 1950s and 1960s. He lost on both counts, but what he conveyed during these campaigns was an attack on Jews and Blacks. He was a devout antisemite and racist and presented himself as such when campaigning on television in the 1950s. I sat with my parents and siblings and watched him berate Jews as Jews, calling out many by their names. Some were the parents of friends of mine. I was finally beginning to understand antisemitism. The issue of racism for me was yet to come.

My environment as a kid was very much characteristic of a significant portion of the United States today, one of the perversion of law, of oligarchies with wealth and power concentrated in the hands of a few, who play on fear and bigotry to keep working-class whites thinking about something else.

When I left my lily-white public schools of Montgomery in 1960, I entered the all-white University of Alabama and joined my all-white Jewish fraternity. We had fraternities and sororities then for Jews and Christians. And, just in case you think those divisions weren't sufficient, there were Jewish fraternities for Southern Reform Jews, Southern Conservative Jews, and, of course, Yankee Jews. No line left undrawn!

We thrilled to our all-white football team, which gave us the opportunity to occasionally refight the War of Northern Aggression, and show solidarity with our racist governor, George Wallace.

In my junior year, 1962, a fraternity brother, Melvin Meyer of Starkville, Mississippi, wrote an editorial for the school newspaper, *Crimson White*, supporting the integration of the University of Mississippi by James Meredith, a civil rights activist and US Air Force veteran who, that same year, was the first Black student to be admitted to the University of Mississippi. That resulted in a barrage of hate calls to the fraternity house where most of us lived at the time, and a cross was burned in our front yard by the United Klans of America, then headquartered in the university's hometown of Tuscaloosa. So, the Klan was mad at Melvin, while I and many of my contemporaries at the university were mad at Melvin for disrupting our lives and, in my hometown, many Jews were mad at Melvin, wondering why we tolerated such a radical in our midst. It was quite a combination of critics. What Melvin wrote and the way that I and others reacted began to change the course of my thinking and alter my view of the world.

So, in 1966, I graduated from law school, practiced a bit with my dad, then went to Fort Benning (which was changed to Fort Moore in 2023 but then back to Fort Benning[3]), Georgia, for basic infantry officers' training. Back in the day, unless you were a draft dodger like Donald Trump (and yes, Bill Clinton), you likely got drafted, you enlisted, or you came out of college, law school, or graduate school with a two-year ROTC obligation. For me, I was in military intelligence (MI), finished my basic infantry officers' training at Fort Benning, spent six weeks in MI school at Fort Holabird, Maryland, and was prepared to go straight to Vietnam, as had the majority of my infantry and intelligence colleagues. Then New York City intervened.

Surprisingly the Army sent me to Manhattan. I served with the NY field office of the 108th MI Group. What I did get out of my two years in the city was a sense of the larger world; a sense of diversity. I worked with African, Italian, Irish, and Asian Americans, and white and Black women.

Serendipity intervened. In 1969, I returned to Montgomery and met Morris Dees. We tried some cases together, started a law firm, and in 1971, with the help and encouragement of the late Julian Bond, who served as our first president, established the Southern Poverty Law Center (SPLC). I was very lucky. I found a use for my law degree that I never could have imagined. Thank you Melvin and New York City.

At this stage of the book's foreword, you might be wondering why in the world I am writing so much about my personal history. Good question. It's because my history as a young man was engrossed by hate, bias, and bigotry, even if it was not always expressed openly. This book is the most detailed and analytical examination of how these develop. Moreover, the commonality of human experiences is pretty much the same in the Northern Hemisphere and the Southern Hemisphere. Whether or not the bias, bigotry, or hate extend somehow from our brain cells, which are combinations of growth experiences due to our childhood environment or the environments of others into which we may merge, it's there. We see it every day. How can it be addressed?

As noted author Anaïs Nin has put it, "There are very few human beings who receive the truth ... by instant illumination. Most of them acquire it fragment by fragment ..."

I can relate to that. It was my life. These chapters pull together every conceivable aspect of hate, bias, and bigotry. The writings are truly educational and must be read and understood by those who run nongovernmental organizations (NGOs), professors, primary and secondary school teachers, politicians, lawyers, medical professionals, and many others. These issues must be shared and discussed with students, their parents, adults generally, and commentators of all stripes. The world needs to appreciate that there is no absolute "cure" for hate, bias, and bigotry within the human race, but if understood they can be moderated and issues that arise from them can be addressed rationally.

One week after the 2016 US presidential election, I spoke to a chapter of the National Council of Jewish Women in Cleveland, Ohio. The talk had been scheduled before the election, and the topic was supposed to be implicit bias. That's not where I went. I argued that we were back to an era when hate is no longer hidden in the larger population; it is open, and it is extensive.

What was observed during the 2016 US presidential campaign was an invigoration of extremists and extremist groups, ranging from old Klan leaders to neo-Nazis, other white supremacists, and radical anti-immigrant groups. They felt supported and energized. Donald Trump's re-election to the presidency in 2024 will undoubtedly produce a level of validation for extremist groups that intensifies hate for many years.

In January 2019, speaking at a Temple in Teaneck, New Jersey, I struggled to think of something useful to say about what happened in Pittsburgh's Squirrel Hill neighborhood at the Tree of Life Synagogue where eleven Jewish congregants were shot and killed and six wounded. All I could come up with, as angry as that tragedy made me, was it was equally disturbing that I wasn't surprised.

The United States was not alone. For example, in New Zealand in 2019, an attacker murdered forty-nine persons and wounded forty-eight in a rampage at two mosques. This is especially significant because it reinforced my concern that we're looking at a white nationalism of international scope. A hate-filled manifesto reportedly written by the mosque attacker included references to the US Second Amendment to the Constitution (protection of gun ownership), with the gunman opining that he hoped conflicts over firearms would eventually lead to the United States splitting along political, cultural, and racial lines. The attacker also wrote that he supported then-US president Donald Trump "as a symbol of renewed white identity." It hasn't stopped. According to a June 2023 story in *The Guardian*, "almost 7000 hate-driven crimes were recorded [in New Zealand] since January 2022."[4]

As reported by the authoritative Global Project Against Hate and Extremism (GPAHE), "in recent years, far-right extremist and hate movements motivated by white supremacy, xenophobia, anti-LGBTQ+ beliefs, antisemitism, anti-Muslim sentiment, religious discrimination, anti-woman activity, and gender bias have been growing across the globe."[5]

So, here we are, well into the twenty-first century. To me it feels much like the era of my youth, but with an even greater expanse of hate, extremist, and anti-government groups than I experienced then or had been identified by the SPLC during its thirty years of work prior to the beginning of the twenty-first century. The SPLC called out 1,430 hate and extremist groups operating throughout the United States in 2023. The enormous expansion of the internet has only increased the ability of these groups to connect with and expand their base without the necessity of direct contact. That helps explain why all NGOs that track hate crimes and hate and extremist groups have seen such a huge increase in violence over the past quarter century.

Moreover, the US Federal Bureau of Investigation (FBI) recently released its 2023 Hate Crimes Statistic Act report, disclosing a record-breaking 11,862 hate crime incidents in 2023. And the FBI data are presumed to be understated since many state and local law enforcement agencies don't report these crimes.[6]

Hate groups vilify others because of their race, religion, ethnicity, sexual orientation, or gender identity – prejudices that strike at the heart of democratic values and fracture society along its most fragile fault lines. There's more to come.

As I prepared this writing, looked back over the last eighty plus years, and thought about where I started and where we are as a nation and a world now, it brings me back to my main point. Where are we? What world is this? I thought the stories of bigotry and hate had been relegated to the fringes of society. I was wrong. I personally see, smell, and feel the 1950s and 1960s, but what is even more concerning is that I see America's history of pro-Nazi involvement by prominent citizens and politicians in the 1930s and into the 1950s, such as Charles Lindbergh, Henry Ford, and Joseph McCarthy, rising once again in public space.

On July 26, 1920, notable journalist and essayist H.L. Mencken wrote in the *Baltimore Evening Sun*, "As democracy is perfected, the office of the President represents, more and more closely, the inner soul of the people. On some great and glorious day, the plain folks of the land will reach their heart's desire at last, and the White House will be occupied by a downright fool and a complete narcissistic moron." I wonder if Mencken would be surprised that it's happened twice.

So, what is the "inner soul" of our people?

A former autocratic ruler once put it this way: "I use emotion for the many and reserve reason for the few. Through clever and constant application of propaganda, people can be made to see even heaven as hell, and also the other way around, to consider the most wretched sort of life as paradise. The greater the lie, the more readily will it be believed. So, make the lie big, make it simple, keep saying it, and eventually the people will believe it" (Adolf Hitler). And, as Voltaire stated, "If I can get you to believe absurdities, I can get you to commit atrocities." Our current president's words and actions only provide proof for the accuracy of both statements.

Steve Bannon, right-wing extremist, former *Breitbart* editor, and close friend and advisor of Donald Trump, was quoted in *Politico* as saying, "It was always great to hear what the hobbits had to say because at the end of the day, what they had to say mattered most. This whole movement, it's really the top of the first inning."[7]

What inning are we, the world, in now? What can we do to mitigate the hate and rebuild the "inner soul" of our Earth?

Our school systems, public and private, must do a better job of educating our children so that future generations do not fall prey to the same bigotry, bias, and hate that we've seen for far too long. It's all about community. Speak up in the community. Work in the community. When you hear about attacks on immigrants, LGBTQI+ individuals, racial and religious minorities in your communities, whoever the "others" may be, say something. Don't let it go unanswered. Make sure that, in the future, the "inner soul" of our people bends toward truth, compassion, and justice.

The week after the attack on the Tree of Life Synagogue, the Jewish Federation of Central Alabama hosted a community event in Montgomery. Participants included Jews, Christians, Unitarians, Muslims, atheists, and just plain unaffiliated citizens. The most important theme was that "hope" is not enough. We must act!

Winston Churchill once said this, "Life is fraught with opportunities to keep your mouth shut," which leads me to one of Dr. Martin Luther King Jr.'s most important quotes, "In the end, we will remember not the words of our enemies, but the silence of our friends."

Churchill also said, "You can always count on Americans to do the right thing once they've exhausted every other possibility." I hope that applies to the world at large.

I end here with my strong edit of words premised upon a 2001 speech by former president George W. Bush, which I believe is very important in this era of hate, bigotry, and bias: "The [world] has never been united by blood or birth or soil. We [should be] bound by ideals that move us beyond our backgrounds, lift us above our interests and teach us what it means to be [human]. Every child must be taught these principles. Every [person] must uphold them."[8]

Education is the only way to achieve these goals and no educational product other than *Simply Human* better analyzes what those who teach must learn and share in order to address humanity's faults of hate, bigotry, and bias.

Joseph J. Levin Jr.

NOTES

1 As a good friend of mine, Lloyd V. Hackley, put it: "Substituting the 'N-word' is a distortion, indeed, an insult to those of us who endured it, as well as to those, like you, who used it in those days without a full appreciation of its impact on the targets. Don't we all understand what 'N-word' says? [To quote Grigorenko:] 'Concealment of the historical truth is a crime against the people.'" (Hackley is quoting from General Petro G. Grigorenko's letter to the editorial staff of a *samizdat* history journal in the USSR, c. 1975.)

2 Judge Walter B. Jones, "I Speak for the White Race," *Montgomery Advertiser*, Editorial Page, March 4, 1957, https://www.newspapers.com/article /the-montgomery-advertiser-1957-tennessee/30782409/.

3 In 2025, the Trump administration changed the name of the base back to Fort Benning. See Idrees Ali and Phil Stewart, "Pentagon Chief Restores Former Name of Fort Benning," *Montgomery Advertiser*, March 4, 2025, https://montgomeryadvertiser-al.newsmemory.com/?publink=221e5f5bc _134f8e4.

4 Charlotte Graham-McLay, "Exclusive: Racism, Homophobia Fuelling Thousands of Crimes in New Zealand Each Year, Figures Show," *The Guardian*, June 7, 2023, https://www.theguardian.com/world/2023 /jun/08/exclusive-racism-homophobia-fuelling-thousands-of-crimes-in -new-zealand-each-year-figures-show.

5 Global Project against Hate and Extremism, "Our Philosophy," accessed January 1, 2025, https://globalextremism.org/our-philosophy/.

6 Federal Bureau of Investigation, "FBI Releases 2023 Crime in the Nation Statistics," press release, September 23, 2024, https://www.fbi.gov/news /press-releases/fbi-releases-2023-crime-in-the-nation-statistics.

7 Nolan D. McCaskill, "Bannon Tells Breitbart: 'Hobbits' and 'Deplorables' Were Key to Trump's Success," *Politico*, December 30, 2016, https://www .politico.com/story/2016/12/steve-bannon-breitbart-hobbits-deplorables -donald-trump-233074.

8 George W. Bush, "The First Inaugural Address, from West Front, U.S. Capitol, Washington, D.C., January 20, 2001," *Selected Speeches of George W. Bush, 2001–2008*, George W. Bush White House Archives, https:// georgewbush-whitehouse.archives.gov/infocus/bushrecord/documents /Selected_Speeches_George_W_Bush.pdf.

Editor's Preface

Hate is part of the human condition; it always has been, and likely always will be. It is frequently destructive.

It's harder to know what to do about hate, and how to reduce its harmful, sometimes deadly, effects.

I've spent my professional life thinking about this challenge. The goal isn't to find a silver bullet against hate, because there is none, but rather to harness what we do know into a more understandable group of theories. The alternative – to throw up our hands and declare hate "enigmatic" – is not an acceptable answer. Many ideas that help us understand hate do exist. They are, however, like scattered light beams that illuminate little individually. This volume harnesses some of the more important strands, and focuses them together as a unit, not only to guide us in our lives, but more directly to help the change agents we rely on – particularly nongovernmental organizations (NGOs) dedicated to fighting hate or some discreet subset of it – to be more effective.

What you'll find in this volume is the best thinking of world-class experts from different academic fields, sharing not only their insights, but co-creating a volume that underscores why it is important for hate to be reduced, and provides a roadmap for how to do it.

Perhaps more importantly, and in some of the chapters more than others, the value is in identifying what NOT to do, because doing the wrong things, despite good intentions, can make things worse, and waste precious resources that can be used more effectively.

That said, this book doesn't answer all the questions, partly because there are no complete answers, and partly because there are so many other fields that have something to add to our thinking. This book is a start, to guide action today and to suggest how others may contribute to our understanding of hate in the future.

Why is this book dedicated to the late Bill Wassmuth, someone you probably never heard of?

Bill was a parish priest in the panhandle of Northern Idaho in the 1980s, not far from the Aryan Nations' compound. At that time, the Aryan Nations was America's most important neo-Nazi group involved in political violence, including murders, robberies, and bombings. It unabashedly praised Hitler, conducted firearms training with pictures of Jews as targets, and was the go-to gathering spot for white supremacists from around the country. Northern Idaho was a special draw because there were very few non-white people living there. But there were some.

And soon, of course, some of the Blacks and Jews in the community were threatened. Bill spoke out. Then his house was firebombed, with him in it. Luckily, he wasn't injured.

How many of us would have given into the fear of a bomb detonated at our home? Bill, instead, was pissed off. He left the priesthood and founded the Northwest Coalition, a regional group that for many years led the fight against the neo-Nazis, but also against other manifestations of hate, such as anti-gay ballot initiatives.[1]

I was the American Jewish Committee's expert on antisemitism from 1989 to 2014, and Bill's annual conference was the most important meeting I attended every year. He invited me to give workshops on antisemitism, because many people didn't understand what it was beyond dislike of Jews, and he wanted them to know not only the history of antisemitism, but how it functioned as a backbone of white supremacy.

The value of his conferences, beyond the workshops and presentations, was in bringing together people from a variety of organizations who wanted to combat hate; people who wouldn't otherwise meet, let alone connect and perhaps collaborate. There were representatives from human rights groups, religious groups, ethnic groups, law enforcement, and others. The Coalition was the model I urged others around the country to emulate.

One year Bill asked me to give a keynote address. I was honored, and intimidated, and asked him what he would like me to say. He said, "Challenge us to do something we're not already doing."

It was a hard ask, because his group was already doing the best work in the country. But then I realized that while I came to the meetings as part of my "day job," as did most everyone else, the academics who attended did so because they were personally interested. More than that, I realized that even though the Northwest Coalition did incredible work, I hadn't heard an academic at a conference explain how what they studied or taught might be translated into usable theories that might guide the Coalition's (or any other antihate group's) decisions of what to do and not to do.

So my challenge to Bill and the Coalition was to find an academic home that might generate new thinking so that we weren't, as Bill reflected, "shooting in the dark."

Bill approached contacts in various universities in the Pacific Northwest to see if they'd be willing to house a program dedicated to hate studies.[2] "Great idea!" they'd say, followed quickly by "Do you have any money?" We didn't.

A few years later, Bill's conference was to be held at Gonzaga University, in Spokane, Washington. Weeks before the conference convened, the few Black law school students received death threats, and the university took the opportunity to ask Bill for advice. He said, "We have an idea!" and he and I (along with Morris Dees, then of the Southern Poverty Law Center, who was giving the keynote address at that conference) met with university officials and pitched a Hate Studies center. That's how Gonzaga University's Center for the Study of Hate, and the field of Hate Studies, was launched. At its first conference in 2004, we discussed what various academic areas, from psychology to religion to history to law and beyond,[3] might contribute to an interdisciplinary understanding of hatred (and what to do about it). Our hope was also that other universities would build Hate Studies programs. (Gonzaga University has been the anchor for Hate Studies, holding a conference every two years and publishing the *Journal of Hate Studies*.)

As of this writing, there are nine Hate Studies centers around the globe.[4] I direct the Bard Center for the Study of Hate (BCSH), which opened in 2018. In late 2019, BCSH received a grant to convene a half-week meeting of NGO leaders and academics who study some aspect of hate. The goal was to build solid connections between the two – to give NGOs guidance about what they might choose to do or not do. Then COVID-19 appeared. It was clear that people weren't going to travel during the height of the pandemic, and people were less likely to travel for this type of meeting in the aftermath.

So the "plan B" is this book, and a training program for NGOs and others built around it. It turns out that plan B was better than plan A, since you too are now in the conversation that only a few dozen people would have benefited from.

I've asked the experts whose essays follow to answer this question: "Knowing what you know about hate, if you were the director of an NGO focused on hate, or some aspect of it, what would you do, what wouldn't you do, and why?" And as the experts pondered this question, some communicated with NGO leaders over Zoom and email to get a better sense of what makes NGOs tick.

I asked them to write for a general audience, because the insights from the contributors to this book will challenge thinking about hate more broadly, to the benefit of everyone. So what you'll see here is accessible writing with you in mind, because what makes sense for our civil society groups to do also makes sense for philanthropies and governments and businesses and each of us in our daily lives to do.

And because of the commitment of each of the contributors to the overall project who attended joint meetings (virtual and, enjoyably and productively, over days and meals and drinks in person at Bard College in June 2023) and co-created this volume, the final product reads more as an integrated book rather than a stitched together group of unrelated essays. This book is also more than the sum of its parts. It's a blueprint for thought and action.

And it couldn't be timelier. Hate, as I said, has been a constant in the human story, but there are reasons to be more concerned about it now, as we in the United States are still dealing with the aftermath of the January 6, 2021, insurrection and the divisions evident in the 2024 US presidential election cycle and its aftermath that continue to challenge us. Hate has always worked in politics (otherwise politicians wouldn't use it), but the dangers are more pronounced today. It's the ideas that drive people into their strong tribal associations, but the delivery methods matter too. Social media, and the money to be made from cable news programs that blame "them!" – on both the right and the left – for all our ills, heighten the divisions on race, religion, cultural themes, and politics even further. It was predictable before the 2020 election, and in its immediate aftermath, that should Donald Trump win or lose, there would be violence. The combustible ingredients for even more sustained political violence and erosion of basic democratic rights, driven by hate, exist today. There's no better time than the present for this book and what it instructs all of us to do.

$\sim$

Hate may be like the parable of the elephant and the blind men. Each blind person only touches a part of the elephant, and describes what they feel. Some may touch the skin, some a tusk, some the trunk. What each perceives the elephant to be is not only incomplete, but distorted by the centrality of where each blind person makes contact.

Hate is like this in three ways.

First, we tend to look at hate primarily on how it affects or concerns our particular group. If you're Jewish, you may focus on antisemitism;

if you're a woman, on sexism and misogyny; if you're a person of color, on racism; if you're a Muslim, on Islamophobia; and so on. And even the observation called intersectionality, which recognizes that hate in combination may manifest differently than hate in isolation (the challenges a Black woman faces are more than lumping together the separate dynamics of what she faces as a Black person and as a woman), is still just looking at pieces of a puzzle called hate prioritized by how it is experienced by a subset of people.

Second, while philosophers over the ages and academics today in every field have valuable insights into hate, both the insights and the thinkers are too often segregated and siloed. Some focus on hate as an emotion, some as an attitude, some as a behavior. Some look at hate and how it plays out on the smallest scales – our brains – or on the largest ones, like contests for global power. Some look at hate manifested on and by individual human beings, some on hate and the individual as part of a group, some on the group, some on societies, some on theologies, some on ideologies.

Third, just as the blind men lacked a framework to combine their individual perceptions into an accurate description of an elephant (let alone an understanding of how the elephant functions as a living being in the world), we lack a means of bringing together what we know about hate into a larger framework, helping us think about how it works on all these levels simultaneously, allowing us to see what might be successful to make the elephant less dangerous.

The sad fact is that human beings, for as long as there have been human beings, have divided the world into "us" and "them," and too frequently the dehumanization and/or demonization of the "them" becomes a noble mission. Under the right conditions, hatred can lead to discrimination, harassment, intimidation, or worse – enslavement, war, rape, crimes against humanity, apartheid, genocide. And when it does, it's likely that the haters don't see themselves as haters, but as people who are expressing love for their own group. As the Greek playwright Aeschylus observed in 458 BCE, "Unanimous hatred is the greatest medicine for a human community." That medicine unleashes the elephant, trampling our shared humanity, for hate, by definition, puts other human beings outside the concept of community.

This book is an attempt to answer this question: What would have happened if each of the blind men, as they were touching the elephant, knew what each of the other blind men had felt, and integrated that knowledge into their analysis of what they were feeling? And what if each, having direct knowledge of the small piece of the elephant they knew best, then collectively, and magically, were given the power of sight, or at least insight? And what if, being able to see the elephant, but also using all other senses – smelling the elephant, hearing the elephant, perhaps even tasting the elephant (okay, yuk!) – in the quest of knowing how it functioned, in other words knew much more than they otherwise would know about an elephant, the blind men now could also predict, influence, and perhaps better understand what the elephant would do and how it would do it?

~

I'm not sure what the opposite of an elephant might be, but whatever it is, this book also focuses on the "unelephant." Jean-Paul Sartre observed that "hate is a faith." Too often what we try to do about hate is also a matter of faith, rather than of deep analysis and an examination of what works and what doesn't and why.

Part of the problem is that we don't think about hate like other challenges. Perhaps it's too complex, or too ugly to contemplate. Perhaps we don't care so much about it as a consistent danger because all of us hate to some degree, and perhaps even get some pleasure out of the misfortune of others. There's even a German word – *schadenfreude* – to describe this phenomenon.

It's much easier to think of potential solutions to other human challenges, even global warming. We have teams of scientists and others telling us exactly what we have to do, by when, or what the consequences will be.

But what do we do about hate?

Ask, and the answers are usually bromides that sound soothing, but should actually annoy us. Is it really satisfactory, reacting to an antisemitic event, to proscribe "Holocaust education?" Don't get me wrong, Holocaust education is good in and of itself, but as a single-shot vaccine against all types of antisemitism?

Or how about an anti-Black hate crime. Yes, people should be prosecuted, and where appropriate, hate crime laws applied. But is that all? And what about some calls after the murder of George Floyd in 2020 to "defund the police"? While there are logical arguments that the models of community policing should include more social work theory, what about thinking, at the same time, of the political implications of any such slogan, and how it might stoke hate and fear?

And what about the calls to censor speech we might see as hateful? What are the dangers when that becomes our go-to strategy? Does censorship work, or does it make things worse?

And what do we do about leaders who successfully stoke fears of "others," but with whom we agree on a particular third-rail issue (abortion, guns, immigration, Israel/Palestine)? Does it work to pick and choose where we oppose and where we support?

And who is the "we" who can do something anyway?

All of us, as this book will show, can do something, or at least do it better than we currently do.

But the most important groups we look to, ones we presume will do the heavy lifting, are nongovernmental organizations (NGOs), also sometimes referred to as "civil society." After all, such groups proclaim on their websites and in their mass fundraising mailings that they are the leaders targeting hate or some subset of it. We look to them – groups such as the Anti-Defamation League and the National Association for the Advancement of Colored People and the Southern Poverty Law Center, and many more – for clear thought, guidance, and action. Governments rely on their expertise, as do journalists. Philanthropists donate millions of dollars on the presumption that the NGOs are using their resources effectively for good.

But what if we can't prove that what feels good to do is actually doing good? What if some of what's touted as good actually does harm? As Thomas Brudholm and Birgitte Johansen note in chapter 1 in this volume, there's no equivalent of the Hippocratic Oath for people confronting hate, but arguably there should be, or at least some ethical expectation that an NGO can articulate a reason people should believe what they propose to do won't make things worse.

I worked for twenty-five years as the American Jewish Committee's antisemitism expert. I believe my colleagues and I did important work, as did friends in similar organizations. But I don't recall any framing of "what to do" in the scholarship of academics. Academics are usually talking and teaching and thinking and researching and writing among themselves, rather than coordinating, communicating, or advising these civil society groups to which leaders look and philanthropists fund, on the assumption these groups know what they are doing.

One purpose of this book is to create a firm and lasting connection between the important insights into hate from the academic world and have this knowledge help drive decisions of NGOs, from board members to program officials, from fundraisers to those working on messaging and media and social media, to those engaged in legal and legislative work. In other words, to create a multi-tiered and multi-focused set of theories, or at least academically grounded and sound principles, to drive NGO decisions, to make sure that they have the best chance to use their financial and moral capital for good. And, in turn, the NGOs will undoubtedly think more of the academic world as a resource, spurring research into new areas that will be identified by the NGO's need to show to itself, and others, that it is having the impact it alleges in the myths it tells itself and also in its fundraising appeals.

Supporters of these groups will benefit too. First, they can cite these academic principles and theories to ask the NGOs to do more than describe their work, but also to document why and how it is having the desired effect, both short term and long term. Second, the lessons learned from observations on the molecular scale (how our brains are influenced by hate, and thus our thinking and emotions) to the cultural and societal scale (how messaging strategies should take on board the ways in which hateful conspiracy theories grow, and how not to feed them) will give guidance to all of us in our daily lives.

Government will benefit too, from police forces to human rights commissions to legislators wanting to help victims of hatred.

Philanthropies will benefit, and should be eager consumers of this book. Many fund efforts they believe will reduce hate, but this book will help them ask the recipients of their support better-targeted questions about why and how the funding supplied will effect change. The net result, I hope, is that money will be spent more efficiently and in a more targeted way.

Hate, as I said, is complicated, and we've been confounded by it since ancient times.[5] Hate is many things at once. It is emotion, yes, but also behavior and attitude. It is in theology and ideologies. And it is related at times to other parts of the human condition – emotions like anger or jealously or envy, faiths defining who or what is good and who or what is evil.

We human beings too often take the default position of trying to make the complicated simple (that goes for both haters and those of us opposing hate, since we're all human). But to tackle hate more effectively, we have to seek out and engage the complexity. We have to look expansively, not narrowly – with wide lenses. Each of the experts providing chapters in this book provides one of the lenses, and they do so as a team, aware of what each of their colleagues is contributing. Together, they are the team that show us how better to see the elephant.

Kenneth S. Stern

NOTES

1 The authors in this volume, like many others, generally refer to those who suffer gender-identity-based discrimination with different formulations of

acronyms (some shorter, some longer). We will use LGBTQI+ as a standard formula to keep this volume consistent (except in a few places where there is a reason to use a different term).

2 In Kenneth Stern, "The Need for an Interdisciplinary Field of Hate Studies," *Journal of Hate Studies* 3, no. 1 (2004): 7–35, https://jhs.press.gonzaga.edu /articles/10.33972/jhs.18, I define Hate Studies as follows: "Inquiries into the human capacity to define, and then dehumanize or demonize, an 'other,' and the processes which inform and give expression to, or can curtail, control or combat, that capacity."

3 Stern, "The Need for an Interdisciplinary Field of Hate Studies."

4 Bard Center for the Study of Hate, "Hate Studies," accessed January 1, 2025, https://bcsh.bard.edu/hate-studies/.

5 When I teach about hate, I ask students to ponder quotes about hate. Here are some of them:

a. "Hate is a bottomless cup, I will pour and pour." Euripedes, *Medea*

b. "In time we hate that which we often fear." William Shakespeare, *Antony and Cleopatra*

c. "[E]njoying and hating the right thing seem the most important factors in virtue of character." Aristotle, *Nicomachean Ethics*

d. "To die hating them, that was freedom." George Orwell, *1984*

e. "Allow enemies their space to hate; they will destroy themselves in the process." Lisa Du

f. "[S]imple ideas [drive] the logic of hate." Eyal Press, *Beautiful Souls*

g. "Let's not hate the existence of hatred." Toba Beta, *Betelgeuse Incident*

h. "Hate is the father of all evil." David Gemmel, *Fall of Kings*

i. "Hate is a faith." Jean-Paul Satre, *Antisemite and Jew*

j. "Hatred is the coward's revenge for being intimidated." George Bernard Shaw

k. "Unanimous hatred is the greatest medicine for a human community." Aeschylus, *Eumenides*

l. "You can safely assume you've created God in your own image when it turns out that God hates all the same people you do." Anne Lamott

SIMPLY HUMAN

Editor's Introduction to Chapter 1

In 2015 my colleague Roger Berkowitz, director of Bard's Hannah Arendt Center, which "provides an intellectual space for passionate, uncensored, nonpartisan thinking that reframes and deepens the fundamental questions facing our nation and our world," met Thomas Brudholm – a scholar from Copenhagen – at a conference, then introduced us, telling me "I just had a fascinating talk with the only person I've met who thinks about hate as much as you do." Brudholm is, without doubt, one of the most important philosophers writing about hate today. In his early work, he looked at understandings of resentment among advocates of reconciliation after mass atrocity and he argued that victims' resentment can be the expression of a moral protest that is as humane or honorable as the willingness to forgive. Questions about hate have been on his agenda since 2010 and he has contributed to discussions of its nature and ethical implications across several scholarly and political fields, from the philosophy of emotion to studies of hate crime, dehumanization, genocide, and transitional justice. Like many philosophers before him, Brudholm questions what many others tend to assume, including whether hatred is always a matter of prejudice and whether it is always ethically wrong to hate.

In the following chapter, Brudholm has teamed up with his colleague Birgitte Schepelern Johansen, a sociologist with a strong interest in how political actors and organizations conceptualize and tackle hate today. In her works on hate, she has brought attention to aspects that are often overlooked in purely philosophical studies, including the relation between hate and democracy and how hate can materialize in laws and institutions. Writers and philosophers have been wrestling with how to understand and respond to hate for millennia. So it's appropriate to start our exploration with an examination of the conceptual and ethical implications of the combating of hate.

1 The Ethics of Combating Hate

THOMAS BRUDHOLM AND
BIRGITTE SCHEPELERN JOHANSEN

This is a book about how best to combat hate, and in this chapter, we (a philosopher and a sociologist) want to engage with some of the ethical questions that can arise in the struggle. We are aware that asking how best to do something is typically about how to do so as effectively as possible; one needs to know what works best in relation to the stated goal of diminishing or even eliminating hate. For example, is criminalizing hateful speech, as we do in several countries in Europe, an effective means for preventing hate? Or is counterspeech the most beneficial response to hateful speech? Questions about the instrumental value of different means and strategies are deeply important. However, if you listen to those who are engaged in the struggle, what matters is not just efficiency or knowing what works (or what is legally permissible or advisable). What also matters is whether the struggle rests on a just cause, or whether a particular intervention is morally justified; even if everyone agreed that hate is bad, and that the world would be a better place without it, it does not mean that anything goes as one tries to diminish its influence. So, to be responsibly engaged in the combating of hate also means to be able to respond to a variety of ethical questions that emerge in the struggle. Ethics, as a philosophical discipline and as we will apply it here, is certainly about what it is right or wrong to do (or omit doing), but it is also about our moral understanding of things that matter to us (such as hate), about what it is good or bad to be (or allow oneself to become), and about how to live well (for example, in the context of an enduring struggle against injustice).

As part of the research for this chapter, we (with the help of Kenneth Stern) organized two online meetings with leading representatives from around a dozen antihate NGOs based in the United States and Canada. In the preparation for the meetings, we informed our interlocutors that we reached out to them in the conviction that our ethical reflection would be most interesting if informed by conversations with persons who are or have been extensively engaged in the organized struggle against hate. We told them that we were curious about whatever came to their mind under the heading of "the ethics of combating hate," but that we would also like to get their response to some of our ideas about what issues to explore in the chapter. We learned a lot during these conversations, and what follows is our attempt to philosophically elaborate and reflect on the ideas that were exchanged.

Professional and applied ethics include a wide range of highly specialized branches, from the ethics of war to the ethics of education, journalism, nursing, and more. However, there is no established field of research specifically on the ethical challenges facing NGOs dedicated to combating hate.[1] A similar lack of systematic or organized reflection seems to be prevalent within the NGOs themselves. We have not conducted any kind of empirical survey, but it is our impression based on the conversations that when ethical concerns arise in action or practice, they are primarily dealt with informally and privately. Some NGOs offer supervision, for example when staff or activists are exposed to threats and hate mail. Perhaps, sometimes such supervision can be an occasion for scrutiny of specifically ethical concerns. Others rely, at least in part, on what one NGO representative, during one of our meetings, called a culture of "toughening it out." It is not for us to decide whether NGOs should do more to secure an organizational space for thinking about the ethics of combating hate.[2] At this point, what we can contribute is an attempt to clear the view for the reality and diversity of moral issues in the struggle. Heeding the words of John Dewey, our aim is to inspire, among those who are interested in the combating of hate, "a vital conviction of the genuine reality of moral problems and the value of reflective thought in dealing with them."[3] Like Dewey, we have no intentions of developing a comprehensive theory, but we hope that the following reflections can support the ability "to make delicate distinctions, to perceive aspects of good and of evil not previously noticed, [and] to take into account the fact that doubt and the need for choice impinge at every turn."[4]

Finally, a caveat as to the scope of the ensuing discussion. NGOs are engaged in combating hate around the world. Some operate in a context of peace, others in a country at war or in a region plagued by protracted group violence, terror, or even genocide. Some work in a state where civil rights are constitutionally protected, others must deal with authoritarian regimes in blatant disregard of international human rights conventions. The ethical questions, and the types of hate in need of analysis and reflection, are probably not the same across the field. Indeed, another chapter would have to be written, we think, if we were to address the ethical issues faced by NGOs combating hate in, for example, contexts of war, where the hate to be combated is not necessarily the product of prejudice. We leave open the question of the reach of the following reflections to the readers.

Our examination will unfold in three parts. The first dwells on the concept of hate and on what is combated under this banner. The second turns to questions related to "the combating" as such, and the third directs the attention to those who are fighting the fight. The subheadings for each section are all quotes from the conversations.

"Clearly, Clearly Define Hate"

One of the first suggestions brought to the table when we asked NGO representatives what one should attend to in an ethics of combating hate was to "clearly, clearly define hate." Indeed, an organization set up to combat something should of course be able to delimit its target. Simply to assert that one is combating hate works well on the level of slogans and placards, but – if left undefined – the label opens the avenue for uncertainty and abuse. As scholars, we distinguish between different forms of hate, and we don't want to presume that *all* these forms are equally bad, bad in the same way, or even bad at all.[5] At the same time, we recognize that to call something "hate" is, ordinarily, to simultaneously condemn it and those who enact it. This is one reason why one should be able to account for what one means if one claims that something is a matter of hate.

In this section, we will develop a definition of hate that speaks to current and common usage of the term by NGOs. What matters the most is not whether all NGOs can endorse our account, but rather whether the conceptual and normative considerations through which it is developed prompt organizational reflection on how to account for one's use of the term. To clearly define something can mean several things. We should say that our aim is not to provide the kind of binary definition (hate, yes or no) that would satisfy a wish for bright lines or a concept of the essence of hate as such. Instead, we aim at an account that clarifies what standard examples of so-called "hate" have in common. By "standard examples" we mean cases or incidents that clearly count (to the degree that anything can do so) as examples of how the term "hate" is currently and commonly used by antihate NGOs. We will later refer to how hate is conceptualized in philosophy. However, what matters in the discussion that follows is *not* whether the examples we think through fit what would be central or satisfactory to philosophers of hate; what matters is whether we think through a pattern of examples that can be recognized as key or paradigmatic of what NGOs combat when they say they combat hate. Having traversed guides and mission statements of a variety of antihate NGOs (in the United States and Europe), we suggest that the following excerpt provides exactly the kind of exemplification we are looking for, that is, a pattern of cases that aptly illustrate what is targeted as manifestations of hate. The passage is from the Southern Poverty Law Center's *Ten Ways to Fight Hate: A Community Response Guide*:

> A presidential candidate wins election after denigrating Muslims, Latinos, women and people with disabilities. A young white man opens fire and kills nine African Americans who welcomed him into Bible study at a church in Charleston, South Carolina, telling his victims, "I have to do it." A Muslim woman is seated on a bench in front of a coffee shop in Washington, D.C., when a woman begins screaming anti-Muslim epithets. A swastika and other anti-Semitic graffiti appear at an elementary school in Stapleton, Colorado. A lone gunman carrying an assault rifle and a handgun storms a well-known gay club in Orlando, Florida, killing 49 people and wounding 53 others.[6]

If this cluster of incidents is exemplary, what does it tell us about the meaning of "hate"? The excerpt lumps together a very diverse set of acts that are all wrongful, but for different reasons, on different levels of gravity, and with different ramifications. Yelling at another person is one thing; entering a nightclub with the intent of killing and wounding as many people as possible is quite another. Still, we are to expect that for all the differences, the whole cluster is in every case about hate, but what is the nature of this hate? Is it possible to pinpoint a conceptual core? Evidently, across the set there is manifest hostility. Let us take a closer look at the particularities of this hostility: The woman is yelled at *as a Muslim, antisemitic graffiti* appears on an elementary school, the young men in Charleston are killed *as African Americans*, the club in Orlando was targeted *as a gay club*. What unites the cases, one could suggest, is the demonstration of hostility toward collective identity categories with which the individual victims are perceived to be affiliated. This is, however, a too-inclusive formula, because it could include hostility toward others because of their membership in groups against which hostility could be morally justifiable. One can be hostile, for example, toward someone who is a member of a terrorist group, of a racist social club, of a group that indulges in child prostitution, or of a military unit responsible for war crimes. Whatever one thinks about displays of hostility toward such groups or categories, it lies either outside or at least at the periphery of the operational concept of hate; that is, outside or at the periphery of the forms of group-focused hostility that are centrally targeted in the combating of hate. None of the victims from the exemplary excerpt has said or done anything to personally provoke the animus to which they are all exposed: students were attending an elementary school, the Bible study group demonstrated hospitality, the Muslim woman just sat and enjoyed a cup of coffee, and the crowd in the club were just enjoying themselves. In the absence of reasonable provocations, it seems reasonable to infer that the hostility at hand is motivated by the hate itself, for example, by prejudiced, bigoted, or fearful notions, say, of women, disabled persons, Muslims, Jewish students, or Latinos. Thus, we might say that what unites the cases from the excerpt is the demonstration of prejudice-based hostility toward social identity categories with which the individual victims are perceived to be affiliated.

We are, we think, close to an adequate account of the NGO concept of paradigm hate, apart from one additional point. What remains, is recognition that the hostility in focus uniformly targets people who due to their group identity have been or are already exposed to widely distributed forms of prejudice and discrimination or the legacies thereof. This reminds us that the combating of hate today is closely affiliated with a broader civil and human rights struggle against group-focused oppression and injustice. Paradigm hate – when enacted or expressed – involves forms of hate that are primed to echo and activate memories of structural or institutionalized discrimination and persecution. Thus, the meaning of such acts of hate and their ability to create a sense of threat or fear of harm and exclusion cannot be understood without an understanding of the broader societal and historical context. Philosopher Jeremy Waldron has reconstructed the implicit message to members of the minorities targeted by paradigm hate:

> Don't be fooled into thinking you are welcome here. The society around you may seem hospitable and nondiscriminatory, but the truth is that you are not wanted, and you and your families will be shunned, excluded, beaten, and driven out, whenever we can get away with it. We may have to keep a low profile right now. But don't get too comfortable. Remember what has happened to you and your kind in the past. Be afraid.[7]

In sum, we suggest that paradigm hate refers to enactments of prejudice-based hostility that targets people because of their perceived affiliation with groups that are already subjected to discrimination and stigmatization. So, is it *not* hate if a politician with a minority background denigrates people who belong to a majority? Or what if a woman belonging to a stereotyped and marginalized group screams epithets at someone belonging to a privileged group? It is, we would say, not *paradigm* hate, but the very idea of talking about paradigms (rather than criteria or demarcation lines) is that it allows for discussions of conceptual territories with centers and peripheries. In our view, the powerless and marginalized can hate; they can hate the powerful as well as other minorities, or even themselves. The question "who can hate?" (much like the question "who can be racist?") is ethically interesting, but it makes no difference as to our basic point about the nature of paradigm hate.[8]

Pondering how to philosophically articulate the evil inherent in paradigm hate, it can be noticed that it makes a menace of human difference; it creates and projects upon its target a tainted, treacherous, disgusting, or odious character to which it parades as a legitimate reaction. The examples from *Ten Ways to Fight Hate* vary in gravity, but they all involve disrespect of their victims as persons. "To say," as philosopher Stephen Darwall has argued, "that persons as such are entitled to respect is to say that they are entitled to have other persons take seriously and weigh appropriately the fact that they are persons in deliberating about what to do."[9] The perpetrators of hate, as depicted in the excerpt, all fail to do so, in so far as they are treating persons, that is, their victims, as individually replaceable tokens of an intolerable category or group of people.

At this point it is important to emphasize the particularity and limitations of the given account. What characterizes paradigm hate does not necessarily apply to all forms of hate. Forgetting the particularity of paradigm hate, one may, for example, slip into statements that "clearly, prejudice underpins hatred as a human emotion." The claim would be a reasonable claim if it was clearly restricted to the given paradigm, but does prejudice underpin hate in *any* form? Is it essential to the concept of hate as such? We do not think so. The formation of hate can be based on all-too real experience with the target's capacity for violence and cruelty. Our point is not that hatred without prejudice is morally good or right, but only that use of our account becomes ethically problematic if overgeneralized. It is neither reasonable nor fair to consider anyone who hates as someone who is necessarily prejudiced or mistaken about the character of the persons they hate or have hated.[10]

The account of paradigm hate presented above provides, we hope, a clear picture of what lies at the heart of the fight; paradigm hate does not exhaust what can reasonably be understood as hate, but to this it should be added that it also does not exhaust, for example, the anti-racist or antihomophobic struggle. Sometimes NGOs target behaviors, ideas, and attitudes that are not clearly at the center of the paradigm. NGOs can work to raise awareness of the problems with name-calling in schools or the perpetuation of stereotypical images of minorities in the media. Such situations may display *some* features of paradigm hate, for example, group stereotyping or untenable generalizations, but they do not necessarily entail the forms of unreasonable ill-will and deni-grating hostility that characterize hate in the central cases. Granted that the moral condemnation of paradigm hate draws its legitimacy from the center, it is worth considering how far away, toward the periphery, one can move before the label – and hence accusation – of hate becomes problematic or even untenable.

The given account of hate is, finally, limited by being built exclusively on scrutiny of what characterizes paradigmatic examples of the kind of behavior to which the term "hate" is currently applied by NGOs. If one is interested in a deeper and more comprehensive understanding of the nature and complexity of hate, one must engage with expert scholarly investigations of the phenomenon.[11]

"We Want to Win, but There Are Principles"

Even if there is a just cause for working to bring an end to hate, it does not mean that anything goes regarding how to achieve it. "We want," as one of our interlocutors said, "to win, but there are principles." In our conversations with the NGO representatives, we asked them to respond to the question whether there are things they would never do. This elicited a lot of debate and perhaps the question could fruitfully be addressed by all antihate NGOs. Several of our interlocutors expressed a determination to uphold fundamental norms of decency in contexts where one could be tempted to cut moral corners or lower one's stan-dards to the benefit of the just cause. So, for example, appeals were made to never lie to the media and never exaggerate when describ-ing hate groups, pending threats, and so on. In our view, loosening demands for factual accuracy in order to emphasize one's point may be tempting, but it jeopardizes the NGO's credibility, just as it risks misrepresenting the actions or attitudes of those who enact hate. Fur-ther, it is doubtful whether exaggeration helps those who are targeted by hate. For one thing, because exaggerations may create pushbacks from a wider audience, but also because circulating stories about hate incidents can have severe intimidating effects on already vulnerable groups.[12]

Sometimes, exaggerations might be the unintended outcome of what C. Thi Nguyen calls "epistemic bubbles."[13] Epistemic bubbles are social spaces in which knowledge is created and exchanged in such a way that they become self-referential and enclosed to the surroundings, not as a matter of deliberate exclusion of other voices, but rather through communication only with those who share one's experiences and fundamental orientations. The lack of epistemic friction in such bubbles, we would argue, can create an environment in which exaggerations and creations of strawmen can go unnoticed and hence unaddressed. Thus, there is an ethical task for NGOs in considering how to keep their communication and platforms of debate open to questioning and corrections. Antihate NGOs are not academic institutions, but they share with the latter a basic commitment to truthfulness and trustworthiness. Therefore, we wonder whether NGOs could benefit from articulating something akin to the normative principles that university scholars are held to when communicating their research. For example, scholars at Danish universities are officially accountable to the Danish Code of Conduct for Research Integrity. The code rests on three principles of *honesty, transparency,* and *accountability* in research and research communication.[14] Could something similar – both in terms of form and content – be relevant to NGOs fighting hate?

The question, whether there were things our interlocutors would never do, also prompted thoughts about the importance of never breaking the law and never engaging in violence. While this may seem obvious, subsequent discussions also revealed why this is not necessarily easy or self-evidently right, morally speaking. Combating hate sometimes means participating in public demonstrations and parades that may attract counterresponses from hate groups who show up to disrupt the demonstration or harass and attack the crowd. One NGO representative explained how the use of physical force on rare occasions can be justified if a confrontation escalates into violence. The awareness that some upfront encounters are likely to escalate and even erupt into physical violence could be behind another answer elicited by our question, namely, to always try avoiding confrontation with extremists, both because of the risks it entails and because of the limited value of attempts of "talking it out." Even though antihate activism throughout the twentieth century includes many stories of brave nonviolent confrontations, there is an ethical question about the value and limits of such bravery. As Candis Delmas summarized the hard-won experiences of the civil rights movement in the United States during the 1960s, "Too much bravery can be hazardous."[15] However, there is a limit to how much control you can have over public events and if confrontational situations do occur, a right to protect and defend oneself and others may emerge and challenge ideals of absolute nonviolence. The issue of civil disobedience has a long and complex history: from the suffragist movement in Europe to civil rights activism to anticolonial struggles, questions about a right or duty to disobey (unjust laws) have been pivotal.[16] This is not the place for deeper reflection on the question of whether (and if so when) breaking the law or engaging in violence can be morally justified as part of the fighting of hate, but it is a good case to ponder for other contributions to the ethics of the struggle.

Another cluster of responses that resonated among the NGO representatives was captured by the statement, "Do not give oxygen to hate groups." To the extent that hate groups thrive on and grow through public attention, every loud confrontation and every media exposure may add wood to the fire, clicks to stories, more source material for AI-generated hate, and an increased amount of hateful speech in the commentary tracks. In an increasingly mediatized and interconnected world, the concern is no longer solely to make the truth known; the truth becomes a piece in ever more complicated attention games. This situation, we suggest, potentially creates a dilemma, because the ethically important task of witnessing and providing evidence of expressions and enactments of hate has not disappeared. Speaking out, recognizing, and acknowledging hate when it is expressed and enacted can be of important reparative value for those groups that are targeted (that they do not stand alone). Further, it may serve an important purpose of raising awareness among people who are not themselves targeted.[17] So how to balance the need for public recognition and truth-telling with the wish to "smother the fire"? There are no easy answers, but an important step is to recognize exactly this: staying with the difficulty, not rushing toward the solution that *feels* good. For example, as the *Community Guide for Opposing Hate* from the Bard Center for the Study of Hate explains, it might feel instinctively good to make efforts to stop hateful speech, but,

> [i]n most instances, such an attempt [to stop hateful speech] would be both a legal and tactical mistake. That doesn't mean letting hate go unaddressed. It means knowing that calls for censorship most times backfire. Not only do they usually fail to stop the haters from speaking, they actually help amplify the hateful message and sometimes even make the haters seem sympathetic. What feels good sometimes doesn't do good, and in fact can do harm.[18]

The quote also illustrates another way that antihate activism may give oxygen to hate groups: not by sharing news and knowledge about hate, but by trying to block verbal expressions of it. Such attempts, instead of stopping the hateful message from spreading, may increase the circulation and create legitimacy for "haters" as free speech "martyrs." The best strategies for stopping hateful speech may be different for NGOs working in societies with hate speech laws. For example, it is not, at least not de facto, a legal mistake to try to stop speech that is in fact criminalized. However, the risk of amplification is still present, and in any case, the important point is to allow sufficient time to consider whether and when one's activities may, however unintentional, give oxygen to hate groups. These considerations mainly revolve around pragmatic concerns whether one's activities risk doing harm to the cause. Beneath this, there is of course a more fundamental ethical and legal discussion about whether hateful speech is a kind of wrong that deserves criminalization or not.

As mentioned in the prior section, the combating of hate is also a fight for certain values such as equality and nondiscrimination. It could be a guiding principle for NGOs, across the board, to embody and exemplify such values in their own practices. On such a principle, it matters morally whether and how the combating of hate privileges particular groups. Many antihate NGOs fight hostility toward a particular social category or group. For example, the Disability Hate Crime Network, in the UK, works to challenge hate crime against disabled people; ILGA-Europe focuses on hostility and violence against LGBTQI+ people; and the mission of the Anti-Defamation League is "to stop the defamation of the Jewish people."[19] This is not in itself ethically problematic.[20] There are, however, ways of caring particularly about one group or category that become morally dubious or neglectful. This might be the case, for example, if the combating of "hate" against a particular group is attended by a systematic indifference to the well-being of or threats to other groups, or if one is only ready to call out hate when it targets those for whom one fights. When working for the rights and protection of particular groups becomes excluding in this way or biased in recognition, it may contribute to polarization and enforce what sociologist Arlie Russell Hochschild has termed "empathy walls" between social groups.[21]

Enacting the values in whose name the combating takes place would also oblige NGOs not to call out hate too quickly, without sufficient evidence or without clear marking of the degree of certainty with which one speaks (clearly, this point ties back to the overlap between the principles of good research communication and good NGO communication). NGOs combating hate must be vigilant and effective, but they should also take care not to rush too quickly to judgments, condemning acts or expressions as hateful, antisemitic, homophobic, and so on. It might be tempting to speak out assertively and quickly to show commitment and resolve, especially when the case seems obvious. However, granted that judging hate implies a strong moral accusation, perhaps even stigmatization of the accused, it is something that one should only do upon careful consideration. A too-hasty judgment may damage the moral authority of the NGO in the long term if the accusation turns out to be unfounded. Likewise, using the word hate – or any of its more group-specific synonyms – without careful deliberation risks robbing the word of its power.

A case worth considering in relation to this last point is the aftermath of an exceptionally heinous murder of a young man in a forest outside of the main town on the island of Bornholm in Denmark in the summer of 2020.[22] The victim was Black; the perpetrators, two brothers who severely mistreated and killed him, were white. The three men were also close acquaintances, and according to several locals they had been friends. Anyway, for many people, including Black Lives Matter in Denmark, the crime was clearly a racist hate crime or at least it had to be prosecuted as such. Not only because of the racial characteristics of the brothers and their victim, but also because one of the brothers had a Nazi tattoo and one of them had placed a knee on the throat of the victim, reminding everyone of the killing of George Floyd. However, the police and the prosecutor consistently denied that the killing was motivated by racist hate and focused instead on an intimate relation between the deceased and the accused's mother as a possible motive. In the eyes of antiracist scholars and activists, this was a morally outrageous denial of or, at best, blindness to a clear racist hate motive. Black Lives Matter and other antiracist activists went to demonstrate in front of the court on the island where the trial took place. They were met by a group of local counterdemonstrators who contested the allegations of racism. In their view, the antiracist NGOs ran roughshod over the concrete reality of the case. In the end, the brothers were punished harshly for their brutal murder, but the Danish penalty enhancement clause for crimes enacted with a hate motive was not applied, neither in the local court on Bornholm nor in the appeals trial that followed. For some, this was evidence of systemic racism or a morally offensive blindness to hateful racism, but for others – including a criminologist who followed the case – the authorities' stance was more likely to be expressive of either a closer appreciation of the details of the concrete case or of a particular goal-oriented mode of rationality focused on securing the harshest possible sentence as cost-effectively as possible.[23]

We cannot say whether the NGOs' "verdict" was ultimately correct or not. What matters for the focus of this chapter is something different, namely, how to fight hate justly and wisely. The haste and lack of caution with which the NGOs proceeded seems to us to be risky, polarizing, and ethically inadequate. To ensure trustworthiness and reliability, NGOs should only make strong claims when they can be based on evidence, they should be accurate, and they should be transparent as to the eventual limitations of their data and uncertainty of their judgments, especially if they are accusing others – whether it is private individuals, authorities, or entire societies – of harboring hate or acting out racism.[24]

We hope that it has become clear that combating hate is an enterprise rife with complex and interesting ethical questions. Let us offer a few considerations on how best to sustain and integrate ethics in organizational practice. Could it, for example, make sense to introduce some kind of commitment for NGOs to "do no harm"? Such commitments can take the form of joint declarations that aim to articulate and safeguard the ethics of a particular profession or organization. Ancient and modern declarations – such as the ancient Hippocratic Oath[25] or the Declaration of Geneva from 1948[26] – have served, and continuously serve, as normative guidelines and tools for creating a shared language about the ethics of a profession or an organization. This is not the place for making an actual attempt, but the idea of some kind of joint declaration seems to us interesting, and in the section on the principles of the struggle, we found inspiration in similar codes of integrity from the Universities Denmark organization. We leave it to the reader, especially readers from NGOs dedicated to the combating of hate, to decide whether the idea of a declaration should be taken further. We would simply like to add that even if declarations and written standards have value, they are only banisters for the prevention of malpractice and wrongdoing. Rules and declarations must never be an excuse for ethical laziness or nonthinking about the content of given normative standards.[27] Arguably, what matters the most, ethically speaking and for the prevention of doing wrong in the name of fighting for the good, is not an official declaration, but rather that NGOs are willing to nurture and actively engage in a vibrant culture of common ethical deliberation. In closing: Yes, some kind of Hippocratic Oath or joint commitment could be valuable, but only if accompanied by critical, Socratic questioning.

"Don't Let the Hate Consume Who You Are"

Antihate NGOs clearly need funding, organization, and effective tech-nologies. However, and perhaps most fundamentally, they also need *people* who are able and willing to engage in a long-term struggle. There must be those who will speak up publicly, do the teaching, provide legal counsel, show up at demonstrations, deal with threats and hate mail, and more generally endure the ups and downs of the antihate work. Participation in such a struggle can be enriching and meaning-ful, but it can also affect or transform people – their selves, their char-acter, or their social dispositions – in potentially harmful and morally regrettable ways. In various branches of professional and applied eth-ics, scholars discuss the value of more systematic attention to different forms of moral damage, distress, or injury to the self. For example, in relation to combat veterans there is much discussion of *moral injury* and in the ethics of health care there is a focus on *moral distress*. The ques-tion is whether a concern with the well-being of those who are engaged in the combating of hate should, likewise, attend to various forms of moral damage. To test whether the topic would resonate among our interlocutors, we asked them to consider what long-term engagement in the fighting of hate can imply for those engaged in it, including dis-cussion of how one manages various emotions emerging in response to participation in the struggle.[28] The ensuing discussion with and between our interlocutors was deeply interesting, and we recommend that NGOs make space and time for similarly focused conversations. We recognize, as already indicated, that participation in the struggle can also affect the "combatants" in morally valuable ways (by develop-ing virtues of integrity, moderation of indignation, toleration, etc.), but we leave consideration of this potential for another occasion.

Let us begin with the cautionary remark that we used above as the title for this section, that is, the warning against letting "the hate con-sume who you are." It was suggested during our conversations by a senior activist and scholar with decades of personal experience with antihate work, including the organization of demonstrations against US-based neo-Nazis. To be consumed, unwittingly, by the evil one set out to fight – that is, to become hateful yourself – would surely repre-sent a regrettable form of moral damage. Let us, however, postpone for a moment the elaboration of this interpretation of the statement, because if we understood our interlocutor correctly, what he had in mind was not the danger of developing a hateful self. At stake, rather, was the danger of becoming so passionately absorbed in the fighting of hate that one neglects caring about anything else. Combating hate arguably requires people who care passionately about (in)justice and who are, at least periodically, willing to engage beyond the limits of duty. Yet there is a point where laudable, passionate commitment transforms into what might be called the vice of moral *obsession*. Enduring moral obsession can be a cause of real damage, both to the self and to those who otherwise depend on the activist. The warning, to not let "the hate consume who you are," presupposes – and reasonably so – that you are, perhaps, also a parent or a child, a friend, and indeed yourself a person worthy of care and respect. Persons who are driven in their life choices and being with others by nothing but rage against hate fail to pay adequate attention and give adequate care to the obligations issuing from these other roles. Stories of this – at once heroic and tragic, laudable and pitiable – figure are easily brought to mind. Remember, for example, Heinrich von Kleist's story about Michael Koolhaas, an offended horse dealer on an obsessive quest for revenge; a classic story about the dangers – both to the self, family, and society – of passionate obsession with (in)justice.[29]

In the history of thinking about passions, it has indeed been common to make passion itself, by definition, uncontrollable and dangerous. For example, according to Immanuel Kant, to be subject to passion is to suffer a serious illness of the mind, an illness that bars the exercise of reason and moderation.[30] Still, the ethical significance of our interlocutor's statement relies not least on the implicit recognition that the damage of moral obsession is avoidable. Those who have *let* hate consume who they are must – at least in part – themselves be responsible for the kind of character they have (allowed themselves to) become. However, in our opinion the responsibility is shared by the organization that can do its bit to prompt a balanced commitment among its volunteers and staff. Hesitation in blaming persons who have "let" hate consume who they are can also stem from acknowledgment that in some cases responsibility for the moral obsession lies, in part, with the community that has failed to respond adequately to the obsessed person's attempt to protest injustice. Several of our interlocutors knew, from personal experience, about feelings of moral frustration, why others "don't get it," where "it" referred to the moral importance of actively fighting hate.

Now, let us return to the first-mentioned interpretation of the statement, namely, as a warning against somehow developing *oneself* as a hateful character, as a tragic effect of participation in the fighting of hate. Who you are has become hard to distinguish from the kind of people you originally set out to fight; you have let yourself become hateful, intolerant, prejudiced. On this interpretation, the statement echoes Friedrich Nietzsche's warning that "he who fights with monsters should be careful lest he thereby become a monster."[31] It also echoes the notion of so-called "cycles" of hatred, according to which there is a risk that we, in our response to wrongdoing, will recycle or mirror the wrong that was done to us.[32] Clearly, this differs from moral obsession and should be labeled and considered independently. Persons who have let hate consume who they are, in this sense, are either what we might call morally *tainted* or *spoiled* by the evil they set out to diminish. In the worst case, one has allowed hate to fester in oneself. Perhaps, what began as anger or rage has transformed into something indistinguishable from hate, but there is also the possibility that one has let certain *aspects* of hate influence who one is. Think, for example, of someone who has succumbed to prejudiced stereotypes of "the haters," or to an untenably zero-tolerant attitude, all too hastily advocating the elimination, removal, firing, or cancellation of something or someone.[33]

Finally, we would like to present what seems to us a particular form of so-called "moral distress." Moral distress occurs, roughly speaking, when you know what the right thing to do is, but it is impossible to do it due to situational constraints.[34] The phenomenon of moral distress has been described and discussed primarily with a focus on health care professionals, but we think it might also be relevant to NGOs combating hate. That paradigm hate is an evil worth fighting is beyond dispute, but the fight can take its toll on people if its goals are not properly conceived. Among those who are engaged in the fighting of hate one sometimes comes across expressions that state eradication of hate as the end goal: the aim is ultimately to eliminate hate "for good" (Anti-Defamation League), to "create a world without racism" (Council of Europe), or to "step up to help bring homophobia, biphobia and transphobia to an end" (Schweppe and Walters, chapter 7, in this volume). These appeals may express a genuine belief that such a goal is achievable, or they may express what one takes to be a regulative ideal that may never be reached, but still points in the right direction. This way of conceiving the nature and aim of the combat invites ethical reflection. Surely, what sociologist Ruth Levitas calls "social dreaming"[35] is indispensable for social activism, because it allows us to imagine different and perhaps better futures. But it is ethically significant how we do so. The framing of the goal as a progressive (forward or upward) movement toward a time where hate no longer exists can be inspiring, but its flipside is the image of Sisyphus rolling the stone uphill (forward, upward) everyday, just to see it roll down again. There are no indications that hate will be overcome for good, so maybe we are better off with different images than the progressive ones?

Writing on the perpetual struggles that human beings face when fighting evil, philosopher Kathryn J. Norlock invites us to develop an ethics not for idealized versions of a world that probably will never come, but for the present nonideal world, inhabited by imperfect human beings, who will continue to do evil.[36] Such an ethics starts out by questioning the linear, progressive models, because they build on an imagination of a world populated with increasingly perfect human beings – and this is not the world we live in. Furthermore, it is questionable whether it is a world that we should wish to live in. While linear, progressive models may inspire movement and action, they may also contribute to burnout and disillusion. So instead of thinking forward and upward (and then downward again), we should, according to Norlock, realize that "there is no hill."[37] There are ongoing maintenance and renewed commitments, there are victims that need support, and there will continue to be victims that need support. An ethics for this kind of work is one that appreciates not so much the ability to continuously push forward, but "diligence in rehearsing skills, consistency in repeated reapplication, taking turns, sharing burdens that can't be put down and must, therefore, be traded, and cultivating receptivity to a renewal of promises."[38] This way of striving does not lack aim or goals, but the goals will be local and temporary. There are plenty of stories of local successes, lives that have been changed, communities that have stood together, and hostile acts that have been prevented or contained because of the persistent work of NGOs combating hate. Such work can make an enormous difference, without there being any chance of eliminating hate for good.

Acknowledgments

We wish to thank Ken Stern for securing, with exceptional care, an inspiring context for the writing of this chapter. Thanks also to the other contributors for responses offered at The Center for Hate Studies, Bard College, June 2023. For helpful and critical comments to draft versions, thanks to Alessandro Salice, Daniel Berthold, Andrew Schaap, Bice Maiguasha, and the Ethics and Violence Cluster at the Department for Cross-Cultural and Regional Studies, University of Copenhagen. A special thanks is owed here to the anonymous NGO representatives who set aside time to meet and talk with us. The writing of this chapter has been supported by funding from Velux Fonden (project: Afterthoughts: An Investigation of the Ethical Aspects of Responses to Wrongdoing) and the Danish Research Council (project: *In terrorrem*: On the Social Ramifications of Hate Crime).

NOTES

1 To the best of our knowledge, scholarly studies of the ethics of combating hate have all been focused on the realm of states and governmental organizations (national as well as international). There is a literature on the ethics of criminalizing and punishing hate; see, for example, Jeremy Waldron, *The Harms of Hate* (Boston: Harvard University Press 2012), and Antony Duff and Sandra Marshall, "Criminalizing Hate," in Thomas Brudholm and Birgitte S. Johansen, eds., *Hate, Politics, Law* (Oxford: Oxford University Press, 2018). For discussions of ethical concerns related to different conceptualizations of international hate crime legislation, see, for example, David Brax, "Hate Crime Concepts and Their Moral Foundations: A Universal Framework?" and Thomas Brudholm, "Conceptualizing Hate Globally: Is Hate Crime a Human Rights Violation?," both in Mark Walters and Jennifer Schweppe, eds., *The Globalization of Hate: Internationalizing Hate Crime?* (Oxford: Oxford University Press 2016).
2 For an interesting discussion of the role of the ethicist and ethics consulting in practice, see Margaret Urban Walker, "Keeping Moral Space Open: New Images of Ethics Consulting," *The Hastings Center Report* 23, no. 2 (1993): 33–40, https://doi.org/10.2307/3562818.
3 John Dewey, *Ethics* (London: n.p., 1910), iii.
4 John Dewey, "Three Independent Factors in Morals," *Educational Theory* 16, no. 3 (1966): 197–209, trans. J.A. Boydston, reprinted in John Dewey, *The Later Works of John Dewey, 1925–1953*, vol. 5 (Carbondale: Southern Illinois University Press, 1985), 280.
5 For examples of deeper discussions of the morality of hate and hating, see several chapters in Noell Birondo, ed., *The Moral Psychology of Hate* (Lanham, MD: Rowman & Littlefield, 2022); Jeffrie Murphy and Jean Hampton, *Forgiveness and Mercy* (Cambridge: Cambridge University Press, 2019); Thomas Szanto, "Can It Be or Feel Right to Hate?," *Filozofija i drustvo* 32, no. 3 (2021): 341–68, https://doi.org/10.2298/FID2103341S; and Thomas Brudholm and Johannes Lang, "On Hatred and Dehumanization," in Maria Kronfeldner, ed., *The Routledge Handbook of Dehumanization* (London: Routledge, 2021).
6 Southern Poverty Law Center, *Ten Ways to Fight Hate: A Community Response Guide*, August 14, 2017, https://www.splcenter.org/20170814/ten-ways-fight-hate-community-response-guide.
7 Jeremy Waldron, *The Harm in Hate Speech* (Boston: Harvard University Press, 2014), 2.
8 For further discussion of the relationship between hate and power, see Claudia Card, *The Atrocity Paradigm* (Oxford: Oxford University Press, 2002).

For an analogous discussion of racism, hate, and power, see Susan E. Babbitt and Sue Campbell, eds., *Racism and Philosophy* (Ithaca, NY: Cornell University Press, 1999).

9 Stephen L. Darwall, "Two Kinds of Respect," *Ethics* 88, no. 1 (1977): 38, https://doi.org/10.1086/292054.

10 We have elsewhere written on the nature and limits of current conceptions of hate: Thomas Brudholm, "What Is Hate?," in Robert J. Sternberg, ed., *Perspectives on Hate: How It Originates, Develops, Manifests, and Spreads* (New York: American Psychological Association); Birgitte S. Johansen, "Hate as a Political Outcast," *Ethnologia Europea* 45, no. 2 (2015): 70–85, https://doi.org/10.16995/ee.1169.

11 For some recent contributions to the philosophical literature, see Berit Brogaard, *Hatred* (Oxford: Oxford University Press, 2020); Bennet W. Helm, "Hate, Identification, and Othering," *American Philosophical Quarterly* 60, no. 3 (2023): 289–310, https://doi.org/10.5406/21521123.60.3.06; Alessandro Salice, "I Hate You. On Hatred and Its Paradigmatic Forms," *Phenomenology and the Cognitive Sciences* 20, no. 4 (2021): 617–33, https://psycnet.apa.org/doi/10.1007/s11097-020-09668-0.

12 There is a growing literature on such intimidating effects, so-called "in terrorem" effects, of hate crime and hate incidents. See James Weinstein, "First Amendment Challenges to Hate Crime Legislation: Where's the Speech?," *Criminal Justice Ethics* 11, no. 2 (2010): 6–20, https://doi.org/10.1080/0731129X.1992.9991917; Paul Iganski, "Hate Crimes Hurt More," *American Behavioral Scientist* 45, no. 4 (2001): 626–38, https://doi.org/10.1177/0002764201045004006; and Barbara Perry and Shahid Alvi, "'We Are All Vulnerable': The *in terrorem* Effects of Hate Crimes," *International Review of Victimology* 18, no. 1 (2012): 57–71, https://doi.org/10.1177/0269758011422475.

13 C. Thi Nguyen, "Echo Chambers and Epistemic Bubbles," *Episteme* 17, no. 2 (2018): 141–61, https://doi.org/10.1017/epi.2018.32.

14 Ministry of Higher Education and Science, *The Danish Code of Conduct for Research Integrity*, November 2014, https://ufm.dk/en/publications/2014/the-danish-code-of-conduct-for-research-integrity.

15 Candis Delmas, *A Duty to Resist: When Disobedience Should Be Uncivil* (Oxford: Oxford University Press, 2018), 4.

16 For a recent discussion and overview, see Delmas, *A Duty to Resist*. Also, during our conversations with NGO representatives, the famous Battle of Cable Street was discussed as an example of the use of violence that was, arguably and in hindsight, justifiable. See Mike Cole, "The Battle of Cable Street," Historic UK, accessed January 2, 2025, https://www.historic-uk.com/HistoryUK/HistoryofBritain/Battle-Of-Cable-Street/.

17 See Norman Geras, *The Contract of Mutual Indifference: Political Philosophy after the Holocaust* (London: Verso, 1998), for a thought-provoking analysis of the moral significance of passive bystanding to violence.

18 Bard Center for the Study of Hate, Western States Center, and the Montana Human Rights Network, *A Community Guide for Opposing Hate*, 67, accessed January 2, 2025, https://bcsh.bard.edu/files/2022/05/Opposing HateGuide-single-pages-8M-5-3.pdf.

19 Anti-Defamation League, "Who We Are," accessed January 2, 2025, https://www.adl.org/about/who-we-are.

20 The consideration of equal concern for different groups weighs much more heavily on the shoulders of states and inter-state human rights instruments, and the modern history of antihate legislation in criminal law is, at least in part, a story about a long fight for recognition or inclusion of this or that category on the lists of protected characteristics. For example, across the European Union there has been ongoing discussion about the inclusion of sexual orientation and gender identities in national hate crime legislations and policing.

21 Arlie Russell Hochschild, *Strangers in Their Own Land: Anger and Mourning on the American Right* (New York: The New Press, 2016).

22 The case reached several international media outlets, including the *New York Times*.

23 See David Sausdal, "Police Prejudice or Logics? Analyzing the 'Bornholm Murder Case,'" *Conflict and Society: Advances in Research* 8, no. 1 (2022): 1–19, https://doi.org/10.3167/arcs.2022.080101.

24 For another case of debate as to the reality of hate-motivation in the US context, see Kenneth Stern, "What If Matthew Shepard's Murder Wasn't an Anti-Gay Hate Crime?," *Forward*, September 9, 2013, https://forward.com/opinion/183494/what-if-matthew-shepards-murder-wasnt-an-anti-gay/.

25 See Hippocrates, "Hippocratic Oath," accessed January 2, 2025, http://www.perseus.tufts.edu/hopper/text?doc=Perseus:text:1999.01.0252.

26 See World Medical Association, "Declaration of Geneva: The 'Modern Hippocratic Oath,'" accessed January 2, 2025, https://www.wma.net/what-we-do/medical-ethics/declaration-of-geneva/.

27 See Hannah Arendt, "Thinking and Moral Considerations: A Lecture," *Social Research* 38, no. 3 (1971): 417–46, https://www.jstor.org/stable/40970069.

28 Asking how *one* manages the struggle, we did not assume that *one* is uniform. One can be engaged in the struggle in many ways, from a variety of social positions, and with different degrees of resilience. For some, combating hate is a professional occupation and a matter of allyship (supporting marginalized groups without belonging to one oneself).

For others, hate is a threat to be fought, so to say, around the clock, because they themselves belong to one or several stigmatized groups. To this it should be added, as indicated in our introduction, that the terrain at hand would have been even more complex if we had also focused on NGOs located in countries and regions plagued by war, terror, and protracted group violence.

29 For a free online reproduction of the German story, see Heinrich von Kleist, "Michael Kohlhaas: Aus einer alten Chronik" (1810), Project Gutenberg-DE, accessed January 2, 2025, https://www.projekt-gutenberg .org/kleist/kohlhaas/kohlhaas.html.

30 See Immanuel Kant, "Book III: On the Faculty of Desire," in *Anthropology from a Pragmatic Perspective*, ed. and trans. Robert B. Louden (Cambridge: Cambridge University Press, 2006). First published 1798 (Germany).

31 Friedrich Nietzsche, Chapter IV, "Apophthegms and Interludes," no. 146, in *Beyond Good and Evil*, trans. Helen Zimmern, Project Gutenberg Ebook, updated January 19, 2019, https://www.gutenberg.org/cache/epub /4363/pg4363-images.html.

32 For a discussion of the notion of cycles of hatred, see Margaret Walker, "The Cycle of Violence," *Journal of Human Rights* 5, no. 1 (2006): 81–105, https://doi.org/10.1080/14754830500485890.

33 Lurking behind these forms of vicious mimicry lies the discussion whether "the hate" in response to "hate" should sometimes be acknowledged as a less vicious form of hate, or perhaps even moral hatred. For further discussion, see Marilyn Friedman, "Racism: Paradigms and Moral Appraisals (A Response to Blum)," in Susan E. Babitt and Sue Campbell, eds., *Racism and Philosophy* (Ithaca, NY: Cornell University Press 1999), 98–107.

34 For one of many interesting attempts to develop the concept, see David Batho and Camilla Pitton, "What Is Moral Distress? Experiences and Responses," Green Paper, The University of Essex, February 2018, https:// powerlessness.essex.ac.uk/wp-content/uploads /2018/02/MoralDistressGreenPaper1.pdf.

35 Ruth Levitas: *Utopia as Method: The Imaginary Reconstitution of Society* (New York: Palgrave Macmillan, 2013).

36 Kathryn J. Norlock, "Perpetual Struggle," *Hypatia* 34, no. 1 (2019): 6–19, https://doi.org/10.1111/hypa.12452.

37 Norlock, "Perpetual Struggle," 16.

38 Norlock, "Perpetual Struggle," 15.

Editor's Introduction to Chapter 2

When the Hate Studies initiative opened at Gonzaga University in the late 1990s, and we surveyed the different academic disciplines that had something useful to say about hate, I don't recall anyone suggesting brain science. A few years later I was speaking at a conference in Scottsdale, Arizona, about the Holocaust. I always address antisemitism in the context of what we know about hate, and toward that end I mentioned the Hate Studies work at Gonzaga. A retired neuroscientist in the audience named Edmund Glaser approached me afterwards. He had also spoken at the conference – about his experience as a photographer at the Nuremberg trials. He wondered what his field had to say about hate. I encouraged him to investigate, and write an article for the *Journal of Hate Studies*, which he did.[1] I found the idea that we could get insights into hate by putting people into magnetic resonance imaging (MRI) machines fascinating.

Since that time much more has been written, including by brain scientists such as Robert Sapolsky.[2] So, as we explore the different fields, after thinking about philosophy – which asks what we think about hate and the ethics of those choices – it made sense to look at the most basic level of our thoughts – how the brain works. We are, after all, human beings – animals. And our brain is the central area in our bodies that controls much of how we think and feel.

To combat hate, we have to take our brains on board, as they are. That means thinking about our messaging and programs, and are they designed to elicit a response from the parts of the brain that make us see a "them," or are they designed to activate the parts of the brain more likely to encourage empathy, and allow us to think more expansively about who is the "us." That's hard, because in times of perceived conflict against whomever we see as an "us," we tend to retreat into our tribal tents. It may be somewhat inevitable that our immediate reaction at these times is to strengthen the binary that, instead, makes people in our group feel more self-righteous and part of a team opposing a "them."

We are fortunate to have Adriana Galván, who is both the dean of undergraduates at UCLA and active in its Hate Studies program, guide us through brain science and hate – what we know and what we don't. Whether you remember the science she describes or not, the point is clear: all of us, whether those who promote hate or those who combat it, have brains poised to see "us" and "them." That's an observation that is hard for some of us to grasp. A few years ago, when teaching a group of Jewish communal professionals about antisemitism as a form of hate, one executive vehemently objected to the idea that hate was a part of the human condition. He preciously said, "I don't hate anyone – except antisemites."

NOTES

1 Edmund M. Glaser, "Is There a Neurobiology of Hate?," *Journal of Hate Studies* 7, no. 1 (2009): 7–19, https://repository.gonzaga.edu/jhs/vol7/iss1/2/.
2 See Robert Sapolsky, "This Is Your Brain on Nationalism: The Biology of Us and Them," *Foreign Affairs*, March/April 2019, https://www.foreignaffairs.com/world/your-brain-nationalism; and Robert Sapolsky, "Hate and the Brain," Bard Center for the Study of Hate, YouTube, May 13, 2020, video, 1:01:41, https://www.youtube.com/watch?v=S5g_LAoUYZQ&ab_channel=BardCenterfortheStudyofHate.

2 Elucidating the Brain Mechanisms That Underlie Hateful Behavior

ADRIANA GALVÁN

Précis

Hate is a complex construct that is undoubtedly influenced by many factors. The majority of chapters in this book provide commentary and synthesize scholarship on the factors that influence, create, and perpetuate hate. This chapter diverges from others in that it instead focuses on the (very limited) brain science related to hate. Is there hate in the brain? Do certain brain architectures lead to feelings of hate? The field of neuroscience has not evolved enough to answer such complex questions, but it has made significant strides in understanding how the human brain represents constructs very closely related to hate, including prejudice, bias, negative emotions, and threat. Neuroscientists and psychologists have identified brain regions that "light up" when experiencing these negative feelings and biases; these studies are summarized in the chapter. For most readers, the details of which brain regions are activated when an individual is experiencing prejudice, for example, will not be of particular interest so they can skim over explanations of the methods, experiments, and brain regions. What is important for the reader to glean is that these studies demonstrate how adaptable the brain is to one's environment and how the brain uses regions that have evolved for very basic reasons (e.g., the detection of threat, the feelings of fear) and hijacked them for more sophisticated purposes, such as the feeling of hate.

The chapter also highlights research on "dehumanization" and "us versus them" distinctions. The brain does not have a region that has evolved to dehumanize others but what research in this area shows is that the brain instead uses the very basic function of categorization (i.e., parsing out information into different categories) to make quick judgments about others. The ability to do this helps the brain work

efficiently. This is not to suggest that being able to categorize individuals into those who are "with us" versus those who are "against us" is
good, but rather, it provides a potential explanation for why humans
seem to make these distinctions almost automatically. It is because our
brains do it at the millisecond level – faster than the blink of an eye.

A latter section in the chapter examines why. Why do people hate –
is there something rewarding about hate? Based on the large body of
research that examines how the brain processes reward, this section
examines whether engaging in hateful behavior or bonding with others
about hatred toward a particular group elicits feelings of reward in the
brain. If so, this might also help explain what motivates individuals to
hate others, and to encourage others to hate. The very limited number
of neuroimaging studies that have examined hate provide some preliminary evidence that reward may play a role in perpetuating hateful
behavior.

The brain research summarized in this chapter is dense. However, it
may provide a preliminary view into the neural basis of the very complex behaviors that undergird hate. Similar to how brain science has
been used to predict, redirect, or mitigate other problematic behaviors,
the emerging research on the neuroscience of hate may also provide
another dimension in our understanding and eradication of hate.

∼

The goal of this chapter is to provide an overview of what is currently
known about the neural underpinnings of hate. The short answer is:
not much. The field of neuroscience has not kept pace with the extensive scholarship, interest, and relevance of studying hate now and
throughout history. There is no subfield on the "neurobiology of hate."
However, there *is* a rich literature on neural representations in the brain
of various constructs and mechanisms that are tightly related to hate –
such as anger, fear, prejudice, bias, power, and emotion. This chapter
will begin with a synthesis of current knowledge of the neurobiology
of these constructs and how they may relate to our understanding of
hate. The latter half of this chapter will provide an overview of the few
studies (and their methodological limitations) that have aimed to identify circuits in the brain that process hate. Due to the multi-semantic
nature of hate, the chapter is written to encompass various disciplines
and perspectives. As such, I begin the discussion in each subsection
by stipulating the context and definitions used. Although the focus of
this chapter will be on the neurobiology that may contribute to hateful

behavior, I draw on social-psychological perspectives to examine hate from a multifaceted lens.

As the reader reviews the research presented here, I invite them to consider the following: What is the value of examining questions of hate from the perspective of neuroscience? Whether particular brain regions are active when experiencing feelings of hate is not alone going to advance understanding and/or mitigation of hate. However, there may be some insights derived from understanding the neural mechanisms that underlie feelings of hate and/or hateful behavior. First, neuroimaging offers a unique way of uncovering participants' automatic, nonconscious responses to stimuli.[1] As the reader will note, the brain imaging studies reviewed here illustrate how constructs related to hate elicit both overlapping and distinct activation among key neural networks. Second, research indicates that functional magnetic resonance imaging (fMRI) studies – the most widely used tool to estimate how the brain functions – can accurately predict real-world human behavior,[2] supporting its valuable role in complementing psychological studies.[3] Despite these contributions, there are limits to what neuroscience can offer on this topic. The most glaring limitation is that emulating real-world feelings, events, and behaviors in a brain scanner is nearly impossible. Cognitive neuroscientists rely on images or videos or induction exercises to engage the brain's response to particular psychological states – including those reviewed here. Therefore, we can never exactly "prove" that the stimuli are actually inducing the psychological state of interest so ecological validity is not ensured. Second, fMRI has poor temporal resolution. This means that the brain response measured is delayed relative to the actual neuronal response,[4] which may make it challenging to discern which brain regions are responding to a particular stimulus. Third, analysis of fMRI data varies by research lab. If corrections for multiple comparisons are not statistically accounted for, the chances of finding false positive results are greatly inflated because brain imaging studies yield hundreds of thousands of datapoints.[5] Another complication is that there is no single way to acquire, preprocess, or analyze fMRI data.[6] The final results are significantly influenced by each analytical choice the researchers make.

Perhaps the most challenging issue with brain imaging research is that interpreting fMRI data is not straightforward. When researchers see a particular brain region exhibit greater (or less) activation in response to stimuli, they typically infer the meaning of the activation based on previous research of that brain region. For example, the amygdala, a brain region that will feature prominently in this chapter, is often referred to as the seat of emotion processing. Although emotion processing is one known function of the amygdala, it is also involved during learning, face processing, when presented with a novel object, and also in helping the organism stay alert during times of uncertainty.[7] Thus, when the amygdala is activated during an fMRI study the researcher must infer *why* the amygdala is engaged – in response to images the researcher believes to elicit feelings of threat (a gun for example) the researcher may assume the amygdala is processing (and reflective of feelings of) threat. This interpretation is quite plausible and reasonable based on extant research, but an alternative explanation may be that the amygdala is instead responding to the novelty of the gun if the research participant has limited familiarity with it. Yet another alternative is that the amygdala is monitoring both feelings of threat and novelty. To better approximate the reason why the particular brain region is active, appropriate and rigorous controls must be included in the experimental design. To disentangle the brain response to threat versus novelty, for example, research participants should be shown the "threatening" images (e.g., gun) and images that are also novel to participants but not threatening (e.g., perhaps an obscure tool). If the amygdala responds to both objects, the researchers might conclude that it is reflecting novelty, but if it exhibits greater activation to the gun versus the obscure tool, then the researchers may have greater confidence in the hypothesis that the amygdala activation is reflective of feelings of threat. The complex and multifaceted nature of hate makes experimental design particularly challenging because there is no perfect control condition – should the control condition be images that represent the opposite of hate (i.e., love) or indifference? Or is a better control condition one that invites the brain to compare hated (but unfamiliar) persons with unfamiliar persons to isolate the feelings of hate irrespective of close contact? Researchers grapple with challenging questions such as these when studying complex emotions. So too must consumers of brain imaging studies consider the limitations when evaluating the utility of them in studies of complex human behaviors and motivations. Nonetheless, the study of emotion and other complex psychological constructs has benefited from understanding the neural underpinnings and may help us better understand hate.

Is Hate an Emotion?

In the scientific literature, there is disagreement as to whether hate is an emotion. There is actually little consensus about what an emotion is.[8] The first documented discussion of the issue was presented by the American psychologist William James in 1884 who asked, "What is an emotion?"[9] James would be disappointed to know that his astute question remains unanswered today, as scientists continue to grapple with how emotions should be defined, where the thresholds are for what constitutes an emotion, and the universality of emotions. Over a century later, neuroscientist Joseph LeDoux noted that "one of the most significant things ever said about emotion may be that everyone knows what it is until they are asked to define it."[10] On the one hand, emotions are considered "functional states" that undergird behavior (e.g., the emotion of fear helps in evading a predator) and are fairly universal.[11] Another view is that emotions are both consciously and unconsciously experienced (e.g., the internal milieu of the body that is not consciously observed) and, therefore, everybody's experience of emotion is different and partially based on their previous experience of the emotion[12] that constructs their "social reality."[13] The fact that feelings cannot be measured directly makes it quite challenging to conduct research on feelings and emotions. Instead, researchers rely on "outward expression of emotional responses"[14] or on what humans state they feel.

Emotions generally fall into two subcategories: basic emotions and complex emotions. Basic emotions are those that are universally expressed and recognized in people around the world, conserved in our close animal ancestors, and supposedly hard-wired into brain circuits by evolution.[15] The original list of basic emotions was fear, anger, happiness, sadness, disgust, and surprise[16] but these have been challenged.[17] A hallmark of basic emotions is that they are associated with universally recognizable facial expressions. Complex emotions, defined by the 2018 edition of the *American Psychological Association Dictionary of Psychology* as an emotion that is an aggregate of two or more others, include awe, disgust, embarrassment, envy, guilt, jealousy, pride, remorse, shame, and worry.[18] According to the dictionary, hate is "considered a fusion of anger, fear, and disgust."[19] To the extent that hate can be defined within the context of emotion, it stands to reason that it is best defined as a complex emotion that draws on multiple brain circuits and feelings to produce a unique expression of behavior. However, greater exploration of the definition space is warranted.[20] Fischer and colleagues propose that the goal of hate is "not merely to hurt, but to ultimately eliminate or destroy the target, either mentally (humiliating, treasuring feelings of revenge), socially (excluding, ignoring), or physically (killing, torturing), which may be accompanied by the goal to let the wrongdoer suffer (Ben-Ze'ev, 2008)."[21] In other words, they define hate on the social functional perspective on emotions[22] – based on the desired outcomes, not simply on the negativity associated with the feelings it elicits.

A major challenge with determining whether hate is an emotion is the vast within-category variability of what hate means to different people and how liberally the word is used. Hate is used to describe hatred and intense negative feelings toward a group of individuals or a culture or a religion, but it is also used to describe relatively petty nuisances we all "hate" such as traffic or sitting on the tarmac for a delayed flight. One of hate's core characteristics is that it is enduring (unlike, say, fear or anger), and not typically a reaction to a specific event.[23] A second issue with thinking of hate as an emotion is that emotions are generally considered to be essential for survival.[24] Fear is necessary for us to identify threat in the environment, and anger is helpful in motivating behavior, but is hate necessary for the survival of the human species?

How the Brain Processes Threat and Fear

Neuroscientists have spent decades meticulously identifying how the brain processes threats in the environment. This literature is relevant to hate insofar as hateful behavior is the consequence of feeling threatened, afraid, or suspicious of the hated. There is strong evidence for "defense circuits" in the brain[25] that are found even in single-celled organisms.[26] It is also clear that a perceived threat is species-specific: rats are threatened by predator odors,[27] particular auditory stimuli,[28] and bright open spaces,[29] whereas primates trigger defense circuits at the sight of snakes and spiders[30] and human primates trigger defense circuits at the sight of fearful and aggressive faces of conspecifics.[31] For example, a complex multi-region response is triggered when rodents smell odors that signal predators, one that involves signaling among sensory regions (e.g., the olfactory system), homeostatic regions (e.g., the hypothalamus), and emotion regions (e.g., the amygdala).[32] This coordinated response leads to defensive behavior, which may include freezing behavior, or the "fight-or-flight response," which was first described by Walter Bradford Cannon[33] and that has been extensively studied since.

In humans, feelings of threat and fear are complex. Although considered a "basic emotion," fear is nuanced. In fact, in the English language there are more than thirty words that are used to rank and classify feelings of fear (including fear, panic, anxiety, worry, terror, dismay, suspicion, foreboding, and apprehension) and even colloquial phrases (e.g., the "creeps," "heebie-jeebies"). Thousands of studies on the neural circuits that underlie fear and "threatening" stimuli have coalesced around a general fear/threat circuit in the human brain. This is pretty remarkable because the stimuli used to elicit feelings of fear vary by

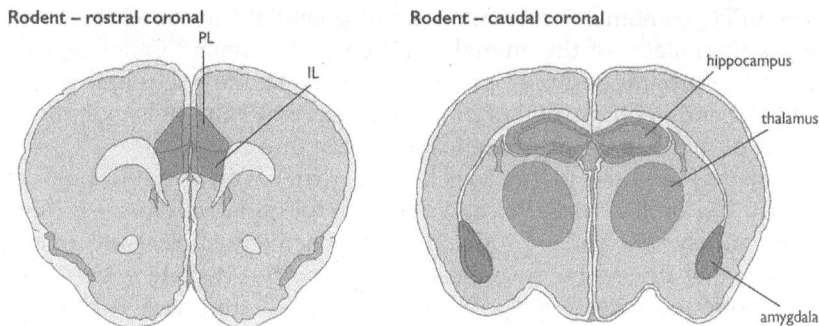

Figure 2.1. Brain regions involved in threat detection and fear.

Source: M. Alexandra Kredlow et al., "Prefrontal Cortex, Amygdala, and Threat Processing: Implications for PTSD," *Neuropsychopharmacology* 47 (2022): 247–59, https://doi.org/10.1038/s41386-021-01155-7. Reproduced with permission from *Springer Nature*.

stimulus type (e.g., images of angry faces, specific threats such as guns or fire) and modality of delivery (e.g., pictures, electric shocks) across fMRI studies. Researchers know that these stimuli are imperfect, recognizing that whether images of an angry person or one wielding a knife actually elicit feelings of threat or fear in a research participant is questionable, but without better alternatives they are the best option. Using these stimuli, presented to research participants while undergoing a brain scan, neuroscientists have identified the key regions of the fear/threat circuit as the amygdala, hypothalamus, medial prefrontal cortex (mPFC), and hippocampus.[34] This circuit, illustrated in figure 2.1, is among the most well understood behavioral circuits in neuroscience.[35] In addition to serving as a threat detector and to learn about potential threats,[36] the amygdala serves to communicate the salience of the threat cue to the mPFC.[37] As one node in the threat circuit, the hippocampus encodes contextual information about a threat and, through memory processing, helps the animal determine whether the threat in question is one previously encountered.[38] If it is a new threat, it stores the information to create a new memory that will aid the animal in sensing and avoiding the threat in future encounters,[39] a process that is supported by nuclei in the thalamus.[40] As described in an excellent review by Kredlow and colleagues,[41] the mPFC serves as an integration hub of inputs from subcortical structures, including the amygdala, hippocampus, ventral striatum, hypothalamus, periaqueductal gray, and cerebellum, among others, that it then uses to modify "behavioral decisions on a moment-to-moment basis."[42] In particular, the mPFC combines information about potential threats with current behavioral states of the animal to influence behavior.[43] Other regions of the prefrontal cortex – namely, the dorsolateral prefrontal cortex (dlPFC) and ventromedial prefrontal cortex (vmPFC) – help extinguish a fear or regulate the response to a potential threat.[44]

A neural response to threats is necessary for survival, but it comes at a cost. The brain's resources and attention for other activities – including nourishment and reproduction – are actively suppressed in the presence of threats because these other activities deplete energy and metabolic resources.[45] Response to threats and suppression of other activities has primarily been studied in nonhuman animals, but there is evidence that humans also diminish attentional resources to activities that detract from a focus on the threat.[46] Since the majority of this human research has focused on acute threats and suppression of other activities, it would be interesting to examine whether focus on a perceived threat over a prolonged amount of time also dampens attention to other key activities over time.

Prejudice in the Brain

Prejudice and stereotypes together influence social behavior toward outgroup members.[47] Prejudice is defined as an evaluation of, or an emotional response toward, a social group grounded in preconceptions based on its group membership. Stereotypes are the cognitive component of intergroup bias and the conceptual attributes associated with a particular social group.[48] Are there brain regions that categorize the psychological phenomenon of "us versus them"? As the neurobiologist and primatologist Robert Sapolsky notes: "Dividing the world into Us and Them is deeply hard-wired."[49]

Neuroscience studies of prejudice and stereotypes have shown engagement of brain regions that are also implicated in threat detection (figure 2.2). In general, the amygdala is involved in the rapid processing of social category cues, including racial groups, in terms of a potential threat or reward. However, the multiple nuclei in the amygdala seem to independently contribute to different aspects of prejudice. Sensory inputs enter the lateral nucleus of the amygdala (LA) and, depending on the context and nature of the stimuli, this signal is directed to the central nucleus of the amygdala (CeA), which supports a threat response, or to the basal nucleus of the amygdala (BA), which supports an instrumental response.[50] An early fMRI study of implicit prejudice focused on the amygdala response to Black and white faces.[51] A behavioral index of implicit prejudice collected from research participants

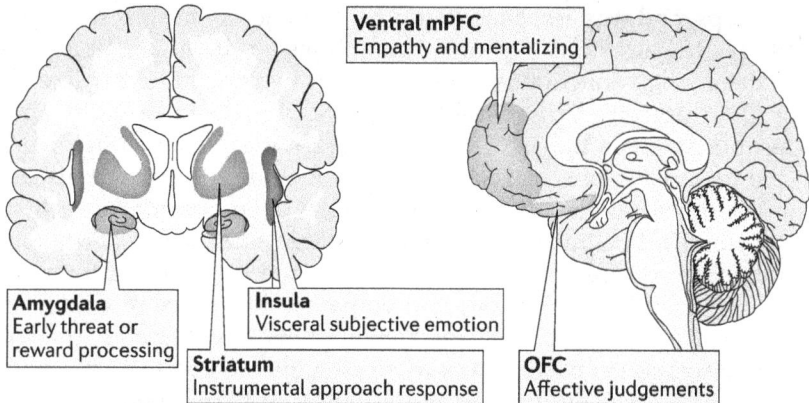

Figure 2.2. Brain regions in the "Prejudice Network" – an interactive set of neural structures that underlie components of a prejudiced response.

Source: David M. Amodio, "The Neuroscience of Prejudice and Stereotyping," *Nature Reviews Neuroscience* 15, no. 10 (2014): 670–82, https://doi.org/10.1038/nrn3800. Reproduced with permission from *Springer Nature*.

was associated with amygdala activity in response to Black compared with white faces.[52] Many subsequent brain imaging studies have also observed a relationship between activation in the amygdala and behavioral indices of implicit bias or prejudice. Much of this research suggests that the amygdala response reflects an immediate (or implied) threat response to racial outgroup members.[53] For example, in white subjects viewing images of Black faces, amygdala activation is greater in response to faces with darker rather than lighter skin tone.[54] However, there is a dampened difference in the amygdala response to outgroup versus ingroup faces when there is greater familiarity with racial outgroup members,[55] which seems to emerge in adolescence.[56] Together, these findings may be evidence for the notion from social psychology theories that implicit prejudice reflects a type of threat processing.[57]

Although the majority of research on the neuroscience of prejudice has focused on the amygdala, it does not work in isolation. For example, the striatum, a brain region typically associated with responding to reward, shows the opposite response from that of the amygdala: there is greater activation of the striatum when participants viewed pictures of ingroup versus outgroup members.[58] The insula, which has been implicated in a variety of neural processing, including disgust, exhibits a greater response to racial outgroup versus ingroup members.[59] This finding reflects a negative visceral reaction, such as disgust, to racial outgroups, and was associated with white subjects' implicit negative attitudes toward outgroup members. However, it should be noted that the insula's function is more than simply responding to visceral stimuli or perceived disgust – it is also responsive to empathy and other positive emotions.[60] The medial prefrontal cortex is involved in the processing of social information,[61] including forming impressions of other people, perspective-taking, and empathy.[62] As such, a diminished mPFC response to a social target has been interpreted to be a form of prejudice that is characterized by a lack of humanization (i.e., dehumanization) and empathy. One piece of evidence that might corroborate this interpretation is that there is greater mPFC activation in participants when viewing members of esteemed groups associated with pride and admiration than when a subject views members of perceived low-status groups associated with disgust and disregard.[63]

In contrast to prejudice, which seems to elicit greater activation in subcortical brain regions, stereotyping elicits greater engagement of cortical structures. These regions are those that support more general forms of semantic memory, object memory, retrieval, and conceptual activation, such as the temporal lobes and inferior frontal gyrus (IFG), as well as regions that are involved in impression formation, such as the mPFC[64] (figure 2.3). Specifically, the anterior temporal lobe (ATL), which stores and represents social knowledge[65] represents stereotype-related information.[66] The ATL provides input to the mPFC, which is involved in the formation of impressions about an individual.[67] This is the mechanism by which social stereotypes "stored" in the ATL are thought to influence trait impression processes associated with activation in the mPFC. The application of stereotypes to behavior seems to involve regions of the lateral PFC that are associated with goal representation and response inhibition.[68] Together, the structures in this network may support the storage, activation, and behavioral expression of social stereotypes.

These exemplars illustrating how cognitive neuroscientists have aimed to identify the neural bases for prejudice highlight the notion that there is *no one* brain region implicated in prejudice, nor that activation in a particular brain region is necessarily evidence for prejudice, but rather that neural activation patterns are as complex as the psychological feelings and multilayered attributions that yield prejudiced behavior. Furthermore, regions implicated in threat and prejudice, such as the amygdala, are also responsive to novel faces, so greater activation in response to an outgroup may also be reflective of less familiarity with outgroup faces.[69]

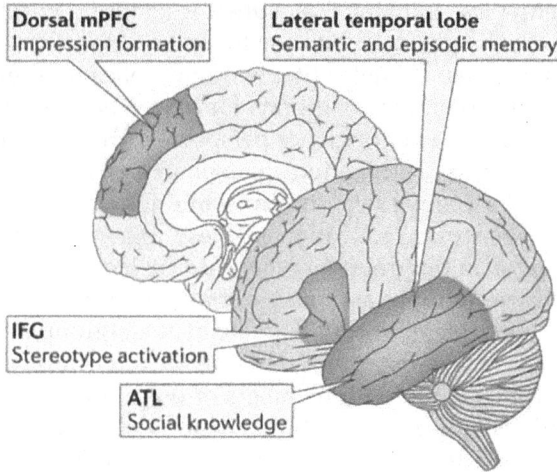

Figure 2.3. Neural structures that underlie components of intergroup stereotyping.

Source: David M. Amodio, "The Neuroscience of Prejudice and Stereotyping," *Nature Reviews Neuroscience* 15, no. 10 (2014): 670–82, https://doi.org/10.1038/nrn3800. Reproduced with permission from *Springer Nature*.

Several pieces of evidence point to a basic human aversion to physically harming others.[70] So then how does an intergroup threat lead to violence? Throughout human evolution, belonging to a group was intimately tied to survival.[71] Indeed, neuroimaging studies show that activation patterns in the brain differentiate "us versus them." Brain regions that respond to pain perception and empathy, including the anterior cingulate cortex (ACC) and anterior insula (AI), exhibit greater activity when seeing ingroup versus outgroup members in pain.[72] Regions involved in more basic functions such as face processing (i.e., the fusiform face area) exhibit an increased neural response in response to ingroup (versus outgroup) faces.[73] According to intergroup threat theory, outgroup threats can take the form of a realistic or symbolic threat.[74] Realistic threats are those presenting direct danger to the ingroup's physical safety, power, or resources, while symbolic threats risk the ingroup's traditions, values, ideology, religion, and cultural customs. In one recent fMRI study, non-Muslim Caucasian participants observed stereotypically Muslim-looking men make threatening or reconciliatory statements toward their ingroup.[75] The authors found that threatening statements increased activity in areas previously related to the detection and processing of threat (i.e., amygdala and insula), stereotypical thinking (i.e., superior temporal gyrus and temporal poles), and heightened attention to semantic information (i.e., the supramarginal gyrus).[76] Walter Stephan and colleagues suggest that one of the most prominent conditions for perceived intergroup threat is uncertainty.[77] From a neuroscience perspective, this may help explain why there is increased activation in regions associated with uncertainty, including the amygdala, striatum, anterior cingulate cortex, and insula.[78] In other words, activation in these regions when presented with an image of an outgroup member may be less of an "emotional" response as it was at times assumed, but rather a reflection of the lack of familiarity (i.e., greater uncertainty) about an outgroup member. One way to mitigate uncertainty may be to provide opportunity for greater exposure and interaction with members of outgroups. Indeed, neuroimaging findings indicate that rehumanization of targets may be possible when actively trying to engage in mentalization.[79]

Dehumanization

Dehumanization, the deprivation of positive human qualities to a person or group – and thus associating them with an entity less than human – contributes to prejudice and hateful behavior. While we have an aversion toward harming other human beings, this aversion is less for nonhuman entities, enabling violence toward dehumanized individuals.[80] Collectively, fMRI studies have found robust evidence that the brain quickly categorizes objects and humans along a dehumanization spectrum. For example, Harris and Fiske report that when viewing pictures of dehumanized groups, participants showed diminished activity in the mPFC,[81] which is a key brain region involved in perspective-taking.[82] When attributing less humanity to a target, participants also exhibited greater neural activity in the ACC.[83] A separate study examined participants' neural responses to viewing images of stereotypically dehumanized groups compared to viewing affectively negative images of control targets (e.g., a couple in a cemetery or a soldier firing a gun); results revealed greater activation in the mPFC (along with activity in several temporal and occipital regions) in response to control targets compared to dehumanized targets.[84]

Is Hate Rewarding?

All organisms are motivated by reward. When a stimulus/behavior/ individual elicits feelings of reward, we act to achieve more of that reward. This psychological state is represented in the extensively studied mesolimbic circuit in the brain. This network, including the striatum, ventral tegmental area, amygdala, thalamus, hippocampus, and other limbic and cortical areas, has been consistently associated with reward processing. A reward, any stimulus that an organism finds appetitive, elicits increased approach behavior. The neural regions that govern these behaviors share a few characteristics. First, they are rich in the neurotransmitter dopamine and bidirectionally project to one another, comprising what is known as the "reward system." Second, the neural systems that process reward are conserved across age, organisms, and species.

Dopamine is a neurotransmitter that is critically involved in detecting, responding to, and learning from rewarding events.[85] Dopamine neurons fire vigorously in response to rewards,[86] social interactions,[87] and unexpected events or stimuli.[88] Neurocircuitry involved in reward processing is comprised of regions rich in dopamine and/or which receive innervation from dopaminergic neurons. At the center of this network is the cortico-ventral basal ganglia circuit, which consists of a distributed neural network that includes the ventral striatum, the anterior cingulate cortex, the orbitofrontal cortex, the ventral pallidum, and midbrain dopamine neurons.[89] Additionally, auxiliary structures, including the dorsolateral prefrontal cortex, amygdala, hippocampus, thalamus, habenula, and regions in the brainstem help regulate reward neurocircuitry.[90] This network works to integrate reward-related information and translate motivation into motor output.[91]

The ventral striatum (VS) is the striatal region that has been most strongly implicated in reward. It includes the nucleus accumbens and the broad continuity between the caudate nucleus and putamen ventral to the rostral internal capsule, the olfactory tubercle, and the rostrolateral portion of the anterior space adjacent to the lateral olfactory tract in primates.[92] Most input to the VS is from the orbitofrontal cortex, insular cortex, cingulate cortex, and amygdala,[93] regions discussed previously for their role in threat processing and prejudice. Together, this complex network facilitates the coordinated effort that is required for an organism to predict, evaluate, and respond to a reward.

Why is a discussion of reward relevant for a chapter on hate? From a mechanistic perspective, the brain regions implicated in reward overlap, and/or receive projections from, those that represent psychological constructs associated with hate – threat, prejudice, dehumanization. There is also a deeper conceptual link. Individuals who feel hatred toward a particular group of people often feel a sense of cohesion with other individuals. In other words, hatred is a shared, and unifying, experience. The mesolimbic reward circuit undergirds the deeply gratifying feeling of being aligned with, connected to, and accepted by others. Might the pleasurable feelings of being united in hatred sustain hateful feelings and motivate hateful behavior? There is some evidence for this. In an excellent review piece by Joseph Walther, he notes that "a theory of online hate based on social approval suggests that individuals and collaborators generate hate messages to garner reward, for their antagonism toward mutually hated targets, by providing friendship and social support that enhances perpetrators' well-being as it simultaneously deepens their prejudices."[94]

The need to belong is a fundamental human motivation first described by Roy Baumeister and Mark Leary[95] in a landmark paper that has since been researched extensively by others.[96] Baumeister and Leary's basic premise is that all of us seek out interpersonal attachment that is not only a desire but a basic human need. Some individuals achieve that sense of belonging through their community, family, or other personal relationships. Indeed, feeling close to others – whether through romantic love,[97] friendships,[98] or parent-child bonding – elicits activation in a broad network of brain regions often associated with emotion, attention, perspective-taking, and reward processing. Research suggests that those who hate may also experience rewarding feelings when they form affiliative bonds with others who have a similar hatred toward a particular group. Some join online and offline hate groups precisely to form friendships and cultivate a sense of belonging.[99] For example, people generate hate messages online primarily to accrue signals of admiration and praise from sympathetic online peers and to make friends.[100] An approval-seeking theory of online hate suggests that a primary motivation for individuals to express hate online is the interaction among haters they experience and the gratifications that they glean from mutual social attention and social approval[101] from both unknown in-group partisans as well as from those with whom they develop intensely interpersonal relationships online.[102] In a study with right-wing nationalists, Sahana Udupa contends that participation in hateful behavior and speech is also fun for the haters. In particular, participants have fun with making their hateful speech funny or witty, as well as when they hold meme contests and celebrate hashtag trending.[103] In other words, the social acceptance, bonding, and understanding is itself rewarding, thus fulfilling the "need to belong."

Another consideration is that in addition to fulfilling a need to belong, might hate be fulfilling the need to contribute? Long-standing scholarship demonstrates that as an intensely social species, humans demonstrate the propensity to contribute to other individuals and groups by providing support, resources, or helping to achieve a shared goal.[104] People voluntarily give time, energy, and resources to their social group.[105] Providing assistance to others may be a mechanism by which to satisfy the fundamental needs of helping, autonomy, relatedness, and competence posited by self-determination theory.[106] Other theorists cite the evolved social imperative of humans as the reason why we give to and help others.[107] There are also social, psychological, and health benefits of contributing to others[108] across the lifespan.[109] Those who engage in hateful behavior presumably feel justified in their hate toward a particular group and may feel as though they are contributing to (or defending) their own group. This in and of itself elicits feelings of reward. Brain imaging studies have demonstrated that brain regions and networks involved in processing reward, social cognition, and cognitive control engage in response to helping behavior.[110] Activation in the ventral striatum and ventral tegmental area correlate with actual giving behavior during experiments in which participants had the opportunity to give to charities or others, perhaps reflecting the psychosocial rewards of helping.[111]

Whether or not hateful speech and behavior is initially motivated by reward, it is quite plausible that rewards – a sense of affiliation, belonging, and contribution – help sustain the actions and feelings that perpetuate hate. It is thus unsurprising that the few studies that have examined hate using brain imaging (reviewed below) report a vast network of brain regions previously implicated in a range of psychological constructs, including emotion, prejudice, and reward.

Preliminary Studies on the Neural Basis of Hate

All of the constructs described thus far, including emotions, threat, prejudice, and stereotype, have received extensive neuroscientific attention. Thousands of brain imaging studies have identified the neural regions and networks that represent these psychological processes in the human brain. For that reason, it is particularly surprising that research to identify neural circuits implicated in hateful behavior is extremely limited. One reason may be because the definition of hate, as described above, remains rather elusive. Another is because there are some methodological challenges in this type of research that make the data particularly challenging to interpret.

In an fMRI study, Semir Zeki and John Paul Romaya presented research participants with images of a person they hated – in most cases an ex-lover or competitor at work – as well as images of acquaintances for whom they had neutral feelings.[112] Relative to viewing an acquaintance, viewing a hated person yielded increased activation in several brain regions, including the medial frontal gyrus, right putamen, premotor cortex, and the insula (figure 2.4). Due to the small sample size,

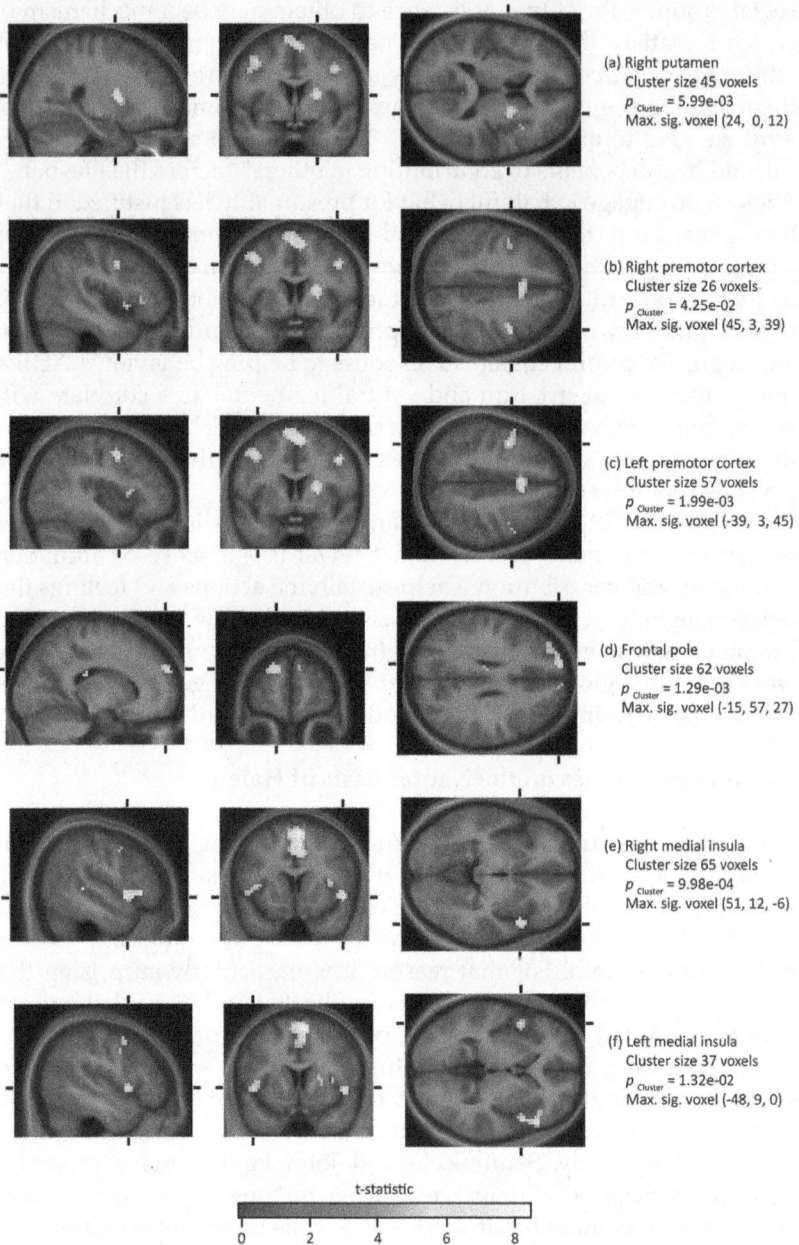

Figure 2.4. Activation for the contrast of hated faces versus neutral faces in the right putamen (a); right premotor cortex (b); left premotor cortex (c); frontal pole (d); right medial insula (e); and left medial insula (f).

Source: Semir Zeki and John Paul Romaya, "Neural Correlates of Hate," *PLoS One* 3 no. 10 (2008): e3556, https://doi.org/10.1371/journal.pone.0003556.

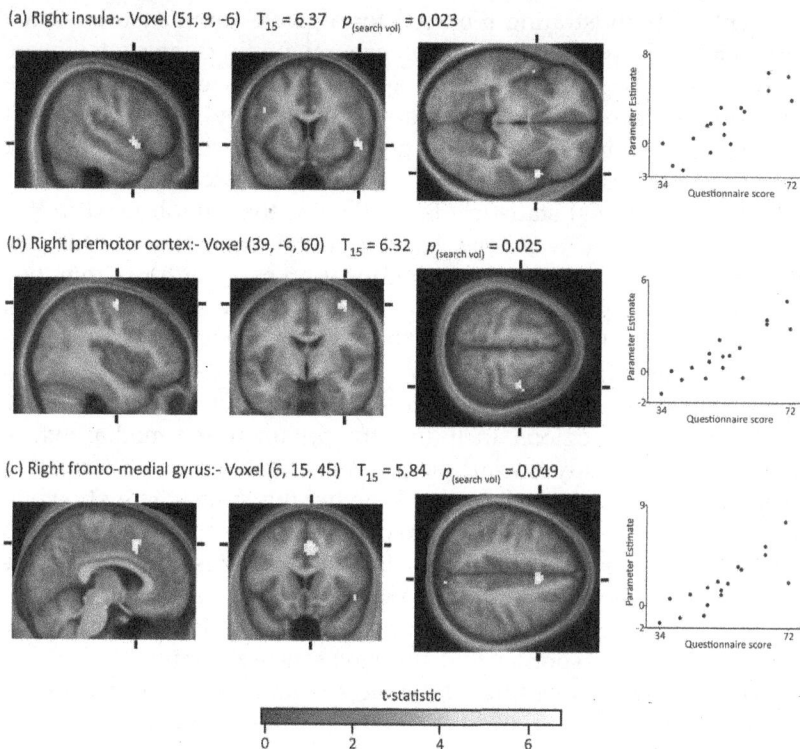

(a) Right insula:- Voxel (51, 9, -6) T_{15} = 6.37 $p_{(search\ vol)}$ = 0.023

(b) Right premotor cortex:- Voxel (39, -6, 60) T_{15} = 6.32 $p_{(search\ vol)}$ = 0.025

(c) Right fronto-medial gyrus:- Voxel (6, 15, 45) T_{15} = 5.84 $p_{(search\ vol)}$ = 0.049

t-statistic

Figure 2.5. The relation between hate scores and brain activation in the insula (a); right premotor cortex (b); and right fronto-medial gyrus (c).

Source: Semir Zeki and John Paul Romaya, "Neural Correlates of Hate," *PLoS One* 3 no. 10 (2008): e3556, https://doi.org/10.1371/journal.pone.0003556.

interpretation of the results is challenging but it does implicate neural regions that have previously been associated with evaluation, action, and disgust. Participants also completed a questionnaire (the Passionate Hate Scale [PHS]) that provided a "hate score." Individuals with higher PHS scores exhibited greater activation in the insula, right premotor cortex, and right medial frontal gyrus (figure 2.5).

This research is innovative in being among the first studies to tackle this question but there are a few limitations to note. One, as noted above, is the very small sample size. When this study was published in 2008, an fMRI study with only seventeen participants was considered modest in size for statistical power but not too uncommon. In present day, a study with seventeen participants in neurotypical humans would struggle to get published because of statistical advancements in recent years illustrating the need for a greater number of research participants. Second, although the general findings presented were analyzed using rigorous statistical approaches (corrected for multiple comparisons using Gaussian random field theory), activations that specifically examined brain activation to a hated versus neutral face were only significant at an uncorrected (less statistically rigorous and potentially spurious) statistical level. Finally, the stimuli used in this study is confounded with love. The object of hate for many of the participants (exact number not provided) was an ex-lover for whom they presumably had passionate feelings of love before strong feelings of hate. Participants were not asked if they retained feelings of love for the person they hated; therefore, activation in the brain that may have been attributed to love – rather than hate – is not accounted for. Indeed, the authors note that regions, including the putamen and medial insula, activated in this study toward the hated person were also activated in an earlier study of romantic love.[113] Whether this similar activation pattern indicates that hate and love are closely related or that the research participants in this particular study had both feelings of love and hate while viewing the images is unknown. However, the insula is a brain region that has been implicated in responding to disgust[114] and more broadly in neural responses to distressing sensory stimuli.[115]

A different study identified differences among individuals who suffer from depression compared to those who do not in what was called a "hate circuit"[116] – defined as activation in the superior frontal gyrus, insula, and putamen. Specifically, the researchers observed differences in co-activation among these brain regions in those with depression as compared to those without depression. It should be noted that no other research group has used this terminology to describe brain activation related to hate, and these researchers use that term only because these are the same brain regions observed in the Zeki and Romaya study described above. No hate data were collected in this study – in other words, activation in these brain regions was not related to any measure of hate in the research participants – so attributing differences in activation among depressed versus nondepressed participants to a "hate circuit" is questionable.

A recent study took a different approach to the study of hate in the brain. They examined whether exposure to "hate speech,"[117] defined as "a derogatory language based on racial, religious, or sexual prejudice,"[118] influences neural mechanisms of empathy toward an ingroup versus an outgroup. Agnieszka Pluta and colleagues recruited Polish research participants in Poland to an fMRI study in which they were exposed to either hateful or neutral comments. An example of a hateful comment directed against immigrants and refugees used in this study was, "We need to defend Europe against the hordes."[119] The neutral comments consisted of comments related to current economic and legal issues. Participants were then exposed to narratives depicting individuals of Polish (ingroup) and Arab (outgroup) descent in pain. Arabs were chosen as the outgroup because of recent geopolitical circumstances in which they have "been subject to political attacks in the Polish media."[120] Findings indicate that hateful comments about Arabs attenuated neural responses in the temporal parietal junction (TPJ) to someone else's pain, irrespective of whether the person in pain was in the ingroup or outgroup. This is interesting because the TPJ has been previously shown to be associated with perspective-taking[121] and empathy,[122] so perhaps this finding helps explain how hateful speech may lead to desensitization and harm intergroup relations.[123] Indeed, the authors interpret the data as supporting the psychological numbing hypothesis, that repeated exposure to negatively charged messages with a high emotional intensity leads to psychological desensitization.[124] This aligns with a different study showing that people show diminished brain activity of the anterior cingulate cortex in response to physical pain experienced by others of different ethnicities.[125]

Conclusion

Complex emotions and feelings, fueled by tangled individual and cultural histories, underlie hateful behavior. Accordingly, hate draws upon a parallel complexity at the neuronal level with a highly interconnected network of brain regions. Although brain regions each have their own "specialty," they are each also involved in representing numerous psychological processes, particularly one as complicated as hate. As reviewed in this chapter, brain regions that are known to be involved in processing emotion, prejudice, and threat – the exact psychological constructs that are likely associated with hate – likely underlie hate. Additionally, the brain's reward circuit may play a role in the positive feelings those who hate may experience when bonding with others over their shared hatred. However, I must reiterate that the brain is not designed with a "hate circuit" but, rather, the brain utilizes existing information processing networks to represent hate.

It is intriguing that hate remains an understudied topic in psychology and neuroscience. Hate is a complex phenomenon that is hard to operationalize and for most psychological and neuroscientific studies, the construct of interest needs to have been clearly defined. However, current geopolitical events may serve as the impetus to draw attention to hate and the need to understand it from a multidisciplinary perspective.

NOTES

1 Dorottya Lantos and Pascall Molenberghs, "The Neuroscience of Intergroup Threat and Violence," *Neuroscience & Biobehavioral Reviews* 131 (2021): 77–87, https://doi.org/10.1016/j.neubiorev.2021.09.025.

2 Elliot Berkman and Emily Falk, "Beyond Brain Mapping: Using Neural Measures to Predict Real-World Outcomes," *Current Direction in Psychological Science* 22, no. 1 (2013): 45–50, https://doi.org/10.1177/0963721412469394.

3 Lantos and Molenberghs, "The Neuroscience of Intergroup Threat and Violence."

4 Jason C. Coronel and Emily Falk, "Functional Magnetic Resonance Imaging and Communication Science," in Jörg Matthes, Christine S. Davis, and Robert F. Potter, eds., *The International Encyclopedia of Communication Research Methods* (New York: John Wiley, 2017), https://doi.org/10.1002/9781118901731.iecrm0108.

5 Nikolaus Kriegeskorte et al., "Circular Analysis in Systems Neuroscience: The Dangers of Double Dipping," *Nature Neuroscience* 12 (2009): 535–40, https://doi.org/10.1038/nn.2303.

6 Russell A. Poldrack et al., "Scanning the Horizon: Towards Transparent and Reproducible Neuroimaging Research," *Nature Reviews Neuroscience* 18 (2017): 115–26, https://doi.org/10.1038/nrn.2016.167.

7 Oriel FeldmanHall, "The Functional Roles of the Amygdala and Prefrontal Cortex in Processing Uncertainty," *Journal of Cognitive Neuroscience* 31, no. 11 (2019): 1742–54, https://doi.org/10.1162/jocn_a_01443.

8 Joseph LeDoux, "Rethinking the Emotional Brain," *Neuron* 73, no. 4 (2012): 653–76, https://doi.org/10.1016/j.neuron.2012.02.004.

9 William James, "What Is an Emotion?," *Mind* 9, no. 34 (1884): 188–205, https://www.jstor.org/stable/2246769.

10 Joseph LeDoux, *The Emotional Brain* (London: Simon & Schuster, 1996), 66.

11 Ralph Adolphs, Leonard Mlodinow, and Lisa Feldman-Barrett, "What Is an Emotion?," *Current Biology* 29 (2019): R1055–69, https://www.cell.com/current-biology/pdf/S0960-9822(19)31168-6.pdf.

12 Adolphs, Mlodinow, and Feldman-Barrett, "What Is an Emotion?"

13 Lisa Feldman-Barrett, "Emotions Are Real," *Emotion* 12, no. 3 (2012): 413–29, https://psycnet.apa.org/doi/10.1037/a0027555.

14 LeDoux, "Rethinking the Emotional Brain."

15 Charles R. Darwin, *The Expression of the Emotions in Man and Animals* (London: John Murray, 1872); Paul Ekman, Wallace V. Friesen, and Phoebe Ellsworth, *Emotion in the Human Face: Guidelines for Research and an Integration of Findings* (New York: Pergamon Press, 1972); Paul Ekman, Wallace V. Freisen, and Sonia Ancoli, "Facial Signs of Emotional

Experience," *Journal of Personality and Social Psychology* 39, no. 6 (1980): 1125–34, https://psycnet.apa.org/doi/10.1037/h0077722; Paul Ekman, "Expression and Nature of Emotion," in Klaus R. Scherer and Paul Ekman, eds., *Approaches to Emotion* (Hillsdale, NJ: Lawrence Erlbaum, 1984); Paul Ekman, "Basic Emotions," in Tim Dalgleish and Mick J. Power, eds., *Handbook of Cognition and Emotion* (New York: John Wiley & Sons, 1999); Carroll E. Izard, "Basic Emotions, Relations among Emotions, and Emotion-Cognition Relations," *Psychological Review* 99 (1992): 561–5, https://psycnet.apa.org/doi/10.1037/0033-295X.99.3.561; Antonio Damasio, *The Feeling of What Happens: Body and Emotion in the Making of Consciousness* (New York: Harcourt, 1999); Jaak Panksepp, *Affective Neuroscience: The Foundations of Human and Animal Emotions* (New York: Oxford University Press, 1998); Jaak Panksepp, "The Neurodynamics of Emotions: An Evolutionary-Neurodevelopmental View," in Marc D. Lewis and Isabela Granic, eds., *Emotion, Development, and Self-Organization: Dynamic Systems Approaches to Emotional Development* (Cambridge: Cambridge University Press, 2000); Jessse J. Prinz, *Gut Reactions: A Perceptual Theory of Emotion* (Oxford: Oxford University Press, 2004).

16 Ekman, Friesen, and Ellsworth, *Emotion in the Human Face.*

17 For example, Lisa Feldman-Barrett et al., "Of Mice and Men: Natural Kinds of Emotions in the Mammalian Brain? A Response to Panksepp and Izard," *Perspectives on Psychological Science* 2, no. 3 (2007): 297–311; https://doi.org/10.1111/j.1745-6916.2007.00046.x.

18 *American Psychological Association Dictionary of Psychology*, s.v. "Emotion," updated April 19, 2018, https://dictionary.apa.org/emotion.

19 *American Psychological Association Dictionary of Psychology*, s.v. "Hate," updated April 19, 2018, https://dictionary.apa.org/hate.

20 David M. Lydon-Staley et al., "Hunters, Busybodies, and the Knowledge Network Building Associated with Deprivation Curiosity," *Nature Human Behavior* 5, no. 3 (2021): 327–36, https://doi.org/10.1038/s41562 -020-00985-7.

21 Agneta Fischer et al., "Why We Hate," *Emotion Review* 10, no. 4 (2018): 309–20, https://doi.org/10.1177/1754073917751229.

22 Agneta Fischer and Antony S.R. Manstead, "Social Functions of Emotion and Emotion Regulation," in Lisa Feldman Barrett, Michael Lewis, and Jeannette M. Haviland-Jones, eds., *Handbook of Emotions*, 4th ed. (New York: Guilford Press, 2016).

23 Katherine Aumer-Ryan and Elaine C. Hatfield, "The Design of Everyday Hate: A Qualitative and Quantitative Analysis," *Interpersona: An International Journal on Personal Relationships* 1, no. 2 (2007): 143–72, https://doi.org/10.5964/ijpr.v1i2.11.

24 LeDoux, "Rethinking the Emotional Brain."

25 LeDoux, "Rethinking the Emotional Brain"; Elizabeth A. Phelps and Joseph E. LeDoux, "Contributions of the Amygdala to Emotion Processing: From Animal Models to Human behavior," *Neuron* 48, no. 2 (2005): 175–87, https://doi.org/10.1016/j.neuron.2005.09.025.

26 LeDoux, "Rethinking the Emotional Brain."

27 Jerome H. Pagani and Jeffrey B. Rosen, "The Medial Hypothalamic Defensive Circuit and 2, 5-dihyro-2,4,5,-trimethylthiazoline (TMT) Induced Fear: Comparison of Electrolytic and Neurotoxic Lesions," *Brain Research* 1286 (2009): 133–46, https://doi.org/10.1016/j.brainres.2009.06.062.

28 Fabio Bordi and Joseph LeDoux, "Sensory Tuning beyond the Sensory System: An Initial Analysis of Auditory Response Properties of Neurons in the Lateral and Amygdaloid Nucleus and Overlying Areas of the Striatum," *Journal of Neuroscience* 12, no. 7 (1992): 2493–503, https://doi.org/10.1523/JNEUROSCI.12-07-02493.1992.

29 Robert Thompson and Joseph E. LeDoux, "Common Brain Regions Essential for the Expression of Learned and Instinctive Visual Habits in the Albino Rat," *Bulletin of the Psychonomic Society* 4, no. 2-A (1974): 78–80, https://doi.org/10.3758/BF03334199.

30 David G. Amaral, "The Amgydala, Social Behavior, and Danger Detection," *Annals of the New York Academy of Sciences* 1000, no. 1 (2003): 337–47, https://doi.org/10.1196/annals.1280.015; Susan Mineka and Arne Öhman, "Phobias and Preparedness: The Selective, Automatic, and Encapsulated Nature of Fear," *Biological Psychiatry* 52, no. 10 (2002): 927–37, https://doi.org/10.1016/S0006-3223(02)01669-4.

31 A conspecific is a member of the same species. See Ralph Adolphs, "Fear, Faces and the Human Amygdala," *Current Opinion in Neurobiology* 18, no. 2 (2008): 166–72, https://doi.org/10.1016/j.conb.2008.06.006; F. Caroline Davis et al., "A Tale of Two Negatives: Differential Memory Modulation by Threat-Related Facial Expressions," *Emotion* 11, no. 3 (2011): 647–55, https://psycnet.apa.org/doi/10.1037/a0021625.

32 Wenfei Han et al., "Integrated Control of Predatory Hunting by the Central Nucleus of the Amygdala," *Cell* 168, nos. 1–2 (2017): 311–24, https://doi.org/10.1016/j.cell.2016.12.027.

33 Walter Bradford Cannon, *Bodily Changes in Pain, Hunger, Fear, and Rage* (New York: Appleton-Century-Crofts, 1915), 211.

34 Luiz Pessoa, "How Many Brain Regions Are Needed to Elucidate the Neural Bases of Fear and Anxiety?," *Neuroscience & Biobehavioral Reviews* 146 (2023): 105039, https://doi.org/10.1016/j.neubiorev.2023.105039.

35 M. Alexandra Kredlow et al., "Prefrontal Cortex, Amygdala, and Threat Processing: Implications for PTSD," *Neuropsychopharmacology* 47 (2022): 247–59, https://doi.org/10.1038/s41386-021-01155-7; Phelps and LeDoux, "Contributions of the Amygdala to Emotion Processing."

36 Joseph E. LeDoux et al., "Different Projections of the Central Amygdaloid Nucleus Mediate Autonomic and Behavioral Correlates of Conditioned Fear," *Journal of Neuroscience* 8 (1988): 2517–29, https://doi.org/10.1523 /JNEUROSCI.08-07-02517.1988.

37 Elisabeth A. Murray and Lesley K. Fellows, "Prefrontal Cortex Interactions with the Amygdala in Primates," *Neuropsychopharmacology* 47 (2022): 163–79, https://doi.org/10.1038/s41386-021-01128-w.

38 Mazen A. Kheirbek et al., "Differential Control of Learning and Anxiety along the Dorsoventral Axis of the Dentate Gyrus," *Neuron* 77, no. 5 (2013): 955–68, https://doi.org/10.1016/j.neuron.2012.12.038.

39 Kredlow et al., "Prefrontal Cortex."

40 Nancy Padilla-Coreano, Fabricio H. Do-Monte, and Gregory J. Quirk, "A Time-Dependent Role of Midline Thalamic Nuclei in the Retrieval of Fear Memory," *Neuropharmacology* 62, no. 1 (2012): 457–63, https://doi .org/10.1016/j.neuropharm.2011.08.037.

41 Kredlow et al., "Prefrontal Cortex."

42 Kredlow et al., "Prefrontal Cortex," 248.

43 Kredlow et al., "Prefrontal Cortex."

44 Esther Kristina Diekhof et al., "Fear Is Only as Deep as the Mind Allows: A Coordinate-Based Meta-Analysis of Neuroimaging Studies on the Regulation of Negative Affect," *Neuroimage* 58, no. 1 (2011): 275–85, https://doi.org/10.1016/j.neuroimage.2011.05.073; Jason T. Buhle et al., "Cognitive Reappraisal of Emotion: A Meta-Analysis of Human Neuroimaging Studies," *Cerebral Cortex* 24, no. 11 (2014): 2981–90, https:// doi.org/10.1093/cercor/bht154.

45 Steven L. Lima and Larry Dill, "Behavioral Decision Made under the Risk of Predation: A Review and Prospectus," *Canadian Journal of Zoology* 68, no. 4 (1990): 619–40, https://doi.org/10.1139/z90-092.

46 Josh M. Cisler and Ernst H.W. Koster, "Mechanisms of Attentional Biases towards Threat in the Anxiety Disorders: An Integrative Review," *Clinical Psychology Review* 30, no. 2 (2009): 203, https://doi.org/10.1016/j.cpr .2009.11.003.

47 David M. Amodio and Patricia G. Devine, "Stereotyping and Evaluation in Implicit Race Bias: Evidence for Independent Constructs and Unique Effects on Behavior," *Journal of Personality and Social Psychology* 91, no. 4 (2006): 652–61, https://psycnet.apa.org/doi/10.1037/0022-3514 .91.4.652.

48 David M. Amodio, "The Neuroscience of Prejudice and Stereotyping," *Nature Reviews Neuroscience* 15, no. 10 (2014): 670–82, https://doi.org /10.1038/nrn3800.

49 Robert M. Sapolsky, *Behave: The Biology of Humans at Our Best and Worst* (New York: Penguin Books, 2017), 10.

50 Joseph E. LeDoux, "Emotion Circuits in the Brain," *Annual Review of Neuroscience* 23 (2000): 155–84, https://doi.org/10.1146/annurev .neuro.23.1.155; Amodio, "The Neuroscience of Prejudice and Stereotyping."

51 Elizabeth A. Phelps et al., "Performance on Indirect Measures of Race Evaluation Predicts Amygdala Activation," *Journal of Cognitive Neuroscience* 12, no. 5 (2000): 729–38, https://doi.org/10.1162/089892900562552.

52 Phelps et al., "Performance on Indirect Measures of Race Evaluation."

53 David M. Amodio, "The Social Neuroscience of Intergroup Relations," *European Review of Social Psychology* 19 (2008): 1–54, https://psycnet .apa.org/doi/10.1080/10463280801927937; Jennifer T. Kubota, Mahzarin R. Banaji, and Elizabeth A. Phelps, "The Neuroscience of Race," *Nature Neuroscience* 15, 940–948 (2012), https://doi.org/10.1038/nn.3136; Adam M. Chekroud et al., "A Review of Neuroimaging Studies of Race-Related Prejudice: Does Amygdala Response Reflect Threat?," *Frontiers in Human Neuroscience* 8 (2014): 179, https://doi.org/10.3389/fnhum.2014.00179.

54 Jaclyn Ronquillo et al., "The Effects of Skin Tone on Race-Related Amygdala Activity: An fMRI Investigation," *Social Cognitive and Affective Neuroscience* 2, no. 1 (2007): 39–44, https://doi.org/10.1093/scan /nsl043.

55 Phelps et al., "Performance on Indirect Measures of Race Evaluation"; Andreas Olsson et al., "The Role of Social Group in the Persistence of Learned Fear," *Science* 309, no. 5735 (2005): 785–7.

56 Eva H. Telzer et al., "Amygdala Sensitivity to Race Is Not Present in Childhood but Emerges in Adolescence," *Journal of Cognitive Neuroscience* 25, no. 2 (2013): 234–44, https://doi.org/10.1162/jocn_a_00311.

57 Amodio, "The Neuroscience of Prejudice and Stereotyping."

58 Jay J. Van Bavel, Dominic J. Packer, and William A. Cunningham, "The Neural Substrates of In-Group Bias: A Functional Magnetic Resonance Imaging Investigation," *Psychological Science* 19, no. 11 (2008): 1131–9, https://doi.org/10.1111/j.1467-9280.2008.02214.x.

59 Ronquillo et al., "The Effects of Skin Tone"; Matthew D. Lieberman et al., "An fMRI Investigation of Race-Related Amygdala Activity in African-American and Caucasian-American Individuals," *Nature Neuroscience* 8 (2005): 720–2, https://doi.org/10.1038/nn1465; Jennifer A. Richeson et al., "An fMRI Investigation of the Impact of Interracial Contact on Executive Function," *Nature Neuroscience* 6 (2003): 1323–8, https://doi.org/10.1038 /nn1156.

60 Tania Singer et al., "Empathy for Pain Involves the Affective but Not Sensory Components of Pain," *Science* 303, no. 5661 (2004): 1157–62; Tania Singer et al., "Empathic Neural Responses Are Modulated by the Perceived Fairness of Others," *Nature* 439 (2006): 466–9, https://doi.org/10.1038 /nature04271; Claus Lamm, Andrew N. Meltzoff, and Jean Decety, "How

Do We Empathize with Someone Who Is Not Like Us? A Functional Magnetic Resonance Imaging Study," *Journal of Cognitive Neuroscience* 22, no. 2 (2010): 362–76, https://doi.org/10.1162/jocn.2009.21186.

61 David M. Amodio and Chris D. Frith, "Meeting of Minds: The Medial Frontal Cortex and Social Cognition," *Nature Review Neuroscience* 7, no. 4 (2006): 268–77, https://doi.org/10.1038/nrn1884.

62 Chris D. Frith and Utah Frith, "Interacting Minds – a Biological Basis," *Science* 286, no. 5445 (1999): 1692–5; Mina Cikara, Emile G. Bruneau, and Rebecca R. Saxe, "Us and Them: Intergroup Failures of Empathy," *Current Directions in Psychological Science* 20, no. 3 (2011): 149–53, https://doi.org/10.1177/0963721411408713.

63 Lasana T. Harris and Susan T. Fiske, "Dehumanizing the Lowest of the Low: Neuro-Imaging Responses to Extreme Outgroups," *Psychological Science* 17, no. 10 (2006): 847–53, https://doi.org/10.1111/j.1467-9280.2006.01793.x.

64 Amodio, "The Social Neuroscience of Intergroup Relations"; Amodio, "The Neuroscience of Prejudice and Stereotyping"; Ingrid R. Olson et al., "Social Cognition and the Anterior Temporal Lobes: A Review and Theoretical Framework," *Social Cognitive and Affective Neuroscience* 8, no. 2 (2013): 123–33, https://doi.org/10.1093/scan/nss119; Susanne Quadflieg and C. Neil Macrae, "Stereotypes and Stereotyping: What's the Brain Got To Do with It?," *European Review of Social Psychology* 22, no. 1 (2011): 215–73, https://doi.org/10.1080/10463283.2011.627998.

65 Olson et al., "Social Cognition and the Anterior Temporal Lobes."

66 Juan M. Contreras, Mahzarin R. Banaji, and Jason P. Mitchell, "Dissociable Neural Correlates of Stereotypes and Other Forms of Semantic Knowledge," *Social Cognitive and Affective Neuroscience* 7, no. 7 (2012): 764–70, https://doi.org/10.1093/scan/nsr053.

67 Jason P. Mitchell, Todd F. Heatherton, and C. Neil Macrae, "Distinct Neural Systems Subserve Person and Object Knowledge," *Proceedings of the National Academy of Science of the United States of America* 99, no. 23 (2002): 15238–43, https://doi.org/10.1073/pnas.232395699.

68 Amodio, "The Neuroscience of Prejudice and Stereotyping."

69 Mary L. Phillips et al., "Neurobiology of Emotion Perception I: The Neural Basis of Normal Emotion Perception," *Biological Psychiatry* 54, no. 5 (2003): 504–14, https://doi.org/10.1016/S0006-3223(03)00168-9.

70 Fiery Cushman et al., "Simulating Murder: The Aversion to Harmful Action," *Emotion* 12, no. 1 (2012): 2–7, https://psycnet.apa.org/doi/10.1037/a0025071.

71 Robert Kurzban and Mark R. Leary, "Evolutionary Origins of Stigmatization: The Functions of Social Exclusion," *Psychological Bulletin* 127, no. 2 (2001): 87–208, https://psycnet.apa.org/doi/10.1037/0033-2909.127.2.187.

72 Luis Sebastian Contreras-Huerta et al., "Racial Bias in Neural Empathic Responses to Pain," *PLoS One* 8, no. 12 (2013): e84001, https://doi.org/10.1371/journal.pone.0084001; Xiaojing Xu et al., "Do You Feel My Pain? Racial Group Membership Modulates Empathic Neural Responses," *Journal of Neuroscience* 29, no. 26 (2009): 8525–9, https://www.jneurosci.org/content/jneuro/29/26/8525.full.pdf.

73 Jay J. Van Bavel, Dominic J. Packer, and William A. Cunningham, "Modulation of the Fusiform Face Area following Minimal Exposure to Motivationally Relevant Faces: Evidence of In-Group Enhancement (Not Out-Group Disregard)," *Journal of Cognitive Neuroscience* 23, no. 11 (2011): 3343–54, https://doi.org/10.1162/jocn_a_00016.

74 Walter G. Stephan, Oscar Ybarra, and Kimberly Rios Morrison, "Intergroup Threat Theory," in T.D. Nelson, ed., *Handbook of Prejudice, Stereotyping and Discrimination* (New York: Psychology Press, 2009).

75 Dorottya Lantos et al., "The Neural Mechanisms of Threat and Reconciliation Efforts between Muslims and Non-Muslims," *Social Neuroscience* 15, no. 4 (2020): 420–34, https://doi.org/10.1080/17470919.2020.1754287.

76 Lantos et al., "The Neural Mechanisms of Threat and Reconciliation Efforts."

77 Stephan, Ybarra, and Rios Morrison, "Intergroup Threat Theory."

78 FeldmanHall, "The Functional Roles of the Amygdala and Prefrontal Cortex."

79 Lasana T. Harris and Susan T. Fiske, "Social Groups That Elicit Disgust Are Differentially Processed in mPFC," *Social Cognitive and Affective Neuroscience* 2, no. 1 (2007): 45–51, https://doi.org/10.1093/scan/nsl037.

80 Lantos and Molenberghs, "The Neuroscience of Intergroup Threat and Violence."

81 Harris and Fiske, "Dehumanizing the Lowest of the Low."

82 Amodio, "The Neuroscience of Prejudice and Stereotyping."

83 Lasana T. Harris and Susan T. Fiske, "Dehumanized Perception: A Psychological Means to Facilitate Atrocities, Torture, and Genocide?," *Zeitschrift Für Psychologie/Journal of Psychology* 219, no. 3 (2011): 175–81, https://psycnet.apa.org/doi/10.1027/2151-2604/a000065.

84 Anne C. Krendl, Elizabeth A. Kensinger, and Nalini Ambady, "How Does the Brain Regulate Negative Bias to Stigma?," *Social Cognitive and Affective Neuroscience* 7, no. 6 (2012): 715–26, https://doi.org/10.1093/scan/nsr046.

85 Wolfram Schultz, Peter Dayan, and P. Read Montague, "A Neural Substrate of Prediction and Reward," *Science* 275, no. 5306 (1997): 1593–9.

86 Mitchell Roitman et al., "Real-Time Chemical Responses in the Nucleus Accumbens Differentiate Rewarding and Aversive Stimuli," *Nature Neuroscience* 11 (2008): 1376–7, https://doi.org/10.1038/nn.2219.

87 Donita L. Robinson, Michael L.A.V. Heien, and R. Mark Wightman, "Frequency of Dopamine Concentration Transients Increases in Dorsal and Ventral Striatum of Male Rats during Introduction of Conspecifics," *Journal of Neuroscience* 22, no. 23 (2002): 10477–86, https://doi.org/10.1523/JNEUROSCI.22-23-10477.2002.

88 Yuji K. Takahashi et al., "The Orbitofrontal Cortex and Ventral Tegmental Area Are Necessary for Learning from Unexpected Outcomes," *Neuron* 62, no. 2 (2009): 269–80, https://www.cell.com/action/showPdf?pii=S0896-6273%2809%2900202-5.

89 Suzanne Haber, "Neuroanatomy of Reward: A View from the Ventral Striatum," in Jay A. Gottfried, ed., *Neurobiology of Sensation and Reward* (Boca Raton, FL: CRC Press, 2011).

90 Suzanne Haber and Brian Knutson, "The Reward Circuit: Linking Primate Anatomy and Human Imaging," *Neuropsychopharmacology* 35 (2010): 4–26, https://doi.org/10.1038/npp.2009.129.

91 Barry J. Everitt and Trevor W. Robbins, "Neural Systems of Reinforcement for Drug Addiction: From Actions to Habits to Compulsion," *Nature Neuroscience* 8 (2005): 1481–19, https://doi.org/10.1038/nn1579.

92 Lennart Heimer et al., "The Human Basal Forebrain. Part II," in Floyd E. Bloom, A. Bjorkland, and T. Hokfelt, eds., *Handbook of Chemical Neuroanatomy* (Amsterdam: Elsevier, 1999).

93 Haber, "Neuroanatomy of Reward."

94 Joseph B. Walther, "Social Media and Online Hate," *Current Opinion in Psychology* 45 (2022): 101298, https://doi.org/10.1016/j.copsyc.2021.12.010.

95 Roy F. Baumeister and Mark R. Leary, "The Need to Belong: Desire for Interpersonal Attachments as a Fundamental Human Motivation," *Psychological Bulletin* 117, no. 3 (1995): 497–529, https://psycnet.apa.org/doi/10.1037/0033-2909.117.3.497.

96 For example, Kelly-Ann Allen et al., "The Need to Belong: A Deep Dive into the Origins, Implications, and Future of a Foundational Construct," *Educational Psychology Review* 34 (2022): 1133–56, https://doi.org/10.1007/s10648-021-09633-6.

97 For example, Arthur Aron et al., "Reward, Motivation, and Emotion Systems Associated with Early-Stage Intense Romantic Love," *Journal of Neurophysiology* 94, no. 1 (2005): 327–37, https://doi.org/10.1152/jn.00838.2004; Bianca P. Acevedo et al., "Neural Correlates of Long-Term Intense Romantic Love," *Social Cognitive and Affective Neuroscience* 7, no. 2 (2012): 145–59, https://doi.org/10.1093/scan/nsq092; Andreas Bartels and Semir Zeki, "The Neural Basis of Romantic Love," *NeuroReport* 11, no. 17 (2000): 3829–34, https://journals.lww.com/neuroreport/fulltext/2000/11270/the_neural_basis_of_romantic_love.46.aspx.

98   For example, Andrik I. Becht et al., "Beyond the Average Brain: Individual Differences in Social Brain Development Are Associated with Friendship Quality," *Social Cognitive and Affective Neuroscience* 16, no. 3 (2021): 292–301, https://doi.org/10.1093/scan/nsaa166; Ullrich Wagner et al., "Beautiful Friendship: Social Sharing of Emotions Improves Subjective Feelings and Activates the Neural Reward Circuitry," *Social Cognitive and Affective Neuroscience* 10, no. 6 (2015): 801–8, https://doi.org/10.1093/scan/nsu121.

99   Pete Simi et al., "Addicted to Hate: Identity Residual among Former White Supremacists," *American Sociological Review* 82, no. 6 (2017): 1167–87, https://doi.org/10.1177/0003122417728719.

100 Walther, "Social Media and Online Hate."

101 William J. Brady et al., "How Social Learning Amplifies Moral Outrage Expression in Online Social Networks," *Science Advances* 7, no. 33 (2021), https://www.science.org/doi/10.1126/sciadv.abe5641.

102 Walther, "Social Media and Online Hate."

103 Sahana Udupa, "Nationalism in the Digital Age: Fun as a Metapractice of Extreme Speech," *International Journal of Communication* 13 (2019): 3143–63, https://ijoc.org/index.php/ijoc/article/view/9105/2715.

104 Andrew J. Fuligni, "The Need to Contribute during Adolescence," *Perspectives on Psychological Science* 14, no. 3 (2019): 331–43, https://doi.org/10.1177/1745691618805437.

105 Michael A. Hogg, "Intergroup Relations," in John DeLamater and Amanda Ward, eds., *Handbook of Social Psychology* (Dordrecht, Netherlands: Springer, 2013).

106 Frank Martela and Richard M. Ryan, "The Benefits of Benevolence: Basic Psychological Needs, Beneficence, and the Enhancement of Well-Being,' *Journal of Personality* 84, no. 6 (2016): 750–64, https://doi.org/10.1111/jopy.12215; Richard M. Ryan and Edward L. Deci, *Self-Determination Theory: Basic Psychological Needs in Motivation, Development, and Wellness* (New York: Guilford Press, 2017); Netta Weinstein and Richard M. Ryan, "When Helping Helps: Autonomous Motivation for Prosocial Behavior and Its Influence on Well-Being for the Helper and Recipient," *Journal of Personality and Social Psychology* 98, no. 2 (2010): 222–44, https://psycnet.apa.org/doi/10.1037/a0016984.

107 Michael Tomasello and Amrisha Vaish, "Origins of Human Cooperation and Morality," *Annual Review of Psychology* 64 (2013): 231–55, https://doi.org/10.1146/annurev-psych-113011-143812.

108 Stephanie L. Brown et al., "Providing Social Support May Be More Beneficial Than Receiving It: Results from a Prospective Study of Mortality," *Psychological Science* 14, no. 4 (2003): 320–7, https://doi.org/10.1111/1467-9280.14461; Elizabeth B. Raposa, Holly B. Laws, and

Emily B. Ansell, "Prosocial Behavior Mitigates the Negative Effects of Stress in Everyday Life," *Clinical Psychological Science* 4, no. 4 (2016): 691–8, https://doi.org/10.1177/2167702615611073; Yunqing Li and Kenneth F. Ferraro, "Volunteering and Depression in Later Life: Social Benefit or Selection Processes?," *Journal of Health and Social Behavior* 46, no. 1 (2005): 68–84, https://doi.org/10.1177/002214650504600106.

109 Nancy Morrow-Howell et al., "Effects of Volunteering on the Well-Being of Older Adults," *The Journals of Gerontology Series B: Psychological Sciences and Social Sciences* 58, no. 3 (2003): S137–45, https://doi.org/10.1093/geronb/58.3.S137; Jonas G. Miller, Sarah Kahle, and Paul D. Hastings, "Roots and Benefits of Costly Giving: Children Who Are More Altruistic Have Greater Autonomic Flexibility and Less Family Wealth," *Psychological Science* 26, no. 7 (2015): 1038–45, https://psycnet.apa.org/doi/10.1177/0956797615578476; Hannah M.C. Schreier, Kimberly A. Schonert-Reichl, and Edith Chen, "Effect of Volunteering on Risk Factors for Cardiovascular Disease in Adolescents: A Randomized Controlled Trial," *JAMA Pediatrics* 167 (2103): 327–32, https://doi.org/10.1001/jamapediatrics.2013.1100.

110 Fuligni, "The Need to Contribute during Adolescence."

111 Naomi I. Eisenberger, "An Empirical Review of the Neural Underpinnings of Receiving and Giving Social Support: Implications for Health," *Psychosomatic Medicine* 75, no. 6 (2013): 545–56, https://doi.org/10.1097/PSY.0b013e31829de2e7; Jorge Moll et al., "Human Fronto–Mesolimbic Networks Guide Decisions about Charitable Donation," *Proceedings of the National Academy of Sciences USA* 103, no. 42 (2006): 15623–8, https://doi.org/10.1073/pnas.0604475103.

112 Semir Zeki and John Paul Romaya, "Neural Correlates of Hate," *PLoS One* 3, no. 10 (2008): e3556, https://doi.org/10.1371/journal.pone.0003556.

113 Bartels and Zeki, "The Neural Basis of Romantic Love."

114 Hannah A. Chapman and Adam K. Anderson, "Understanding Disgust," *Annals of the New York Academy of Sciences* 1251 (2012): 62–76, https://doi.org/10.1111/j.1749-6632.2011.06369.x.

115 Richard D. Lane et al., "Neuroanatomical Correlates of Happiness, Sadness, and Disgust," *American Journal of Psychiatry* 154, no. 7 (1997): 926–33, https://doi.org/10.1176/ajp.154.7.926.

116 Haojuan Tao et al., "Depression Uncouples Brain Hate Circuit," *Molecular Psychiatry* 18, no. 1 (2013): 101–11, https://doi.org/10.1038/mp.2011.127.

117 Editor's note: Throughout this volume, unless there is a reason (such as citing a law or article) to do otherwise, we avoid the term "hate speech" and use "hateful speech" instead. In the American context, some people believe there's an exception to the First Amendment for speech that expresses hate; there isn't. See, for example, "To Fight 'Hate Speech,'

Stop Talking about It," *Washington Post*, June 3, 2016, https://www
.washingtonpost.com/posteverything/wp/2016/06/03/we-dont-need
-laws-banning-hate-speech-because-it-doesnt-exist/; and Chris Marchese,
"Suzanne Nossel Criticizes 'Incoherent' Concept of 'Hate Speech,'" FIRE:
Foundation for Individual Rights and Expression, June 7, 2016,
https://www.thefire.org/news/suzanne-nossel-criticizes-incoherent
-concept-hate-speech.

118 Agnieskza Pluta et al., "Exposure to Hate Speech Deteriorates
Neurocognitive Mechanisms of the Ability to Understand Others' Pain,"
Scientific Reports 13 (2023): Article 4127, https://doi.org/10.1038
/s41598-023-31146-1.

119 Pluta et al., "Exposure to Hate Speech."

120 Pluta et al., "Exposure to Hate Speech," 2.

121 David Dodell-Feder et al., "fMRI Item Analysis in a Theory of Mind
Task," *NeuroImage* 55, no. 2 (2011): 705–12, https://doi.org/10.1016
/j.neuroimage.2010.12.040.

122 Nicholas Fallon, Carl Roberts, and Andrej Stancak, "Shared and Distinct
Functional Networks for Empathy and Pain Processing: A Systematic
Review and Meta-Analysis of fMRI Studies," *Social Cognitive and Affective
Neuroscience* 15, no. 7 (2020): 709–23, https://doi.org/10.1093/scan
/nsaa090.

123 Pluta et al., "Exposure to Hate Speech."

124 Pluta et al., "Exposure to Hate Speech."

125 Xu et al., "Do You Feel My Pain?"

Editor's Introduction to Chapter 3

The organizers for an International Conference of Hate Studies (held virtually at Gonzaga University during the COVID-19 pandemic) asked me to moderate a session of leading thinkers about hate. I had suggested some of the people mentioned or published in this volume (including Thomas Brudholm and Robert Sapolsky), but someone else suggested Mengyao Li, a leading young social psychologist. I had never heard of her, but a quick google search impressed me. She was a 2012 graduate of Bard College, and her thesis advisors (Tom Keenan of the Human Rights Project and Kristin Lane of the psychology department) are two of the academics with whom I work most closely. Both spoke glowingly about her, and it was impressive that, only a decade after graduating, she secured her PhD, a post-doctoral appointment, and was then working at one of the leading think tanks in the world, the Max Planck Institute for Research on Collective Goods in Bonn, Germany (she now teaches at Queen's University Belfast). I read her Bard senior thesis (on schadenfreude), and a number of her cutting-edge articles about hate, intergroup violence, identity, and related topics. It's no surprise she received an award for best manuscript in an early career.

Her field – social psychology – is central to understanding how hatred plays out on a group level. For NGOs focused on hate, it's essential to think through many of the characteristics of group hate. Why it might be a longer-lasting emotion than some others. Why we may default to seeing outgroup members as having bad intentions, or even as evil. When these hateful tendencies become particularly destructive, it's important to look at how they intersect with ideologies and theologies, how they relate to issues of anger, feelings of powerlessness, communal narratives and memories of past communal trauma. We also want to know how the power of social norms, the human need to have a sense of belonging, and the impact of world events – like the terrorist attacks of 9/11, the insurrection at the US Capitol on January 6, the Hamas massacre and kidnapping of Israelis on October 7, and the massive Israeli response in Gaza – "stir things up," to use the words of novelist Dashiell Hammett.

Li artfully guides us through the wide-ranging insights social psychology offers about hate, and provides guidance for NGOs that might try and intervene against it.

3 The Social Psychology of Group-Based Hate: Characteristics, Origins, and Implications for Interventions

MENGYAO LI

Psychology, especially its subfield of social psychology, has come a long way in its pursuit of understanding the origins and consequences of intergroup conflicts. While extensive literature exists on the psychological mechanisms and processes underlying intergroup violence, group-based hate or hate experienced on behalf of a group against another group as one of the most potent catalysts for extreme violence has received relatively limited attention. Nonetheless, psychology offers crucial insights into the nature of hate and its role in intergroup relations. From a theoretical perspective, psychology contributes a micro-level analysis of hate by centering on individuals' feelings, experiences, and understandings of hate. With its rich tradition of exploring complex human emotions, psychological research has also revealed distinct features of hate in terms of the associated motivation, cognition, and behavior, while the broader interdisciplinary literature on conflicts and violence often conflates "hate" with related concepts such as anger, contempt, prejudice, and feelings of revenge. From an applied perspective, recognizing the unique properties of hate is important for critically evaluating existing interventions and developing better strategies to mitigate its detrimental impact.

Drawing heavily from the empirical psychological research on hate in intergroup contexts, this chapter aims to review the psychological literature on hate and discuss how this understanding can inform NGOs and practitioners in combating this destructive force in intergroup relations. The chapter consists of three parts. First, it offers a multidimensional conceptualization of group-based hate, as characterized by unique patterns of cognition, motivational goals, and behavioral tendencies. By examining these attributes, I will show that hate is closely linked to, but still distinct from, various related concepts. Second, this chapter will provide an overview of psychology's primary accounts of why people hate. Here, the discussion centers on two levels of analysis: the individual level and the group level. At the individual level, feelings of insecurity and shame, for example, emerge as probable predictors of hate. At the group level, prior experiences of collective victimization, societal norms, and leadership dynamics can all contribute to the emergence and spread of hate. Finally, the chapter will discuss how the psychological understanding of hate can shed light on efforts to address hate effectively. On the one hand, the psychological properties of hate make it particularly difficult to eradicate or transform. Therefore, many well-established, well-meaning interventions that have been shown to reduce negative intergroup emotions and attitudes (e.g., prejudice, anger) might not be effective in reducing hate. On the other hand, recognizing these difficulties may be the first step toward identifying interventions and societal mechanisms to confront hate and its destructive consequences.

What Is Hate? The (Social) Psychological Perspective

The concept of hate has been the subject of diverse definitions and interpretations. This complex nature is reflected in the plethora of ways in which scholars from various disciplines have attempted to describe the essence of hate, both interpersonal and intergroup.[1] Some have portrayed hate, for example, as a syndrome,[2] an "extreme dislike,"[3] a negative generalized evaluation,[4] a normative judgment,[5] a motive to devalue others,[6] a justice construct implicated throughout the dynamic process of harming others,[7] or an emotion[8] and emotional attitude.[9] Recent philosophical analysis of hate has attempted to grasp its complexity by considering its cognitive, evaluative, conative, structural, and material aspects.[10] Rather than embarking on yet another journey to define the concept of hate,[11] I will review the psychological research that has dealt with some of the key characteristics of hate and critically discuss the existing empirical evidence on these characteristics.

The psychological perspective on hate or hatred[12] has primarily viewed it as an emotion or an affective phenomenon while acknowledging its complex and multifaceted nature.[13] Eran Halperin and Drew E. Schwartz, for example, describe hate as a "secondary, extreme, and continuous emotion that is directed at a particular individual or group and denounced them fundamentally and all-inclusively."[14] Despite the rich theorizing about what hate is, only a handful of studies have empirically investigated the various conceptualizations of hate, and even fewer have addressed specifically group-based hate.[15] The scarcity of empirical studies on hate is, to a certain extent, a result of the general reluctance in people to admit that they experience such extreme, negative feelings toward others.[16] In a 2008 interview study with Jewish Israeli participants, Halperin explored people's lay conceptions of "hatred" in intergroup contexts.[17] Interestingly, none of the participants reported ever having experienced "hatred" toward another social group,[18] despite living in the midst of one of the world's most "intractable" conflicts.[19] In the meantime, almost all participants perceived (group-based) hatred as an immoral or nonlegitimate emotion.

This is not to suggest, however, that hate is impossible to study or measure due to its profound social undesirability. According to Halperin, participants were willing to acknowledge that Palestinians were subject to hate by Israelis and were more willing to disclose their own feelings of hate after being told that it is a legitimate and common emotion.[20] In fact, in the same line of research, Jewish Israeli participants were willing to admit feelings of hatred when asked to indicate the degree to which they felt hatred toward Palestinians on a rating scale after being reminded of the recent "acts of terror and destruction of Israel" by various Palestinian groups.[21] Although participants in the study rated their feelings of hatred the lowest, compared to other negative emotions such as fear and anger, the average rating of hatred was above the mid-point of the scale, indicating the presence rather than the absence of such an extreme emotion. Given the highly limited geopolitical locations of the existing or published studies of hate, it remains unknown how socially undesirable or illegitimate hate is perceived in other social, cultural, and political contexts. Indeed, self-report measures of hate have been developed and used successfully in recent research in the United States, Canada, and South Korea, among other countries.[22] In the following sections, I provide an evidence-based account of the unique characteristics of hate.

Duration and Intensity

Unlike other negative emotions such as anger, which tends to dissipate relatively quickly, hatred has been found to be one of the most enduring emotions.[23] Studies conducted among the Israeli-Jewish population revealed that lay individuals perceived hate as long-lasting, extreme, and highly emotional in nature,[24] and reported more long-term rather than short-term hate toward other social groups.[25] Of course, people are capable of experiencing short-term hate in response to "unusual, most destructive, and violent" events.[26] Research has also successfully distinguished between "immediate hatred" and "chronic hatred," which predicted differential political outcomes.[27] These two types of hatred, however, could reinforce each other in the sense that frequent experiences of events that elicit immediate hate might lead to the development of chronic hate, while "chronic haters" might be especially prone to reacting with acute, immediate hate when encountering their targets.

Previous theorizing of hate has also attempted to provide a taxonomy of hate based on the intensity of the emotion along with other dimensions.[28] These classifications of hate, however, have not been substantiated with robust empirical evidence. The psychological literature has generally agreed that feelings of hate – group-based hate, in particular – are characterized by extraordinary intensity. Recent empirical work in the United States has provided preliminary evidence for this notion, showing that hate was more arousing and more intense than some of the commonly experienced moral emotions such as anger and contempt.[29]

Cognitive and Moral Appraisals

Not only is intergroup hate more intense and enduring than many other negative intergroup emotions, but it is also qualitatively distinct in terms of the accompanied cognitive[30] and moral appraisals.[31] Hate toward an outgroup involves the perception that outgroup members possess malevolent intentions and are evil by nature.[32] Importantly, such appraisals are not based on the specific actions of the hated group, but rather the belief about their stable, dispositional attributes. Comparing the cognitive appraisals associated with anger versus hate, researchers have further suggested that hate involves the belief that the hated outgroup will never undergo positive change,[33] whereas anger (without hatred) is not necessarily accompanied by such feelings of lack of control and targets of anger could be seen as capable of change.[34] In terms of moral appraisals of hate targets, a recent set of qualitative and quantitative studies conducted in Canada and the United States revealed that compared to dislike, feelings of hate were more connected to participants' moral beliefs and convictions.[35] This finding resonates with the earlier research on hate groups in the United States, which shows that members of hate groups are particularly likely to refer to issues of a moral nature (e.g., group preservation) as sources of their hate.[36] Not surprisingly, the appraisals of the target as immoral, dangerous, and incapable of change are further associated with specific behavioral tendencies toward the hated outgroups.

Behavioral Tendencies

The action tendencies associated with hate are generally believed to be highly destructive. Hate has been shown to predict a variety of attack-oriented behavioral tendencies, such as verbal aggression, moral exclusion, physical attack, and extreme violence.[37] While most of this work has been conducted in Western countries (Israel, the United States, and Canada), a recent study in South Korea similarly demonstrated that group-based hate emerged as the most potent emotional predictor of support for military policy against North Korea, compared to other negative emotions (i.e., anger, fear, angst, despair).[38] Among all the predictors tested (e.g., political ideology, ingroup identification, right-wing authoritarianism), hatred was second only to the belief that the Korean conflict was a zero-sum game in its predictive power of military support.

It has been argued that although the actions born of hate and other intergroup emotions (e.g., anger, disgust, contempt, humiliation, and revenge) can be quite similar, the motivational goals associated with these different emotions are not.[39] Due to the associated cognitive and moral appraisals of the target being unable to change its malicious and evil nature, the motivational goal of hate is not merely to harm the outgroup, but to remove outgroup members from the ingroup's social and physical environment and even to ultimately destroy the outgroup.[40] Intergroup anger, on the other hand, does not always stem from the belief that the outgroup cannot improve, and is therefore not necessarily a catalyst of destructive intergroup behavior. Empirical studies have indeed demonstrated that anger can lead to both destructive responses and constructive responses such as support for reconciliation and negotiations to achieve peace.[41] Hate can also be differentiated from other negative emotions associated with the goal of socially excluding others (contempt),[42] protecting the self (humiliation),[43] or restoring equity in suffering (desire for revenge).[44]

How the motivational goal of hate translates into action will likely vary, depending on the specific intergroup context, the history between the ingroup and the outgroup, the collective narrative, societal norm, leadership, and the available means. As mentioned earlier, hate-driven actions may range from social distancing and exclusion to more extreme forms of violence, including genocide and mass killing.[45] Research has not yet clearly identified the conditions in which hate is more or less likely to translate into extreme violence. Examining the diversity in the behavioral manifestation of hate can potentially provide important insights into the prevention of hate crimes and political radicalization.

Notwithstanding this gap in the literature, it is clear that group-based hate is not an inevitable precursor to intergroup violence. It is also crucial to recognize that not all acts of violence and extreme intergroup behavior are a result of hate. In fact, violence can be instrumental in achieving specific collective goals without being moralized.[46]

One notable limitation of the empirical studies reviewed above is their tendency to focus on one side of the conflict – most often the more powerful side (e.g., Jewish Israelis in the Israeli-Palestinian conflict, South Koreans in the Korean conflict). It remains unknown whether hate maintains these unique features among members of the less powerful, minoritized, or historically oppressed groups in asymmetrical conflicts. For example, to what extent are hate and anger distinguishable from the perspective of the less powerful party in a conflict? One of the key differences between these two negative emotions is the unique feeling of powerlessness associated with hate, and the constructive potential of anger lies largely in the sense of control over the situation.[47] It could thus be more challenging to discern the constructive outcomes of anger among groups lacking power in contrast to the powerful.

Why Do We Hate?

In this section, I will explore some of the socio-psychological explanations of group-based hate, again drawing predominantly from the empirical literature. These explanations primarily fall within two levels of analyses: micro level (i.e., centering on individual experiences) and macro level (i.e., centering on collective experiences). These two levels of analysis are not mutually exclusive; rather, they are often interlinked, working in concert to give rise to group-based hate. Further, micro-level mechanisms can be shaped by macro-level factors and processes, and vice versa. Group identification, for example, operates at the micro-level by essentially capturing how individuals view themselves in relation to their social groups.[48] The strength and quality of identification, however, can be shaped by collective experiences such as intergroup conflict and collective narrative.[49] Volumes have been written about the origins, foundations, and sources of hate.[50] In chapter 2 of this volume, Galván reviews empirical studies revealing the neural basis of hate, whereas in chapter 5, Lowe and Jimenez discuss the role of media in shaping hate toward immigrants. It is beyond the scope of this chapter to offer an exhaustive list of reasons behind this phenomenon. Instead, my goal is to highlight the multi-layered pathways to hate, which further illuminates both the challenges and opportunities in mitigating hate and its destructive impact.

Micro-Level Factors

Frustration of basic needs. In Staub's analysis of the origins and evolution of hate, he emphasizes the importance of understanding basic human needs and childhood experiences in exploring the roots of hate. According to Staub, the frustration of basic human needs such as the need for connection, security, certainty, and belongingness can set the stage for the development of extreme intergroup emotions and attitudes. Early-life experiences of neglect and mistreatment, for example, can plant the seeds for hate in adulthood.[51] Interviews with youths associated with white supremacist groups and "hate groups" in the United States[52] provided evidence for this argument, revealing that many of the interviewees experienced significant childhood losses and lacked meaningful social connections, which are pivotal for developing resilience.[53] Recent quantitative studies provided additional evidence for the appeal of hateful ideologies, demonstrating that hate toward collective entities (but not individuals) can bolster feelings of determination, coherence, and enthusiasm, and thereby increase perceived meaning in life.[54]

Research on radicalization has similarly theorized and demonstrated how frustrated needs can drive the endorsement of extremist ideologies. Feelings of insignificance and uncertainty, for instance, can predispose individuals to identify with radical groups.[55] On the one hand, radical groups provide clear norms, values, meaning, and a sense of belonging. On the other hand, they consider their own group's norms and values as superior to those of others. Identifying with radical groups leads to the next level in the radicalization process – as the ties between the individual and the radical group become strengthened, the individual might even develop a sense of oneness with their group.[56] Finally, encounters with triggering events such as the death of a relative or friend might serve as the direct cause of the determination to commit violence. The last stage of the radicalization process is arguably accompanied by the eruption of intense, immediate hate, which is associated with the perceived urgency and an "explosive motivation" to act.[57] Therefore, while the frustration of basic human needs might not directly lead to hate, it provides fertile ground for hate to emerge, especially when the individual encounters a significant and destructive event.

Group identification. It is nearly impossible to explore the psychological underpinnings of group-based hate without considering the role of group identification. Individuals experience emotions on behalf of their group as a result of social categorization and group identification.[58]

Decades of research have been devoted to uncovering the link between positive sentiments directed toward one's ingroup and biases, hostility, and hate directed toward the outgroup. One of the most robust findings in social psychology is that when an outgroup is perceived to be a threat to the ingroup – whether a threat to the material (e.g., land, resources, power) or symbolic (e.g., value, culture, identity) existence of the ingroup – love for the ingroup becomes particularly prone to transform into hatred for the outgroup.[59] On the one hand, the intensity of emotional response to perceived collective threats is closely linked to the strength of ingroup identification.[60] On the other hand, individuals who strongly identify with their ingroup are more likely to perceive threats in the first place.[61] In other words, high levels of identification can lower the threshold of perceiving collective threats, thereby sowing the seeds for group-based hate.

Research on group identification has also illuminated important differences in the antecedents of interpersonal and intergroup hate. Studies in the interpersonal domain have suggested that feelings of humiliation can elicit hate. The perception of being betrayed or humiliated by one's partner, for example, has been linked to the emergence of hate.[62] In the intergroup domain, however, more recent studies on exclusionary, defensive modes of ingroup identification – for example, collective narcissism,[63] and ingroup glorification[64] – have suggested that while intergroup hate might also rise from feelings of humiliation, haters do not necessarily have low self- or collective esteem. Instead, it may be the perceived threat to a grandiose view of one's group that motivates hatred and violence toward another group. Considerable research in various contexts of intergroup conflict has demonstrated the destructive consequences of identifying with one's ingroup in a glorifying manner. These consequences include but are not limited to hostile intergroup attitudes, support and moral justification for intergroup violence, and desire for revenge.[65] Although these studies did not directly examine group-based hate as an outcome, they all point to the possibility that identification with one's group, particularly when marked by a grandiose perception of the group, can be a catalyst for outgroup hate. This becomes especially probable when the very existence of the outgroup is viewed as a threat to such group identity.

Macro-Level Factors

Beyond individual-level factors, group-based hate also finds roots in many collective, macro-level processes, some of which are closely tied to the concepts of group identification and collective threat, as previously mentioned. These macro-level factors not only contribute to the emergence of group-based hate but also fuel its propagation and intensification within social groups.

Collective victimization. The aftermath of the 9/11 attacks serves as a compelling example of how collective experiences of victimization can give rise to generalized hate, extending to groups unrelated to the initial source of the threat. In the two decades following the attacks, a strong sense of collective victimization rallied many Americans behind the official survivor mission – the "war on terror" – against countries with no clear connection to the 9/11 attacks.[66] This example resonates with a large body of research in psychology (and other disciplines) that typically views collective victimhood as a conflict-supportive belief, yielding negative and even violent outcomes for intergroup relations.[67]

Experiences of collective victimization have a profound and long-lasting impact on the way group members perceive, evaluate, and respond to social processes and intergroup events, even when the traumatic events took place in the distant past.[68] This is especially true for groups that have suffered extreme violence such as genocide – they tend to view current intergroup situations through the lens of historical trauma, indistinguishable from the pain and suffering of the past.[69] Indeed, reminders of collective victimhood can lead to prejudice, discrimination, and even hatred toward groups and individuals viewed as associated with perpetrators of the original trauma or in conflict with the ingroup in present times. For example, when reminded of various events where the ingroup was victimized, Jewish Israelis who had a perpetual ingroup victimization orientation, or the belief that the ingroup is constantly victimized by different enemies, increased attributions of malevolent intentions to outgroup members in ambiguous situations in the present.[70] A series of studies revealed that antisemitism in Greece built on the legacy of the Holocaust such that perceived collective victimhood – especially competition over victim status – contributed to antisemitic prejudice in Greece, the nation with the strongest antisemitic sentiments in Europe.[71]

When discussing how hate spreads within groups, Fischer and colleagues highlight the role of collective processes in the flourishing of hate at the group level.[72] Notably, members of victim groups tend to share their emotional experiences through collective narratives, which can be transmitted across generations.[73] The knowledge that other ingroup members share the feeling of hatred can reinforce both the experience and the expression of one's emotions.[74] In turn, the sharing of collective emotions reinforces collective narratives about victimization, which further intensifies and prolongs the feeling of hatred. Thus, collective victimhood is associated with a variety of collective processes that contribute to the emergence, prolongation, and escalation of group-based hate.

Social norms. Social norms constitute another powerful force that shapes individuals' expressions of hate and prejudice toward other groups, such as racist, xenophobic, and discriminatory speech.[75] Research has provided empirical evidence that the public expression of prejudice toward social groups strongly correlates with perceived societal approval of that expression.[76] A study on online hateful speech revealed that in the absence of a strong norm against hateful speech, residents in Germany were more likely to express hate against refugees (but not other minority groups) in an online forum after two consecutive Islamist terrorist attacks in the country.[77] These findings have collectively revealed the important role of social norms in fostering and restraining the expression of hate.[78]

While hate-tolerant social norms can shape the behavioral manifestations of hate and prejudice, they are not necessarily internalized or lead to hostile personal beliefs toward other groups. Psychological research has demonstrated that social norms can directly influence behavior, independent of personal beliefs and attitudes.[79] Across fifteen Western countries, researchers examined the implications of the increasing normalization of far-right political groups in the media.[80] The evidence suggests that greater media exposure to the far-right was associated with a greater perceived prevalence of the far-right (i.e., increased descriptive norm). Importantly, such increased perceived prevalence predicted stronger rejection of the far-right, indicating that the changing group norm was not necessarily internalized. It is therefore important to distinguish personal feelings of hate from expressions of hate when considering the role of social norms in group-based hate.

In sum, psychological research sheds light on a wide range of factors underlying group-based hate. These micro- and macro-level factors can interact with one another, working in tandem in giving rise to hateful sentiments toward another group or the expression and spread of hate. For instance, narratives about collective victimhood can shape the way individuals identify with their group, which in turn influences attitudes and feelings toward other groups.[81] It is also worth noting that many other psychological processes and societal mechanisms also contribute to group-based hate.[82] The aim here is to illustrate the complexity of these influences, which is crucial for understanding the challenges and possibilities in addressing hate.

Implications for Combating Hate

So far, I have reviewed the diverse (mostly) psychological literature on the core characteristics of group-based hate and the various factors and processes contributing to such a phenomenon. In this section, I will discuss how the psychological understanding of hate illuminates the various challenges in addressing hate and how it can guide NGOs and practitioners in effectively combating this destructive force in intergroup relations.

Limitations of Psychological Interventions

Along with the plethora of explanations of group-based hate and other extreme forms of intergroup negativity, social psychology has developed numerous interventions that aim to reduce biases and prejudice in ongoing conflicts and post-conflict societies. Many of the widely applied theories and interventions – for example, promoting a common ingroup identity,[83] facilitating positive intergroup contact,[84] and fostering perspective-taking with the outgroup[85] – have been shown to be successful in reducing prejudice and negative intergroup emotions in empirical research. Some researchers even went as far as arguing that psychological, prejudice-reduction interventions are essentially about regulating intergroup emotions.[86] These theoretical and empirical developments have led to programs and policies highlighting psychological interventions to fight hate and related societal issues.[87] The effectiveness of these interventions in mitigating hate – an exceptionally intense and enduring intergroup emotion – remains uncertain for several reasons. Some of these reasons apply to psychological interventions in general and others are specific about using these interventions to reduce hate.

   Limited evidence from the real world. In 2009, Paluck and Green published an influential review showing that an overwhelming majority of prejudice-reduction interventions had not received rigorous evaluations in the real world, casting doubts on their actual effectiveness.[88] Although the field has now seen rapid growth in research evaluating these interventions, evidence for their effectiveness remains ambiguous. In a recent meta-analytical review, Paluck and colleagues reviewed over 400 experiments on psychological interventions that were reported between 2007 and 2019.[89] The researchers concluded that the positive effects of these interventions tend to be exaggerated due to publication bias and their long-term benefits remained unclear. Furthermore, the most well-designed and well-executed studies on prejudice-reduction interventions in the real world (e.g., interventions involving face-to-face intergroup contact and perspective-taking, diversity training) produced modest positive effects that were "limited in size, scope, or duration."[90] Interestingly, the review of these "landmark" studies also revealed a marked gap between attitude and behavior, such that interventions tended to be more effective in reducing discriminatory behavior than negative intergroup attitudes. Although most of the studies reviewed did not measure hate as an outcome, this review reveals the limitations of psychological interventions in achieving their intended goals, which often include shifting from negative to positive psychological orientations toward the outgroup.

Selective target populations. Research evaluating psychological interventions has been conducted primarily on (less prejudiced) college students and, much less frequently, on the general population.[91] This not only limits the generalizability of research findings to the real world but also means that we know little to nothing about the effects of these interventions on individuals who have felt hatred toward other groups. Even studies on hate or other extreme forms of intergroup negativity rarely investigate members of real hate groups or extremists.[92] Insights into how members of radical groups, or individuals particularly prone to experiencing and acting on hate, respond to antihate interventions are therefore severely lacking. This is not to say that research on reducing hate among the general public is not valuable. Rather, tackling extreme intergroup emotions requires insights into those who regularly experience those emotions. Such efforts are also crucial for understanding and addressing the rising prevalence of hate groups, as seen in various parts of the world, including the United States.[93]

Unique characteristics of hate. The distinct properties of hate – its endurance, intensity, and rigid cognitive basis – may render it particularly difficult to downregulate compared to other negative intergroup emotions.[94] Consider perspective-taking as an example: instructing individuals to step into the shoes of members of an outgroup that they feel angry about (but do not hate) might help them appreciate external circumstances as contributing to their actions, thereby lowering the intensity of anger. The same intervention, however, may not be effective for someone holding essentialized beliefs about the outgroup's evil intentions and nature (i.e., when the outgroup is a target of hatred). In the same vein, conciliatory intergroup gestures such as offering apologies and reparations might be effective for recipients who believe that the outgroup is capable of change and reduce their feelings of anger,[95] but not for those who have no faith in the outgroup's ability to improve.

Such gestures can even backfire when they are viewed as disingenuous or when preexisting levels of intergroup trust are low.[96] Positive contact between members of groups, while generally effective in reducing prejudice,[97] also seems to have limited utility in changing more deeply engrained beliefs about intergroup relations.[98] Furthermore, it seems rather unlikely that individuals harboring intense, extremely negative sentiments toward the outgroup would find themselves in situations conducive to sustained positive contact with members of the hated group.

Lack of attention to macro-level factors. While group-based hate is rooted in both micro- and macro-level factors, the vast majority of psychological interventions focus on eliciting attitudinal and behavioral changes by influencing micro-level processes, for example, perspective-taking, emotion regulation, and social identification.[99] Only a small minority of social psychological theories and interventions center on macro-level factors or explicitly take those factors into account.

The power dynamics between groups, for example, have been repeatedly demonstrated to influence the efficacy of various prejudice-reduction strategies.[100] Many well-intended interventions prove ineffective or even backfire for one side of an asymmetrical conflict – in most cases, the low-power side.[101] Overlooking macro- or structural-level factors not only limits the effectiveness of interventions, but also risks impeding constructive societal changes. In many cases, negative intergroup emotions, including hate, are legitimate reactions to structural issues such as systematic injustices, oppression, and victimization.[102] These issues are inevitably sidelined when the attention is solely on individual-level cognitive and affective changes.

Relatedly, traditional psychological models of conflict intervention have largely failed to consider the vast differences between victim and perpetrator groups.[103] Although I focused on experiences of collective victimhood in my analysis of the origins of hate, hate is evidently present among both victim and perpetrator groups of conflict. Strategies to reduce hate, however, are unlikely to induce sustainable changes at a large scale if they fail to address the divergent needs of victim versus perpetrator groups following a conflict. According to the needs-based model of reconciliation,[104] victims' loss of agency and status during the conflict results in a heightened need for empowerment, whereas perpetrators' loss of reputation and moral status results in a heightened need for acceptance. These divergent needs thus motivate group members to respond differently to interventions depending on whether the intervention meets their respective needs.

Hopeful Takeaways and Constructive Approaches to Tackling Hate

The current body of research portrays a somewhat pessimistic outlook on many psychological interventions in their applications to combat group-based hate. This research, nevertheless, also suggests that interventions and practices can benefit from addressing the unique characteristics and multilayered antecedents of hate. Below I summarize several tentative but encouraging takeaways that can be drawn from this literature.

Even extremists can change. The long-enduring nature of hate does not mean that those who experience hate are bound to it forever. Research indeed suggests that deradicalization or disengagement is not uncommon, even among members of extremist groups.[105] Among the diverse reasons underlying individuals' decisions to leave hate groups, one important factor is the feeling of burnout and exhaustion stemming from their associations with these groups.[106] This resonates with the psychological understanding of hate as an emotion of immensely high intensity. Enduring such a high-intensity negative emotion can arguably take a toll on the individual. An ethnographic study of former neo-Nazis in Scandinavia found that many people left their groups due to the demanding lifestyles and constant involvement in violence, requiring "a steady supply of rage" that eventually began to dissipate.[107] Thus, although most intervention efforts focus on moderates rather than extremists (for understandable reasons), the latter should not be considered a "lost cause" – rather, they are capable of undergoing meaningful and constructive change.

Not all negative emotions are (equally) destructive. The empirical research reviewed above underscores the need to differentiate between negative intergroup emotions with various levels of destructiveness. In particular, it is important to recognize the constructive role that anger sometimes plays in promoting support for peace and nonviolent collective action.[108] Anger toward other groups, when not accompanied by the belief that the outgroup cannot change, can motivate support for conciliatory policies.[109] Hence, when devising policies and interventions to reduce intergroup hostility, not all negative intergroup emotions should be treated uniformly.

Although targeting a specific negative emotion without affecting closely related ones may prove challenging in practice, interventions can potentially benefit from explicitly acknowledging the legitimacy and usefulness of certain negative emotions. Developing strategies to prevent these emotions from further escalating into more destructive ones, such as hatred, could present a promising avenue for future intervention design.

Challenging the rigid cognitive basis of hate. I have discussed a number of reasons that should give us pause when applying traditional psychological approaches to addressing intergroup hostilities. Recent advancements in psychological interventions, however, have illuminated several promising directions. One such intervention aims to reduce hate by changing the perception that members of the hated outgroup are inherently evil and all the same.[110] This intervention exposes individuals to narratives about outgroup members who risked important aspects of their lives to help others from different groups, such as rescuers during the Holocaust. These stories of *moral exemplars* challenge the rigid categorizations of groups as exclusively good or bad, victim or perpetrator, "us" or "them," and thereby present an opportunity to diminish hatred.[111]

Another promising intervention strategy focuses on promoting the belief that groups, in general, have a malleable (as opposed to fixed) nature that allows for change over time.[112] This intervention is believed to reduce hatred by targeting the appraisal of the antagonistic outgroup as incapable of altering its destructive nature. Studies across different intergroup contexts have provided indirect evidence for this idea, showing that shifting beliefs about group malleability can indeed generate positive changes in intergroup orientations and foster forgiveness in the presence of a collective apology.[113]

Fostering inclusive, non-defensive group identities. Alongside the cognitive approaches discussed earlier, interventions targeting hate can potentially benefit from transforming defensive, exclusionary aspects of group identity into non-defensive, inclusive ones. Collective victimization, for example, is typically believed to elicit defensive, threat-oriented responses including the perception of the ingroup as having suffered uniquely, exclusively, and perpetually. More recent research, however, challenges this view on victimhood, showing that experiences of collective victimization do not necessarily lead to hatred and violence. Instead, group members can view their suffering through an inclusive lens, recognizing shared experiences among victim groups.[114]

Embracing an inclusive victim identity can give rise to a variety of positive, prosocial intergroup outcomes, many of which are essential for preventing and fighting hatred (e.g., activism to prevent genocide and promote peace).[115] This body of work further points to the importance of exposing people to victim narratives from other (non-adversarial) groups to foster an inclusive sense of victimhood. Vollhardt recommends facilitating such exposures through educational programs, dialogues, media, as well as panels featuring survivors of mass violence.[116] However, it is worth cautioning that emphasizing similarities in suffering might have negative consequences for low-power groups if the power difference is not acknowledged.[117]

Targeting social norms rather than personal beliefs. As discussed earlier, the behavioral manifestations of hate are varied, and hate does not inevitably drive individuals to violence. Indeed, social norms can function as behavioral "inhibitors," breaking the link between hate and violence.[118] There is evidence that changes in group norms can potentially lead to changes in the expression of hate, even without group members endorsing the new norm.

In a year-long field experiment in Rwanda, Paluck examined the impact of exposure to a radio program promoting messages about reducing prejudice and violence in fictional communities on listeners' intergroup attitudes and behavior.[119] Compared to the control group that listened to a neutral radio program, listeners in the experimental group showed changes in perceived social norms regarding intergroup relations. These changes were accompanied by changes in behavior such as active participation in negotiation, open expression of sensitive topics, and cooperation. Changes in perceived social norms and behavior, however, did not translate into changes in personal beliefs or attitudes regarding intergroup violence and trauma. Although this research did not measure intergroup hate as an outcome, the findings suggest that interventions may be more effective in targeting perceived social norms than personal beliefs.

Promoting structural changes to effect individual-level changes. The above review also highlights the need to address the structural roots of hate in order to facilitate sustainable societal changes. This is not to downplay the importance of individual-level factors and processes contributing to hate; rather, these processes should be considered within the broader social and political context. As discussed earlier, collective experiences of conflict, injustices, victimhood, and perpetration not only directly fuel feelings of hate, but also indirectly contribute to it by frustrating individual needs, fostering defensive group identities, and heightening perceptions of threats. It thus stands to reason that interventions promoting support for structural changes can be paramount in the fight against hate by facilitating individual-level transformations.

Indeed, research has shown that societal mechanisms, such as judicial approaches (i.e., trials and punishment) to intergroup violence and formal acknowledgment of wrongdoings by perpetrator groups, can help fulfill victim group members' need for justice and increase their positive orientations toward the perpetrator group.[120] Additionally, shifting collective narratives to include the adversarial group's suffering has demonstrated potential in reducing defensive modes of ingroup identification (e.g., ingroup glorification).[121] Considerations of structural processes can thus guide interventions in determining their targets and approaches.

Concluding Remarks

Transforming deep-seated hatred into mutual acceptance and respect between groups can take years and even generations. It is important to recognize both the potential and limitations of interventions as no single intervention can address all dimensions or origins of hate, and there is no one-size-fits-all solution to it. Effective interventions should consider micro- and macro-level factors in tandem, the idiosyncratic context in which they operate, as well as the challenges presented by the unique features of hate. It is equally important to acknowledge that hate can be a justified response to injustices. Following mass violence or systemic human rights violations, rushing into dialogues and negotiations to promote positive intergroup emotions might be ineffective or even harmful if the intergroup dynamic is characterized by oppression or severe power imbalance. Hence, enabling structural changes is a necessary step toward positive affective changes within individuals.

NOTES

1 Thomas Brudholm, "What Is Hate?," in Robert J. Sternberg, ed., *Perspectives on Hate: How It Originates, Develops, Manifests, and Spreads* (Washington, DC: American Psychological Association, 2020), https://doi.org/10.1037/0000180-004; Agneta Fischer et al., "Why We Hate," *Emotion Review* 10, no. 4 (2018): 309–20, https://doi .org/10.1177/1754073917751229; Edward B. Royzman, Clark McCauley, and Paul Rozin, "From Plato to Putnam: Four Ways to Think about Hate," in Robert J. Sternberg, ed., *The Psychology of Hate* (Washington, DC: American Psychological Association, 2005), https://doi.org/10.1037 /10930-001.
2 Alexander Faulkner Shand, *The Foundations of Character: Being a Study of the Tendencies of the Emotions and Sentiment*, 2nd ed. (London: Macmillan, 1920).
3 Gordon W. Allport, *The Nature of Prejudice* (Reading, MA: AddisonWesley, 1954).
4 Aaron Ben-Ze'Ev, "Emotional and Moral Evaluations," *Metaphilosophy* 23, no. 3 (1992): 214–29, https://www.jstor.org/stable/24438865.

5 Jack Levin and Jack McDevitt, *Hate Crimes: The Rising Tide of Bigotry and Bloodshed* (New York: Springer, 1993), https://doi.org/10.1007/978-1-4899-6108-2.

6 John K. Rempel and Christopher T. Burris, "Let Me Count the Ways: An Integrative Theory of Love and Hate," *Personal Relationships* 12, no. 2 (2005): 297–313, https://doi.org/10.1111/j.1350-4126.2005.00116.x.

7 Susan Opotow and Sara I. McClelland, "The Intensification of Hating: A Theory," *Social Justice Research* 20, no. 1 (2007): 68–97, https://doi.org/10.1007/s11211-007-0033-0.

8 Jon Elster, *Alchemies of the Mind: Rationality and the Emotions* (Cambridge: Cambridge University Press, 1999).

9 Paul Ekman, "An Argument for Basic Emotions," *Cognition and Emotion* 6, no. 3–4 (1992): 169–200, https://doi.org/10.1080/02699939208411068.

10 Thomas Brudholm and Birgitte Schepelern Johansen, "Pondering Hatred," in Thomas Brudholm and Johannes Lang, eds., *Emotions and Mass Atrocity: Philosophical and Theoretical Explorations* (Cambridge: Cambridge University Press, 2018), https://doi.org/10.1017/9781316563281.005.

11 For a discussion on the ethical importance of defining hate, see Brudholm and Johansen, chapter 1, in this volume.

12 In keeping with the psychological literature, "hate" and "hatred" are used interchangeably throughout this chapter.

13 For example, Daniel Bar-Tal, *Intractable Conflicts: Socio-Psychological Foundations and Dynamics* (Cambridge: Cambridge University Press, 2007); Fischer et al., "Why We Hate"; Eran Halperin, "Group-Based Hatred in Intractable Conflict in Israel," *Journal of Conflict Resolution* 52, no. 5 (2008): 713–36, https://doi.org/10.1177/0022002708314665; Robert J. Sternberg, "A Duplex Theory of Hate: Development and Application to Terrorism, Massacres, and Genocide," *Review of General Psychology* 7, no. 3 (2003): 299–328, https://doi.org/10.1037/1089-2680.7.3.299; Janne van Doorn, "Anger, Feelings of Revenge, and Hate," *Emotion Review* 10, no. 4 (2018): 321–2, https://doi.org/10.1177/1754073918783260. See also Galván, chapter 2, in this volume.

14 Eran Halperin and Drew E. Schwartz, "Emotions in Conflict Resolution and Post-Conflict Reconciliation," *Les Cahiers Internationaux de Psychologie Sociale* 87, no. 3 (2010): 430, https://doi.org/10.3917/cips.087.0423.

15 Halperin, "Group-Based Hatred"; Eran Halperin, Daphna Canetti, and Shaul Kimhi, "In Love with Hatred: Rethinking the Role Hatred Plays in Shaping Political Behavior," *Journal of Applied Social Psychology* 42, no. 9 (2012): 2231–56, https://doi.org/10.1111/j.1559-1816.2012.00938.x; Cristhian A. Martínez, Jan Willem van Prooijen, and Paul A.M. van Lange, "Hate: Toward Understanding Its Distinctive Features across Interpersonal and Intergroup Targets," *Emotion* 22, no. 1 (2021): 46–63, https://doi

.org/10.1037/emo0001056; Clara Pretus et al., "The Psychology of Hate: Moral Concerns Differentiate Hate from Dislike," *European Journal of Social Psychology* 53, no. 2 (2023): 336–53, https://doi.org/10.1002/ejsp.2906. See also Fischer et al., "Why We Hate," for a review.

16 Michael J.A. Wohl, Nassim Tabri, and Eran Halperin, "Emotional Sources of Intergroup Atrocities," in L.S. Newman, ed., *Confronting Humanity at Its Worst: Social Psychological Perspectives on Genocide* (Oxford: Oxford University Press, 2020), https://doi.org/10.1093/oso/9780190685942.003.0004.

17 Halperin, "Group-Based Hatred," Study 1.

18 See Fischer et al., "Why We Hate"; Wohl et al., "Emotional Sources of Intergroup Atrocities."

19 Bar-Tal, *Intractable Conflicts*.

20 Halperin, "Group-Based Hatred." See also Wohl, Tabri, and Halperin, "Emotional Sources."

21 Halperin, "Group-Based Hatred," Study 3.

22 Martínez, van Prooijen, and van Lange, "Hate"; Nimrod Nir, Eran Halperin, and Juhwa Park, "Intergroup Hate in Conflict: The Case of the Korean Conflict," in Juhwa Park et al., eds., *Annual Reports of Attitude of Koreans toward Peace and Reconciliation* (Seoul: Korea Institute for National Unification, 2019); Pretus et al., "The Psychology of Hate."

23 Philippe Verduyn and Saskia Lavrijse, "Which Emotions Last Longest and Why: The Role of Event Importance and Rumination," *Motivation and Emotion* 39, no. 1 (2015): 119–27, https://doi.org/10.1007/s11031-014-9445-y.

24 Halperin, "Group-Based Hatred."

25 Halperin et al., "In Love with Hatred."

26 Fischer et al., "Why We Hate," 312.

27 Halperin et al., "In Love with Hatred."

28 Sternberg, "A Duplex Theory of Hate."

29 Martínez, van Prooijen, and van Lange, "Hate."

30 Eran Halperin et al., "Anger, Hatred, and the Quest for Peace: Anger Can Be Constructive in the Absence of Hatred," *Journal of Conflict Resolution* 55, no. 2 (2011): 274–91, https://doi.org/10.1177/0022002710383670; van Doorn, "Anger, Feelings of Revenge, and Hate."

31 Pretus et al., "The Psychology of Hate."

32 Halperin, "Group-Based Hatred."

33 Halperin, "Group-Based Hatred," Study 2.

34 Halperin et al., "Anger, Hatred, and the Quest for Peace."

35 Pretus et al., "The Psychology of Hate."

36 Jack Glaser, Jay Dixit, and Donald P. Green, "Studying Hate Crime with the Internet: What Makes Racists Advocate Racial Violence?," *Journal of*

Social Issues 58, no. 1 (2002): 177–93, https://doi.org/10.1111/1540
-4560.00255; Hoover et al., "Investing the Role of Group-Based Morality."

37 Tirza Leader, Brian Mullen, and Diana Rice, "Complexity and Valence
in Ethnophaulisms and Exclusion of Ethnic Out-Groups: What Puts the
'Hate' into Hate Speech?," *Journal of Personality and Social Psychology* 96,
no. 1 (2009): Article 1, https://doi.org/10.1037/a0013066; Martínez et al.,
"Hate"; Opotow and McClelland, "The Intensification of Hating."

38 Nir and Halperin, *Intergroup Hate in Conflict.*

39 Fischer et al., "Why We Hate."

40 Halperin, "Group-Based Hatred"; Halperin et al., "Anger, Hatred and the
Quest for Peace"; Martínez van Prooijen and Lange, "Hate."

41 Agneta H. Fischer and Ira J. Roseman, "Beat Them or Ban Them: The
Characteristics and Social Functions of Anger and Contempt," *Journal of
Personality and Social Psychology* 93, no. 1 (2007): 103–15, https://doi.org
/10.1037/0022-3514.93.1.103; Eran Halperin et al., "Promoting the Middle
East Peace Process by Changing Beliefs about Group Malleability," *Science*
333, no. 6050 (2011): 1767–9, https://doi.org/10.1126/science.1202925;
Shuman et al., "Anger as a Catalyst for Change?"

42 Tausch et al., *Explaining Radical Group Behavior.*

43 Liesbeth Mann et al., "Withdraw or Affiliate? The Role of Humiliation
during Initiation Rituals," *Cognition & Emotion* 30, no. 1 (2015): 1–21,
https://doi.org/10.1080/02699931.2015.1050358.

44 Elise Seip, "Desire for Vengeance and Revenge: An Emotion-Based
Approach to Revenge" (PhD diss., University of Amsterdam, 2016).

45 Fischer et al., "Why We Hate"; Opotow and McClelland, "The
Intensification of Hating"; Sternberg, "A Duplex Theory of Hate."

46 Ervin Staub, "The Origins and Evolution of Hate, with Notes on
Prevention," in Robert J. Sternberg, ed., *The Psychology of Hate*
(Washington, DC: American Psychological Association, 2005), https://doi
.org/10.1037/10930-003.

47 Fischer et al., "Why We Hate."

48 Sonia Roccas et al., "Toward a Unifying Model of Identification with
Groups: Integrating Theoretical Perspectives," *Personality and Social
Psychology Review* 12, no. 3 (2008): Article 3, https://doi.org/10.1177
/1088868308319225.

49 Quinnehtukqut McLamore, Levi Adelman, and Bernhard Leidner,
"Challenges to Traditional Narratives of Intractable Conflict Decrease
Ingroup Glorification," *Personality and Social Psychology Bulletin* 45, no. 12
(2019): 1702–16, https://doi.org/10.1177/0146167219841638.

50 For example, Sternberg, *The Psychology of Hate.*

51 Staub, "The Origins and Evolution of Hate."

52 Raphael S. Ezekiel, "An Ethnographer Looks at Neo-Nazi and Klan Groups: The Racist Mind Revisited," *American Behavioral Scientist* 46, no. 1 (2002): 51–71, https://doi.org/10.1177/0002764202046001005.

53 S. Alexander Haslam et al., "Social Identity, Health and Well-Being: An Emerging Agenda for Applied Psychology," *Applied Psychology* 58, no. 1 (2009): 1–23, https://doi.org/10.1111/j.1464-0597.2008.00379.x.

54 Abdo Elnakouri, Candice Hubley, and Ian McGregor, "Hate and Meaning in Life: How Collective, but Not Personal, Hate Quells Threat and Spurs Meaning in Life," *Journal of Experimental Social Psychology* 98 (2022): 104227, https://doi.org/10.1016/j.jesp.2021.104227.

55 Michael A. Hogg, Arie Kruglanski, and Kees van den Bos, "Uncertainty and the Roots of Extremism: Uncertainty and Extremism," *Journal of Social Issues* 69, no. 3 (2013): Article 3, https://doi.org/10.1111/josi.12021; Arie Kruglanski et al., "The Psychology of Radicalization and Deradicalization: How Significance Quest Impacts Violent Extremism," *Political Psychology* 35, no. S1 (2014): Article S1, https://doi.org/10.1111/pops.12163.

56 William B. Swann Jr. et al., "Identity Fusion: The Interplay of Personal and Social Identities in Extreme Group Behavior," *Journal of Personality and Social Psychology* 96, no. 5 (2009): 995–1011, https://doi.org/10.1037/a0013668.

57 Halperin et al., "In Love with Hatred."

58 Diane M. Mackie and Eliot R. Smith, "Group-Based Emotion in Group Processes and Intergroup Relations," *Group Processes & Intergroup Relations* 20, no. 5 (2017): 658–68, https://doi.org/10.1177/1368430217702725.

59 Marilynn B. Brewer, "Identity and Conflict," in Daniel Bar-Tal, ed., *Intergroup Conflicts and Their Resolution: A Social Psychological Perspective* (New York: Psychology Press, 2011).

60 Mackie and Smith, "Group-Based Emotion."

61 Eliot Smith, Charles Seger, and Diane M. Mackie, "Can Emotions Be Truly Group Level? Evidence regarding Four Conceptual Criteria," *Journal of Personality and Social Psychology* 93, no. 3 (2007): Article 3, https://doi.org/10.1037/0022-3514.93.3.431.

62 Julie Fitness and Garth J.O. Fletcher, "Love, Hate, Anger, and Jealousy in Close Relationships: A Prototype and Cognitive Appraisal Analysis," *Journal of Personality and Social Psychology* 65, no. 5 (1993): 942–58, https://doi.org/10.1037/0022-3514.65.5.942.

63 Aleksandra Cichocka, "Understanding Defensive and Secure In-Group Positivity: The Role of Collective Narcissism," *European Review of Social Psychology* 27, no. 1 (2016): 283–317, https://doi.org/10.1080/10463283.2016.1252530.

64 Mengyao Li et al., "National Glorification and Attachment Differentially Predict Support for Intergroup Conflict Resolution: Scrutinizing

Cross-Country Generalizability," *European Journal of Social Psychology* 53, no. 1 (2023): 29–42, https://doi.org/10.1002/ejsp.2881; Sonia Roccas, Yechiel Klar, and Ido Liviatan, "The Paradox of Group-Based Guilt: Modes of National Identification, Conflict Vehemence, and Reactions to the In-Group's Moral Violations," *Journal of Personality and Social Psychology* 91, no. 4 (2006): Article 4, https://doi.org/10.1037/0022-3514.91.4.698.

65 Li et al., "National Glorification"; Roccas, Klar, and Liviatan, "The Paradox of Group-Based Guilt"; Hema Preya Selvanathan and Bernhard Leidner, "Modes of Ingroup Identification and Notions of Justice Provide Distinct Pathways to Normative and Nonnormative Collective Action in the Israeli–Palestinian Conflict," *Journal of Conflict Resolution* 64, no. 9 (2020): 1754–88, https://doi.org/10.1177/0022002720907660; Özden Melis Uluğ et al., "Obstacles to Reconciliation and Forgiveness among Victim Groups of Unacknowledged Past Trauma and Genocide," *European Journal of Social Psychology* 51, no. 2 (2021): 313–25, https://doi.org/10.1002/ejsp.2740.

66 Robert Jay Lifton, "Americans as Survivors," *The New England Journal of Medicine* 352, no. 22 (2005): 2263–5, https://doi.org/10.1056/NEJMp 058048.

67 Tadek Markiewicz and Keren Sharvit, "When Victimhood Goes to War? Israel and Victim Claims," *Political Psychology* 42, no. 1 (2021): 111–26, https://doi.org/10.1111/pops.12690; Johanna Ray Vollhardt and Rashmi Nair, "The Two-Sided Nature of Individual and Intragroup Experiences in the Aftermath of Collective Victimization: Findings from Four Diaspora Groups," *European Journal of Social Psychology* 48, no. 4 (2018): 412–32, https://doi.org/10.1002/ejsp.2341.

68 For reviews, see Mengyao Li et al., "From Threat to Challenge: Understanding the Impact of Historical Collective Trauma on Contemporary Intergroup Conflict," *Perspectives on Psychological Science* 18, no. 1 (2022): 190–209, https://doi.org/10.1177/17456916221094540; Masi Noor et al., "When Suffering Begets Suffering: The Psychology of Competitive Victimhood between Adversarial Groups in Violent Conflicts," *Personality and Social Psychology Review* 16, no. 4 (2012): 351–74, https://doi.org/10.1177/1088868312440048.

69 Gilad Hirschberger and Tsachi Ein-Dor, "A Temporal Account of Collective Victimization as Existential Threat Reconsidering Adaptive and Maladaptive Responses," in Johanna R. Vollhardt, ed., *The Social Psychology of Collective Victimhood* (Oxford: Oxford University Press, 2020), https://doi.org/10.1093/oso/9780190875190.001.0005; Vamik D. Volkan, *Bloodlines: From Ethnic Pride to Ethnic Terrorism* (New York: Farrar, Straus and Giroux, 1997).

70 Noa Schori-Eyal, Yechiel Klar, and Yarden Ben-Ami, "Perpetual Ingroup Victimhood as a Distorted Lens: Effects on Attribution and

Categorization," *European Journal of Social Psychology* 47, no. 2 (2017): Article 2, https://doi.org/10.1002/ejsp.2250.

71 Georgios Antoniou, Elias Dinas, and Spyro Kosmidis, "Collective Victimhood and Social Prejudice: A Post-Holocaust Theory of Anti-Semitism," *Political Psychology* 41, no. 5 (2020): 861–86, https://doi.org/10.1111/pops.12654.

72 Fischer et al., "Why We Hate."

73 See also Li et al., "From Threat to Challenge."

74 Fischer et al., "Why We Hate."

75 See, for example, Fletcher Blanchard et al., "Condemning and Condoning Racism: A Social Context Approach to Interracial Settings," *Journal of Applied Psychology* 79, no. 6 (1994): 993–7, https://doi.org/10.1037/0021-9010.79.6.993; and Kevin Munger, "Tweetment Effects on the Tweeted: Experimentally Reducing Racist Harassment," *Political Behavior* 39, no. 3 (2017): 629–49. For a review on different sources of norms, see Elizabeth Levy Paluck, "What's in a Norm? Sources and Processes of Norm Change," *APA PsycNET* 96, no. 3 (2009): 594–600, https://doi.org/10.1037/a0014688.

76 Chris S. Crandall, Amy Eshleman, and Laurie O'Brien, "Social Norms and the Expression and Suppression of Prejudice: The Struggle for Internalization," *Journal of Personality and Social Psychology* 82, no. 3 (2002): 359–78, https://doi.org/10.1037/0022-3514.82.3.359.

77 Amalia Álvarez-Benjumea and Fabian Winter, "The Breakdown of Antiracist Norms: A Natural Experiment on Hate Speech after Terrorist Attacks," *Proceedings of the National Academy of Sciences of the United States of America* 117, no. 37 (2020): 22800–4, https://doi.org/10.1073/pnas.2007977117.

78 For a more in-depth discussion on norms around hateful speech and counterspeech in online discourses, see Buerger, chapter 9, in this volume.

79 Elizabeth Levy Paluck, "Reducing Intergroup Prejudice and Conflict Using the Media: A Field Experiment in Rwanda," *Journal of Personality and Social Psychology* 96, no. 3 (2009): 574–87, https://doi.org/10.1037/a0011989.

80 Hema Preya Selvanathan et al., "Far-Right Movements in the Western World: How Media Exposure Relates to Normative Beliefs and Attitudes toward the Far-Right," *Group Processes & Intergroup Relations* 28, no. 4 (2025), https://doi.org/10.1177/13684302241309554.

81 McLamore, Adelman, and Leidner, "Challenges to Traditional Narratives."

82 For example, Staub, *The Origins and Evolution of Hate*.

83 Samuel L. Gaertner et al., "The Common Ingroup Identity Model: Recategorization and the Reduction of Intergroup Bias," *European Review of Social Psychology* 4, no. 1 (1993): 1–26, https://doi.org/10.1080/14792779343000004.

84 Thomas F. Pettigrew and Linda R. Tropp, "How Does Intergroup Contact Reduce Prejudice? Meta-Analytic Tests of Three Mediators," *European Journal of Social Psychology* 38, no. 6 (2008): 922–34, https://doi.org/10.1002/ejsp.504.

85 C. Daniel Batson, Shannon Early, and Giovanni Salvarani, "Perspective Taking: Imagining How Another Feels versus Imagining How You Would Feel," *Personality and Social Psychology Bulletin* 23, no. 7 (1997): 751–8, https://doi.org/10.1177/0146167297237008.

86 Sabina Čehajić-Clancy et al., "Social-Psychological Interventions for Intergroup Reconciliation: An Emotion Regulation Perspective," *Psychological Inquiry* 27, no. 2 (2016): 73–88, https://doi.org/10.1080/1047840X.2016.1153945.

87 For example, Robert J. Cramer et al., "Hate-Motivated Behavior: Impacts, Risk Factors, and Interventions," Health Affairs Health Policy Brief, November 9, 2020, https://www.healthaffairs.org/do/10.1377/hpb20200929.601434/full/; Petra C. Gronholm et al., "Interventions to Reduce Discrimination and Stigma: The State of the Art," *Social Psychiatry and Psychiatric Epidemiology* 52, no. 3 (2017): 249–58, https://doi.org/10.1007/s00127-017-1341-9.

88 Elizabeth Levy Paluck and Donald P. Green, "Prejudice Reduction: What Works? A Review and Assessment of Research and Practice," *Annual Review of Psychology* 60, no. 1 (2009): 339–67, https://doi.org/10.1146/annurev.psych.60.110707.163607.

89 Paluck and Green, "Prejudice Reduction."

90 Elizabeth Levy Paluck et al., "Prejudice Reduction: Progress and Challenges," *Annual Review of Psychology* 72, no. 1 (2021): 553, https://doi.org/10.1146/annurev-psych-071620-030619.

91 Paluck and Green, "Prejudice Reduction."

92 For examples of exceptions, see Joe Hoover et al., "Investigating the Role of Group-Based Morality in Extreme Behavioral Expressions of Prejudice," *Nature Communications* 12, no. 1 (2021): 4585, https://doi.org/10.1038/s41467-021-24786-2; and Pretus et al., "The Psychology of Hate."

93 Hoover et al., "Investigating the Role of Group-Based Morality."

94 Fischer et al., "Why We Hate."

95 Čehajić-Clancy et al., "Social-Psychological Interventions."

96 Matthew J. Hornsey and Michael J.A. Wohl, "We Are Sorry: Intergroup Apologies and Their Tenuous Link with Intergroup Forgiveness," *European Review of Social Psychology* 24, no. 1 (2013): 1–31, https://doi.org/10.1080/10463283.2013.822206.

97 Pettigrew and Tropp, "How Does Intergroup Contact Reduce Prejudice?"

98 Brooke Burrows et al., "How Intergroup Contact Shapes Intergroup Attitudes and Construals of Relations between Ethnic Groups: Evidence

from Bosnia and Herzegovina," *Peace and Conflict: Journal of Peace Psychology* 28, no. 3 (2022): 372–83, https://doi.org/10.1037 /pac0000629.

99 Čehajić-Clancy et al., "Social-Psychological Interventions."

100 Mengyao Li and Bernhard Leidner, "Understanding Intergroup Violence and Its Aftermath from Perpetrator and Victim Perspectives," in Leonard S. Newman, ed., *Confronting Humanity at Its Worst: Social Psychological Perspectives on Genocide* (New York: Oxford University Press, 2020), https://doi.org/10.1093/oso/9780190685942.003.0007.

101 For example, Emile G. Bruneau and Rebecca Saxe, "The Power of Being Heard: The Benefits of 'Perspective-Giving' in the Context of Intergroup Conflict," *Journal of Experimental Social Psychology* 48, no. 4 (2012): 855–66, https://doi.org/10.1016/j.jesp.2012.02.017; John F. Dovidio, Samuel L. Gaertner, and Tamar Saguy, "Another View of 'We': Majority and Minority Group Perspectives on a Common Ingroup Identity," *European Review of Social Psychology* 18, no. 1 (2007): 296–330, https://doi.org /10.1080/10463280701726132.

102 Mengyao Li, Daniel R. Rovenpor, and Bernhard Leidner, "Regulating the Scope of an Emotion Regulation Perspective on Intergroup Reconciliation," *Psychological Inquiry* 27, no. 2 (2016): 117–23, https:// doi.org/10.1080/1047840X.2016.1163960; Johanna Ray Vollhardt and Michelle S. Twali, "Emotion-Based Reconciliation Requires Attention to Power Differences, Critical Consciousness, and Structural Change," *Psychological Inquiry* 27, no. 2 (2016): 136–43, https://doi.org/10.1080 /1047840X.2016.1160762.

103 Rezarta Bilali and Johanna Ray Vollhardt, "Victim and Perpetrator Groups' Divergent Perspectives on Collective Violence: Implications for Intergroup Relations," *Political Psychology* 40, no. S1 (2019): 75–108, https://doi.org/10.1111/pops.12570; Li and Leidner, "Understanding Intergroup Violence."

104 Nurit Shnabel et al., "Promoting Reconciliation through the Satisfaction of the Emotional Needs of Victimized and Perpetrating Group Members: The Needs-Based Model of Reconciliation," *Personality and Social Psychology Bulletin* 35, no. 8 (2009): 1021–30, https://doi.org/10.1177 /0146167209336610.

105 John Horgan, "Deradicalization or Disengagement?: A Process in Need of Clarity and a Counterterrorism Initiative in Need of Evaluation," *Perspectives on Terrorism* 2, no. 4 (2008): 3–8, http://www.jstor.org /stable/26298340.

106 Bryan F. Bubolz and Pete Simi, "Leaving the World of Hate: Life-Course Transitions and Self-Change," *American Behavioral Scientist* 59, no. 12 (2015): 1588–608, https://doi.org/10.1177/0002764215588814.

107 Michael Kimmel, "Racism as Adolescent Male Rite of Passage: Ex-Nazis in Scandinavia," *Journal of Contemporary Ethnography* 36, no. 2 (2007): 215, https://doi.org/10.1177/0891241606298825.

108 For example, Eric Shuman, Eran Halperin, and Michal Reifen Tagar, "Anger as a Catalyst for Change? Incremental Beliefs and Anger's Constructive Effects in Conflict," *Group Processes & Intergroup Relations* 21, no. 7 (2018): 1092–106, https://doi.org/10.1177/1368430217695442; Nicole Tausch et al., "Explaining Radical Group Behaviour: Developing Emotion and Efficacy Routes to Normative and Non-normative Collective Action," *Journal of Personality and Social Psychology* 101, no. 1 (2011): 129–48, https://doi.org/10.1037/a0022728.

109 Shuman et al., "Anger as a Catalyst for Change?"

110 Sabina Čehajić-Clancy and Michal Bilewicz, "Moral-Exemplar Intervention: A New Paradigm for Conflict Resolution and Intergroup Reconciliation," *Current Directions in Psychological Science* 30, no. 4 (2021): 335–42, https://doi.org/10.1177/09637214211013001.

111 Čehajić-Clancy et al., "Social Psychological Interventions." For a discussion on the potential pitfalls of this intervention, see Michal Bilewicz and Sabina Čehajić-Clancy, "The Promise and Limits of Moral Exemplars for Intergroup Conflict Resolution and Reconciliation," *Conflict Resolution Quarterly* 41, no. 1 (2023): 7–18, https://doi.org/10.1002/crq.21386.

112 Halperin et al., "Promoting the Middle East Peace Process."

113 Halperin et al., "Promoting the Middle East Peace Process"; Michael J.A. Wohl et al., "Belief in the Malleability of Groups Strengthens the Tenuous Link between a Collective Apology and Intergroup Forgiveness," *Personality and Social Psychology Bulletin* 41, no. 5 (2015): 714–25, https://doi.org/10.1177/0146167215576721.

114 For example, Levin, chapter 4, in this volume; and Johanna Ray Vollhardt and Rezarta Bilali, "The Role of Inclusive and Exclusive Victim Consciousness in Predicting Intergroup Attitudes: Findings from Rwanda, Burundi, and DRC," *Political Psychology* 36, no. 5 (2015): Article 5, https://doi.org/10.1111/pops.12174.

115 For a comprehensive review of the implications of inclusive victimhood for policies and practices, see Johanna Ray Vollhardt, "Inclusive Victim Consciousness in Advocacy, Social Movements, and Intergroup Relations: Promises and Pitfalls," *Social Issues and Policy Review* 9, no. 1 (2015): 89–120, https://doi.org/10.1111/sipr.12011.

116 Vollhardt, "Inclusive Victim Consciousness in Advocacy."

117 Andrew McNeill and Johanna Ray Vollhardt, "'We All Suffered!' – The Role of Power in Rhetorical Strategies of Inclusive Victimhood and Its Consequences for Intergroup Relations," in Johanna Ray Vollhardt, ed.,

Social Psychology of Collective Victimhood (New York: Oxford University Press, 2020), https://doi.org/10.1093/oso/9780190875190.003.0016.

118 See also Leonard Berkowitz, "On Hate and Its Determinants: Some Affective and Cognitive Influences," in Robert J. Sternberg, ed., *The Psychology of Hate* (Washington, DC: American Psychological Association, 2005), https://doi.org/10.1037/10930-008.

119 Paluck, "Reducing Intergroup Prejudice."

120 Mengyao Li et al., "The Role of Retributive Justice and the Use of International Criminal Tribunals in Post-Conflict Reconciliation," *European Journal of Social Psychology* 48, no. 2 (2018): O133–O151, https://doi.org/10.1002/ejsp.2326; Johanna Ray Vollhardt, Lucas B. Mazur, and Magali Lemahieu, "Acknowledgment after Mass Violence: Effects on Psychological Well-Being and Intergroup Relations," *Group Processes & Intergroup Relations* 17, no. 3 (2014): 306–23, https://doi.org/10.1177/1368430213517270. See also Schweppe and Walters, chapter 7, in this volume.

121 McLamore, Adelman, and Leidner, "Challenges to Traditional Narratives."

Editor's Introduction to Chapter 4

Some of the most difficult challenges – the ones that push even some antihate groups into their tribal corners – arise when historical memories clash, or group A is seen as trivializing the trauma of group B for political purposes.

I've written extensively on Holocaust denial, and it of course doesn't surprise me that antisemites will twist the memory of the Holocaust, like they do other things, to paint Jews as conspirators who are bent on harming non-Jews.

But it disturbed me years ago when some colleagues at a conference opposing white supremacy referenced the Holocaust for at best gratuitous, and likely more disturbing, purposes. A Native American woman, speaking eloquently about the discrimination her people faced daily, said in passing that the genocide of American Indians was "worse than" the Holocaust and that Hitler could not get his hands on any Indians, so he went after Jews. Forgetting the absurdity of the notion that Hitler wanted to go after American Indians, the idea that the genocide of American Indians was "worse than" the Holocaust is bizarre. On what scale can one measure genocide? How can you rank these tragedies? It makes no sense to say that the Holocaust was "worse than" slavery, for example. How do you factor in the number killed, the percentage of the population destroyed, the time it took to commit the murder? Each genocide is unique. (What is unique about the Holocaust to me was the priority that killing Jews took over winning the war effort.) Each is another example of people's capacity to classify an "other," to dehumanize that "other," and when dehumanization becomes either central to one's ideology or commonplace and unremarkable, to kill that "other."

Then came a Hispanic poet who spoke passionately about the problems of getting quality public education for Hispanic children. He said that many teachers assumed that a Hispanic child would not amount to much, so these children were neglected and not challenged to succeed. "This is a crime worse than Hitler," he said. "While Hitler attacked the body, these teachers attack the mind." Later he talked about the deportation of farm workers across the border back to Mexico in the first half of the twentieth century and said, "This was the same as the Holocaust." Even allowing for poetic license, this was too much. As racist as those deportations were, farm workers were not lined up on the border and summarily shot nor taken to gas chambers, killed, had their gold fillings removed, and their bodies burned. There is a Holocaust era picture of a girl hastily scribbling a note to someone as she was about to be taken from her home and deported, presumably to one of the camps. Given the choice, she would have willingly suffered sitting in a classroom, being ignored by a racist teacher.[1]

I had a sense, both from this incident and from participating in a clash over memory (around the term "concentration camp") between Jewish and Asian Americans examined in chapter 4 below, that when memories of history of hate intersect, they can cause personal angst, anger even, and cause groups that otherwise share similar goals – Jews, Native Americans, Latinx people, and Asian Americans have powerful reasons to combat white supremacy, which targets them all, for example – to focus on each other instead.

But I had never heard of a theory that looks at how historical memory actually works, and how to think about it more constructively in order to combat contemporary hate more effectively, let alone how to try to avoid the unproductive and unnecessary clashes among organizations and communities.

In 2022 I co-taught an online class on antisemitism, the Holocaust, gender identity, and colonialism. One of the faculty members was Adam Levin, a postdoctoral research fellow from South Africa. He's a literature scholar, but his framing of memory allowed the discussion of the various streams of the class to be connected. He spoke about something I had never heard of before: the theory of multidirectional memory, which is introduced by literary scholar Michael Rothberg in his book *Multidirectional Memory: Remembering the Holocaust in the Age of Decolonization*.[2]

History, in a way, is like our elephant we met in the preface. We tend to focus on one aspect – the Holocaust, or colonialism, for example. Multidirectional memory instructs us to look at history as synonymous with memory. What do we remember and why? There are, of course, collective narratives of each group – what we remember we remember as part of a group. But there is also individual memory.

Memory is all factors together – personal, political, historical. Collective memory is a shared experience. But what happens when each collective experience is seen in competition with another?

The Holocaust, of course, is something that happened to Jews. Is seeing the lessons as important for humankind, for instance, something that degrades, or even erases, the memory of the Holocaust itself? When we look at history to combat hate, what are we actually doing? And does how we look at past events help, or hinder, how we respond to current challenges, or even think about setting useful foundations to better tackle future ones?

The Holocaust, of course, is not the only human tragedy of hate, and when we put it in conversation with other tragedies, and there are comparisons, what happens? Multidirectional memory instructs us to recognize that comparison implies both differences and similarities, and creates hierarchies.

Following Rothberg, Levin argues that historical memory and ritual commemoration are nothing if not a refiguring of present lives in light of a remembered past. You have to look at yourself in the past to understand yourself in the present. In a sense, everyone and the reservoir of their historical memories is a metaphor, and requires comparison. You have to look back at other histories to understand your own. Or at least you should. Part of the dysfunction around issues like the Israel/Palestine conflict is that while these two historical narratives are glued together as part of the same overall story, each either ignores the other's narrative or only treats it as a secondary story and as an obstacle, rather than as something essential to incorporate to get a complete historical understanding.

And this wider lens isn't only about thinking of the memory of group A to understand the history of group B. It also is about looking at political and other memories. Think about how many of today's conflicts associated with hate revolve around memory. In Europe there's constant evidence of this, from the breakup of Yugoslavia to the Russian war on Ukraine (and the memory of Imperial Russia and the "glory" of the former USSR), hate today is frequently stoked by employing memory as a weapon that both vilifies and dehumanizes the "other" and reaffirms the noble goals of those considered to be part of "us."

The same can be said about some of the debates in the United States. Donald Trump's political slogan "Make America Great Again" directly calls out to memory. But what memory? What myths? A poor white person, whose family never had it "great," might be animated by the illusion that at least as a white person he/she was perceived to be "better" than another. To a Black person, the slogan might recall the memory of enslavement. And when these memories intersect – when it comes to such symbolic issues as whether to remove statues of Confederate leaders, or of America's founders who were slaveholders – the memories are indeed in conflict and competition. So too in controversies such as how to teach American history to students. Too often the binary aspect of these contests block out the other part of the story. Some prioritize wanting young people to feel pride in the memories of what indeed made America great (like the ideas of liberty to which we all owe a debt to Thomas Jefferson); others on memories of what made America a travesty to these ideals of liberty (like Jefferson's owning of other human beings).

But is looking at memories as inherently in conflict and competition – something NGOs addressing hate, and the rest of us, frequently do – the only way to think about it? Can the idea of multidirectional memory point to another possible way forward for NGOs, governments, and all of us yearning for better ways to combat hate? Can we create new memories of a more expansive "us" informed by the otherwise competing memories of different groups?

Levin's chapter helps us think about these questions and their challenges. Notably, the majority of the chapter is rooted in his own local context. Engaging with the complexities of multidirectional memory through the social, cultural, and political struggles of contemporary South African society offers a valuable framework through which to explore the issues at hand.

His first draft was completed before the Hamas attack of October 7, 2023, and the Israeli response. That day shook things up, and not only in Israel/Palestine. Groups that had found common cause because of shared concerns and similar memories now had different memories, concerns, and alliances to consider. When we rely on memory as a tool to combat hate, especially in coalition with other groups, it's important to remember that memory isn't static.

NOTES

1 Parts of this section first appeared in Kenneth S. Stern, *Antisemitism Today: How It Is the Same, How It Is Different, and How to Fight It* (New York: American Jewish Committee, 2006).

2 Michael Rothberg, *Multidirectional Memory: Remembering the Holocaust in the Age of Decolonization* (Stanford: Stanford University Press, 2009).

4 Multidirectional Memory in the NGO Sector: The Case of the Hate Crimes Working Group and the Value of Cross-Sector Engagement

ADAM LEVIN

In this chapter, I will examine how the field of Memory Studies can make a valuable contribution to advancing the work that has been undertaken by NGOs whose work is focused on the areas of religious and cultural identity, human rights, and social justice. My particular interest is in how the different communities, which form these NGOs, can develop collaborative relationships in their efforts to combat hate.

In demonstrating how these collaborative relationships may occur through the aid of Memory Studies, I will refer specifically to how literary scholar Michael Rothberg's theory of multidirectional memory can be used as a guiding framework through which to establish and develop these collaborations. Rothberg's theory highlights how, what he refers to as, different collective memories of trauma and oppression can engage in a productive and reciprocal dialogue with one another. This dialogue, he proposes, is one that, if implemented effectively, may create "new forms of solidarity and new visions of justice,"[1] and "new communal and political identities."[2]

To elaborate on how multidirectional memory can be implemented in an NGO context, I will refer to the Hate Crimes Working Group (HCWG), which was established in South Africa, as a case study. The HCWG was founded with the aim of formulating (what its website refers to as) "a multi-sectoral network of civil society organizations set up to spearhead advocacy and reform initiatives pertaining to hate crimes in South Africa and the region."[3] Among the members of this working group are those which represent cultural and religious groups, migrant and refugee rights, restorative justice and human rights, advocacy against gender-based violence and LGBTQI+ rights. Each of these member groups stems from different histories of oppression. Within South African society, the various group members also occupy differing economic, social, cultural, and political positions. These differences may present conflicts in facilitating collaborations between the different NGOs. Yet the HCWG has, to an extent, found ways to engage with these differences in a manner that presents the possibility of creating (to return to Rothberg's words) "new forms of solidarity and new visions of justice."

Given that the HCWG is the first group of its kind, it provides a valuable model through which to think through how collaborative interactions may occur between NGO groups within other global contexts. Using the ideas represented by multidirectional memory as an evaluative tool, I will outline the conflicts and complexities that may occur in following the HCWG's model. I will then reflect on how the initiatives the HCWG has developed and undertaken since its inception highlight productive approaches through which to grapple with these differences and, consequently, seek out solidarity and social justice. As a starting point, I will first outline the field of Memory Studies more broadly, illuminating how it may be of value in fulfilling the objective of combating hate.

Using Memory Studies to Combat Hate

To understand how the ideas and theories posited within Memory Studies can be utilized by NGOs in combating hate, it is important to first establish its characteristics as a field of study. To do so, it is helpful to establish the meanings attached to the term "memory" itself, particularly with regards to how it will be used in this chapter. Acknowledging that "memory" occupies different meanings within different contexts, Astrid Erll provides a preliminary definition of the term, offering a valuable foundation from which the study of memory may occur. As Erll puts it, "memory" is "an umbrella term for all those processes of a biological, medial, or social nature which relate past and present (and future) to sociocultural contexts."[4] Though often conflated with the term "history," memory can be distinguished from it for two reasons. The first of these is that history, which offers a factual rendering of events, is produced through memory as it is constructed via how events are remembered. The second is that whereas history places emphasis on how events are shaped and impacted by the social and political conditions under which they occur, memory's focus is orientated toward how these events are shaped by the individuals and collectives who experience them. Because they are so deeply rooted in human experience, Erll suggests that memories do not provide "objective images of past perceptions, even less of a past reality."[5] Rather, they occur as "highly selective reconstructions, dependent on the situation in which they are recalled."[6] Consequently, memory does not reflect on the historical past as a fixed, unchanging entity. Instead, it presents the past as fluid and ever-changing, particularly as it is consistently reenvisioned and reinterpreted through the "needs and interests of the groups doing the remembering in the present."[7] Developing from this definition, Memory Studies is a field that is not preoccupied with "the shape of the remembered pasts."[8] Rather, it is concerned with how this past is remembered in, as well as shapes, the present.

NGOs may themselves be interpreted as institutions that are founded and formed through the framework of memory. Whether they are focused on preserving human rights or on the uplifting of interfaith and cultural groups, the work of NGOs is almost always informed by the memories of the people and communities they represent. Their aims and objectives are dictated by how these memories are manifested in the present lived realities of these people. Some NGOs directly utilize memory as a center point from which they develop their endeavors to combat hate. Corporación Zoscua, for instance, is a Colombian NGO that actively draws upon the memory of the victims of armed conflict in Colombia to create a platform to advocate for social justice. Zoscua uses mediums such as performance and visual arts, particularly within public spaces, to bring "public visibility and conscious acts of resistance to the misrepresentation of victims or abandonment of their memory."[9] In doing so, Zoscua has employed memory as a pivotal mechanism through which to engage in a "pursuit of justice, reconciliation, and full reparations for victims."[10]

The use of memory in the formation of NGOs may also occur through the application of a transnational lens. In their introduction to *Memory Unbound: Tracing the Dynamics of Memory Studies*, Lucy Bond, Stef Craps, and Pieter Vermeulen define the concept of transnational memory as one that encompasses "the transmission, circulation, mediation, and reception of memory between and beyond ethnic, cultural, or national groups."[11] The notion of memory as an entity that is able to move "beyond and between" different groups opposes prior interpretations that suggest that memory is inherently bound to the identity of one particular nation-state. It suggests that while singular national memories remain present, they are almost always connected to the memory politics of other nations. This makes memory an entity that is increasingly globally orientated.[12] As Chiara De Cesari and Ann Rigney observe, the move toward focusing on memory through a transnational lens serves to identify "the significance of national frameworks alongside the potential of cultural production both to reinforce and transcend them."[13] Furthermore, it also creates "new possibilities for examining the interplay and tensions between cultures and institutions."[14]

The development of Amnesty International, a human rights organization that promotes global protest with the aim of gaining "justice and freedom"[15] for all, is an example of an NGO that was founded on and continues to operate within the framework of transnational memory. In an article entitled "Forgotten Prisoners," published in *The Observer* in 1961, Peter Benenson, the British lawyer who founded the organization, referred to a range of collective memories that were clearly integral to the formation of, what began as, an amnesty campaign. In the conclusion of his article, he highlighted that 1961 was a suitable year to introduce an amnesty campaign because it coincided with "the centenary of President Lincoln's inauguration ... and ... the beginning of the Civil War which ended with the liberation of American slaves."[16] He connected this American national memory to the "centenary of the decree that emancipated the Russian Serfs."[17] Reflecting on the transnational connections between these memories in the present aided Benenson in his process of thinking through the significance of public opinion in altering the course of history and securing human rights for all. In doing so, it also aided him in conceptualizing how his campaign could build on the foundation provided by these pivotal moments of liberation to form a global movement that would, as he put it, "insist on the same freedom for a man's mind as it would for his body."[18]

The success of Amnesty International's work demonstrates the value that drawing on a transnational memory framework (and, consequently, Memory Studies more broadly) can provide in shaping the objectives and discourses employed by NGOs. In the next section, I will use the case study of the Hate Crimes Working Group and the application of multidirectional memory to demonstrate how this framework can also be used as a lens through which to build relationships between different NGOs.

Establishing the Hate Crimes Working Group

On May 11, 2008, horrific acts of xenophobic violence broke out in South Africa, beginning in Alexandra, a township based in Johannesburg, and spreading throughout the country's nine provinces. The xenophobic attacks were a response to a growing fear that the continuing migration of foreign nationals, originating from other African countries, would take away job opportunities and resources from South African nationals. Although acts of xenophobic violence had been documented since the mid-1990s, the attacks of 2008 occurred on a larger scale. According to the Human Rights Watch world report of 2009, the attacks resulted in sixty-two deaths, the injuring of thousands, and 40,000 foreign nationals leaving the country.[19] A further 50,000 foreign nationals were internally displaced.[20] In response to the xenophobic violence, human rights and faith-based NGOs were proactive in their efforts to help the displaced migrants. Some helped by setting up temporary accommodation for the migrants. Others, such as the faith-based NGOs, mobilized their communities to donate and deliver items of clothing and food to the migrants. Some NGOs perceived their efforts at assistance as a humanitarian act toward their fellow humans. In contrast, faith-based NGOs, in particular, saw assisting the migrants also as a necessary duty because of the connections they identified between the migrants' experiences in the present and their community's own past experiences of violence and displacement.

In reflecting on these connections, Zev Krengel, who then served as the national chairman of the South African Jewish Board of Deputies (SAJBD), the representative body of the country's Jewish community, said the following:

> The SAJBD believes that the indiscriminate targeting of foreign nationals is reminiscent of some of the darkest periods of Jewish history, when helpless Jews were subjected to murderous attacks by the host nations amongst whom they lived. It is further reminiscent of the terrible sectarian violence that has resulted, and continues to result, in genocidal atrocities in other parts of the continent.[21]

In referring to the xenophobic attacks as being "reminiscent" of the "darkest periods of Jewish history" and other "genocidal atrocities," Krengel, albeit indirectly, applied a transnational and, consequently, multidirectional lens as he attempted to highlight the connections between different groups' experiences of violence and displacement. In doing this, he alluded to the necessity of establishing solidarity between these groups on account of their shared experiences of oppression, whether they be based in the past or in the present.

Seeking out connections between different groups' experiences of othering and oppression in an effort to combat hate was a central concern in the formation of the Hate Crime Workers Group (HCWG), a year after the attacks occurred. In an interview I conducted with Alana Pugh-Jones Baranov, a former HCWG steering committee member, she explained that the xenophobic attacks and their ramifications prompted many individuals, communities, and organizations to contemplate the root causes of the hate, which produced the attacks, and, consequently, seek out long-term solutions. Baranov recalled that while many conversations around these issues occurred through government organizations and think tanks, it was also felt that there was a need to establish "a network within civil society of different groups who were interested in tackling hate crimes"[22] and would come together to find solutions through which to do so. Following an invitation from the Consortium for Refugees and Migrants South Africa (CoRMSA), the network, comprised of a "multidisciplinary group of organizations and individuals,"[23] came together to form the HCWG. The network aimed to create a dialogue between victims of xenophobia and other groups that have experienced discrimination, be it by virtue of their race, religion, ethnicity, gender, sexuality, or any other identity marker that would label them as "other." Its ultimate goal was to advise and influence government policy on hate crimes.

The HCWG has consisted of, among others, NGOs focused on promoting refugee rights and integration (Consortium for Refugees and Migrants in South Africa, Congolese Civil Society of South Africa), advancing justice and women's rights (Sonke Gender Justice), campaigning for the equality and inclusion of the LGBTQI+ community (Out Wellbeing, The Triangle Project), and representing the voices of interfaith and cultural communities (SAJBD, South African Muslim Network, and the Chinese Association). The group has also incorporated NGOs and other organizations that are focused on broader issues of human rights and social justice issues (Amnesty International, Center for the Study of Violence and Reconciliation). Membership to the group is permitted on the grounds that, as stipulated by the terms of reference, the applying individual's or organization's "aims, policies and programmes are consistent with the ethos of the HCWG."[24] As Baranov indicated to me, a key consideration is that the applying individuals or organizations have not been connected with hate crimes themselves.[25]

When considered analytically, the dialogue that emerges between the NGOs and the respective groups they represent prompts two points of reflection. The first of these relates to engaging with the connections but also distinctions between the experiences of hate that each group has been exposed to in the present. The second concerns the connections, but also distinctions, between the respective groups' collective memories and, ultimately, their histories of trauma and oppression. This second point, in particular, highlights the complexities inherent in developing a collaboration between these different groups. In chapter 1 of this volume, Thomas Brudholm and Birgitte S. Johansen discuss the goals of NGOs that engage in the fighting of hate in order to curtail or control and ultimately eradicate or eliminate hate. While the

NGOs may indeed share this goal, how the communities they represent understand hate, as well as the ways it has affected them, may differ from one another.

For the sake of this study, I will focus on how these complexities are illuminated when placing experiences of antisemitism in South Africa in dialogue with those of xenophobia. In applying the concerns of multidirectional memory to evaluating this dialogue, I intend to demonstrate the conflicts that may arise if the HCWG's model were to be followed in other global contexts. Yet I will also examine the HCWG's approach to dealing with these conflicts and, ultimately, how thinking through the concerns of multidirectional memory can be valuable to this process.

Multidirectional Mapping

In order to demonstrate multidirectional memory's value as an evaluation tool in the NGO space, it is useful to utilize the mnemonic map Rothberg has produced in an effort to provide a "formula" through which multidirectionality can be assessed (figure 4.1). In *The Implicated Subject: Beyond Victims and Perpetrators*, Rothberg establishes that this map possesses a "four-part distinction in which multidirectional memories are located."[26] The map positions the formulation of multidirectional memories between two axes. The first axis is an "axis of comparison," which encompasses a "continuum stretching from equation to differentiation."[27] The second is an "axis of political affect," which encompasses a "continuum stretching from solidarity to competition."[28] In practice, what the combination between these axes suggests is that in order for multidirectionality to occur effectively a two-step process needs to be followed. First, in engaging in a comparison between different collective memories, one must seek out points of connection, but not equation. As a term, "equation" implies "sameness," suggesting that one memory can be connected to another by virtue of how the events and details represented by one memory can be aligned with the other. Conflating events and details of separate collective memories with one another creates the risk of each memory losing its uniqueness. Because of this, Rothberg suggests that differentiation is necessary. This implies acknowledging the historical differences between these collective memories, suggesting that their commonality lies in the didactic messages they represent, as opposed to factual similarities. Turning to the axis of political affect, Rothberg suggests that approaching multidirectionality from this perspective avoids the potential for competition that inevitably occurs when the factual details of different collective memories

Figure 4.1. Four-Part Distinction in which Multidirectional Memories Are Located

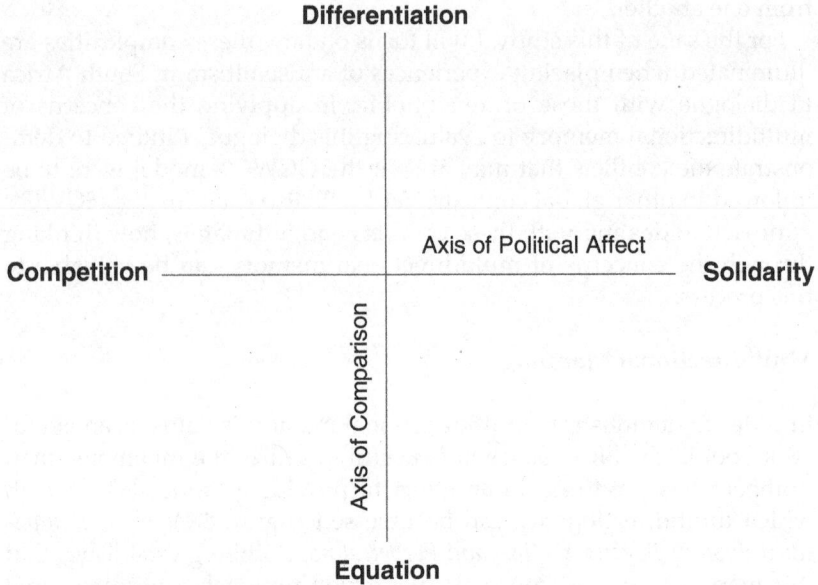

Differentiation

Axis of Political Affect

Competition ———————————————— **Solidarity**

Axis of Comparison

Equation

are compared with one another. Rather, it creates potential for solidarity as separate groups find ways of coming together via, what he terms, a form of "empathetic identification."

To clarify how, what may be termed, "multidirectional mapping" may occur in practice, it is helpful to refer to an exchange that occurred between the American Jewish Committee (AJC), an American Jewish advocacy organization, and the Japanese American National Museum (JANM), a museum dedicated to preserving the history and culture of Japanese Americans. The exchange occurred following the mounting of a museum exhibition titled *America's Concentration Camps: Remembering the Japanese American Experience*, which took place at the Ellis Island Immigration Museum in 1998. The exhibition, which focused on the incarceration of 110,000 Japanese Americans during World War II, provoked a debate between American Jewish and Japanese American communities. At the center of this debate was the use of the term "concentration camps" in the exhibition's title. In the context of the exhibition, this term was used to refer to the camps that the interned Japanese Americans were forced to occupy due to their ancestry. The image of these camps, which were "encircled by barbed wire and guarded by armed sentries,"[29] bears parallels with that of the Nazi concentration camps that European Jews were forced to occupy during World War II. Yet, for certain members of the Jewish American community, using "concentration camps" as a universal term that encompassed both the Jewish and Japanese American experience was problematic. This is because they believed that the use of the same term created a situation in which these experiences were equated.

David A. Harris, who was the director of the AJC at the time, argued that this act of equation served to "[dilute] what we have come to understand as the meaning of concentration camps."[30] Furthermore, he noted that "[since] the Second World War, these terms have taken on a specificity and a new level of meaning which deserves protection."[31] Harris's suggestion that using "concentration camps" as an umbrella term would serve to minimize the Jewish experience was contested by Karen Ishizuka. During this period, Ishizuka served as the senior curator at the Japanese American National Museum. She is also a third-generation Japanese American whose parents and grandparents were imprisoned during the war.[32] Ishizuka argued that they did not refer to the Japanese American camps as "concentration camps" to be provocative. As she put it, "There's no intent to compare or mitigate the absolute horror of the Holocaust ... This happens to be our experience, and it is our responsibility to tell it the way we experienced it."[33] The opposition between the Jewish American and Japanese American communities inevitably led to a sense of competition between them.

To address this issue, members of the AJC met with museum curators. Their discussion culminated in a decision to include a poster at the entrance to the exhibition, explaining the origins of "concentration camp" as a term, as well as its "shades of meaning."[34] The poster brought emphasis to the history of the term, tracing its early origins to the "turn of the century in the Spanish-American and Boer Wars,"[35] noting the important distinctions between America's concentration camps and those in Nazi Germany (e.g., many Nazi camps were factories of death), and, finally, drawing attention to the more recent iterations of concentration camps that have "existed in the former Soviet Union, Cambodia, and Bosnia."[36] Crucially, the poster's explanation concluded: "Despite differences, all had one thing in common: the people in power removed a minority group from the general population and the rest of society let it happen."[37] In these words, the AJC and the museum curators highlighted a *differentiation* between their understandings of the term and its location within their respective histories. On the other hand, however, they found a point of connection as they emphasized that despite the differences in their experiences, they were bonded by their position as persecuted minority groups who were moved from a society that simply "let it happen." The content of the poster prompted a sense of *solidarity* and "empathetic identification" between the two groups based on their shared experiences of trauma. The feelings of solidarity were affirmed by Ishizuka who stated, "On both sides, we reiterated the commonalities we have had, the past work we have done together and the future work we hope to do together."[38]

The Conflicts of Xenophobia and Antisemitism

In applying multidirectional mapping to a reflection on the tensions between antisemitism and xenophobia in South Africa and, consequently, the conflicts that may arise in following the HCWG model, it is necessary to first establish the state and nature of xenophobia in contrast to that of antisemitism within South African society today.

In elaborating on the distinctions between these two forms of hate, it is necessary to highlight the differences between the terms "hateful speech" and "hate crime." A consideration of these differences is crucial to evaluating South African xenophobia and antisemitism in relation to one another. Though it is often difficult to settle on a concrete definition of "hate crime" as a term, it is perhaps best defined as "a crime perpetrated against people, property or an organization, which constitutes a criminal offense under existing legislation (such as an assault, robbery or murder)."[39] (See further discussion of hate crimes in Schweppe and Walters, chapter 7, in this volume.) What distinguishes it from other forms of crime is that it is motivated specifically by selection in that the perpetrator of the hate crime chooses the victim based on "a characteristic (real or perceived) that is a fundamental or core aspect of identity shared by a group, such as race, religion, sexual orientation or nationality."[40] Hateful speech is connected to hate crime in that it too is formed through selection. Yet it differs to it in that it occurs primarily through an utterance or expression of hate about or toward specific individuals and/or groups. In South Africa, activists and researchers whose work focuses on issues related to hate crimes most often share the view that hateful speech possesses the potential to create "fertile ground for physical forms of hate-motivated victimization,"[41] which take the form of hate crimes.

South African xenophobia occurs frequently in the mode of hate crimes that are triggered and enforced by acts of hateful speech. In their reflections on the motivations behind and affect of xenophobia in South

Africa, Duncan Breen and colleagues observe that it is an example of South African violence that is "at times condoned as an expression of citizens' frustrations."[42] Michael Neocosmos traces the emergence of these frustrations back to the apartheid era. During this period, physical labor, which included activities such as mining, farming, and working in domestic households, was predominantly performed by Black South Africans. In order to increase their labor force, the apartheid regime imported workers from African countries. These workers were easier to exploit because they were vulnerable and unable to claim rights within South Africa.[43] Their presence fueled resentment amongst native Black South Africans. The reason for this was that the foreign African workers were awarded the same status as Black South Africans. This gave them equal claim to employment opportunities. Because of this, Black South Africans perceived African laborers as intruders who were after their jobs and increased their struggle in fighting for labor rights.[44] This sentiment has continued to be evident in present-day South Africa, albeit in a different context. Today, South Africa is governed by the African National Congress (ANC), a political party whose members are predominantly Black South Africans. The ANC government has taken an uneasy stance on xenophobia. On one hand, it has condemned xenophobic violence, deeming it to be out of line with the country's constitution. On the other, it has increasingly drawn attention to the perception that "illegal" foreign nationals are continuously taking jobs and business opportunities that should be reserved for South Africans, and that foreign nationals are responsible for the acts of criminality occurring in the country.[45]

This perception has created a clear basis for acts of hateful speech that, when elevated to the level of incitement, have created an environment in which hate crimes occurred. In 2015, for instance, Zulu King Goodwill Zwelitheni, who was an influential figure within the Zulu ethnic group, incited a wave of xenophobic violence in the city of Durban after he called for foreign nationals to "pack their bags" and leave the country. In recent years, initiatives such as Operation Dudula have pushed the spread of xenophobic violence even further. Founded in the township of Soweto in 2021, Operation Dudula is a movement that was initially started with the aim of addressing incidents of criminality in the city of Johannesburg.[46] Over time, however, the movement has gained a reputation as a group dedicated to enforcing the removal of foreign nationals, particularly within the township of Soweto. Apart from issuing calls for the "mass deportation of undocumented immigrants,"[47] the group has also raided businesses that are owned by foreign nationals and forced them to close.[48]

As Krengel's aforementioned statement highlights, there are indeed multidirectional parallels between xenophobia and the collective memory of the Jewish pogroms. This suggests that the South African Jewish community possesses feelings of "empathetic identification" with foreign nationals. The experience of hate encountered by the South African Jewish community, particularly today, is connected to very different concerns. It also most often takes the form of hateful speech as opposed to hate crime. As studies undertaken by the SAJBD and the HCWG indicate, the rise in hateful speech in relation to antisemitism is frequently connected to the "escalation in the conflict between Israel and Palestine."[49]

As with xenophobia, there are integral links between these occurrences of hateful speech and the opinions expressed by the South African government. The Israeli/Palestinian conflict, particularly as it manifests in the Occupied Territories, has most often been considered by many scholars and human rights organizations as following the United Nations' (UN) definition of "apartheid." In a document based on the findings at the 1976 International Convention on the Suppression and Punishment of the Crime of Apartheid, as adopted by the UN General Assembly, it is stipulated that the term "crimes of apartheid" applies to "inhuman acts committed for the purpose of establishing and maintaining domination by one racial group of persons over any other racial groups or persons and systematically oppressing them."[50] These acts include legislative measures that have been undertaken to "divide the population along racial lines by the creation of separate reserves and ghettos for the members of a racial group or groups."[51] The document stipulates that "crimes of apartheid" would include "policies and practices of racial segregation and discrimination,"[52] which are similar to those applied in apartheid South Africa. According to the UN Special Rapporteur's report on the status of human rights in Palestinian territories, which have been occupied since 1967, the international community has not fully recognized Israel as an apartheid state. However, "the concept that Israeli occupation meets the legal threshold of apartheid is gaining traction."[53] Because of this, the ANC government has frequently sided with Palestine, based on what they view as commonalities between the laws and practices implemented in apartheid South Africa and those enforced on Palestinians in Gaza. In late 2023, for instance, South African president Cyril Ramaphosa, wearing a Palestinian keffiyeh, controversially declared the ANC's allegiance to Palestine, a week after the Hamas massacre occurred in Southern Israel, and South Africa filed a case against Israel in the International Criminal Court, alleging that Israel's actions after the Hamas attack violate conventions against genocide. The interim ruling for this case put forward provisional measures that are legally binding in Israel and cannot be appealed. Israel was ordered to submit reports to the South African government, outlining the progress made in implementing these measures.

Members of the South African Jewish community are targeted by anti-Israel groups and individuals, based on their religious and cultural connections to Israel. In the early months of 2009, for instance, protesting groups burnt Israeli flags and carried signs with images of Nazi swastikas and blood-soaked Stars of David during a protest at Beyachad, the Johannesburg-based center in which most Jewish community organizations operate. During this period, threats were also made toward the community's livelihoods if they stood in support of Israel. Protests of this nature have continued, most notably in the City of Cape Town where, since the beginning of 2023, a Jewish community center encountered conflicts with anti-Israel lobbyists who, in their protests, called for the "deaths of Zionists"[54] and openly expressed their support for Hamas, Palestinian Islamic Jihad, and Hezbollah.[55] Following the October 7, 2023, Hamas massacre in Southern Israel, antisemitic graffiti was displayed on a seafront wall during the Cape Town marathon. The graffiti included the words "Holocaust, Oct '23" in red spray paint, as well as two Israeli flags with the words "I stand with genocide" and "'Israel Est. Never' (Israel: established: never)."[56] As horrific as these types of incidents were, they rarely escalated into hate crimes.

In following the formula of multidirectional mapping in establishing a group such as the HCWG, there are two points of conflict that could arise when seeking out connections between the hate experienced by foreign nationals and Jews living in South Africa. First, there is the problem of equation. The South African Jewish community's historical lineage, particularly in relation to European Jewry, provides them with an understanding of the violence and othering encountered by the foreign nationals. This gives both groups a valuable entry point through which to facilitate a dialogue with one another. However, though they possess these historical commonalities, antisemitism and xenophobia represent different forms of hate in a South African context. Consequently, an attempt to equate them with one another and evaluate them within the same framework presents a risk. This is because it may lead to the development of interventions that are ill-suited to engage with the different natures and conditions of each form of hate.

Second, there is the problem of competition. This issue can arise when considering (a) the number of hate-related incidents that each hate group has experienced and (b) the nature of the hate-related incidents. In 2022, the SAJBD's annual report on cases of antisemitism in South Africa indicated that 68 incidents of antisemitism were recorded between the months of January and November.[57] In 2023, these numbers rose as a result of developments in the Israeli/Palestinian conflict. At the time of writing this chapter (late spring 2024), 156 cases were reported.[58] The number of cases continued to escalate in 2024. Although there has been a significant rise in cases of antisemitism in South Africa, they are still not at the level of those that have been experienced globally. They also differ greatly in comparison to the escalating cases of xenophobia. There are no official reports on the number of xenophobic cases in South Africa. However, Xenowatch, an open source system that collects data pertaining to xenophobic incidents, recorded up to 1,041 cases that occurred between 1994 and November 2023.[59] Given that these were the only reported cases, the number of incidents is likely to be much higher.

While both xenophobia and antisemitism may have been influenced by hateful speech, the consequences for each group are different. According to Xenowatch, the hate crimes committed toward foreign nationals have resulted in incidents of displacement, shop looting, physical assault, and murder.[60] Jewish South Africans encounter threats of violence and death, but these are rarely acted upon. In 2023, a total of five physical assaults were reported.[61] These incidents mainly involved such acts as kicking, punching, or spitting at community members. None of these incidents resulted in hospitalization or death.

Because the number of xenophobic hate crimes and their consequences differ significantly to those of antisemitism, there is a danger of creating a discourse in which one experience of suffering is perceived as being worse than the other. In this instance, antisemitic hate crimes are seen as "losing" to xenophobic hate crimes, precisely because they occur in fewer numbers and have a lesser impact. This may also create the perception that, within a South African context, xenophobic hate crimes require more immediate attention than antisemitic hate crimes. Thinking in terms of, what may be deemed, a "hierarchy of suffering" would serve to break down the dialogue that a group such as the HCWG would endeavor to construct.

Consequently, in order to maintain this dialogue and ensure that it is productive, groups that follow the HCWG model must develop an approach that does not attempt to equate the hate crimes of the different groups with one another. The proposed approach should also not result in a competition between the groups. Rather, it should acknowledge how the hate crimes can be differentiated from each other, while also establishing ways in which the groups can work in solidarity with one another.

Hate Crime Monitoring: Engaging with the Differences between Hate Crimes to Achieve Solidarity

In my interview with Baranov, she indicated that the different civil society organizations involved in the HCWG grappled with the conflicts of reconciling different experiences of hate with one another by connecting through the broader ideas represented by hate and its impact on the country as a whole.

In pursuing this endeavor, the HCWG developed the Hate and Bias Crime Monitoring Initiative. This initiative's objective was to address the absence of methods to obtain "comprehensive data to understand the extent of ... victimization on a local or national level"[62] and the absence of systems to "effectively collect or assess data on hate incidents."[63] At the time, these absences were largely due to the fact that there was no hate crime legislation in place in South Africa.[64] Therefore, in response to this, members of the HCWG developed the Hate Crime Monitoring Form. The purpose of this form was to collect data that could be used to improve the "long-term monitoring of hate crime cases as well as [aid in the development of an] improved judicial response to hate crimes."[65] By doing this, the HCWG aimed more broadly to "determine and describe the nature as well as psychological and societal impact of hate crimes in South Africa."[66] Under the auspices of the HCWG, the form was created by a group of academics from the psychology department at the University of South Africa (commonly known as UNISA). The group's objective was to monitor the evolution of hate crimes over a five-year period, beginning in 2013 and concluding in 2017. While this initiative was the first of its kind in Africa, it also endeavored to address the issues identified in similar forms that were being used in the UK, the US, and European countries. One of these issues was that it was too "sector-specific."[67] In its efforts to create cross-sector engagement, the HCWG's Hate and Bias Crime Monitoring Initiative promoted inclusivity by drawing attention to the range of different hate crimes occurring within South African society.

In their study of the process of developing the Hate and Bias Monitoring Form, Juan A. Nel, one of the form's developers, together with Zindi Venter and Vanessa Stratford, observed that in order for the form to be as comprehensive as possible, it needed to be created in collaboration with the diverse range of groups that form the HCWG. A key factor they acknowledged in their assessment was that the HCWG is comprised of a "very diverse range of sectors serving very specific constituencies, and their interests, with sometimes polar opposite values and beliefs regarding matters of religion, sexual orientation and/or gender expression [as well as] non-nationality."⁶⁸ While they acknowledged that bringing these groups together was a strength of the HCWG, it also did create challenges when developing the form because it was necessary for the end product to be representative of "all these groups' needs."⁶⁹ Within the context of "multidirectional mapping," these words highlight the significance of differentiating between the groups and the experiences of hate they represent. This involves acknowledging the complex notion that, ultimately, one group's understanding of hate may sharply oppose another's. Each group is also not monolithic. This implies that even understandings of hate within the groups themselves may be divisive. The SAJBD, for instance, consistently encounters opposition from South African Jews for Palestine (SAJFP), a group of South African Jews who oppose Zionism and, consequently, the SAJBD's understanding of antisemitism. In a statement on the SAJFP website, the group refers to the SAJBD's accusations of antisemitism as being "manipulative and alarmist."⁷⁰ This is because, as the SAJFP perceives it, the SAJBD's definition of antisemitism "includes certain criticisms of Zionism and Israel,"⁷¹ which it views as having been weaponized to distract from the plight of the Palestinians. The challenge, then, is to engage with and negotiate between these different understandings in ways that address their specific concerns, while also finding points of solidarity between them.

The final version of the form was one that addressed the nature and consequences of hate crimes from numerous angles in its efforts to encapsulate the HCWG's members' different concerns. The form was divided into the following sections: victim details and background, current incident details, alleged offender's details, police involvement, access to court procedures, access to health care assistance and support, and previous incident details. Under these sections, the questions asked pertained to the hate crime victim's sexual orientation, nationality, community relations, as well as the type of incident. In connection with this particular question, the form inquired about the factors that played a role in identifying the incident as a hate crime. The factors included the language and words used during or prior to the incident, the location of the incident, as well as whether the incident may have occurred due to the victim's sexual orientation and gender identity, nationality, religious affiliation, race, or occupation. In allowing the victim of the hate crime to select multiple categories, the form made provisions for those whose experience occurred due to prejudices connected to multiple facets of their identities. In doing this, it made provisions not only for the specific groups but also for those whose identity overlaps between different groups.

Although, since 2017, the Hate Crimes Monitoring Initiative has not been used on a sustained basis,[72] it has nevertheless proven to be of great value in developing a database of evidence that can be used by policymakers.[73] More than this, as Nel, Venter, and Stratford have observed, it has highlighted the "severe impact of hate crime incidents, not only on individual victims, but also on greater communities and on society."[74] The evidence gathered from this initiative also provided a valuable resource for the HCWG to draw on in its efforts to contribute to the drafting of the Prevention and Combating of Hate Crimes and Hate Speech Bill that was introduced to the National Assembly in April 2018. This bill intended to address "frequently occurring and sometimes violent conduct of persons who are motivated by clear and defined prejudices."[75] The implementation of the bill was significant, given that, up until that point, South Africa did not record "hate crime as a crime category"[76] and, therefore, did not provide hate crime statistics. To address this concern, the bill was formulated with the objective of, for the first time in South African law, "collecting and reporting hate crimes, both to Parliament and to the public."[77] Although the bill lapsed in May 2019, it was revived in October 2019, and offered a call for comment from the Portfolio Committee on Justice and Constitutional Development in 2021.

Based on the 2018 release of the Hate and Bias Crime Monitoring report, which captured the findings of the Hate Crime Monitoring Initiative, the HCWG compiled an advocacy brief in response to this call. The brief's objective was to provide policymakers and lawmakers with an indication of hate crimes, hateful speech, and prejudice manifested within South African society. It detailed some of the hate crimes recorded by the HCWG's member groups in 2021. The layout of the brief offered a monthly breakdown of the hate crime or "hate speech" offenses that occurred throughout the year. In this breakdown, only three cases of antisemitism were recorded in contrast to the multitude of xenophobic, homophobic, and transphobic cases featured in the brief. Yet their addition was significant in demonstrating and highlighting the various forms in which hate manifests itself. In this instance, it is crucial that the different hate crimes were not separated out and categorized separately from one another. Listing the hate crimes in a manner that demonstrated how they occurred concurrently served to establish a dialogue. This dialogue did not bring them together in a manner that equated them with one another. Rather, it created a context in which solidarity between the groups could occur.

This solidarity was expressed further when, in May 2023, the HCWG made submissions on the draft of the Prevention and Combating of Hate

Crimes and Hate Speech Bill. In its assessment of the bill, the HCWG reflected significantly on whether the bill was broad enough to be inclusive of the various forms of hate crime and hateful speech that occurred within South African society. In considering the bill's preamble, the HCWG identified that it made reference to only two of the country's international commitments: the Declaration adopted at the United Nations World Conference against Racism, Racial Discrimination, Xenophobia and Related Intolerance held in Durban (the Durban Declaration), and the International Convention on the Elimination of All Forms of Racial Discrimination (CERD). The bill, in particular, highlighted the CERD requirement that State Parties declare the following:

> [An] offence punishable by law all dissemination of ideas based on racial superiority or hatred, incitement to racial discrimination, as well as acts of violence or incitement to such acts against any race or group of persons of another colour or ethnic origin.[78]

In its submissions, the HCWG suggested that the bill's emphasis on the Durban Declaration and CERD served to foreground racism and racial discrimination at the expense of other acts of discrimination. The Durban Declaration was a particularly contentious addition given that the Durban conference, which took place in 2001, was accused of sidelining, and even promoting, antisemitism and empowering the Israel-apartheid analogy. Consequently, the HCWG observed that the bill "appears to create a hierarchy of prejudice and discrimination, prioritizing racial discrimination at the top."[79] To remedy this, the HCWG proposed that all other applicable international instruments should be referenced in the bill in order to capture "the importance of the intersectionality that exists in preventing and combating hate crimes."[80] These instruments included those that reflected human rights more broadly (the Universal Declaration of Human Rights, the African Charter on Human and People's Rights) and those that focused on a specific type of discrimination (Resolution 275 of the African Commission on Human and Peoples' Rights, "Resolution on Protection against Violence and other Human Rights Violations against Persons based on their real or imputed Sexual Orientation or Gender Identity"). In advocating for the inclusion of these different instruments, the HCWG, indeed, followed a multidirectional approach in its submissions. It did so, on the one hand, by implying that the Prevention and Combating of Hate Crimes and Hate Speech Bill should aim to differentiate between different forms and experiences of hate crime and hateful speech. And, on the other hand, by emphasizing the need for an equal focus on these different forms and experiences, the HCWG advocated for finding points of solidarity between them.

Challenges to Solidarity after October 7, 2023, and Conclusion

The work of the HCWG on the Hate Crimes Monitoring Initiative and its submissions on the draft of the Prevention and Combating of Hate Crimes and Hate Speech Bill demonstrate how multidirectional dialogues can occur effectively between different civil society organizations. However, as of this writing (early 2025), the future of the HCWG, or at least its ability to have the type of broad communal support it had in the past, is open to question. Shortly after the events of October 7, 2023, the SAJBD withdrew from the HCWG. It did so because of differences that occurred between the SAJBD and the other organizations. The circumstances under which the SAJBD departed suggest that each group's own ideals and values may inevitably present a consistent challenge to maintaining solidarity between the different groups within the HCWG. Collectively, the HCWG will also need to develop approaches that will allow it to grapple with more complex memory narratives (such as that represented by the Gaza War) in more nuanced ways.

This challenge that the HCWG has encountered post–October 7 resonates with the conflicts some cultural groups in the United States have faced in their dealings with Jewish organizations. Recall the successful negotiation between the Japanese American community and the mainstream American Jewish community over the contested term "concentration camp." The shared history of being separated from the rest of society formed a memory that, in the end, was stronger than competition over who got to use a term. That resolution was no doubt aided by another memory: Some American Jewish groups, particularly the American Jewish Committee, remembering the Jewish quest to secure reparations from Germany for Holocaust victims, were strong partners for Japanese Americans seeking reparations for their incarceration.

Yet younger Japanese Americans viewed Israel's response to the Hamas attacks, and more particularly to the defense of Israel by mainstream Jewish groups, as beyond the pale. They saw the Palestinians, particularly in Gaza, as experiencing devastation and discrimination that resonated much more with their perspective on the world, and what it meant to be Japanese Americans. This generational divide continues to be a source of controversy, particularly inside the Japanese American Citizens League, perhaps the pre-eminent NGO representing Japanese Americans.[81]

So, while multidirectional memory can help bring communities together, we end where we started – that memories aren't static; they negotiate with each other, can change over time, and are influenced by events. The challenge for NGOs, like HCWG and others, is to be aware of how the academic field of Memory Studies can be of value in relationship-building between NGOs that engage with issues of hate from different social, cultural, and political vantage points, and how much work may be required to maintain these relationships in difficult moments.

NOTES

1 Michael Rothberg, *Multidirectional Memory: Remembering the Holocaust in the Age of Decolonization* (Stanford: Stanford University Press, 2009), 5.
2 Rothberg, *Multidirectional Memory*, 11.
3 Hate Crimes Working Group, "About Us," accessed August 29, 2023, https://hcwg.org.za/about/.
4 Astrid Erll, *Memory in Culture*, trans. Sara B. Young (Basingstoke, UK: Palgrave Macmillan, 2011), 7.
5 Erll, *Memory in Culture*, 8.
6 Erll, *Memory in Culture*.
7 Erll, *Memory in Culture*.
8 Erll, *Memory in Culture*.
9 Claire L. Taylor et al., "Archives of Human Rights and Historical Memory: An Analysis of Archival Practices 'From Below' in Four NGOs in Colombia," *Journal of Contemporary Archival Studies* 8 (2021): 6, https://elischolar.library.yale.edu/jcas/vol8/iss1/3.
10 Taylor et al., "Archival of Human Rights."
11 Lucy Bond, Stef Craps, and Pieter Vermeulen, "Introduction: Memory on the Move," in Lucy Bond, Stef Craps, and Pieter Vermeulen, eds., *Memory Unbound: Tracing the Dynamics of Memory Studies* (New York: Berghahn Books, 2017), 3.
12 Bond, Craps, and Vermeulen, "Introduction," 4.
13 Chiara De Cesari and Ann Rigney. "Introduction," in Chiara De Cesari and Ann Rigney, eds., *Transnational Memory: Circulation, Articulation, Scales* (Berlin: De Gruyter, 2014), 4.
14 De Cesari and Rigney, "Introduction," 4.
15 Amnesty International, "About Us," accessed January 13, 2025, https://www.amnesty.org/en/about-us/.
16 Peter Benenson, "Forgotten Prisoners," *The Guardian*, May 28, 1961, https://www.theguardian.com/uk/1961/may/28/fromthearchive.theguardian.

17 Benenson, "Forgotten Prisoners."

18 Benenson, "Forgotten Prisoners."

19 Human Rights Watch, "South Africa: Events of 2008," accessed September 12, 2023, https://www.hrw.org/world-report/2009/country-chapters /south-africa.

20 Human Rights Watch, "South Africa."

21 David Saks, "South African Jews Condemn Violence, Support Victims," *World Jewish Congress*, May 21, 2008, https://www.worldjewishcongress .org/en/news/south-african-jews-condemn-violence-support-victims.

22 Alana Pugh-Jones Baranov (steering committee, Hate Crimes Working Group), in discussion with the author, September 2023.

23 Baranov discussion with author.

24 Hate Crimes Working Group, *Terms of Reference for the Hate Crimes Working Group*, May 29, 2018, 8, http://hcwg.org.za/wp-content/uploads /2019/02/HCWG-ToR-2018.pdf.

25 Baranov discussion with author.

26 Michael Rothberg, *The Implicated Subject: Beyond Victims and Perpetrators* (Stanford: Stanford University Press, 2019), 124.

27 Rothberg, *The Implicated Subject*.

28 Rothberg, *The Implicated Subject*.

29 Somini Sengupta, "What Is a Concentration Camp? Ellis Island Exhibit Prompts a Debate," *New York Times*, March 8, 1998, https://www.nytimes .com/1998/03/08/nyregion/what-is-a-concentration-camp-ellis-island -exhibit-prompts-a-debate.html.

30 Sengupta, "What Is a Concentration Camp?"

31 Sengupta, "What Is a Concentration Camp?"

32 Sengupta, "What Is a Concentration Camp?"

33 Sengupta, "What Is a Concentration Camp?"

34 Somini Sengupta, "Accord on Term 'Concentration Camp,'" *New York Times*, March 10, 1998, https://www.nytimes.com/1998/03/10/nyregion /accord-on-term-concentration-camp.html.

35 Japanese American National Museum (JANM), "American Jewish Committee, Japanese American National Museum Issue Joint Statement about Ellis Island Exhibit Set to Open April 3," March 13, 1998, https:// www.janm.org/press/release/american-jewish-committee-japanese -american-national-museum-issue-joint-statement.

36 JANM, "American Jewish Committee."

37 JANM, "American Jewish Committee."

38 Sengupta, "Accord on Term."

39 Juan A. Nel and Yolanda Mitchell, "Victims of Hate Crime," in Robert Peacock, ed., *Victimology in Africa*, 3rd ed. (Pretoria: Van Schaik Publishers, 2019), 272.

40 Nel and Mitchell, "Victims of Hate Crime."

41 Duncan Breen et al., "Hate Crimes in Transitional Societies: The Case of South Africa," in Jennifer Schweppe and Mark Austin Walters, eds., *The Globalization of Hate: Internationalizing Hate Crime?* (Oxford: Oxford University Press, 2016), 130.

42 Breen et al., "Hate Crimes," 129.

43 Michael Neocosmos, *From "Foreign Natives" to "Native Foreigners": Explaining Xenophobia in Post-Apartheid South Africa Citizenship and Nationalism, Identity and Politics* (Dakar: CODESRIA, 2010), 19–58.

44 Neocosmos, *From "Foreign Natives."*

45 Aretha Oluwakemi Asakitikpi and Joanah Gadziḳwa, "A Critical Discourse Analysis of Online YouTube News Coverage of South African Discourses on Xenophobia in Democratic South Africa," *Politikon: South African Journal of Political Studies* 47, no. 4 (2020): 484–7, https://doi.org/10.1080/02589346.2020.1840022.

46 Nomathamsanqa Masiko-Mpaka, "Xenophobia Rears Its Ugly Head in South Africa: Foreigners Scapegoated for Country's Problems," Human Rights Watch, September 28, 2023, https://www.hrw.org/news/2023/09/28/xenophobia-rears-its-ugly-head-south-africa.

47 Masiko-Mpaka, "Xenophobia."

48 Masiko-Mpaka, "Xenophobia."

49 Nel and Mitchell, "Victims of Hate Crime," 274.

50 United Nations, *International Convention on the Suppression and Punishment of the Crime of Apartheid*, Doc. A/9030 (1974), July 18, 1976, Article II, https://www.un.org/en/genocideprevention/documents/atrocity-crimes/Doc.10_International%20Convention%20on%20the%20Suppression%20and%20Punishment%20of%20the%20Crime%20of%20Apartheid.pdf.

51 United Nations, *International Convention.*

52 United Nations, *International Convention.*

53 Francesca Albanese, *Report of the Special Rapporteur on the Situation of Human Rights in the Palestinian Territories Occupied since 1967* (New York: United Nations General Assembly, 2022), 5, https://www.un.org/unispal/wp-content/uploads/2022/10/A.77.356_210922.pdf.

54 Tali Feinberg, "Cape Town Jews Doubly Victimised as Antisemitism Rages," *South African Jewish Report*, October 19, 2023, https://www.sajr.co.za/cape-town-jews-doubly-victimised-as-antisemitism-rages/.

55 Feinberg, "Cape Town."

56 Feinberg, "Cape Town."

57 Alana Pugh-Jones Baranov, email correspondence with the author, November 14, 2023.

58 David Saks, the associate director of the SAJBD, email correspondence with the author, November 15, 2023. Saks compiles the annual SAJBD reports on antisemitism.

59 Xenowatch, "Dashboard and Statistics," accessed November 15, 2023, https://www.xenowatch.ac.za/statistics-dashboard/.

60 Xenowatch, "Dashboard and Statistics."

61 Saks, email correspondence.

62 Hanlie van Wyk and Juan A. Nel, "The Role of Organized Psychology in Inspiring Hope and Preventing Hate Victimization: Recommendations from a South African Hate and Bias Monitoring Initiative," *Journal of Hate Studies* 18, no. 1 (2023): 22, https://doi.org/10.33972/jhs.230.

63 Wyk and Nel, "The Role of Organized Psychology."

64 Wyk and Nel, "The Role of Organized Psychology."

65 Hate Crimes Working Group, "Hate and Bias Crime Monitoring Form," accessed August 29, 2023, https://hcwg.org.za/hate-bias-crime -monitoring-form/.

66 Breen et al., "Hate Crimes," 136.

67 Juan A. Nel, Hanlie van Wyk, and Konzi Mbatha, *Hate Crime and Bias Crime Monitoring Form: User Guide* (Pretoria: Hate Crimes Working Group, 2013), 11, https://www.hcwg.org.za/HCWG_User%20Guide_Aug2013. pdf.

68 Juan A. Nel, Zindi Venter, and Vanessa Stratford, "Advancing Social Justice: Critical Reflections on the Hate Crime and Bias Monitoring Form," *Acta Criminologica: African Journal of Criminology and Victimology* 3, no. 3 (2022): 53, https://hdl.handle.net/10520/ejc-crim_v35_n3_a3.

69 Nel, Venter, and Stratford, "Advancing Social Justice."

70 South African Jews for a Free Palestine, "SAJFP Rejects Claims of an Environment of Antisemitism in South Africa," accessed April 21, 2024, https://sajfp.org.za/sajfp-rejects-claims-of-an-environment -of-antisemitism-in-south-africa/.

71 South African Jews for a Free Palestine, "SAJFP Rejects Claims."

72 South African Jews for a Free Palestine, "SAJFP Rejects Claims," 65.

73 South African Jews for a Free Palestine, "SAJFP Rejects Claims."

74 Nel, Venter, and Stratford, "Advancing Social Justice."

75 Portfolio Committee on Justice and Correctional Services (National Assembly), *Prevention and Combating of Hate Crimes and Hate Speech Bill [B9B-2018]* (2018), 14.

76 Hate Crimes Working Group, *The State of Hate in South Africa in 2021: Advocacy Brief* (Cape Town: HCWG, 2022), 3, https://za.boell.org/sites /default/files/2022-05/HCWG%20Advocacy%20Brief%202022%2003 %2022.pdf.

77 Hate Crimes Working Group, *The State of Hate in South Africa*.
78 Portfolio Committee on Justice and Correctional Services, *Prevention and Combating*, 3.
79 Hate Crimes Working Group, *Submission of the Hate Crimes Working Group: Prevention and Combating of Hate Crimes and Hate Speech Bill [B9B-2018]*, Submissions, May 2023, 1.
80 Hate Crimes Working Group, *Submission*, 2.
81 Amy Qin, "War in Gaza Causes Surprising Rift within Japanese American Group," *New York Times*, April 18, 2024, https://www.nytimes.com/2024/04/18/us/israel-hamas-asian-american-japanese.html?searchResultPosition=1.

Editor's Introduction to Chapter 5

I asked scores of people who they thought might make a valuable contribution to this volume, and what particular areas the book should cover – both to help us understand hate better (as the preceding chapters do) and to guide our thinking about what may work to combat hate, or at least not make the situation worse. While these topics inevitably overlap (as in Adam Levin's chapter 4), the remaining chapters of this book are more focused on what NGOs ought to consider doing about hate.

Adam Strom, formerly of Facing History and Ourselves and now of Re-Imagining Immigration, was someone whose opinion I sought. He suggested Kevin Jennings, for his cutting-edge work at the Gay, Lesbian and Straight Education Network (GLSEN) years ago. Jennings used data and human stories of the bullying and discrimination faced by gay and lesbian students to drive policy change. He was appointed by then-governor William Weld of Massachusetts to co-chair the Education Committee of the Governor's Commission on Gay and Lesbian Youth, and he was the main author of a report that lead to Massachusetts becoming the first state (in 1993) to prohibit discrimination against students in public schools based on sexual orientation. Jennings now runs LAMBDA, an important NGO addressing anti-LGBTQI+ discrimination. He was eager to contribute to this volume, to offer insights on how data and humanizing stories about those considered "other" at best, or "evil" or "sinful" or "dangerous" at worst, can drive useful policy changes.

But the time-consuming and pressing real-world needs of the community he serves – including increased hate crimes and discrimination, particularly against transgender people – required him to withdraw from this project.

Luckily, just as Jennings had to drop out, I saw an announcement that my friend and former AJC colleague Rebecca Neuwirth had just been appointed to lead Define American, a nonprofit group focused on projecting humanizing stories of another community targeted with hate – immigrants.

When I spoke with Rebecca about her new job, I mentioned the late Gary Rubin, another former AJC colleague who specialized in immigration. He had said that "Americans hate immigration but love immigrants," and he helped AJC chapters around the country plan large public swearing-in ceremonies for new citizens. The images of excited, proud, and newly minted Americans holding small American flags were powerful and humanizing.

I told Rebecca about this book, and that Jennings had to drop out. Rebecca said I had to meet her colleague Sarah Lowe, whose work focused on humanizing immigrants and analyzing the success and failure of those efforts.

What you'll see in this chapter, written by Define American's Sarah Lowe and cultural strategist Charlene Jimenez, is a slightly different approach from what Jennings was prepared to offer, but with the same goal in mind for an NGO's work: What works best to create emotional empathy for human beings who are targeted as a "them"?

Not every group in the NGO space is going to have the capacity to work with media companies the way Define American does, but the principle of how we can create images and stories to help see a potential "them" as a real and relatable human being is an important part of the work.

5 "Intimacy at a Distance": Using Parasocial Interaction to Reduce Prejudice

SARAH E. LOWE AND CHARLENE JOY JIMENEZ

Think of your favorite television character. Think of their face. Would you know their laugh if you heard it from the next room? It probably feels like you know them, and in a sense you do. Even if your favorite character is an antihero, chances are you find them relatable in some way, a well-drawn character that you love to hate. The phenomenon of feeling a closeness, or kinship, with a performer in a mass media program – such as television, radio, or online media like YouTube – is known as parasocial interaction.[1] Sociologist Donald Horton and anthropologist R. Richard Wohl, who developed the term "parasocial relationship," described the interaction as "intimacy at a distance."[2] Since the 1950s, social scientists have been studying how intergroup contact reduces prejudice[3] and how the mediated contact through mass media broadcasts can foster a connection akin to friendship.[4] Just like with real friends, our imagined relationships with television characters can influence our attitudes about others, educate us about other ways of being in the world, and even change our actions,[5] for better or worse.

Narrative change is the process by which dominant stories that guide a society's attitudes, knowledge, beliefs, and actions are shifted over time.[6] NGOs can leverage parasocial interaction – these imagined friendships – in narrative change intervention tactics for prejudice reduction by collaborating with media creators to leverage the intimacy of media. The immigrant rights organization Define American, for which we have worked – Sarah E. Lowe as the director of Narrative Research and Charlene Joy Jimenez as the former director of Entertainment Partnerships & Advocacy – has been committed to understanding the capability and limits to narrative change since the organization's inception in 2012. We are not alone in the herculean endeavor. Developing in the 2000s to the present, advocacy organizations like GLAAD, Coalition of Asian Pacifics in Entertainment, Color of Change, Illuminative, the Muslim Public

Affairs Council, National Domestic Workers Alliance, Pillars Fund, the Storyline Partners Collective, and others have developed consultancy programs to assist the TV and film industry on storylines for accuracy and nuance around the impacted communities they represent.

Opportunities exist for NGOs working with noteworthy allies in media to create cultural content to reduce prejudice in mass audiences. In this chapter, we will explore how to use research and consulting on media representation to transform TV consumption into real-world action. We use our own narrative change work as a case study for the use of parasocial contact for shifting attitudes, knowledge, beliefs, and actions of general audiences. However, research shows that parasocial interaction can be leveraged in far-reaching ways beyond just scripted television. Fruitful outcomes have been seen with celebrities, sports figures, actors, musicians, and social media influencers.[7] We offer our experiences as a basic roadmap to implementing a feedback loop of research, practice, and evaluation to ensure that narrative-based interventions are manageable, sustainable, effective, and measurable over time.

Defining Hate

Deep societal value is gained from parasocial interaction when mass audiences regularly tune into or binge on TV series that feature characters from a community that is different from their own,[8] which has been linked to prejudice reduction in real intergroup interaction.[9] Using video content for prejudice reduction guides a viewing audience to develop understanding about differences without someone who identifies as being from a marginalized community performing the emotional – and often unpaid – labor of teaching about differences. The one-way mediated version of the relationship can actually alter behavior in the two-way interactions of real life. As Mengyao Li discusses in chapter 3 in this volume, studies in intergroup theory show us that meaningful connection with one's ingroup can guide the way we act toward others. Television is a cultural space for audiences to see outgroup members in intimate ways: as worried parents, as job seekers, as baseball fanatics, as brokenhearted or overcaffeinated or weepy when sentimental. The intimacy of television allows space for a character in an outgroup to become part of the audience's ingroup through identities of basic human connection. Psychologists Thomas F. Pettigrew and Linda R. Tropp[10] found in a meta-analysis of 713 samples from 515 studies, that intergroup contact reduces prejudice despite differences in the participant groups and study settings. Likewise, the outcomes can be seen through the mediated form of contact of parasocial interaction that mass audiences have with personalities and fictional characters in mass media.

Prejudice reduction is not the only benefit to a parasocial relationship. Symbolic annihilation[11] refers to a phenomenon where a lack of representation – or symbolism – in popular media also denies the existence of marginalized communities in society itself. Sociologist George Gerbner and screenwriter Larry Gross describe it this way: "Representation in the fictional world signifies social existence; absence means symbolic annihilation."[12] The US media landscape for television and film continues to show signs of symbolic annihilation today of people of color, including immigrants.[13]

Can we classify structural violence, like symbolic annihilation, as hate? Erasure alone could seem like a stretch, but consider erasure paired with underrepresentation in positions of power within the entertainment industry and the kinds of stories that may result from that lack of representation. In 2017, the racial justice organization Color of Change commissioned research from sociologist Darnell Hunt[14] about Hollywood television writers' rooms. Of the 234 TV series analyzed, 86 per cent of the writers were white. Of the showrunners who made key decisions about what progressed to our televisions, 91 per cent were white and 80 per cent were men. Our organization, Define American, commissioned a longitudinal research project with the nonpartisan research organization the Norman Lear Center, beginning with that same television season – 2017–18 – by examining 143 episodes of forty-seven shows. Our first report in the study, *Immigration Nation: Exploring Immigrant Portrayals on Television*, revealed that women immigrants in every racial group were underrepresented in comparison to their real life counterparts as well as Asian immigrants and undocumented Black immigrants.[15] American audiences saw predominantly Latine (85 per cent) men representing the immigrant community on TV. In reality, the immigrant community was fairly evenly split between women (52 per cent) and men (48 per cent), and the largest populations were Latine (45 per cent) and Asian (26 per cent). Immigrants on television were also overrepresented as criminals, overrepresented as incarcerated, and portrayed as less educated than their real life counterparts.[16] Less than 1 per cent of immigrants in the United States were incarcerated, in 2017 through 2024, but the 2017–18 TV season represented 11 per cent of immigrants as incarcerated and 34 per cent were portrayed as associated with a crime. In the 2017–18 television season, 91 per cent of showrunners produced TV shows where immigrants were depicted as predominantly people of color who were less educated than their real life counterparts, overrepresented in association with crime, and ten times more likely to be incarcerated. The United States is a nation made up of 45 million immigrants; an estimated 11.8 million are undocumented, meaning they had visas that lapsed or they crossed a US border without authorization. Immigrants have been scapegoated by US mass media since the inception of the country with recurring narratives of criminalization, victimization, disease/contamination, and other stereotypes and tropes being carried forward from generation to generation and that are still present in our mass media today. The specific groups of immigrants dehumanized throughout the years have changed, yet many tropes remain the same. Immigrants are either criminals to be feared or victims to be saved, and most often we see immigrants of color being feared or victimized with protectors and saviors depicted as white citizens. Though an increase in inclusive hiring in Hollywood is helping to change the landscape of who is in front of and behind the cameras, historically TV has been made mostly by white cis-gender men and the stories produced into television largely reflect it.

How did we get here? The first immigration law in the United States was the Nationality Act of 1790,[17] which stated that "free white men" who had lived in the country for two years or more were the only people eligible for citizenship. Additionally, the category of "alien" was introduced, meaning all others who were not citizens. Indigenous Americans, Asian Americans, African Americans, and all women were targeted for exclusion of human rights, establishing a system of racist, xenophobic, and sexist laws, the remnants of which still plague US immigration policies. Immigrants from Asia, facing deep racial discrimination and with less familiarity with the Romance languages than those from Europe, were the first migrant population specifically targeted for exclusion. The 1875 Page Act denied entry into the United States of "any subject of China, Japan, or any Oriental country."[18] All were seen as a form of indentured servants to other peoples. Furthermore, xenophobia and racism were passed into law with the Chinese Exclusion Act of 1882 that banned Chinese laborers from entry for ten years. Families who planned to reunite were faced with a problem: remain separated for a decade or find unauthorized ways of entering the United States. The Immigration Act of 1924 limited visas to 2 per cent of the populations that were already represented in the country at the time of the 1890 census.[19] The result was 70 per cent of all visas issued to those from just three regions: Great Britain, Germany, and Ireland. The result of mass exclusion was an influx of undocumented immigrants, primarily of Asian origin, which prompted the creation of the US Border Patrol the same year, 1924.

The quota cap on immigrants by nationality, established by the US Immigration and Nationality Act of 1924, created dire consequences for German Jewish immigrants in the following decade. The German-Austrian cap in 1939 was 27,370 people annually, forcing Jewish people fleeing the Holocaust onto waiting lists that were years long.[20] Similar quotas are embedded in our current US immigration system. A quota by nationality is associated with refugees and asylum seekers as well as green card holders. In 2020, the United States reported that 1,224,062 people of Mexican origin were backlogged for green card processing.[21] Some people in visa queues will wait up to twenty-five years, separated from their grown children, siblings, and extended family members for decades, while the US government processes their applications for legal authorization to travel to and reside in the United States. Those who get trapped in the system because they are in the country when their visa and/or status lapses or who cannot tolerate immigration bureaucracy standing in the way of pressing life decisions become undocumented.

We noted in our 2020 report with the Norman Lear Center, describing our study of ninety-seven episodes of fifty-nine shows in the 2018–19 television season, that a new storyline had emerged on television that reflected real-life events happening in the United States at that time: 34 per cent of the immigrant population on TV was depicted as being held in immigration detention facilities. In reality, 3 per cent of the immigrant population was held in detention facilities. TV creators and writers drew characters and plotlines directly from the news that consumed the nation in the summer of 2017. Photos, videos, audio recordings, and stories of immigrant children separated from their parents filled our newsfeeds during the Zero Tolerance policy enforcement by the first Trump administration. According to Immigration Customs and Enforcement data, 500,000 immigrants were detained in 2019. In television, it seemed to be a moment when Hollywood understood its power to use storytelling to illuminate the nuance of what was happening with these immigrant families.

However, an analysis of characters and storylines found a major difference in what types of immigrants were deemed worthy of exploration. Of all episodes analyzed, the storylines that focused on immigrant *characters* prominently featured white immigrants (31 per cent) from European countries (21 per cent) who were naturalized citizens or permanent residents. Storylines that centered on *immigration plots* predominantly featured Latine (61 per cent) characters from Latin American countries (59 per cent) that were undocumented (62 per cent) and either incarcerated (20 per cent) due to illegal activity or in detention centers (34 per cent) for crossing the border without authorization. White immigrants had backstories; immigrants of color were criminals in a white character's hero-journey.

These depictions of criminalization also paralleled the language used to describe immigrant characters, particularly undocumented immigrant characters. In the 2018–19 television season, we observed the term "illegal" and "illegal immigrant" used frequently in scripted series.[22] Define American then made it a point in its entertainment consultations to educate TV creators about the real-world harm this language can cause. The term "illegal" is dehumanizing and replaces complex legal circumstances with an assumption of guilt. We encouraged the use of terms such as "undocumented" or "unauthorized," which offer options for neutral terminology. In 2022, we saw a substantial decrease in the use of the term "illegal": from 22 per cent of all episodes in our 2020 research to 5 per cent in 2022. The term "undocumented" was also used far more often than "illegal(s)" in our 2022 research: 50 instances in 30 episodes of television, compared to 11 instances in 8 episodes, respectively.

Define American was founded as a survival strategy in the midst of this immigration policy turmoil. In 2011, Jose Antonio Vargas, then a Pulitzer Prize–winning journalist with a big secret, was about to leave his job at *The Washington Post* and out himself as an undocumented resident in the United States in a *New York Times Magazine* essay. He and three friends, who were all high-level media professionals, developed a "coming out" campaign to target mass media. Vargas, along with Jake Brewer, Jehmu Greene, and Alicia Menendez, sparked a nationwide conversation around immigration and the power of visibility and invisibility in the media. Their campaign grew into Define American, and shaped its goal to combat harmful rhetoric about immigrants in mass media, believing that we cannot change the politics of immigration until we change the culture through which immigrants are seen.

From the forming of the nation as a country of "free white men" and everyone else as "alien," we see the legacy of the white supremacist structure of oppression still represented in television. Many television creators have biases, both acknowledged and unconscious, that are amplified to the nation and around the world, representing who and what "American" means. The stereotypes that exist in their minds can manifest into the characters they draw and those narrow understandings can surface in the storylines we see on TV. The power of television creators' points of view is magnified. Therefore changing the perception of immigrants requires changing how we tell these cultural stories.

Define American's name originated from the principle that a country is defined by its residents, who are not necessarily represented

authentically in dominant culture or dominant media. As an organization, it believes that being "American" is defined by the civic participation of all that reside in the nation. To fix the politics, Define American
believes you must first influence people. The hate we tackle can often
be in the form of erasure but is most frequently seen as misrepresentation and stereotypes that add fuel to the fires burning in culture and
politics around immigrant communities. We aim, both in our work to
combat mis- and disinformation about immigrants in social media and
our work in television and film, to increase nuanced representation in
media and reduce stereotypical depictions. In other words, to humanize immigrants for who they are: people just like everyone else.

Cultivating "Intimacy at a Distance"[23]

Social commentary, satire, and propaganda permeate mass media's history. Fictional programming could be used as a tool of social and political influence, both to promote hate in films like D.W. Griffith's *Birth
of a Nation*, and for hate reduction in films like Charlie Chaplin's *The
Great Dictator*, Joseph L. Mankiewicz's *No Way Out*, and Elia Kazan's
Gentleman's Agreement. Television, however, brought about an opportunity to speak to – and educate – audiences on a regular basis and in the
intimacy of their own homes. In the 1950s and 1960s, television creators
began to develop the concept of educating audiences as a strategy in
children's programming, seen in shows like *Watch Mr. Wizard*, *Captain
Kangaroo*, and *Mr. Roger's Neighborhood*. In 1969, the Public Broadcast-
ing Network (PBS) introduced the beloved and longest-running educational entertainment program on US television, *Sesame Street*.[24] PBS
has produced numerous educational programs throughout the years,
including *Arthur*, *The Magic School Bus*, *Reading Rainbow*, and a vast
array of current programming for children's enjoyment and learning.

Though National Geographic television specials also began in the
1960s, the traction for adult audiences' consumption of educational
entertainment, or edutainment, did not see an uptick in viewership
until the late 1970s. The Discovery Channel was launched in 1985,
focusing on documentaries and docuseries. Since its inception it has
become a popular cable television channel globally, featuring a wide
range of educational and documentary programming across various
genres, including science, nature, history, and technology. Also during
the 1970s, some scripted TV shows began to grapple with contemporary issues and incorporate social messaging into their storylines. Many
of these originated from the legendary producer Norman Lear. His hit
television show *All in the Family* (1971–9) featured a racist, bigoted

father paired with a doting and tolerant mother. Lear said he based Archie Bunker, the father, on his own dad and fashioned Edith Bunker, the mother, as Christ-like, to model unconditional love and tolerance within one family. The social modeling of diverse viewpoints set amidst relatable family dramas was a hit, and Lear went on to produce *Sanford and Son* (1972–7), *Good Times* (1974–9), *One Day at a Time* (1975–84), *The Jeffersons* (1975–85), and others that leveraged the technique of depicting and confronting social conflict in families. The roots of parasocial interaction for prejudice reduction and fostering intergroup empathy can be seen in all of these shows. Their popularity laid the groundwork for further issue exploration on iconic shows like *Family Ties* (1982–9) and *The Cosby Show* (1984–92).

Recognizing the impact of media representation, several nonprofits focusing on narrative change for social justice were inspired by a collaboration that developed in 2002 between the Centers for Disease Control and Prevention (CDC) and the University of Southern California (USC), called Hollywood, Health & Society.[25] The program partnered with writers of the primetime television medical drama *ER* (Emergency Room; 1994–2009) to embed accurate health information into the show's plot lines. *ER* featured doctors – and the rising Hollywood star George Clooney – in an ensemble cast working in a Chicago hospital. Hollywood, Health & Society provided health experts and resources to the writers and producers of *ER* to ensure the accurate portrayal of medical issues and health-related storylines on the show. While the concept of edutainment was not new, mass collaborations across nonprofit and for-profit sectors for better public health was a new innovation. In 1988, all of the major television networks in the United States collaborated with the Center for Health Communication at Harvard University on seeding the idea of having a "designated driver" if planning to drink alcohol socially.[26] The initiative, called the Harvard Alcohol Project, is credited as the reason the concept of a designated driver is widely used in the United States today. The collaboration was a formal endorsement in the longevity of edutainment as a tool for social norm change around public health topics.

Ten years later, the TV show *Will & Grace* (1998–2006) premiered, featuring some of the first openly gay lead characters in a US primetime television series. The popularity and cultural response to the show has been colloquially dubbed the "Will and Grace effect," describing how parasocial interaction with the fictional character of Will changed attitudes, knowledge, and beliefs of much of US society toward gay people and gay rights.[27] Studies showed that the parasocial relationship strongly correlated to prejudice reduction particularly for audience members who self-reported that they had no real life contact with gay people. The nonprofit Gay and Lesbian Alliance Against Defamation (GLAAD), founded in 1985, lauded the television representation. Other nonprofits also took note of the power of television for social change.

The character of Mateo on NBC's *Superstore* created an opportunity for Define American to understand how research and practice could connect to generate a clearer understanding of how television creators could shift real world action. In 2016, the creators of *Superstore* approached the consulting team at Define American; they wanted to reveal that the series regular Mateo was undocumented. Having heard about Define American's work in Hollywood, they invited our consulting team to advise on the character development so that the details of the character's beliefs, motivations, actions, and overall storyline were accurate. Mateo's "coming out" experience unfolded over a few episodes, and secured a lasting partnership between the *Superstore* writing team and the Define American consulting team until the show's end in 2021.

Over those years, we worked with the writers to improve accuracy around immigration law points and to pitch storylines that were both comical and realistic. Humanizing Mateo's narrative was important to the show's writers as well as the advocates on our team. When the writers needed a deeper understanding of the challenges of obtaining a visa, we facilitated an in-person conversation with an undocumented storyteller from our network who shared, in detail, his experience navigating the US immigration system. He also told us about how he was mugged near his home, and that his friends jokingly congratulated him because he would be eligible for a U-Visa, a four-year visa granted to victims of crimes who assist authorities in apprehending perpetrators. Currently, there is no pathway to citizenship for the 11.8 million undocumented people in the United States, but the U-Visa does carry with it the path to a green card. This real-life story made its way to the air in early 2018 when Mateo urges a co-worker to rough him up in an attempt to "fix" his immigration status. The writers used both comedy and tragedy to educate viewers about the challenges that someone who is undocumented has to face in order to obtain a visa.

By season 5, the *Superstore* team wanted to explore what would happen if *Superstore* experienced a raid by Immigration Customs and Enforcement, and Mateo was detained. The conversation between our two teams illustrated the vulnerability and instability that an undocumented status carries. As various scenarios were discussed, the weight of reality fell over the teams. The character of Mateo could not be saved by his colleagues in the season finale. He was handcuffed, put in the back of a car, and taken away, leaving tearful and shocked colleagues behind. The episode reflects reality and a scenario that too many have faced in the United States.

Superstore was the first network primetime comedy with an undocumented series regular. Media scholars Caty Borum Chattoo and Lauren Feldman[28] chronicled the importance of comedy for social change as an emerging strategy of edutainment, using *Superstore* as a case study. The opportunity was exciting to our team because the character of Mateo already existed on television; he had an identity prior to the reveal that he was undocumented. The sequence of meeting someone and finding out later about their immigration status closely mirrors how that information is shared between most people in the United States. However, on television we often see immigrant characters who are defined first or solely by their undocumented status.

In Define American's work to achieve parity with real life, the experience of *Superstore* presented a good case study for parasocial contact interaction. Twenty episodes aired over the course of three years in Mateo's storyline. This timeline is important because our research with the Norman Lear Center suggests that there is greater impact when a viewer sees a portrayal over a period of time rather than just once.[29] In a survey of regular viewers of twelve shows featuring regular or recurring immigrant characters, the more often viewers across political ideologies watched the shows, the more likely they were to believe that diversity is a valuable asset to society, report greater knowledge of immigration-related issues, and take action in support of immigrants.

We decided with the Norman Lear Center research team to study the parasocial interaction of *Superstore* viewers in our 2020 report. Those who saw Mateo's storyline experienced feelings of friendship with him.[30] *Superstore* viewers that participated in the study felt that Mateo was down-to-earth (74 per cent) and they felt comfortable with him in a similar way that they felt comfortable with their own friends (69 per cent). Viewers that felt a parasocial connection to Mateo were also more likely to support an increase in immigration to the United States. The phenomenon was seen clearest with those who self-reported having little or no real-life contact with immigrants. For the first time in Define American's history, we could see narrative change translating to real-life attitude and belief change in a mass media audience. Our 2020 report showed more than just changing minds; immigration storylines sustained across a single season of television were translating into real-world action. *Superstore* viewers who had seen the immigration-related episodes took more immigration-related actions in real life than unexposed participants.

Two years later, we saw similar behavior change with characters from two other television shows: CBS's *Bob Hearts Abishola* and Netflix's *Never Have I Ever*. Define American and the Norman Lear Center decided to study the effects of these two shows that prominently feature immigrants. We were interested in the degree of understanding experienced when immigrant characters were regularly featured in multiple episodes over time.

Authenticity has been a key element in the creation of *Bob Hearts Abishola*, which centers on Abishola, a Nigerian immigrant nurse who falls in love with her patient Bob, a white middle-aged compression sock salesman. The daughter of Nigerian immigrants herself, co-creator Gina Yashere insisted on hiring writers and actors who are African and Black. In its first season, *Bob Hearts Abishola* was CBS's highest-rated new sitcom, with over five million viewers consistently every week. Yashere has said, "It's opened doors because now everybody's looking at our show and going, 'Oh, we can do shows like this and they can be successful, and all of America can enjoy the show.' It doesn't have to be just Black people or just Nigerians. Everybody can enjoy the show for what it is, which is a great show."[31]

Bob Hearts Abishola viewers experienced significant parasocial interaction with the central character of Abishola.[32] The show increased 34 per cent of viewers' understanding of immigrant experiences; 29 per cent said it increased their comfort around meeting a recent immigrant to the United States; 44 per cent said it increased their understanding of the sacrifices people must make to emigrate. On average, *Bob Hearts Abishola* viewers – regardless of their political ideologies – agreed that diversity is a valuable asset to society.

Additionally, viewers of the series *Never Have I Ever*, a coming-of-age comedy-drama about the complicated life of a first-generation Indian American teenage girl, were more likely to agree that diversity is a valuable asset to society and express comfort in sending their children to a school where the majority of students are immigrants.[33] These outcomes were driven in part by parasocial interaction with the regularly occurring character Nalini, the Indian immigrant mother of the show's main character, Devi. Viewers of *Never Have I Ever* were also more likely to support increased immigration to the United States. These feelings of friendship with Nalini partially compensated for limited real-life contact with immigrants. Specifically, stronger feelings of friendship were associated with greater support for immigration primarily among those who have few or no relationships with immigrants in reality. *Never Have I Ever* viewers also reported several positive changes in their attitudes toward immigrants. Compared to non-viewers, they were more likely to report greater knowledge of immigration-related issues, greater comfort with the idea of sending their children to schools where the majority of students are immigrants, and moving to neighborhoods with many immigrants. They also demonstrated lower prejudice toward immigrants as measured by the Realistic Threats scale and had a stronger belief in the value of diversity to society. Why does this matter for prejudice reduction? Parasocial relationships are one mechanism through which entertainment storylines influence audience attitudes and beliefs. The more feelings of friendship viewers experience with an immigrant character, like Mateo, Abishola, or Nalini, the more likely they are to believe immigrants contribute to society, and that diversity is a valuable asset.

Putting Parasocial into Practice

Define American is dedicated to advancing our strategies through meticulous research aimed at enhancing impact on the US media landscape. This process typically involves conducting comprehensive landscape analyses, dissecting the gaps and limitations present in media representations within specific mediums, and proposing recommendations to close those gaps. Additionally, we conduct audience surveys to gauge perceptions and understanding of characters and storylines related to immigrants and immigration.

Doing the Research

A small constellation of US-based research organizations partner with nonprofits to study representation of impacted communities on television. Three nonpartisan research hubs exist within the Annenberg School of Communications at the University of Southern California (USC): Hollywood, Health & Society; the Norman Lear Center; and the Media Impact Project. Hollywood, Health & Society continues to research health, security, and safety while the Norman Lear Center explores cultural, social, economic, and political issues in mass media. The Media Impact Project's focus is on the ways in which mass media influences audiences' attitudes, beliefs, and actions. At the University of California Los Angeles (UCLA) sits the Center for Storytellers and Scholars with research interests in the landscape of children and youth television programming across the globe and its impact on young people as well as the Entertainment & Media Research Initiative (EMRI), which publishes the UCLA Hollywood Diversity Report. The Center for Media and Social Impact (CMSI) at the American University examines how entertainment can be used for social change. The Geena Davis

Institute on Gender and Media – founded by the renowned actress and activist Geena Davis – uses an intersectional lens to examine the landscape of media around gender, identity, disabilities, race, age, and body image. GLAAD has monitored the representation of the LGBTQI+ community for over twenty-five years and uses the findings of its own original research to push for change in mass media industries to positive effect for its cause.

Define American did not begin with big research projects, however. Our processes started with steps that many NGOs are already putting into practice. One such strategy was conducting informal audience tests using social media content and associated analytics platforms. Platforms like Facebook Insights, X Analytics, and Instagram Insights offered valuable information on our audience demographics, engagement rates, and content performance, which helped paint a preliminary picture of our audience's attitudes about immigrants and immigration. These platforms provided real-time data on our audience's interests. Additionally, our communications team was already using Sprout Social as a tool for social media management. We leveraged Sprout Social's sentiment analysis feature to more deeply investigate how audiences were reacting to media narratives on various social media platforms. Using social media analytics, NGOs are provided a real-time indication of public sentiment and can help identify areas of concern or success with narrative agendas.

Our social media audiences do not necessarily reflect our target audience of media gatekeepers or even our secondary audience of mass media consumers who are moveable on immigration issues. Instead, they reflect our base, the people who are already with us and bought into our mission. In an age of media filters, it can be hard to bridge-build using social media platforms. When our budget for testing grew, we invested $5,000– $10,000 in paid ads on Facebook, X, and YouTube to target audiences more specifically outside of our own social media followers. We could have also chosen to leverage free-to-low-cost tools for audience surveying like Google Forms, SurveyMonkey, or Typeform to design and distribute audience surveys. Ultimately, we did not for a number of reasons. These less costly services produce a lot more data that need to be parsed and analyzed, which did not match up with our staff capacity when looking at the return on investment for implementation.

As our organizational investment and threshold for research grew, we began working with the research organizations Change Research and Swayable to better understand the way our static image posts and videos were resonating with audiences we wanted to reach rather than who we could pay to target through social media ads. Dedicating a budget in the range of $15,000–$25,000 allowed us to uncover insights about demographics and ideologies of a moveable-on-immigration audience who also regularly consumes media on a number of platforms.

Our founder, board, and senior leadership invested in the idea of being a research-led organization early in our organizational history and made decisions on how to allocate funding to grow the program. We are lucky to have that forward-thinking investment, which is not always the case, especially in smaller nonprofits. At every level, though, well-targeted audience research provides a case for deeper investment. As a research department, we fully align each research project to practical application and have an internal benchmark that each research project should feed into our whole team's consulting programs for two years. Any investment then can be cost-shared in value across two years, with key indicators set for evaluation to ensure we understand how the research is being used in the field. We create one-pagers, guides, social media assets, and other products whose usage can be monitored and tracked as well as consultancies, meetings with stakeholders, panels, and other forms of distribution that can also be monitored and tracked.

As we grew, we wanted comprehensive and more conclusive research on a variety of topics to move our expertise in the field of narrative change for culture change to the next level. Scholars whose work aligns with NGOs can work together to produce research that has little-to-no cost for the NGOs. As community partners, the organizations provide access to the communities impacted by the issues or internal data on how advocacy advances – or does not – in real time. Collaborations with scholars are often funded through grants to the researchers and can be mutually very beneficial. The drawbacks are that it can take time to find the right collaboration, the funding, and align on research outputs and timelines. Define American has also commissioned research from scholars and research organizations due to the nature of our timelines and the types of research we require. When our budgets grew to $45,000 and upward, we were able to commission research specific to our needs.

Character and Story Development

Once we had a comprehensive understanding of the media representation landscape – in this case on television and with our research partner, the Norman Lear Center – and audience attitudes, knowledge, beliefs, and actions regarding immigrants and immigration in a specific medium, we tailored our consulting practice to address the identified gaps. The goal is to shift audience perspectives toward greater understanding and advocacy for immigrants in the United States. At the same time, ongoing monitoring of activities in the field allows us to identify stakeholders who are instrumental in fostering a media landscape more conducive to humanized immigrant representation.

Our organization's theory of change centers on activating media industry gatekeepers. By influencing these key decision-makers, Define American seeks to open the gates for greater immigrant representation, thereby altering the national programming and dominant harmful narratives present in US media.

Once the representation landscape and audience attitudes are understood, NGOs can tailor strategies to address identified gaps and effectively influence public perceptions. Using these data to inform direct collaboration with media gatekeepers and industry insiders is crucial, as they play a pivotal role in shaping media narratives. Activating these gatekeepers, whether they be content creators, producers, or executives, can open new avenues for representation and influence the broader cultural dialogue. To enhance the effectiveness of strategies tailored to address representation gaps and influence public perceptions, NGOs can integrate these additional steps into the feedback loop between research and practice, fostering a more comprehensive and dynamic approach.

We purposely hire individuals from the media industries where we hope to implement narrative change strategies and build the field. Bringing on key team members who possess professional experience and also identify with immigrant communities has been critical to facilitating successful consultations. NGOs interested in narrative change interventions in pop culture can similarly seek to support their efforts with staff who possess notable industry experience or at least a working understanding of media hierarchies and production, in addition to deep knowledge about their issue area in the community of interest. This is a critical skill set that enables the use of common language of those industries, the ability to identify key milestones in media production pipelines at which changes can realistically be implemented, and the ability to identify and build relationships with gatekeepers, thus more effectively building trust in creative collaborations.

There can be a misconception in media fields, and particularly in the entertainment industry, that the goal of advocacy organizations is simply to be a watchdog. In the age of "cancel culture," it is important to debunk that notion and find common ground *as storytellers* in order to build trust at initial stages of collaboration, create an environment that fosters open dialogue, productively challenge harmful tropes and stereotypes, and find creative solutions for accurate and nuanced storytelling.

In addition to industry fluency and building trust, we have also found it effective to engage individuals from impacted communities who are willing to be storytellers, and then introduce them to TV writers' rooms or film production executives. In these spaces, which have already been primed by way of deep relationship-building, we have been able to facilitate conversations between the TV and film people and the storytellers to bring humanity and depth to immigrant characters and immigration storylines. We have been able to find great storytellers through our own immigrant artist fellowship program and the community of artists we cultivated through other creative collaborations – again, building trust all along the way.

When these interactions produce successful results, it can also encourage repeat collaboration. Many of our past consulting partners have returned to us to collaborate on new and related projects. We also follow trade publications to identify and proactively pitch creative teams who are writing immigrant characters as well as provide comprehensive and approachable workshops that educate creatives and industry professionals about our research, the harms of stereotyped characters on audiences, and the societal benefits of creating relatable and nuanced immigrant stories.

Above all else, our research has been a foundational element to all of our creative consultations and partnerships. By introducing hard data points and marrying them to the fundamentals of storytelling, we have been able to persuade and educate people in the film and TV industries on damaging missteps to avoid and more accurate and even aspirational immigrant storylines to explore.

As previously noted, our 2022 report showed that 40 per cent of all immigrant characters on television were associated with crime – an all-time high since we began our longitudinal study. Actually, immigrants are less likely to commit crime than individuals born in the United States.[34] In one consultation for an episodic streaming series that featured an immigrant character with DACA (Deferred Action for Childhood Arrivals), we found the character and other leads of color in a prison escape room scene wearing prison jumpsuit costumes. While this was not a real event in the context of the scene, we shared our data points around immigrant association with crime and discussed the dangers of perpetuating this misconception. The creative teams understood and moved away from using this imagery out of context in promotional materials.

Finally, sharing our research covering parasocial interaction coupled with anecdotes from the field has been another highly effective method in our consultation process. The previously shared data points around underrepresentation and misrepresentation, although accurate and often effective, can also be disheartening and digested as negative. On the other hand, by introducing our case studies on parasocial contact and highlighting the positive effects that nuanced characters can have in reducing prejudice, we're able to tangibly illustrate inspirational success stories and empower creatives to make better, more nuanced story decisions on their own.

While Define American's work focuses largely on moving away from dehumanizing depictions and racist stereotypes, we also acknowledge that there is a need to depict instances of racism and xenophobia in order to confront it and model healthy conflict. For example, when we encounter a line of dialogue in a script in which an antagonist uses a racial slur against an immigrant character, we must step back and ask a few questions: What are this character's motivations? Does this character exist in real life? Is the immigrant character given the agency to hold the antagonist accountable? Are there allies available to hold them accountable? And does the lesson outweigh any harm in the audience hearing the word used? If an immigrant character or their allies can be depicted as confronting the use of this word, even making a correction, the audience is able to imagine a model for how that conflict may be healthily resolved in real life.

Monitoring and Evaluating

Evaluation was the last piece that Define American added to its feedback loop. When our investment in being a research-led organization grew, so did our data and programs, resulting in the need for an in-house evaluator. This has proved an essential part of the process. Many consider evaluating narrative change for culture change as a behemoth task that is out of reach, but we, as a social change field, are starting to understand that is not the case. Using research to understand the gaps and areas of opportunity, targeting those opportunities, and then monitoring key indicators around change can provide a roadmap to understanding narrative change efforts.

One strategy we use is conducting stakeholder interviews and surveys, including with the media industry. These interactions can provide nuanced insights into their perspectives, challenges, and potential areas for collaboration. Surveys, whether distributed digitally or in person, can capture diverse viewpoints and help identify shared goals and concerns. These qualitative data can be invaluable in understanding the motivations and considerations of key decision-makers in the media landscape.

To understand the breadth, depth, and opportunities in our networks, we established a centralized database – though it could be as simple as a spreadsheet – where we log qualitative information about the media landscape that is cataloged and shared among staff. This repository includes insights gained from meetings, stakeholder interviews, surveys, and other qualitative research. Creating a structured database facilitates knowledge-sharing, enabling staff members to draw on collective insights and experiences, fostering a collaborative and informed organizational culture. Maintaining the database, or tracking in an already existing customer relationship management (CRM) system, provides data on how stakeholders and influencers in the field are amplifying our contributions to the field, like sharing resources or inviting us to speak on panels. By tracking contacts, NGOs can identify emerging leaders, potential collaborators, and key decision-makers who contribute to positive changes, in our case, to better representation on television.

To maximize the feedback loop, Define American chose to invite and train all staff, including operations staff and our senior leadership, in contributing findings to the data tracking. We recognize that this is unique and not feasible for most organizations. Building a culture of continuous evaluation involves creating a sense of collective responsibility for the organization's impact, which can be separate from the actual maintenance of spreadsheets. Even dedicating quarterly meetings with staff to discuss "success and challenges" could be a way of keeping tabs on the activities that are progressing or stifling the mission. Providing opportunities for departments and the full team to collaboratively assess progress and make informed decisions benefits the organization in building a learning culture that is more advanced and sometimes more actionable than just collecting data for grant deliverables.

In these evaluations, it's crucial to consider whether the chosen indicators truly map to the desired cultural change. It's not just about tracking numbers but about understanding the qualitative nuances that contribute to the overall narrative. Leaning into qualitative data becomes imperative to capture engagement that might feel tricky to measure quantitatively. This could involve soliciting feedback from community members, stakeholders, and field experts to gauge the qualitative impact of the organization's initiatives.

Field-building, often underestimated in traditional metrics, should be recognized as a powerful measurement in and of itself. No single NGO can achieve culture change alone, and the collective effort of building a field contributes significantly to the broader societal transformation. The impact of an organization extends beyond its immediate initiatives to the networks it fosters, collaborations it nurtures, and the dialogue it stimulates within media industries. Evaluating these aspects provides a holistic understanding of the organization's role in shaping narratives and fostering cultural shifts.

A feedback loop, coupled with a commitment to ongoing evaluation, positions NGOs not just as passive observers but as active contributors to the evolution of cultural landscapes. By engaging staff in the monitoring process, regularly checking in on metrics, and valuing both qualitative and field-building impacts, NGOs can ensure that their work remains adaptive, relevant, and genuinely impactful in promoting positive cultural change. Additionally, it is also imperative for NGOs as well as funders to monitor, acknowledge, and share learnings about mistakes in order to move the field forward. This dynamic approach not only serves the organization's mission but also contributes to the collective effort of reshaping narratives on a broader scale. By documenting and analyzing efforts year over year, organizations can build a robust understanding of the evolving landscape, ensuring that their work remains relevant and effective in promoting positive cultural change. Ultimately, implementing a feedback loop allows NGOs to not only learn from their experiences but also contribute meaningfully to shaping narratives and fostering cultural shifts.

Conclusion

In light of the powerful insights derived from the exploration of parasocial interaction and narrative change presented, NGOs working toward social justice can draw valuable lessons to shape their own strategies. The phenomenon of feeling a kinship with fictional characters, as described by Horton and Wohl,[35] underscores the potential of mass media in influencing attitudes and behaviors. The innovation of leveraging produced content for prejudice reduction through parasocial interaction is particularly significant, allowing audiences to develop empathy without requiring individuals from marginalized communities to bear the burden of teaching about difference.

For NGOs seeking to learn from and implement practices based on the findings of Define American's narrative change efforts, the following are some key pieces to remember:

1) Create a plan for research and data collection:
> Start with research to understand the current state of representation or the issue you are addressing. Define clear research objectives and collaborate with research institutions or experts to ensure comprehensive and unbiased data collection.

2) Identify key stakeholders and collaborate:

Establish partnerships with relevant stakeholders, such as academic institutions, media creators, and community organizations. Collaborative efforts can provide diverse perspectives, expertise, and resources that enhance the impact of your initiatives.

3) Integrate research and practice:

Align research findings with actionable strategies. The case of NBC's *Superstore* highlights the importance of integrating research into the creative process, influencing storyline development, character representation, and overall narrative construction.

4) Promote authentic representation:

Emphasize the importance of authentic storytelling. Encourage creators to involve individuals from the affected communities in the development process to ensure accuracy, cultural sensitivity, and a nuanced portrayal that resonates with the audience.

5) Establish a feedback loop:

Implement a feedback loop similar to Define American's model. Continuously evaluate the impact of your initiatives, not only in terms of audience reactions but also in measurable changes in attitudes, knowledge, beliefs, and actions. Adjust strategies based on ongoing assessments.

6) Monitor the audience:

Actively engage with your target audience to understand their perspectives, concerns, and preferences. Define American's study on parasocial interactions emphasizes the profound impact of repeated exposure to well-developed characters on audience attitudes.

7) Measure impact beyond awareness:

Go beyond measuring awareness. Define and measure key indicators related to attitudinal and behavioral changes. Assess how narrative change translates into tangible actions or shifts in societal norms.

8) Stay adaptable and open to iteration:

Be prepared to iterate and adapt your strategies based on ongoing feedback and changing societal dynamics. The landscape of media and societal attitudes evolves, and NGOs need to stay responsive to ensure continued effectiveness.

As organizations embark on their narrative change journeys, it is crucial to recognize that narrative strategies can feel daunting and abstract, but the lessons from this chapter can provide a partial roadmap. NGOs can harness the power of storytelling to challenge stereotypes, foster understanding, and drive positive societal change. Just as Define American has demonstrated, the integration of research, practice, and evaluation within a feedback loop can serve as a potent tool for narrative interventions and strategic communication efforts aimed at prejudice reduction. Through concerted efforts, NGOs can contribute to reshaping narratives that might otherwise stigmatize "others," and instead underscore our common humanity through innovations in television, film, radio, social media, journalism, and beyond.

NOTES

1 Donald Horton and R. Richard Wohl, "Mass Communication and Para-Social Interaction," *Psychiatry* 19, no. 3 (1956): 215–29, https://doi.org/10.1080/00332747.1956.11023049.

2 G. Gerbner and L. Gross, "Living with Television: The Violence Profile," *Journal of Communication* 26, no. 2 (1976): 172–99, https://doi.org/10.1111/j.1460-2466.1976.tb01397.x.

3 Gordon W. Allport, *The Nature of Prejudice* (Reading, MA: Addison-Wesley, 1954).

4 Horton and Wohl, "Mass Communication."

5 Sarah E. Lowe et al., *Change the Narrative, Change the World: The Power of Immigrant Representation on Television* (Los Angeles: The Norman Lear Center and Define American, 2022), https://defineamerican.com/research/change-the-narrative; Erica L. Rosenthal et al., *Change the Narrative, Change the World: How Immigrant Representation on Television Moves Audiences to Action* (Los Angeles: The Norman Lear Center and Define American, 2020), https://defineamerican.com/research/change-the-narrative/; Edward Schiappa, Peter B. Gregg, and Dean E. Hewes, "Can One TV Show Make a Difference? *Will & Grace* and the Parasocial Contact Hypothesis," *Journal of Homosexuality* 51, no. 4 (2006): 15–37, https://doi.org/10.1300/J082v51n04_02.

6 Nikki Kalra, Cecilia Borges Farfan, and Sarah Stachowiak, *Measuring Narrative Change: Understanding Progress and Navigating Complexity* (Seattle: ORS Impact, 2021), https://www.orsimpact.com/directory/Measuring-Narrative-Change.htm.

7 Tracy R. Gleason, Sally A. Theran, and Emily M. Newberg, "Parasocial Interactions and Relationships in Early Adolescence," *Frontiers in Psychology* 8 (2017): 255, https://doi.org/10.3389/fpsyg.2017.00255; Jean P.G. Lacap et al., "Parasocial Relationships and Social Media Interactions: Building Brand Credibility and Loyalty," *Spanish Journal of Marketing – ESIC* 28, no. 1 (2023): 77–97, https://doi.org/10.1108/SJME-09-2022-0190.

8 Schiappa, Gregg, and Hewes, "Can One TV Show Make a Difference?"
9 Bradley J. Bond, "Parasocial Contact and Prejudice Reduction," in Jan Van den Bulck et al., eds, *The International Encyclopedia of Media Psychology* (New York: John Wiley & Sons, 2020), 1–4, https://doi.org/10.1002/9781119011071.iemp0205.
10 Thomas F. Pettigrew and Linda R. Tropp, "A Meta-Analytic Test of Intergroup Contact Theory," *Journal of Personality and Social Psychology* 90, no. 5 (2006): 751–83, https://doi.org/10.1037/0022-3514.90.5.751.
11 Gerbner and Gross, "Living with Television."
12 Gerbner and Gross, "Living with Television," 182.
13 Lowe et al., *Change the Narrative, Change the World*; Elisha Marr and Laura B. Luchies, "Symbolic Reality Bites 2: Contemporary Representations of Women and People of Color in Top 100 Films," *Sociological Spectrum* 43, no. 6 (2023): 147–69, https://doi.org/10.1080/02732173.2023.2254431.
14 Darnell Hunt, *Race in the Writers' Room: How Hollywood Whitewashes the Stories That Shape America* (Hollywood: Color of Change, 2017), https://hollywood.colorofchange.org/wp-content/uploads/2019/03/COC_Hollywood_Race_Report.pdf.
15 Johanna Blakely et al., *Immigration Nation: Exploring Immigrant Portrayals on Television* (Los Angeles: The Norman Lear Center, 2018), https://learcenter.s3.us-west-1.amazonaws.com/immigration_nation_report_final_1.pdf.
16 Blakeley et al., *Immigration Nation*.
17 U.S. Capitol Visitor Center, *H.R. 40, Naturalization Bill, March 4, 1790*, accessed January 16, 2025, https://www.visitthecapitol.gov/artifact/h-r-40-naturalization-bill-march-4-1790.
18 U.S. National Park Service, *Ulysses S. Grant, Chinese Immigration, and the Page Act of 1875*, accessed January 16, 2025, https://www.nps.gov/articles/000/ulysses-s-grant-chinese-immigration-and-the-page-act-of-1875.htm.
19 U.S. Department of State, Office of the Historian, *The Immigration Act of 1924 (The Johnson-Reed Act)*, accessed January 16, 2025, https://history.state.gov/milestones/1921-1936/immigration-act.
20 U.S. Holocaust Memorial Museum, *Voyage of the St. Louis*, accessed January 16, 2025, https://encyclopedia.ushmm.org/content/en/article/voyage-of-the-st-louis.
21 National Immigration Forum, *Legal Immigration to the United States: National Quotas and America's Immigration System*, January 30, 2024, https://immigrationforum.org/article/legal-immigration-to-the-united-states-national-quotas-americas-immigration-system/.
22 Rosenthal et al., *Change the Narrative, Change the World*.
23 Horton and Wohl, "Mass Communication."

24 Shalom M. Fisch and Rosemarie T. Truglio, eds., *G Is for Growing: Thirty Years of Research on Children and Sesame Street* (New York: Routledge, 2000), https://doi.org/10.4324/9781410605252.

25 Vicki Beck, "Working with Daytime and Prime-Time Television Shows in the United States to Promote Health," in Arvind Singhal et al., eds., *Entertainment-Education and Social Change: History, Research and Practice* (New York: Routledge, 2003).

26 Center for Health Communication, *Harvard Alcohol Project: Designated Driver*, Harvard T.H. Chan School of Public Health, accessed January 16, 2025, https://www.hsph.harvard.edu/chc/harvard-alcohol-project/.

27 Schiappa, Gregg, and Hewes, "Can One TV Show Make a Difference?"

28 Caty Borum Chattoo and Lauren Feldman, *A Comedian and an Activist Walk into a Bar: The Serious Role of Comedy in Social Justice* (Berkeley: University of California Press, 2020).

29 Lowe et al., *Change the Narrative, Change the World.*

30 Lowe et al., *Change the Narrative, Change the World.*

31 Keisha Hatchett, "*Bob Hearts Abishola*'s Gina Yashere on Being Her Authentic Nigerian Self before Hollywood Thought It Was Cool," TV Line, February 5, 2021, https://tvline.com/interviews/bob-hearts-abishola -gina-yashere-black-history-month-1234636662/.

32 Lowe et al., *Change the Narrative, Change the World.*

33 Lowe et al., *Change the Narrative, Change the World.*

34 Lowe et al., *Change the Narrative, Change the World.*

35 Horton and Wohl, "Mass Communication."

Editor's Introduction to Chapter 6

So far we've examined what philosophy teaches us about approaching hate, how our brains work around "us" and "them," how hatred works on a group level, the question of how memories fuel or might be altered to help combat hate, and how data and humanizing stories can help reduce hatred. Hate harms us morally and ethically; it harms our politics and our institutions and our culture.

To return to (and to mix) the elephant metaphor discussed in the preface, what's the cost of letting the elephant run loose in the china shop? In dollars and cents. What does hate actually cost us?

Whatever that figure is, both massive and difficult to calculate, it is important for NGOs and the rest of us to contemplate this question. We generally don't think problems are serious unless there's some way for us to quantify their cost.

That's why this book contains a chapter from Lee Badgett, an economist who in 2020 wrote the groundbreaking book *The Economic Case for LGBT Equality: Why Fair and Equal Treatment Benefits Us All*.

You most likely care about hate for reasons having nothing to do with money. You may care about the harm hate has on people who look like you or pray like you or share your ethnic background or politics. You yourself may have been victimized by hate. Or you may feel empathy for people oppressed by hate around the world today simply because they, like you, are human beings first.

But others may only care about hate when it targets them personally. They don't think that hate of others has anything to do with them. But it does. It costs them. Money. So let's pause for a moment and consider something less tied to empathy and more to crass self-interest. There may be times when moral principles outweigh economic calculations – I don't know anyone who will change their view of abortion based on alleged costs in either direction. But when we hear of the societal costs of obesity or smoking or pollution or drunk driving or gun violence, some of which hit our pocketbooks directly (such as in higher insurance rates), we understand better the need to address these problems.

What if each of us knew that the economic cost of hate cost us, in our own pocketbooks? What if we thought of the cost of hate as a tax, one that isn't for the common good (like we pay taxes for paving our roads and keeping street lights on or collective security), but rather one paid because we don't do enough to reduce the costs hate imposes, in other words a tax that ideally should be avoidable, and in practice can be reduced? And what if NGOs, in making their case against whatever type of hatred concerns them, also point to this most tangible of societal costs?

6 How NGOs Can Use Economic Arguments to Undermine Hate: A Case Study of Hate against LGBTQI+ People

M.V. LEE BADGETT

After Proposition 8 passed in California in 2008, eliminating a six-month-old right to marry for same-sex couples in that state, a new social media meme emerged: the NOH8 campaign (imagine a red 8 to give the pronunciation "no hate").[1] Tens of thousands of people painted NOH8 onto one cheek and covered their mouths with a strip of duct tape to symbolize the silencing of voices by Prop 8. The NOH8 Campaign, an NGO, turned this into one of the most prominent memes on LGBT Twitter (now X), judging from my own friends and followers, and people still post those photos on their social media profiles. Hate is much less popular than prejudice and stigma, it seems, as many famous people felt comfortable condemning hate, including Cindy McCain, the wife of 2008 Republican presidential candidate Senator John McCain.

By 2015, the same-sex marriage issue had been decided by the US Supreme Court in *Obergefell*, with a narrow 5–4 vote that same-sex couples have a constitutional right to marry. Or was it finally decided? Perhaps because of impressive increases in support for allowing same-sex couples to marry before and after 2015, it was a very shocked chill that went up the spines of married same-sex couples in 2022 when Supreme Court Justice Clarence Thomas argued that *Obergefell* should be revisited after the Court overturned *Roe v. Wade*.[2]

As that push to reconsider a settled case implies, opinion polls have also documented persistent reservoirs of hate and its close cousins – prejudice, stigma, and discriminatory intent – toward LGBTQI+ people.[3] Vocal and powerful minorities remain opposed to giving LGBTQI+ people the right to marry or the right to be protected against discrimination in workplaces and schools. Sparks of hatred, fanned by political and financial incentives for right-wing organizations to pursue deeply harmful policies against unpopular minorities, have once again ignited in many states and at the federal level with new attacks on DEI (diversity, equity, and inclusion).[4] In 2022, thirty-nine states considered

315 anti-LGBTQI+ bills, of which 29 passed and were signed into law, censoring discussion of LGBTQI+ issues in schools and curtailing the rights of young transgender people to decide which bathroom they will use or teams they can play on, or the ability of their physicians to prescribe gender affirming health care.[5]

Those opponents of equality and inclusion continue to exercise the power to define all or some subgroup of LGBTQI+ people as an "other" not worthy of basic human rights. It appears that hate against LGBTQI+ people has never been eradicated, and we are now seeing the rekindling of that sentiment in the United States and in many parts of the world.

Rather than fight fire with fire, this chapter proposes a cooler, broader argument against contemporary laws and practices that demonize and prevent LGBTQI+ people from experiencing their full human rights. This economic strategy has long been used to estimate the cost of doing nothing to address discrimination and hatred in other contexts. For example, economists estimated that racial discrimination in the United States cost as much as $20 billion per year in 1965, just as federal nondiscrimination laws were passed.[6] The cost of intimate partner violence (primarily against women) has been calculated to have an enormous cost on economies globally, ranging from 0.35 per cent of gross domestic product (GDP) to 1.91 per cent of GDP in developed countries and 1.6–6.5 per cent of GDP in developing countries.[7] This chapter also draws on the author's experience in debates over LGBTQI+ rights to show how NGOs and activists might use these arguments for LGBTQI+ rights issues and potentially for a much wider range of NGOs addressing different types of hate.

What I broadly call "the economic case for LGBTQI+ equality" starts with the harms of denying rights to LGBTQI+ people themselves, a human rights issue, and shows how they turn into a drag on the overall economy and affect everyone, regardless of sexual orientation and gender identity. The harms of hatred and stigma include reducing key parts of what economists call "human capital" – the skills, knowledge, energy, and creativity that are essential to the economy. Bullying in schools, minority stress and health disparities, and poor treatment in the workplace all hold LGBTQI+ people back from getting the education, jobs, and lives that they want. And that means that they are not able to contribute as much as they are capable of in the economy. This argument has been applied to the workings of businesses, government budgets, and whole economies in different contexts, providing a positive incentive to adopt nondiscriminatory laws and practices that became visible to decision-makers in those contexts, largely through the deployment of the economic case by many LGBTQI+ NGOs.

By appealing to a different strand of American values – the importance of equal opportunity and broad prosperity – and more universal human rights, in some situations NGOs have been able to shift the narrative on LGBTQI+ issues to this more positive one that focuses on the value of inclusion for all. In this chapter I will discuss the strategic use of this framing in three different contexts in the movement to recognize the human rights of LGBTQI+ people in the United States and in other countries. The first context that emerged for this type of argument came from businesses who began to cite it to justify their adoption of more inclusive policies for LGBTQI+ employees. The economic logic of the "business case" for LGBTQI+ equality then made its way into the second context I will address: the marriage equality debate in the United States. The third context I will describe is the broad economic case for LGBTQI+ equality as a tool for LGBTQI+ inclusive economic development in middle- and low-income countries. In the final section of the chapter, I will respond to concerns about using this argument in a human rights context and will suggest how similar economic arguments might be expanded into other movements against hate. In all cases, NGOs were crucial in turning the economic arguments into strategic talking points about the importance of creating more equal policies and practices.

Using the "Business Case" to Undo Homophobic and Transphobic Practices

Businesses play important roles in the lives of LGBTQI+ people, as with all people. They are sources of employment, of course, but they also have major impacts on culture through their products and marketing and on politics through their lobbying efforts. The business world first discovered something positive about LGBTQI+ people in the marketing context, mainly because of marketing surveys that suggested gay men and lesbians (in particular) were an affluent, underserved market.[8] Even though economic research revealed that the image of gay affluence is an inaccurate stereotype, companies caught on quickly.

During the 1990s, the American market witnessed a notable increase in visibility of gay individuals and couples in advertising. This included portrayals such as gay couples featured in Ikea ads selling dining-room tables, attractive men modeling Calvin Klein underwear on billboards in major cities, and advertisements for financial planning services tailored for affluent same-sex couples. Additionally, companies began investing in advertising space in gay and lesbian publications, sponsoring events organized by LGBTQI+ organizations, and participating in Pride Parades.

Also, starting in the 1990s, LGBTQI+ employees began to lobby and educate their employers about discrimination against LGBTQI+ people and the need for fairer policies, as research has continued to document evidence of discrimination.[9] To address the inequities, employee groups asked for internal policies against discrimination against LGBTQI+ employees and for making benefits equal for people with same-sex partners and for transgender employees.[10] These activists also came together to create NGOs to address these workplace issues, such as Out & Equal and the Human Rights Campaign (HRC) in the United States, and Stonewall in the UK, generating a platform for the propagation of the business case across companies.

The LGBTQI+ NGOs and employee groups soon realized that the interest in the LGBTQI+ consumer could be a compelling argument in persuading employers to provide explicit nondiscrimination protections, health care benefits for same-sex partners, gender affirming care coverage for transgender employees, and other inclusive practices. They argued that companies trying to capitalize on the gay market needed to integrate equality into their corporate values and brand identity. This carrot dangled in front of their employers was a juicy one, with as much as $1 trillion in LGBTQI+ buying power in the United States alone in 2018, according to one estimate.[11]

Over time, a stick emerged to be paired with the carrot: equal treatment and inclusion of LGBTQI+ people in all aspects of business is essential for the company's ability to compete in the marketplace. This "business case for LGBTQI+ equality" argues that equal treatment is good for the bottom line, since businesses are primarily driven by the goal of maximizing profits. One way companies can improve their profits is by reducing their costs of doing business. This includes expenses such as employee wages and benefits, as well as the costs of purchasing goods and services necessary for their operations. By treating LGBTQI+ workers fairly and inclusively, companies can potentially reduce costs associated with turnover, absenteeism, and employee dissatisfaction, leading to a more efficient and productive workforce. Fairness and inclusion become a competitive necessity as companies compete with each other to attract an inclusive and talented workforce. Combine that with the other way to improve the bottom line – increasing business revenue. This can be achieved by expanding the customer base and appealing to new markets. By embracing diversity and inclusivity, including the fair treatment of LGBTQI+ individuals, companies can attract a wider range of customers who value these principles, not just LGBTQI+ consumers. This can lead to increased sales and revenue growth.

In summary, the business case for LGBTQI+ equality argues that treating LGBTQI+ people fairly is not only a matter of ethics but also a smart business decision with financial benefits. Businesses can not only enhance their reputation and employee satisfaction through equitable policies but also reduce costs and increase revenue, ultimately leading to higher profits.

NGOs played a crucial role in disseminating information about the business case through publications, small meetings, and large annual conferences convened by Out & Equal and HRC. The Human Rights Campaign began the Corporate Equality Index to track employers' progress in adopting these fairer practices. This softer form of activism and networking across companies was a key factor in enhancing employers' willingness to make voluntary changes, alongside efforts to promote nondiscrimination laws at the local, state, and federal levels that could add muscle to the voluntary channel. NGOs and workplace activists also had economic competition on their side, as companies in competitive labor markets had to keep up with other employers seeking to hire workers with sought-after skills.[12] Productivity, recruitment, and retention are key considerations for employers when they announce more inclusive policies for LGBTQI+ workers.[13]

Subsequent changes suggest that this strategy worked. As of 2019 data collected by HRC's Corporate Equality Index, we can see a significant shift toward fairer practices, with 93 per cent of Fortune 500 companies incorporating sexual orientation into their nondiscrimination policies, and 85 per cent including gender identity. Moreover, among these major corporations, 49 per cent extended domestic partner benefits, and 62 per cent offered health care benefits inclusive of transgender individuals. Many companies cite economic factors as primary motivations for publicly announcing pro-LGBTQI+ policies, emphasizing the positive impact on the bottom line.[14] And the employers gain as well, as a growing body of evidence documents better financial outcomes for companies with LGBTQI+ inclusive policies – higher profits, higher productivity, and higher stock prices than for companies without inclusive policies.[15] Although some backlash efforts have emerged from time to time over the decades, employers have maintained these workplace policies and continue to argue for the importance of the business case, even as they might downplay some of their marketing efforts.[16]

The benefits of the business case also extend beyond any single company or marketplace into the public policy realm, thanks to the use of research findings by NGOs. Under pressure from customers and employees, as well as drawing on company values related to inclusion, forward-thinking companies have leveraged the business case for LGBTQI+ inclusion to advocate for nondiscrimination protections for LGBTQI+ workers before Congress and state legislatures. With the encouragement of NGOs, these companies have submitted testimony, signed friend-of-the-court briefs, and supported public petitions advocating for marriage equality in various countries (considered further in the next section), including the United States, Ireland, Australia, and Taiwan. In countries where homosexuality is still criminalized (approximately sixty-seven to seventy countries), companies are engaging in discreet dialogues with policymakers to make an economic argument for changing these discriminatory policies. These efforts demonstrate a commitment by many companies to not only promote diversity and inclusion within their own organizations but also to drive broader societal change by advocating for LGBTQI+ rights to become a matter of law as well as voluntary action by companies.

The Economic Benefits of Marriage Equality

Another context where economic reasoning has been deployed alongside arguments about equity was in the marriage equality debate in the US legislatures and courts. The question of equal rights in the treatment of same-sex couples and their access to the important social, cultural, legal, and economic institution of marriage was litigated in courts and legislatures across the United States. The national debate began in the mid-1990s and ended (at least temporarily, given Justice Thomas's recent remarks mentioned earlier) with the 2015 *Obergefell v. Hodges* decision by the US Supreme Court that spread the right of same-sex couples to marry to every state. Economic reasoning was most common in the public and legislative debates and sometimes made its way into court decisions. NGOs in the policy advocacy world and LGBTQI+ legal organizations' litigators often chose to include economic arguments in courtrooms and legislative chambers.

The economic benefits of marriage played a central role in framing the losses to same-sex couples.[17] Attorneys pursuing marriage equality through the courts wanted to quantify the economic value of the benefits of marriage that they had identified as being denied to same-sex couples. The states and federal government structure many laws and programs that provide direct economic rights and pecuniary benefits to married couples, particularly in areas such as taxation, state employee benefits, and dissolution processes. Additionally, third parties, including private employers, often offer economic benefits to married employees, most notably health insurance and retirement benefits. Marriage also offers a legal framework that yields "indirect" economic benefits, which may not be directly financial but are nonetheless significant on both societal and individual levels. These indirect benefits contributed to the argument that the denial of marriage rights to same-sex couples results in economic deprivation. Taken together, the combination of public and private economic aspects of marriage underscores the economic importance of marriage and supports the assertion that the inability to marry represents a form of economic disadvantage for same-sex couples.

Although those private benefits to same-sex couples would constitute economic gains at the social level, too, they were mostly used as ways to demonstrate economic inequities rather than being seen as a potential source of social gains. Indeed, some state legislators looked at those benefits and pronounced them to be too expensive for state governments to pay. As a result of that pushback, NGOs (both state-level and national) encouraged a team that I led at the UCLA School of Law Williams Institute to undertake a series of studies to evaluate whether those concerns were warranted.[18] In state after state, we used data on same-sex couples and state policies to estimate the likely effect on state government budgets of allowing same-sex couples to marry. In every state studied but one, we found that the net effect on state budgets would be positive if same-sex couples could marry. Income tax revenue would rise slightly.[19] Sales and hotel tax revenue would surge as same-sex couples and their friends and families spent money on weddings. State spending on means-tested benefits would drop as families headed by same-sex couples became more economically secure and less in need of (or eligible for) those benefits. Legislators, lawyers, news media, and NGOs (in states and at the national level) all drew on this research to support one of the key messages in the debate: marriage equality was good for same-sex couples and would not hurt anyone else.

Perhaps unsurprisingly, the aspect of the economic and state budget studies that got the most attention were the billions of dollars to be realized in pent-up demand for weddings by same-sex couples. Weddings hold a special significance for couples, often leading them to invite friends and family to celebrate their union. This desire to create a memorable occasion also comes with a willingness to spend significant amounts of money. In 2018, the average cost of an American wedding was reported to be $24,723. Following the US Supreme Court decision that opened up marriage to same-sex couples, researchers Christy Mallory and Brad Sears estimated that approximately 123,000 couples got married and spent around $11,000, resulting in over $1.5 billion in spending within just one year.[20] This surge in weddings created a new market for various industries, including hotels, caterers, restaurants, bands, photographers, jewelers, florists, and others, all of which eagerly expanded their services to cater to this growing demographic (and paid more taxes to the state as a result).

This interest in wedding spending as an argument for same-sex marriages was not limited to the United States, as people around the world also spend significant amounts on weddings. For instance, in 2012, the NGO Australian Marriage Equality invited me to Australia to discuss my research on marriage equality with policymakers, businesspeople, and the public. During my visit, I presented my research on the economic gains from same-sex couples' weddings to the Tasmanian Small Business Council. Tasmania's businesses stood to gain over $161 million if it became the first Australian state to legalize same-sex marriage. While they had not previously considered marriage equality as an issue for small businesses, the council's leaders were persuaded by the economic numbers, realizing the potential business opportunities. They later publicly supported a marriage equality bill introduced in the Tasmanian Parliament, emphasizing the economic benefits and the need for more customers for small businesses.

As noted earlier, some businesses also tied marriage to the business case, arguing to courts and public opinion that marriage equality would help them retain good employees and enhance their productivity.[21] While the business and state budget gains might not have been the most compelling reasons to open marriage to same-sex couples, they were helpful to NGOs that wanted to expand the political coalition of marriage equality supporters. These arguments also implicitly affirmed an overarching message that "marriage equality is good for same-sex couples and not harmful to anyone else" and even explicitly expanded it to make the case that many others would gain from allowing same-sex couples to marry.

Helping Make the Economic Case for Inclusive Development for LGBTQI+ People

A third context that is much more contemporary concerns the question of economic development in middle- and low-income countries. In this context, the economic case argues that countries' economies would be more prosperous if LGBTQI+ people were fully included within education, health, employment, housing, families, and other important social locations.[22] At the country level, LGBTQI+ inclusion means equal and meaningful opportunities for LGBTQI+ people, as well as their achievement of a standard of living and other outcomes that allow them to live in dignity.

Achieving inclusion could be facilitated or even led by global development and financial institutions (such as the World Bank or the Asian Development Bank, for example) and local finance ministries and other government agencies. Those institutions are charged with promoting sustainable economic growth, but like businesses, they are not focused on human rights goals per se. In general, the missions of the World Bank and other such agencies are supposed to be non-political and targeted at economic outcomes, so some of them have commissioned studies of the economy-wide costs of LGBTQI+ exclusion.[23] The economic case research has helped to open the doors of these institutions for NGOs that advocate for LGBTQI+ equality, such as Outright International and many country-level organizations, and it gives them an argument that they can deploy to insist on participation by those agencies in strategies that increase inclusion, such as nondiscrimination in development programs and participation in consultations with those agencies about LGBTQI+ needs.

This version of an economic case is more similar to the business case than to the economic value of marriage. In its most common form, the economic case focuses on the effects of hatred and stigma on what economists call "human capital" – the skills, knowledge, energy, and creativity that are essential to the economy. Evidence of bullying in schools, minority stress and health disparities, and poor treatment in the workplace all show that LGBTQI+ people are held back from getting the education, jobs, and lives that they want and could achieve. As a result, they are not able to contribute to the economy as much as they are capable of. This same basic argument can be (and has been) used by NGOs working for economic inclusion of African Americans, women, people with disabilities, Roma people, and others with marginalized identities.[24]

Country-level studies of the economic cost of exclusion (or its mirror image, the economic benefits of inclusion) have taken the evidence of harms in education, health, and employment and put a monetary value on them based on how much time and effort is lost to the economy. I conducted the first such study of India in 2014 for the World Bank. Looking across studies of India and others done since then for the Philippines, Kenya, South Africa, Caribbean countries, Eastern Europe, and other countries, the research estimates that exclusion of LGBTQI+ people results in a loss of 1 per cent or more of a country's GDP. For comparison purposes, 1 per cent of global GDP would be the size of the entire country of Turkey or the Netherlands, so this is a meaningful loss. Cross-national studies show a positive correlation between the degree of LGBTQI+ inclusion and a country's GDP per capita, confirming the findings of the country-level studies and showing that countries that are inclusive have stronger economies.[25]

In addition to development banks and institutions, who have invited me to present this research to high-level officials and operational staff alike, a wide variety of stakeholders have expressed interest in these studies. Businesses have used them in discussions with countries about having more equitable laws and policies for LGBTQI+ people. I have briefed activists at the country level and global NGOs on this research so they can use it to open up conversations with government policymakers and development institutions. Development institutions have used them with their internal audiences.

Some of my own experiences suggest that the economic case has begun to change the conversation inside those agencies and perhaps to change what those agencies are doing. From my own experience, my research on the economic case has opened the doors of the World Bank, the International Monetary Fund (IMF), the US Agency for International Development, the Asian Development Bank, and many other big national and international economic actors so that I could present the need for more LGBTQI+ inclusion. I've also talked to many powerful people behind closed doors who listened to and later used the economic case to argue for change. Sometime these presentations are on panels where NGOs are also invited to speak about development efforts from their own experiences.

Have these arguments made a difference in what the economic development institutions are doing? One never really knows for sure, but I've given talks that have generated lots of internal discussion, debate, and apparent action. In 2021, I gave an online talk co-hosted by Oogachaga, a local LGBTQI+ NGO, about my book at the US Embassy in Singapore, a country that criminalized homosexuality at the time. Shortly thereafter, the Singaporean government criticized the embassy for meddling in its internal policies.[26] But the following year Singapore's prime minister announced he was urging Parliament to repeal that criminalization law, bringing Singapore into step with other high-income countries.

More directly, some economists recently conducted an experiment testing arguments on LGBTQI+ issues on people in Serbia, Turkey, and Ukraine.[27] That study found that people randomly exposed to the economic case for LGBTQI+ equality were more likely to support equal employment opportunities for LGBTQI+ people. Of particular interest, respondents were also more likely to support equal employment opportunities based on ethnic origin, religion, gender, or disability, as well, after being exposed to the economic case, providing evidence of important potential spillover effects of this economic case in the field. This experiment suggests that NGOs are on the right track when they deploy the economic arguments in local policy discussions.

Lessons Learned in Using Economic Cost or Benefit Arguments in Public Debates

Overall, I think the economic case works very well as a key to open doors of certain kinds of institutions, although the study just mentioned suggests that it should be used more broadly in some settings to change people's minds about LGBTQI+ and other equal rights issues. In this conclusion, I offer some additional thoughts about how NGOs and activists might use these perspectives in the future in LGBTQI+ and other human rights issues.

Economic arguments sometimes seem very technical, and it's true that coming up with convincing and credible estimates means working with an economist or policy analyst. But once the numbers are in place, creating talking points and strategizing about how to use them are more familiar territory for NGOs and activists, who usually know more about communications than economists do. Economic arguments can be framed in multiple ways to fit into campaigns to counteract other arguments. The cost of exclusion could be framed as a "hate tax" of sorts, for example; the benefits of inclusion could be a "fairness dividend."

These arguments might be especially helpful where economic interests are at stake, although this is not so much the case in the so-called US "culture war," where economic arguments play a different role. These economic perspectives move the discussion away from "how the pie is divided" to "making the pie bigger" for everyone.

Another observation is that I have sometimes seen a strategic value in being the first to make an economic argument, especially if it's well-argued and speaks to a potentially harmful issue in a debate. In the marriage equality debate, making arguments in advance about the benefits to state budgets sometimes prevented such issues coming up in the debate. Making economic arguments first also provides opportunities to use good data that dispel harmful stereotypes. For example, the myth of affluence promoted in some marketing contexts (mentioned earlier) has been displaced by the evidence that LGBTQI+ people actually earn less than heterosexual people.[28]

It could be helpful for NGO staff and activists to know that economists are aware that there are costs or benefits that are hard to quantify, such as the value of unpaid labor that many women provide in our economies, or the value of reducing carbon emissions. We know that it's not possible to convey the full value of everything in monetary terms, but leaving them out of a study because we don't have the perfect measure too often results in them being valued at zero, in effect. Economists and policy analysts are good at identifying when other kinds of costs should be added, too. For instance, the legal costs for defending against lawsuits make sense for thinking about state budgets but do not necessarily create larger losses to the economy.

For example, some creative thinking and linking of ideas across studies has made it possible to estimate the economic costs associated with hate crimes, such as the 2012 shooting at the Sikh temple in Oak Creek, Wisconsin. Economist Michael Martell has drawn from a range of data sources to estimate the number of hate crimes in the United States each year.[29] He then applied estimates from other studies of the tangible costs (such as medical care, police response, mental health services, and property damage) and intangible costs (for pain and suffering) of different kinds of crime for victims. These admittedly incomplete costs still add up to a very large number – $3.4 billion – and should be considered a lower bound on the full cost.

I would like to close by considering another strategic issue that I have discussed with many activists in the LGBTQI+ human rights movement that is also likely to be relevant in other contexts. Sometimes activists are less troubled by the technical nature of economic arguments than by the perception that economic arguments displace a more ethical or human rights perspective. I want to emphasize that the economic case for LGBTQI+ inclusion is not a replacement for a human rights or civil rights argument.

Given that concern, perhaps the most important lesson for NGOs considering whether to use economic arguments like these in debates about the human or civil rights of marginalized groups is that they go together nicely. In fact, I would argue that we need both of those perspectives. The relationship between economics and human rights is deeply intertwined. The United Nations Universal Declaration of Human Rights recognizes economic rights, such as the right to work and an adequate standard of living. However, achieving these economic rights often requires more economic resources than countries currently have given their stage of economic development. In that sense, economic development is crucial for realizing certain human rights.

Thinking about the economic argument as complementary to human rights enhances the power of both arguments. Economic arguments can complement the broader human rights framework (and similar arguments) by highlighting the tangible monetary costs of human rights violations to individuals, and to society as a whole. For example, quantifying the lost income, poor health outcomes, or reduced educational opportunities resulting from discrimination can provide a compelling case for the importance of protecting human rights for all individuals as well as an economic case for change. At a moment in history when basic human rights principles related to diversity and inclusion are under attack globally, having an economic argument is especially important. The economic perspective does not mean that human rights are only valuable if they have a monetary value, but rather seeks to demonstrate the tangible harms that result from denying these rights.

In conclusion, while the economic approach to understanding homophobia and transphobia is not a replacement for the human rights framework, it has already been a valuable tool for highlighting the real-world impact of discrimination and strengthening arguments for LGBTQI+ rights in many contexts. By quantifying the costs of homophobic and transphobic exclusion and hate – and other forms of hate – we can better understand the breadth and depth of hate and advocate more effectively for equality and inclusion and other policies designed to counter hate in all contexts.

NOTES

1 See the NOH8 campaign website at http://www.noh8campaign.com/article/about.

2 Sheryl Gay Stolberg, "Thomas's Concurring Opinion Raises Questions about What Rights Might Be Next," *New York Times*, June 24, 2022, https://www.nytimes.com/2022/06/24/us/clarence-thomas-roe-griswold-lawrence-obergefell.html.

3 In this chapter, I follow the practice in the global human rights field and use the acronym LGBTQI+ for lesbian, gay, bisexual, transgender, and intersex people, with the plus sign standing in for other groups of sexual and gender minorities. Although these distinct groups are grouped together in that acronym, not all of the examples apply to each separate group.

4 Adam Nagourney and Jeremy W. Peters, "How a Campaign against Transgender Rights Mobilized Conservatives," *New York Times*, April 16, 2023, https://www.nytimes.com/2023/04/16/us/politics/transgender-conservative-campaign.html?searchResultPosition=5.

5 Movement Advancement Project, *Under Fire: The War on LGBTQ People in America* (Boulder, CO: MAP, 2023), https://www.mapresearch.org/file/Under%20Fire%20report_MAP%202023.pdf. These bills had other effects, as well.

6 M.V. Lee Badgett, *The Economic Case for LGBT Equality: Why Fair and Equal Treatment Benefits Us All* (Boston: Beacon Press, 2020).

7 Sinead Ashe et al., "Costs of Violence against Women: An Examination of the Evidence," Working Paper No. 2, What Works, September 20, 2016, https://www.whatworks.co.za/documents/publications/68-authors-ashe-s-duvvury-n-raghavendra-s-scriver-s-and-o-donovan-d/file.

8 M.V. Lee Badgett, *Money, Myths, and Change: The Economic Lives of Lesbians and Gay Men* (Chicago: University of Chicago Press, 2001).

9 M.V. Lee Badgett et al., "A Review of the Economics of Sexual Orientation and Gender Identity," *Journal of Economic Literature* 62, no. 3 (2024): 948–94, 1–52, https://doi.org/10.1257/jel.20231668.

10 Badgett, *Money, Myths, and Change*; Nicole Raeburn, *Changing Corporate America from Inside Out: Lesbian and Gay Workplace Rights* (Minneapolis: University of Minnesota Press, 2004); Carlos Ball, *The Queering of Corporate America* (Boston: Beacon Press, 2019).

11 LGBT Capital, "Estimated LGBT Purchasing Power: LGBT-GDP 2018," accessed January 20, 2025, http://www.lgbt-capital.com/docs/Estimated _LGBT-GDP_(table)_-_2018.pdf.

12 Badgett, *Money, Myths, and Change*.

13 Badgett, *Money, Myths, and Change*.

14 For examples, see Badgett, *Money, Myths, and Change*; Brad Sears and Christy Mallory, "Economic Motives for Adopting LGBT-Related Workplace Policies," UCLA School of Law Williams Institute, October 2011, https://escholarship.org/uc/item/7sd3f251.

15 Badgett, *The Economic Case for LGBT Equality*.

16 Badgett, *Money, Myths, and Change*; Jordyn Holman, "Target's Sales Hit by Pride Month Merchandise Backlash," *New York Times*, August 16, 2023, https://www.nytimes.com/2023/08/16/business/target-sales-pride -backlash.html.

17 M.V. Lee Badgett, "The Economic Value of Marriage for Same-Sex Couples," *Drake Law Review* 58, no. 4 (2010): 1081–16.

18 These studies were published by the Williams Institute and can be found at the UCLA School of Law Williams Institute, "Search Results 'Economic Impact,'" accessed January 20, 2025, https://williamsinstitute.law.ucla .edu/?s=economic+impact.

19 Other studies at the federal level had similar positive predictions about the impact of same-sex marriage on federal income tax revenue.

20 Christy Mallory and Brad Sears, "The Economic Impact of Marriage Equality Five Years after Obergefell v. Hodges," UCLA School of Law Williams Institute, May 2020, https://williamsinstitute.law.ucla.edu /publications/econ-impact-obergefell-5-years/.

21 Badgett, *The Economic Case for LGBT Equality*.

22 Generally, see Badgett, *The Economic Case for LGBT Equality*, for more detail on this section's argument.

23 M.V. Lee Badgett, "The Economic Cost of Stigma and the Exclusion of LGBT People: A Case Study of India," World Bank, 2014, http://www .worldbank.org/content/dam/Worldbank/document/SAR/economic -costs-homophobia-lgbt-exlusion-india.pdf; Andrew Flores et al., *The*

Economic Cost of Exclusion Based on Sexual Orientation, Gender Identity and Expression, and Sex Characteristics in the Labor Market in the Republic of North Macedonia (Washington, DC: World Bank, 2023), https://openknowledge.worldbank.org/handle/10986/40380.

24 Badgett, *The Economic Case for LGBT Equality.*

25 M.V. Lee Badgett, Kees Waaldijk, and Yana van der Meulen Rodgers, "The Relationship between LGBT Inclusion and Economic Development: Macro-Level Evidence," *World Development* 120 (2019): 1–14, https://doi.org/10.1016/j.worlddev.2019.03.011.

26 Nicolas Yong, "LGBT Policy Is for 'Only Singaporeans to Debate and Decide': MFA to US Embassy," *Yahoo!News*, May 19, 2021, https://sg.news.yahoo.com/lgbt-policy-for-singaporeans-debate-mfa-us-embassy-103223653.html.

27 Cevat Giray Aksoy et al., "Reducing Sexual Orientation Discrimination: Experimental Evidence from Basic Information Treatments," *Journal of Policy Analysis and Management* 42, no. 1 (2023): 35–59, https://doi.org/10.1002/pam.22447.

28 Badgett et al., "A Review of the Economics."

29 Michael E. Martell, "Economic Costs of Hate Crimes," Bard Center for the Study of Hate, March 14, 2023, https://bcsh.bard.edu/files/2023/03/BCSH-Economic-Cost-of-Hate_3-13-23_Online-.pdf.

Editor's Introduction to Chapter 7

When someone writes "Kilroy was here" on your garage door, it's a crime and a nuisance. When someone writes "Kill all [fill-in-the-blanks]" on that door, the harm is exponentially worse. Imagine having to explain one, then the other, to your children. In the first instance, you and your immediate neighbors might be perturbed. In the second, everyone like you in your community might fear being attacked.

When I began working on antisemitism at the American Jewish Committee (AJC) in the late 1980s, I met colleagues who had been instrumental in helping promote the Hate Crime Statistics Act, successfully[1] arguing – much like Badgett in chapter 6 and Lowe and Jimenez in chapter 5 do in this volume – that to tackle a problem, you need data to understand it.

Concern about hate crime can also bring diverse communities together. In chapter 4, Levin discussed how Blacks and Jews came together around hate crimes. When I was at AJC, we, along with the NAACP Legal Defense and Education Fund and the Crown Heights Coalition – a group of Blacks and Jews who came together after the Crown Heights riots of 1991 – filed an Amicus brief in an important hate crime case in the US Supreme Court. Our brief stressed the impact of these crimes while also underscoring the need to protect the right of free speech (arguing that people are entitled to have hateful thoughts, not to select people to be victims of crime based on who they are).

I knew I'd want a chapter to help people understand not only what hate crimes are and why they are important, but also how to reduce the likelihood that they will occur, and when they do occur, what of lasting value might be created out of such a community crisis. The Bard Center for the Study of Hate has published (in partnership with Western States Center and the Montana Human Rights Network) a manual for community groups that includes tips on how to respond to, and organize around, hate crimes.[2] But for this book I wanted new thinking, and Barbara Perry – who runs a Hate Studies center in Canada focused on hate crimes – suggested Mark Walters (from the UK) and Jennifer Schweppe (from Ireland). I had known of Schweppe since I had read some of her essays over the years, but what impressed me about Schweppe's and Walter's work is that they realized, no matter how useful they thought their research might be, their hard work was wasted if it didn't affect what police forces did. They have shown how to take academic thinking and coordinate deeply and meaningfully with law enforcement agencies. Their chapter isn't only about thinking about hate crimes; it offers a model for how scholars should reach out beyond the academy to partner with people who are actually doing the work in the real world, frequently in coordination with NGOs. And even though most of the readers of this book will be Americans, individual US state hate crime laws, like those internationally, vary, and thus the perspective of scholars outside the American context helps us to think about hate crimes more broadly. The main take-away from Schweppe's and Walter's years of work is that NGOs have a crucial role to play when hate turns criminal, both in places that have established protocols and in those that don't.

NOTES

1 That said, the reporting of hate crime data by many law enforcement agencies is still woefully incomplete.
2 Bard Center for the Study of Hate, Western States Center, and the Montana Human Rights Network, *A Community Guide for Opposing Hate*, accessed January 22, 2025, https://bcsh.bard.edu/files/2022/05/OpposingHate Guide-single-pages-8M-5-3.pdf.

7 The Role of Civil Society in Helping to Establish a Framework for the Effective Enforcement of Hate Crime Laws

JENNIFER SCHWEPPE AND MARK AUSTIN WALTERS

In recent decades, countries worldwide have responded to concerns about hate crimes by enacting laws that enhance penalties for offenders motivated by identity-based hostilities. Currently, hate crime laws exist in over 190 jurisdictions globally, spanning all inhabited continents.[1] While these laws are a crucial step in addressing violence and abuse directed at marginalized communities, enacting them is just one facet of a complex public policy strategy to combat hate crime. Therefore, it is essential to establish a comprehensive framework of policies, educational initiatives, and justice interventions alongside these laws to bridge the gap between "the law on the books" and "the law in practice."[2]

Research has shown that a "justice gap" can quickly emerge between what is legally prescribed and what is applied in practice if new legislation is not adequately supported by policies and measures.[3] These include educational campaigns, the development of policies, operational guidance, monitoring mechanisms within criminal justice institutions, and alternative justice interventions, such as restorative justice. Their full implementation can instill public confidence in the seriousness with which hate crime is treated by the state, thereby enhancing reporting rates.[4] Crucially, where such measures are not introduced, the legislative response may be perceived as having failed the victims it is intended to support, leading to further isolation and marginalization from the criminal justice process on the part of these community groups.

This chapter outlines the "next steps" for governments that have enacted hate crime laws to ensure their fair and robust implementation. The chapter presents a framework based on international resources and comparative empirical evidence conducted by the authors, and highlights current practices in jurisdictions with a well-established hate crime policy domain and/or where civil society is respected by the state and indeed often government-funded. It is important to note that the framework's implementation depends on various factors, including available resources, access to expertise, varying regulatory standards, and the existing criminal justice infrastructure. It is also important to note that we do not address hate *crime* in a vacuum, but rather address the multiple ways in which hate and prejudice manifest in society: it is a complex and often intermingled, entangled process, the success of which depends on the criminal justice process operating cooperatively and in engaged, reflective, and reflexive ways.

Civil Society, Nongovernmental Organizations, and Hate Crime Legislation

We believe that a healthy, respected, and well-funded civil society is crucial to the effective implementation of hate crime legislation. This position is now recognized in international human rights law, where the recently adopted Council of Europe Committee of Ministers Recommendation (2024)4 stresses the importance of civil society in the development of hate crime policy, placing obligations on public institutions to engage with civil society organizations for the purposes of "understanding, responding to, preventing and combating hate crime" (para 5). Indeed, that Recommendation sees civil society as so central to developing a comprehensive approach to combating hate crime that it provides that states should provide such organizations with "appropriate funding and resources," as well as promote a "safe, inclusive and enabling online and offline civil space" in which they can operate (para 65). Indeed, as other chapters in this volume have underscored, sometimes victimized groups see other such groups as antagonists. But all have an interest in reducing hate crime, and as Adam Levin underscores in chapter 4, there are opportunities to work together to promote better hate crime structures, and some difficulties too.

We are also aware of the differences in nomenclature with respect to the work we are describing in this chapter versus others in this volume. We adopt the broad understanding of "civil society organizations" as defined by the Organisation for Economic Co-operation and Development (OECD) as "all non-market and non-state organizations ... in which people organize themselves to pursue shared interests in the public domain."[5] Thus, trade unions, universities, and research institutes, under this classification, are civil society organizations.[6] Nongovernmental organizations (NGOs) are, in this context, a subset of civil society, traditionally in the Global South having a role in aid or development cooperation. In our discussion, we use the term "civil society" and "civil society organizations (CSOs)" to describe those groups that work to promote the rights of marginalized and stigmatized groups in promoting social justice for all.

As well, we highlight the importance of civil society in addressing hate crime in a comprehensive way. However, while the significance of an enabling environment for civil society has been recognized by the United Nations, as well as regional human rights bodies, Rachel Hayman and colleagues observe that the reality of civil society in many jurisdictions is that it is a "shrinking space."[7] Indeed, as societies become more divided, and hate is increasingly politicized, the funding and – perhaps more importantly – respect of the work of civil society is under threat. Thus, in this chapter we write to what in many jurisdictions is nothing more than an aspiration, in which the state, through its criminal justice institutions, values and respects the role of civil society in providing a critical and reflective voice through which the experiences and rights of the most vulnerable can be heard and realized.

We recognize in writing this chapter that civil society is not a monolith: organizations and groups (including academics) will often be competing for the same "piece of the pie," and thus there may be jostling and positioning that will create, at best, healthy competition for resources. We also recognize that there are different models for funding, depending on the country. In the United States, for example, much of the funding for these groups comes from philanthropies and individual donors. Elsewhere, such as in many countries in Europe, the bulk of funding is from government sources. But as Lila Corwin Berman explains in chapter 10 of this volume, even the tax-exempt structure in the United States should be viewed as functionally using government funds.

Where CSOs have competing or oppositional policy positions, or oppositional political positions, acrimony may affect good working relationships. The Coalition Against Hate Crime (Ireland), led by Luna Lara Liboni of the Irish Council for Civil Liberties, is a world-class (and perhaps exceptional) example of good practice in civil society. Here, a group of over twenty nationally representative CSOs across all identity groups works using a consensus model to achieve its aims of ensuring Irish law, policy, and practice are reformed in a meaningful way. This type of internal coordination and cooperation across civil society is, in our view, the best means by which the work and expertise of civil society can be heard at a state level.

We also recognize that we are living, working, and writing in jurisdictions (that is, Ireland and England) that, comparatively, have a reasonably well-funded civil society. Equally, there is – at least traditionally – a performance of cordiality on the part of the state in engaging with such organizations. Additionally, in both Ireland and England and Wales, same-sex intimacy or expressions of gender identity are not criminalized. While historical and institutional forms of prejudice may mean that victims of hate crime are less likely to view the police as treating them fairly or respectfully, individuals cannot be *directly* criminalized and sanctioned for holding a specific identity (though it should be noted that irregularly present migrants cannot report without risking deportation). It is from this place of respective jurisdictional advantage that we describe what we see as the best approaches to effectively implementing hate crime legislation and criminal justice practices, informed by the recently adopted Council of Europe Recommendation on combating hate crime.

Approaching the Creation of a Framework

Before detailing the measures and tools for implementing hate crime legislation, and how CSOs can help in this effort, it is essential to explain how and why we constructed and developed a framework. Hate crime legislation has been adopted in a piecemeal fashion at domestic and international levels as a result of the absence of specific international frameworks.[8] To address the uneven approach taken to legislating for hate crime globally, the *UN Declaration on Advancing Crime Prevention, Criminal Justice and the Rule of Law: Towards the Achievement of the 2030 Agenda for Sustainable Development* emphasizes the importance of addressing hate crime, not just through legislation, but in practice, by ensuring that states will commit to its full implementation and "[d]evelop effective strategies, including by enhancing the capacity of criminal justice professionals, to prevent, investigate and prosecute hate crimes, as well as engage effectively with victims and victim communities to build public trust when engaging with law enforcement to report such crimes."[9]

At a regional level, the Council of Europe, made up of forty-six countries (referred to as "Member States") and including all twenty-seven Member States of the European Union, equally recognizes the harms of hate, and that a comprehensive and human-rights-oriented approach to addressing hate is required through its two interwoven recommendations: *Recommendation CM/Rec(2022)16[1] of the Committee of Ministers to member States on combating hate speech;*[10] and *Recommendation CM/Rec(2024)4 of the Committee of Ministers to member States on combating hate crime.*[11] While recognizing the importance of legislative responses to "hate speech"[12] and hate crime, both Recommendations acknowledge the importance of a holistic approach to addressing the phenomena, with the recommendation on combating hate crime having the aim of providing guidance to member States on "developing and implementing measures aimed at combating and preventing hate crime in a comprehensive manner within the framework of human rights, democracy, and the rule of law, and to avoid fragmented approaches to this phenomenon."[13] Such an approach must, while ensuring that those targeted

Figure 7.1. Multipartnership Approach to Implementing Hate Crime Laws

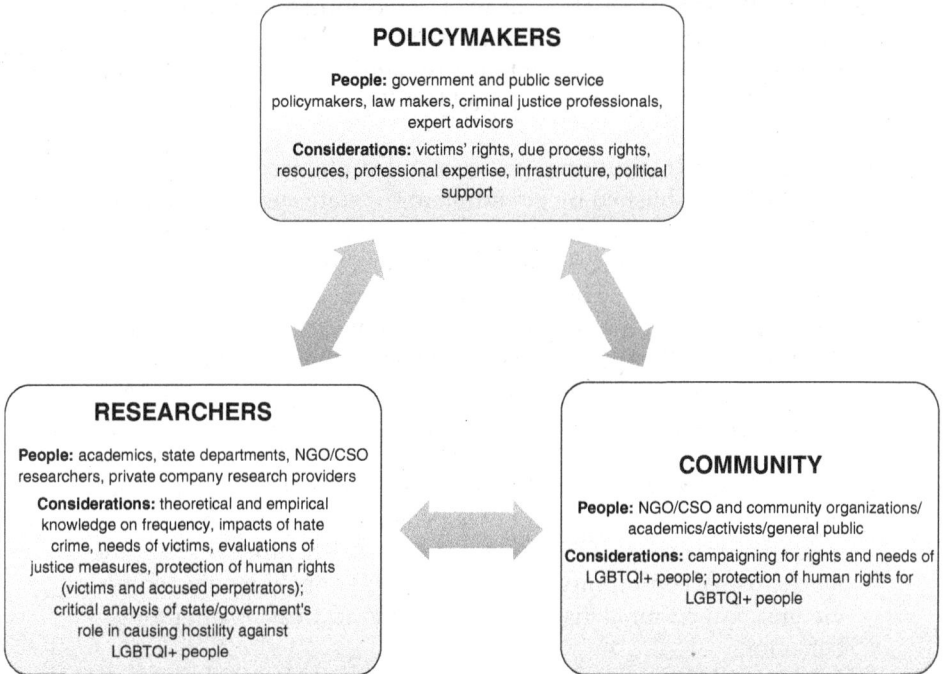

POLICYMAKERS

People: government and public service policymakers, law makers, criminal justice professionals, expert advisors

Considerations: victims' rights, due process rights, resources, professional expertise, infrastructure, political support

RESEARCHERS

People: academics, state departments, NGO/CSO researchers, private company research providers

Considerations: theoretical and empirical knowledge on frequency, impacts of hate crime, needs of victims, evaluations of justice measures, protection of human rights (victims and accused perpetrators); critical analysis of state/government's role in causing hostility against LGBTQI+ people

COMMUNITY

People: NGO/CSO and community organizations/academics/activists/general public

Considerations: campaigning for rights and needs of LGBTQI+ people; protection of human rights for LGBTQI+ people

by hate are protected and their rights realized, equally ensure that those accused of hate crime are treated fairly by the criminal justice system.

We believe that three key domains should drive the development of strategies and measures for hate crime legislation. Each domain involves individuals from various sectors (see figure 7.1). The three domains and the central figures in each are essential for developing, implementing, and reviewing a hate crime law framework. In this multipartnership approach, research, community involvement, and collaboration between policymakers, academics, CSOs, and activists are crucial. This approach aims to engage all stakeholders in a mutually beneficial and responsive process, where information flows in both directions, leading to co-designed research and adaptive policymaking.[14]

At each step of the framework, researchers, activists, and CSOs assist policymakers in co-producing an evolving strategy to combat hate crime. This multiagency approach ensures flexibility and responsiveness to social changes, and it is an ongoing relationship supported by formal structures. The implementation strategy produced as a result of the engagement is not a final point but a stage in an iterative process involving policymakers, civil society, and researchers testing and reviewing the law's operation, as well as recommending revisions.

Within this framework, we have identified three main stages that support the effective implementation of hate crime laws, which can be categorized into three interconnected headings:

1. **National and institutional policies and strategies**: These documents, published by governments or state agencies, outline the goals and objectives for addressing hate crime under the legislative framework. Strategies provide a foundation for other measures and tools to be anchored. They often set targets for criminal justice bodies to ensure policy aims are met. Additionally, there may be other governmental strategies that underscore the importance of legislative, agency, and whole society approaches to reducing hate crime, such as *The U.S. National Strategy to Counter Antisemitism*.[15]

2. **Institutional and community measures and tools**: These practical methods aid the enforcement of legislation, encompassing guidance documents for prosecutors and police officers, reporting mechanisms, community-based programs supporting hate crime victims, and criminal justice interventions addressing offending behavior.

3. **Education initiatives and campaigns**: Operating at national and regional levels, these campaigns may include promoting new legislation, explaining reporting mechanisms, clarifying what constitutes a "hate crime," and educating communities about the impacts of hate crime incidents.

The following sections of this chapter describe various policies, strategies, measures, tools, and education campaigns that have been used to support the implementation of hate crime legislation.[16] We emphasize that the development and implementation of these policies at the domestic level should align with the needs of each community as identified by the multiagency partnership.

Part A: State or National Action Plans and Strategies, and Institutional Policies

National Action Plans

A State or National Action Plan to combat hate crime, along with an implementation action plan, is crucial for the effective implementation of hate crime legislation in a manner that supports and protects human

Figure 7.2. National Action Plan and Institutional Measures Framework

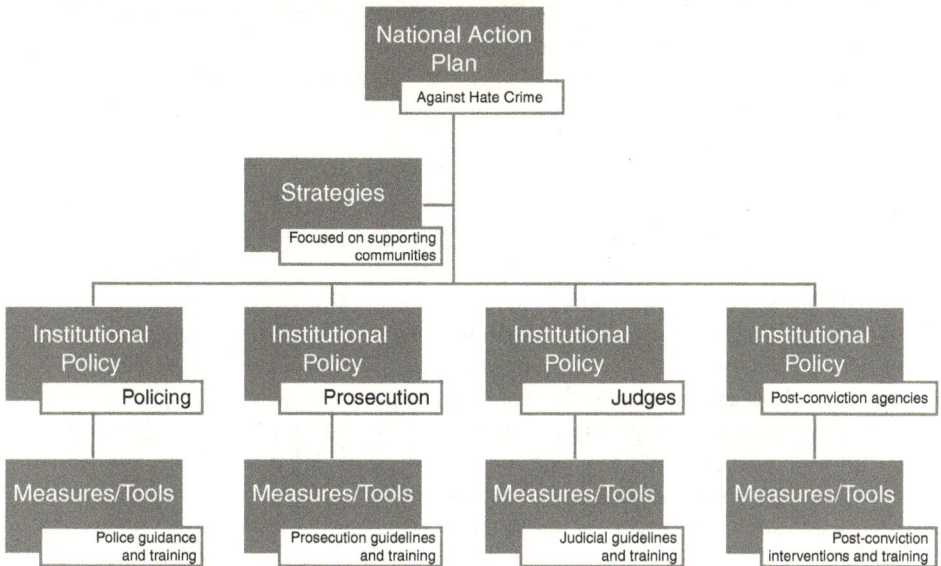

National Action Plan

Against Hate Crime

Strategies

Focused on supporting communities

Institutional Policy	Institutional Policy	Institutional Policy	Institutional Policy
Policing	Prosecution	Judges	Post-conviction agencies

Measures/Tools	Measures/Tools	Measures/Tools	Measures/Tools
Police guidance and training	Prosecution guidelines and training	Judicial guidelines and training	Post-conviction interventions and training

rights, democracy, and the rule of law. CSOs focused on addressing hate, even if their priorities are in other projects and programs, can and should do what they can to help in this effort, and of course, states should facilitate CSOs in doing so. Such plans not only signal the commitment of government to eliminating hate crime but also underscore the prioritization of improving the lives of those commonly targeted. Plans should view hate crime as something that not only traumatizes victims and the groups they belong to but that also tears apart the fabric of a society. We need high-level goals for both legislation implementation and addressing the root causes of hate. The effective implementation of hate crime laws can be hindered when societal prejudices persist;[17] thus, a state or National Action Plan should have as its aim not simply a reaction to hate crime but also a prevention of hate crime, including by way of naming and addressing societal and institutional prejudices.[18]

The plan should include high-level principles, shared definitions, and a common understanding of hate crime, which can be used across institutions. This single document should guide all criminal justice agencies in addressing hate crime internally and in the broader context of the criminal justice process. Key actions that should be covered in this plan include setting up a monitoring and recording system for hate crimes, improving reporting mechanisms, developing guidance for police, prosecutors, and judges, creating effective criminal justice interventions targeting the root causes of hate crime, providing victim support initiatives, and conducting educational campaigns.[19] CSOs focused on hate have expertise that is critical to the success of such plans.

Community-Focused Strategies

Hate crime victims are often members of marginalized communities, and it is important for states to develop action plans that protect their rights and address broader needs. These community-focused strategies should outline ways to build trust between marginalized communities and criminal justice institutions, particularly the police. Hate crime is notoriously underreported, with victims typically stating that they did not report their experience to the police because the police either could not or would not do anything about it.[20] While the first response ("could not") speaks perhaps to objective reasons as to why the report would be in vain – such as the unavailability of witnesses, or the absence of any evidence – the second response ("would not") speaks to subjective factors on the part of the officer. A perception that the police *would* not do anything speaks to a perception that the police would lack interest or would not believe the victim; that there is a sense of general institutional prejudice on the part of the police; or that there is a fear of the police.[21] Thus, in addition to addressing hate crime, these strategies should support diversity, combat intolerance and prejudice, and empower communities to activate their rights and overcome barriers to such activation, both in society and within criminal justice institutions. As will be described later, processes can be put in place to reduce (but of course not eliminate) the capacity of institutional prejudices to nullify the experience of victims.

Developing Plans and Strategies – an Engaged Approach

In developing individual strategies or State or National Action Plans, a multiagency partnership approach is essential to ensure that all perspectives are considered and that workable policies are introduced with support across institutions and communities. This should involve community groups, academic and non-academic experts, criminal justice professionals, and funded independent researchers in order to understand the existing gaps between policy and practice. If government agencies are not proactive in reaching out to CSOs, CSOs should ideally reach out to these officials: though of course it must be acknowledged these advances may not always be well-received. An example of this approach in the United States can be found in Connecticut where, in

Figure 7.3. The Multiagency Partnership Framework in Action

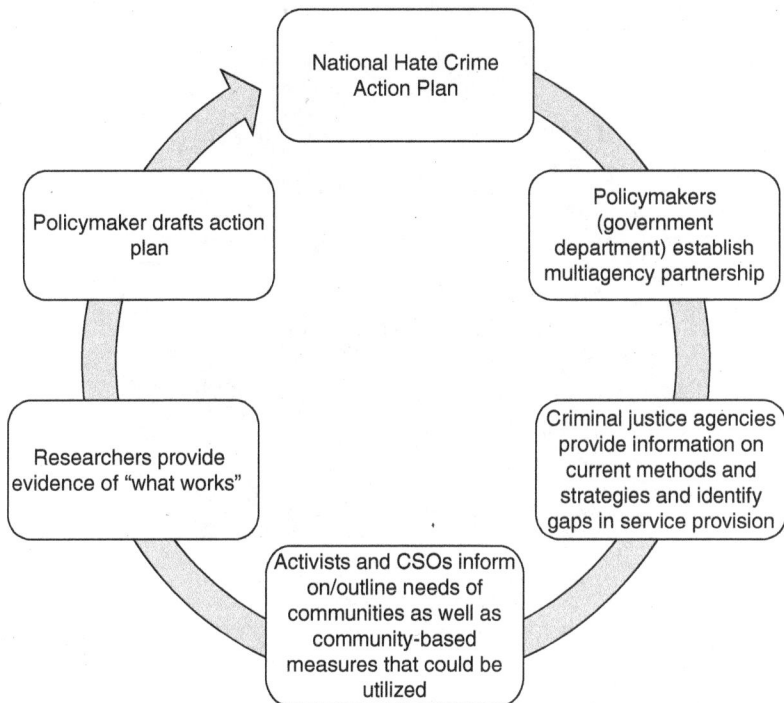

2017, a state-wide Hate Crimes Advisory Council was established.[22] The Council is made up of representatives from the police, prosecution and defense agencies, bar associations, emergency services, as well as thirty representatives from groups committed to decreasing hate crimes. The Council must encourage and coordinate programs to increase community awareness, reporting, and combating of hate crimes.

By using this approach, a core understanding of values and practices can be established, serving as a baseline for identifying institutional needs and necessary support. It also ensures that the policies are tailored to each state's needs while drawing from national and international practices to set future goals.

Institutional Policies

Each criminal justice institution or agency should develop its own policy or strategy that aligns with the State or National Action Plan's broad goals and addresses its specific concerns. These policies should be developed collaboratively across institutions, reflect shared definitions

Figure 7.4. Institutional Policies for Hate Crime Law Enforcement

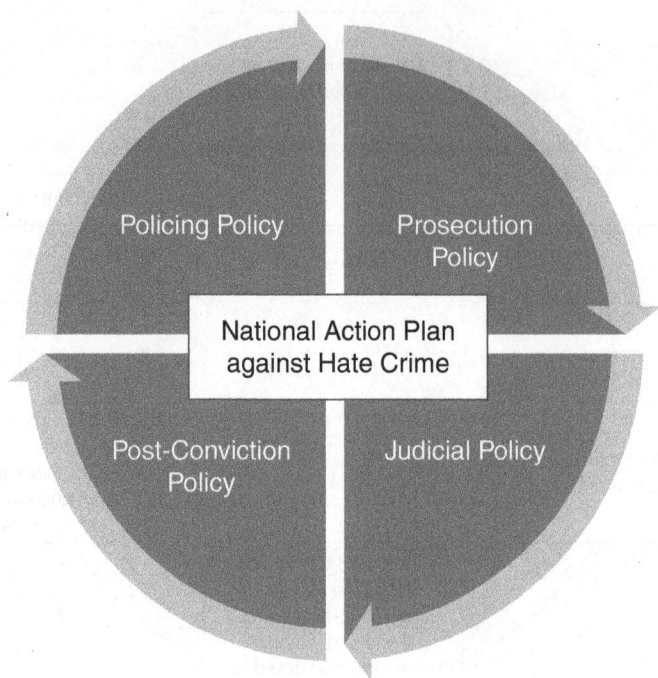

of "hate crimes," and promote interagency collaborations. Oftentimes, such institutions operate in parallel in addressing hate crimes, rather than considering the issues in an intertwined and engaged way.[23] In order to have a comprehensive approach to hate crime, such institutions must engage with one another, in a flexible and reflective way, to ensure a cohesive approach to addressing hate crime in a comprehensive way. Institutional policies should complement the action plan framework, ensuring alignment with its core values, goals, understandings, and directions.

In the next section, we will outline thematic issues that individual policies should contain. To reiterate: it is crucial that all such policies are developed in a manner appropriate to the national context.

Part B: Institutional Measures and Tools

This section delves into the institutional measures and tools required to implement effective State or National Action Plans aimed at preventing and addressing hate crime. For such plans to translate into meaningful action, they must be accompanied by comprehensive documentation that guides the establishment, administration, and evaluation of criminal justice measures targeted at addressing hate crimes. These institutional policies should encompass an array of measures, including reporting mechanisms, practitioner guidance documents, and learning and training resources, all designed to enhance the criminal justice system's capacity to enforce hate crime legislation.[24] Many of the measures set out below aimed at enhancing state responses to hate crime are provided for in the Council of Europe Recommendation on combating hate crime (2024)4 as part of a comprehensive state response to hate crime. Here we focus on how civil society organizations can support these measures. This chapter explores two crucial aspects within this context: reporting mechanisms and monitoring processes, and policing guidance and training.[25] CSOs have an important role to play here too, but it must be recalled that such organizations cannot be expected, in the absence of funding, to perform the duties of the state in addressing criminality and supporting victims. Rather, such organizations should be properly funded and resourced to engage with the state in supporting marginalized communities.

Reporting Mechanisms, Monitoring Processes, and Recording Hate Crime

The effective response to hate crimes begins with victims having accessible and reliable means to report incidents to the police. Without an accessible and robust reporting system, legislative efforts to address hate may prove futile: quite simply, if the criminal justice system is not made aware that a criminal offense has occurred, it cannot address it, nor will CSOs necessarily have the data they need to underscore the harm done by hate crimes to the communities they represent. Hate crime underreporting is a recognized global phenomenon, but it is notably more pronounced within specific communities, such as the transgender community, who report victimization at significantly lower rates.[26] The mere presence of hate crime legislation is insufficient to encourage victims to report. While hate crime is generally underreported, we see particular victim groups or particular contexts in which underreporting will be even more significant. For example, members of the LGBTQI+ community may be unable to identify themselves as victims due to various reasons;[27] crucially, where same-sex intimacy is criminalized, reporting anti-LGBTQI+ hate crime may be particularly complex to encourage on the part of the state. Equally, those with an irregular migrant status may not report due to concerns that their status will be investigated rather than their experience of victimization. Therefore, the criminal justice system must establish measures to support official reporting, ensuring they align with victims' experiences, needs, and perspectives, and in doing so, civil society can act as an important sounding board and information source for support options, as well as a reporting intermediary. This can be achieved by providing alternative reporting mechanisms (such as online reporting) or supporting third-party reporting.

ONLINE/ANONYMOUS REPORTING

As well as civil society reporting mechanisms, online police reporting mechanisms play a pivotal role in facilitating the reporting of hate crimes. They can allow victims to provide information to the police with the expectation of further investigation or formal recording, and while some systems require victims to reveal their identities, others allow for anonymous reporting. Anonymous reporting can empower victims and assist in collecting data to support an evidence-based approach to hate crime prevention.[28] However, police often argue that the absence of victim information can hinder case processing, and some police services may not initiate an investigation without knowledge of the victim's identity; some will not initiate an investigation in the absence of a sworn statement from the victim as to their experiences. The Ottawa Police Service, for example, allows victims of "hate-motivated incidents" to report their experiences online, though again this cannot be done anonymously and those reporting must fill in personal details to make the report. In England and Wales, where there are a range of territorial police forces, there is a single website to specifically facilitate online reporting of hate crime nationally,[29] and while individuals making such reports can provide their personal details so that police officers can contact them, the report can also be made anonymously. By contrast, the Singaporean Police Force, for example, allows only those with a Singpass (a digital identity issued by the state) to report a crime online.[30] Some police services specifically highlight the fact that hate crimes can be reported online.[31] An Garda Síochána, the Irish police service, also operates an additional measure where it will take reports from a CSO and act on that in the absence of a statement from the victim.

THIRD-PARTY REPORTING PROCESSES

CSOs often lack the infrastructure or funding to develop reporting or monitoring systems, and so as well as providing for multiple means by which victims can report their experiences to the police, states should encourage third-party hate crime reporting by collaborating with CSOs or human rights/equality bodies.[32] These entities can share anonymized information about hate crimes, aiding in trend identification and the impact assessment of reporting policies.[33] Monitoring or parallel reporting mechanisms are essential here. A CSO will act as a first (or sometimes, only) contact point for victims to report their experiences.[34] Through that CSO, victims should be supported from a psychological, medicinal, or legal perspective, and additionally be supported in reporting their experiences to the police if that is what they wish to do. Indeed, a well-funded and expert civil society is uniquely qualified to provide such supports in the absence of state involvement. To ensure their effectiveness, it is essential that third-party reporting services are visible, accessible, and well-publicized within communities, leveraging mainstream and minority media, community venues, and social networking sites for outreach.[35]

Third-party monitoring systems, operating parallel to official mechanisms, can supplement limited official recording, challenge official statistics, and offer support to victims in the absence of police reporting. While they serve a valuable role in highlighting the prevalence and reporting gap of hate crimes, their overall value is limited within a comprehensive implementation strategy. Victims are significantly more likely to report to the police when effective reporting mechanisms are in place, rendering third-party monitoring processes less crucial.[36] But even in the absence of a fully robust reporting system, CSOs can, and should where appropriately funded, play a vital role supporting victims, and helping communities understand the societal harm hate crimes produce. With more understanding may come more political will to improve reporting.

Victimization Surveys

It is imperative to uncover true victimization rates, through victimization surveys that are methodologically adjusted to include members from minority communities and where data can be analyzed in a manner that allows for the understanding of reasons behind underreporting and to gain insights into the prevalence and patterns of hate-based violence within communities.[37] Such a survey is carried out in the United States via the National Crime Victimization Survey (NCVS) Series, which collects data on personal and household victimization through an ongoing survey of a nationally representative sample of residential addresses. These data not only assist in evidence-based policy decisions but also help identify hate-based violence patterns, aiding in prevention, response, and future institutional planning to combat this problem. CSOs in other countries might consider advocating for such surveys, and reaching out to CSOs in places where surveys are in place, to understand not only their utility but also how they were constructed.

Recording

As we have established, to formally recognize and effectively address hate crimes within the criminal justice system, the relationship between the police and victims is paramount. Establishing trust between the police and the community is essential, as victims' willingness to report hate crimes is significantly influenced by notions of procedural justice, fairness, and trust.[38] However, victims cannot be required to increase their trust in the criminal process; rather, criminal justice institutions must earn that trust. One means by which this trust can be earned is to ensure that when a victim reports their experience, it is properly recorded on the police database, which increases the likelihood of the hate element of the crime being investigated and thus recognized throughout the process. There are a number of ways in which CSOs can support this process.

The "Perception Test"

Proper recording of hate crimes is crucial as it ensures the "hate element" of an offense is not ignored or overlooked during the criminal justice process. Flagging hate crimes as a specific crime category enables the application of relevant legislative provisions during prosecution and the punishment of perpetrators at sentencing. Moreover, it aids in understanding the extent to which hate crime is a problem, allowing authorities to monitor trends, and measuring the impact of anti-hate crime efforts, while also identifying victims' specific needs.[39] CSOs can have an important role in communicating to criminal justice agencies the need for proper recording by emphasizing the experiences of community members, both in regard to the impacts that such victimization can have, and in turn, the need to measure the extent of the problem.

One approach to recording hate crime that prioritizes victims and targeted communities' service rights has been by using a "perception test." First used in England and Wales, it requires the police to record any criminal offense that is *perceived* by the victim or anyone else to be motivated by prejudice or hostility toward the victim's presumed identity characteristic. This test has now been adopted at a European level, and includes the recording of non-crime prejudice-based incidents (sometimes referred to as "hate incidents"). In the European Commission against Racism and Intolerance's General Policy Recommendation No. 11 on combating racism and racial discrimination in policing, paragraph 14 defines a racist incident as "any incident which is perceived to be racist by the victim or any other person."[40] Crucially, the test operates only at the point of recording, to prompt a thorough investigation of the hate element of the crime – where it is determined that the offense did not contain a hate element, the hate "tag" or "flag" should be removed from the record. Paragraph 35 of the Council of Europe Recommendation on combating hate crime notes the importance of *removing* the flag where necessary, requiring police services to have guidance on "the circumstances, if any, in which a crime should be re-recorded as a non-hate-based offence in the criminal record of a suspect."

This approach to recording is not without criticism; however, in the context of non-crime transphobic hate incidents, the Court of Appeal in England and Wales found the test could fall foul of the freedom of expression protected through Article 10 of the European Convention of Human Rights where recording is carried out without further consideration of free speech rights.[41] This has led to new guidance from the UK Home Office permitting the recording of hate incidents, but officers must first consider whether any interference with a subject's right to freedom of expression is "proportionate" and "necessary."[42]

In addition, as Mason and colleagues note, the test – when used in relation to hate crimes – has the capacity to artificially raise the expectations of the victim by requiring a crime to be recorded as a hate crime though there is no evidence to support that perception.[43] Unfortunately, the test can also result in a misperception by both the general public and the victim that the perception of the victim will determine how the case is prosecuted, including but not limited to what underlying criminal offense was committed. Finally, caution should be exercised in the manner in which the perception of the victim is recorded for the purposes of criminal record checks, and, as noted above, where an investigation determines that there was no such motivation to the offense, the hate element should be removed from the record of the suspect. Equally, the test might be presumed to make the victim responsible for knowing what a hate crime is, as well as the recording mechanism: the test does not of course *preclude* a police officer from recording the crime as a hate crime, but instead offers an additional option for victims to request that it is so recorded. All that said, what is clear is that the approach has resulted in England and Wales officially recording more "hate crimes" than any other country in the world.[44]

Bias Indicators

Identifying jurisdictionally specific and identity group–specific "bias indicators" (i.e., evidence of the "hate element") in collaboration with CSOs is vital for the investigation and in turn prosecution of hate crimes, as they serve as evidential markers to prove the hate element of a crime.[45] These indicators encompass various elements, such as verbal slurs, evidence from electronic devices, background information on the accused, and brutality of violence. Prosecutors' ability to prove a hate element in court hinges on law enforcement's early identification and collation of this critical evidence.[46] Bias indicators can include:

- Complainant and witness testimony of verbal slurs and prejudiced epithets;
- Police-worn cameras and mobile phone footage of verbal slurs;
- Emergency service recordings of incidents that include words spoken in the background;
- Police questioning that may elicit identity-based hostilities;
- Background information of the accused, including
    a. past convictions, membership of hate-based groups, websites, and blogs;
    b. previous conversations with associates evidencing prejudices;
    c. previous convictions for hate-based offenses;
    d. possession of hate-based signs and symbols;
    e. social media posts displaying hateful speech;
    f. text messages expressing identity-based hostility; and
    g. possession of leaflets, letters, or other written documents with hate-content;
- Conduct that specifically targets the identity/perceived vulnerability of the victim (e.g., abuse toward LGBTQI+ sex workers);
- Excessive brutality of violence (often a marker in hate crimes);[47]
- Contemporaneity with trigger events.[48]

Prosecutors play a vital role in proving the hate element in court, particularly when a defendant's motivation is under scrutiny. To assist prosecutors, guidance documentation is invaluable. Several guidance documents are available, such as those from the Office for Democratic Institutions for Human Rights (OSCE/ODIHR) and EU-based projects.[49] In the UK, the Crown Prosecution Service (CPS) provides specific prosecutorial guidance for different hate crime strands, addressing hate crime prioritization, building cases for prosecution, and addressing indicators of bias relating to the victim and the perpetrator.[50]

Victim support is crucial, as many hate crime victims are considered "vulnerable witnesses." The European Union Victims' Rights Directive underscores the importance of measures to support these victims, such as professional interviews, avoiding visual contact with offenders during testimony (such as using screens in court), and the absence of the public during hearings.[51] Though some of these measures can impact on the right of the defendant to confront their accuser, or the right to a trial in public, these "special protection measures," as referred to at a European level, are helpful in ensuring that the rights of victims of hate crimes are upheld through the process. Note that not all are appropriate to every legal system, of course; in Ireland, like the United States, *in camera* proceedings are held very rarely in criminal matters, and largely only where juvenile offenders are involved. However, the EU Victims' Rights Directive is useful insofar as offering a range of potential responses that CSOs can potentially advocate for in supporting victims. CSOs, where appropriately funded, can also support victims by way of court accompaniment services, which are particularly important where legal aid to victims is not provided, where there may be language or ability barriers, or where other access issues could produce a lack of understanding or engagement on the part of the victim.

Training

Ultimately, regardless of the mechanisms employed and introduced, training is the critical component across the criminal justice process, encompassing the content and implications of legislation. Particularly within policing, the establishment of a supportive relationship between law enforcement and commonly targeted communities is vital. In addition to training focused on hate crime, it is crucial to provide training on the recording, investigation, and prosecution of hate crimes.[52] The development of specific policies for hate crime policing, as exemplified by the UK's College of Policing, should be reinforced through training.[53] In addition to general hate crime training, specialized training is essential for officers to effectively record and investigate hate crimes against different victim groups.

CSOs have been active in providing training for law enforcement officers, such as online courses on hate crime and bias indicators.[54] The OSCE/ODIHR also provides a manual on joint hate crime training for police and prosecutors, guiding the setup of training programs using case studies to help officers identify hate crime offenses, bias indicators, investigation techniques, and prosecution. Such training raises awareness of challenges to prosecuting hate crime, including low victim trust in the criminal justice system.[55]

Similar to training for police and prosecution service personnel, it is ideal that training be provided for judges regarding new laws. This training is critical to ensure that judges are knowledgeable about hate crimes and can apply the legislation correctly. It should sensitize judges to the harms of hate and the impact of hate crimes on victims, both direct and indirect, and to the communities of which they are a part, and to democracy itself. The training should also cover the extent to which a sentence can be aggravated and emphasize the importance of judges openly addressing the hate element in the case and its extent.[56]

Judicial Engagement

In most jurisdictions, judges play a crucial role in determining whether the prosecution has met its evidential burden in cases involving hate crime legislation. If a defendant is found guilty or if charges are proven by the prosecution, judges usually also decide on the appropriate punishment. Judicial guidelines provide valuable tools to assist judges in this process, especially in cases where some members of the judiciary may be hesitant to apply laws that increase penalties for hate crime offenders.[57] These guidelines help clarify the significance of these provisions and the procedural aspects of their application.

Some jurisdictions have sentencing bodies that offer guidelines to judges, with the aim of achieving consistency in sentencing across different courts. For instance, the United States Sentencing Commission provides guidelines on sentencing for federal hate crimes, as distinct from other manifestations of offending. Judges in other jurisdictions see such guidelines – or indeed any such policies – as an egregious interference with their closely guarded judicial independence and so may be slow to accept any advice from civil society as to the experiences of victims or the impact of hate crime. Be it through official guidelines, developed with civil society, or through information provided to judges to support their knowledge-base, this guidance can also provide additional information on the common types of aggravation found in hate crime cases and the extent to which they can or should influence the final penalty. Ultimately, the availability of sentencing guidance ensures that hate crime provisions are consistently applied by the courts, promoting uniformity in enforcing the law.

Specialisms

Those responsible for investigating these complex crimes need practical tools, skills, and dedicated policies to interact effectively with victims and deal with the offenses.[58] CSOs can advocate for the development, or support the operation, of specialized police hate crime units that can play a significant role in supporting the implementation of hate crime legislation.[59] Such units can focus on educating police officers and the community about identifying and addressing hate crimes, monitoring and tracking such incidents, and providing outreach to affected communities.[60] That said, police services cannot devolve the responsibility of supporting minority communities to a single unit: the purpose of the unit should be to support the service as a whole in investigating hate crime, and not be the sole unit with competency in this area.

Specialized prosecutors focusing on hate crime cases are also the most effective in ensuring the proper application of hate crime provisions. The complex legal and evidentiary rules for hate crimes, coupled with the unique needs of victims, can necessitate specialized expertise. In England and Wales, each prosecution district designates a "hate crime coordinator" (HCC) who acts as a central point of contact for hate crime–related questions, supports case work across their district, and delivers training to other prosecutors. The HCC Network, which comprises HCCs and an Area Inclusion and Engagement Manager, addresses operational issues raised locally and nationally, enhancing the effective management and prosecution of hate crime cases.

CSOs can play a key role in supporting the work of specialist prosecutors. In England and Wales, regional areas have established "hate crime scrutiny panels" that include representatives from CSOs, whose task is to scrutinize the work of prosecutors and to feed back any concerns they find through reviewing case files and trial outcomes. At the national level the Crown Prosecution Service (CPS) also hosts an "external consultation group" that meets bimonthly. The aim is for the CPS to communicate the work it is carrying out to improve hate crime prosecutions, conviction rates, and the application of sentence uplifts. They also consult CSO representatives on new training activities, guidance documents, and action plans they have developed. Feedback from the group is "actioned" and updates are provided in follow-up meetings.

Institutional Bias

The Council of Europe Recommendation on combating hate crime (2024)4 places central importance on the need for criminal justice systems to "identify, address and take measures to eliminate any institutional bias and discrimination" as a means of supporting access to justice on the part of victims of hate crime. The European Commission against Racism and Intolerance (ECRI) emphasizes the importance of addressing prejudice within policing and underscores the need for the police to guarantee the rights and security of all individuals.[61] It is essential for the police to address biases and discriminatory practices within their own organizations, such as racial profiling, discriminatory behavior, and prejudiced misconduct. To promote positive police-community relations and ensure equality, the ECRI recommends measures including placing the police under a statutory obligation to promote equality, by, for example, training the police in policing diverse societies, proactive efforts to recruit members of underrepresented minority groups, and fostering dialogue and cooperation between the police and minority groups.[62] CSOs can play an active role in providing such train- .ing (as outlined above) while also participating in dialogue with police services, so as to communicate the concerns and perceptions among community members regarding police bias. Criminal justice institu- tions typically vociferously reject accusations of institutional bias: for this reason, we would suggest that rather than ask such institutions to investigate whether institutional bias exists, CSOs ought to emphasize the need for senior police personnel to assume that such biases exist and offer to work with them to address the issue.

Post-Conviction and Out-of-Court Interventions for Hate Crime

While it is beyond the scope of this chapter to comprehensively outline effective criminal justice interventions for hate crime,[63] it is crucial to underscore that effective hate crime legislation should be supported by justice interventions (i.e., mechanisms used to address the underlying causes and consequences of these offenses). These interventions can be used as alternatives to prosecution, especially for minor infractions, or in conjunction with official penalties imposed by the courts after con- viction. Here, civil society can play a crucial role in securing justice.

RESTORATIVE INTERVENTIONS
One innovative justice measure gaining traction for hate crime cases is restorative justice (RJ). RJ brings together community members involved in a hate crime incident through voluntary and inclusive dialogue focused on understanding the harm caused and how it can be repaired. RJ can serve as an alternative to formal prosecution, enabling victims, perpetrators, and other affected community members of hate crimes to engage in a justice process without entering the traditional criminal jus- tice system, or it can be used as part of an offender's sentence.

Some US states have included RJ within hate crime laws in an attempt to focus penal responses on reparative interventions. For instance, sec- tion 422.86. (a) of the Penal Code of California states that among pun- ishment and crime prevention the aim of sentencing hate crime should also include "[r]estorative justice for the immediate victims of the hate crimes and for the classes of persons terrorized by the hate crimes."[64] Other states have specified the use of restorative practices within the "enhanced" element of an offender's sanction. For example, legislation in Colorado includes an option for first-time offenders, at the request of the victim, to be referred "to a restorative justice or other suitable alter- native dispute resolution program."[65] In Connecticut, the state-wide Hate Crimes Advisory Council must also make recommendations for legislation concerning hate crimes, such as "1. restitution for victims of such crimes; 2. community service designed to remedy damage caused by, or related to the commission of such crimes."[66] The growing use of RJ for hate crimes in the United States has coincided with a number of CSOs that have become active in promoting its use in such cases, including the Aspen Institute that has set up a national working group of experts and leaders to focus efforts on how to use restorative justice processes to combat hate crime via its Religion & Society Program.[67] Central to CSO work in this area is the use of research to give evidence of the potential benefits of RJ approaches to addressing the causes and consequences of hate crime. Research indicates that restorative practices can reduce the emotional toll of hate crimes, including anger, anxiety, and the fear of recurrence.[68] Four key variables contribute to improving the emotional well-being of hate crime victims in restorative processes:

- Participants feel they can actively engage in conflict resolution.
- Participants can express the harms they've experienced and discuss their experiences as "different" in the community.
- Participants are supported by restorative facilitators who listen to their accounts.
- The accused perpetrator commits to avoiding further hate incidents.

Restorative processes have the potential to empower victims of hate crimes, especially those who feel voiceless.

Tentative evidence also suggests that RJ can reduce reoffending in hate incidents. In Walters's study in England, eleven out of nineteen separate cases of ongoing hate crime incidents researched ceased directly after the restorative process had taken place.[69] A further six cases stopped after the restorative facilitator included other local agencies and support organizations within the process. These included schools, social services, community police officers, and housing officers. This holistic approach addresses the needs of both victims and perpetrators of hate crimes.

It can also be helpful for CSOs active in this area to demonstrate that RJ is something that communities want as a response to hate crime. Recent research in the UK has shown greater average levels of support among a commonly targeted group for the use of RJ compared with the use of enhanced punishment, with the former being perceived to be better at reducing reoffending and supporting victim needs.[70] The study also revealed that community members who read about the use of RJ for hate crime experienced less anger and sadness about case outcomes and higher levels of satisfaction with the criminal justice system, compared with cases where enhanced punishments were implemented.

While the potential benefits of RJ appear promising, CSOs working in this area should be sensitized to the need for risk management in order to avoid revictimization of victims and other community members. When using restorative practices for hate crimes, research suggests that it is vital to:

- Have experienced and fully trained restorative practitioners facilitate the process.
- Ensure practitioners understand the sensitive dynamics of hate crime victimization.
- Conduct preparatory meetings with each participant to outline the purpose, aims, and objectives of RJ.
- Ensure participation is voluntary and not coerced.
- Encourage a multiagency approach, where facilitators collaborate with various agencies and organizations during restorative meetings, including community-support organizations, schools, neighborhood policing teams, community safety units, and social services.

Post-Conviction Rehabilitation Programs

In many hate crime cases, formal prosecution is necessary, and criminal courts have several options when imposing sentences, including imprisonment or community-based orders. Offenders, post-conviction, become the responsibility of criminal justice agencies like prisons and offender management services, which administer punishment and rehabilitation programs. Rehabilitation aims to change offenders' attitudes and understanding. Educational programs can be integrated into hate crime legislation itself. For example, under a recent amendment to the Illinois Criminal Code:

> [A]ny order of probation or conditional discharge entered following a conviction or an adjudication of delinquency shall include a condition that the offender enroll in an educational program discouraging hate crimes if the offender caused criminal damage to property consisting of religious fixtures, objects, or decorations. The educational program may be administered, as determined by the court, by a university, college, community college, non profit organization, or the Holocaust and Genocide Commission.[71]

It is important to note that whether hate crime offenders can be effectively rehabilitated through educational programs remains largely unproven.[72] Policymakers should recognize that the causes of hate are both individual and structural, stemming from individual animosities and broader societal hostilities toward targeted communities. It is challenging to address identity-based prejudice within a system that has historically subordinated minority identities. While some rehabilitation programs have shown promise,[73] they should be approached with caution.

Rehabilitation programs often include:

- sessions that raise cultural and diversity awareness;
- reflecting on attitudes and beliefs; and
- understanding the impacts of hate crimes on victims and communities.

Long-term evaluations of these programs are limited, but they suggest that one-on-one work is necessary for successful implementation because each perpetrator of a hate crime has unique experiences, beliefs, and needs.

An Iterative Process

Institutional measures in the criminal justice system must be continually reviewed and revised to ensure their effectiveness. Training and guidelines should be updated periodically based on feedback from various interested parties, including police officers, lawyers, and CSOs. Courts' interpretations of legislation and independent research findings should also inform revisions to improve the implementation of hate crime legislation.

A helpful approach to engage with criminal justice professionals, victims, and offenders and assess the legislation's practical impact is the methodology developed as part of the Lifecycle of a Hate Crime project.[74] Periodic legislative reviews should be incorporated into State or National Action Plans, allowing key CSOs to provide input into the review process. This iterative approach ensures that institutional measures continually adapt to the evolving needs and challenges within the criminal justice system.

Part C: Education Campaigns Pre and Post the Enactment of Hate Crime Legislation

Finally, the effectiveness of hate crime laws hinges on public awareness and understanding of their existence. For commonly targeted

Figure 7.5. A Framework of Post-Conviction and Out-of-Court Justice Interventions

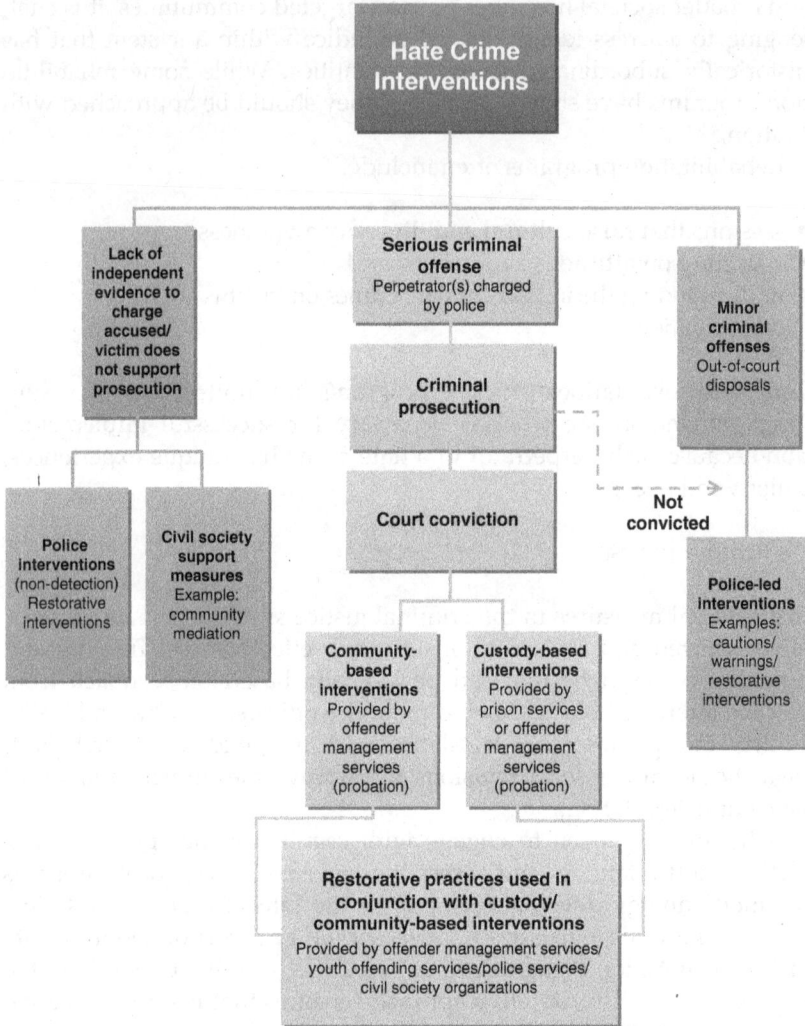

Source: Adapted from Walters, Brown, and Wiedlitzka, "Preventing Hate Crime."

communities, knowledge about hate crime laws is vital to encourage reporting of incidents. Research indicates that victims are hesitant to report hate crimes to the police if they lack confidence that their reports will be taken seriously.[75]

Figure 7.6. The Interactive Process of Enforcing Hate Crime Legislation

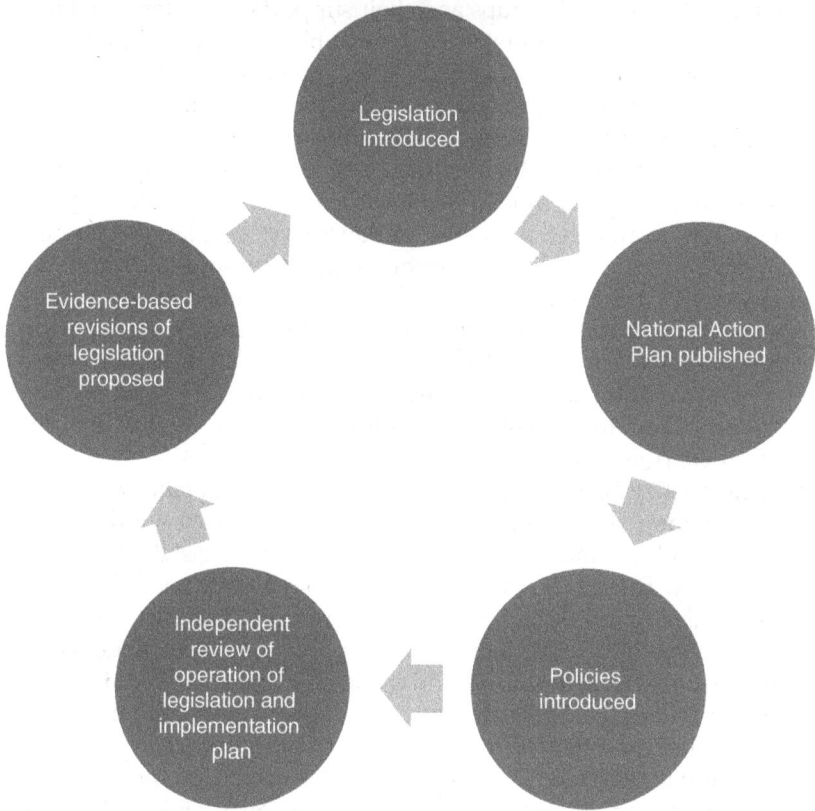

Education campaigns play a crucial role in disseminating information about the aims and significance of hate crime legislation, as well as how individuals can report incidents, and CSOs can play a vital role here. These campaigns also educate the public on what constitutes a "hate crime" and why it is essential for victims to report such incidents to the police. Education campaigns can effectively raise awareness about hate crime legislation and foster support for its implementation. CSOs are best placed to develop such campaigns, and should be supported in doing so. To create an effective education campaign on hate crime, multiagency partnerships should follow specific steps:

1. **Determine the Audience**: Education campaigns should begin by identifying their target audience. This can be achieved through

random sampling and surveys to gauge societal attitudes toward commonly targeted groups and their support or resistance to hate crime legislation. Understanding the public's attitudes allows campaigners to identify sections of society that lack awareness of or harbor hostility toward these groups. Additionally, polls and surveys can help assess the level of societal support for new legislation and which segments of society are most or least supportive. For example, a recent campaign in Belize, "Live and Let Live," conducted a Public Opinion Survey on National Values and Discrimination to gauge public support for anti-discrimination laws for LGBTQI+ individuals. The survey revealed majority support for such laws but also identified sections of society with reservations. Another example is the European Commission–funded "Call It Hate" project, which involved a survey across ten countries to inform public information campaigns on the harms of anti-LGBTQI+ hate crime.[76]

2. **Identify Key Facts**: When crafting messages about hate crime, campaigners should focus on identifying key facts about the nature and dynamics of such offenses and why legislation is necessary. These facts can be obtained from international reports detailing common experiences and impacts of hate crime[77] and the goals of hate crime laws aimed at preventing such incidents.[78] It is also essential to understand the local experiences of targeted communities, including the various forms of victimization they experience and their effects.

3. **Develop a Message**: Those developing the campaign should use the preliminary data gathered on identity group awareness and support or resistance to hate crime legislation as a foundation for shaping their messages. Focus groups can help test ideas and evaluate responses to messages, enabling campaign managers to create the most effective messages. During this process, persuasive messengers can be identified. Individuals who are trusted within the community can effectively convey campaign messages, even across cultural, linguistic, or political barriers. These persuasive messengers can also serve as "change agents," that is, individuals tasked with guiding and facilitating change. They can be from within public sector organizations or be community leaders and activists.

   The "Live and Let Live" campaign, noted above, focused on national values and emphasized that "discrimination isn't a Belizean value." Regarding LGBTQI+ individuals, it highlighted the message that every LGBTQI+ Belizean is someone's family member, and no one should be rejected by their family or denied respect in Belizean society.

4. **Disseminate the Message**: Once sufficient information is gathered on the nature and dynamics of hate crime, the key messages should be disseminated to the target audience(s) (whether specific communities, a particular demographic within broader society, or the public generally). This phase is resource-intensive and may involve various tactics, including public service announcements (PSAs) on radio, TV, YouTube, and social media, coordinated web and social media platforms hosting PSAs and related content, media buys on various platforms, campaign launch events, press releases, post-campaign polling to measure impact, and leveraging poll results in mainstream and social media.

Films, particularly short films, can also be a powerful tool for disseminating campaign messages. They can humanize commonly targeted communities by sharing personal stories of the pain caused by discrimination and hate, and can be developed by states in collaboration with civil society. An example is the film *A Wake Up Call – Hate Crime Law in the Commonwealth* produced by the Human Dignity Trust, which underscores the law's role in protecting LGBTQI+ people from violence. Another example is the Irish campaign "Call It Out," which used an award-winning video titled "Have You Ever Felt?" to convey the message that LGBTQI+ people in Ireland deserve to live free from prejudice and that homophobia, biphobia, and transphobia must be eliminated.

Conclusion

The introduction of hate crime legislation and the better implementation and improvement of the hate crime system where it already exists are important steps in a long process of combating and preventing hate crime. Indeed, this is not a linear process: some jurisdictions may have some policies and practices in place prior to the introduction of legislation; equally, the presence of a holistic and well-established action plan is meaningless in the absence of support and resources from the state. CSOs can operate as a point of connection between the state and its criminal justice institutions on the one hand, and victims on the other. However, the state must take the responsibility of ensuring criminal justice agencies are fit for purpose, and reduce the capacity for revictimization by its employees. CSOs can press the state to take action – most effectively when they are embedded in the process itself. Only when criminal justice institutions earn the trust of those most marginalized in society can hate crime truly be addressed in society.

NOTES

1 Mark Austin Walters, *Criminalising Hate: Law as Social Justice Liberalism* (Cham: Palgrave, 2022).

2 Jennifer Schweppe, Amanda Haynes, and Mark A. Walters, *Lifecycle of a Hate Crime: Comparative Report* (Dublin: Irish Council for Civil Liberties, 2018), https://www.iccl.ie/wp-content/uploads/2018/10/Life-Cycle-of -a-Hate-Crime-Comparative-Report.pdf.

3 Schweppe, Haynes, and Walters, *Lifecycle of a Hate Crime.*

4 Ryken Grattet and Valerie Jenness, "Transforming Symbolic Law into Organizational Action: Hate Crime Policy and Law Enforcement Practice," *Social Forces* 87, no. 1 (2008): 501–27, https://doi.org/10.1353/sof.0.0122.

5 Organisation for Economic Co-operation and Development, *Busan Global Partnership Forum for Effective Development Cooperation* (2011), accessed February 25, 2020, https://www.oecd.org/dac/effectiveness/49650173 .pdf.

6 Ibrahim Natil, "Introducing Barriers to Effective Civil Society Organisations," in Ibrahim Natil, Vanessa Malila, and Youcef Sai, eds., *Barriers to Effective Civil Society Organisations: Political, Social and Financial Shifts* (New York: Routledge, 2020).

7 Rachel Hayman et al., *Legal Frameworks and Political Space for Non-Governmental Organisations: An Overview of Six Countries* (Bonn: European Association of Development Research and Training Institutes, 2013), https://kpsrl.org/sites/default/files/publications/files/legal _frameworks_and_political_space_for_non_governmental_organisations _an_overview_of_six_countries_july_2013.pdf.

8 Walters, *Criminalising Hate*; Schweppe, Haynes, and Walters, *Lifecyle of a Hate Crime.*

9 United Nations, *Kyoto Declaration on Advancing Crime Prevention, Criminal Justice and the Rule of Law: Towards the Achievement of the 2030 Agenda for Sustainable Development* (2021), https://www.unodc.org/documents /commissions/Congress/documents/in-session/Kyoto_Declaration _Advance_Unedited_Version.pdf.

10 See https://search.coe.int/cm?i=0900001680a67955.

11 See https://search.coe.int/cm?i=0900001680af9736.

12 Editor's note: As mentioned in earlier chapters, we use the term "hateful speech" because, especially in the American context, the term "hate speech" is erroneous and misleading. But because Schweppe and Walters are writing about European laws where the term "hate speech" is used, in this chapter we'll use "hate speech" in quotation marks. For more on "hate speech," see Chris Marchese, "Suzanne Nossel Criticizes 'Incoherent' Concept of 'Hate Speech,'" Fire, June 7, 2016,

https://www.thefire.org/news/suzanne-nossel-criticizes-incoherent
-concept-hate-speech.

13 See https://search.coe.int/cm?i=0900001680af9736.

14 Amanda Perry-Kessaris and Joanna Perry, "Enhancing Participatory
Strategies with Designerly Ways for Sociolegal Impact: Lessons from
Research Aimed at Making Hate Crime Visible," *Social and Legal Studies* 29,
no. 6 (2020): 835–57, http://dx.doi.org/10.2139/ssrn.3387479.

15 The White House, *The U.S. National Strategy to Counter Antisemitism*,
May 2023, https://bidenwhitehouse.archives.gov/briefing-room
/statements-releases/2023/06/02/the-u-s-national-strategy-to-counter
-antisemitism-key-actions-by-pillar-2/.

16 In different jurisdictions, terms such as "action plan," "framework,"
"strategy," "guidance," and "policy" are used interchangeably or with
varying definitions. In this chapter, we use these terms consistently with
the following definitions:
- Action Plan: At a state or national level.
- Strategy: At the community level.
- Policy: At the institutional level.
- Guidance: At the subinstitutional level to support the operationalization
of policy.

17 Piotr Godzisz, "The Europeanization of Anti-LGBT Hate Crime Laws in
the Western Balkans," *Crime, Law and Social Change* 71, no. 3 (2019):
291–306, https://doi.org/10.1007/s10611-019-09818-9.

18 Editor's note: The interplay and tensions between preventing prejudice
and hatred, on one hand, and upholding democratic values, like free
speech, on the other, must be considered (see Buerger, chapter 9, in this
volume).

19 Schweppe, Haynes, and Walters, *Lifecycle of a Hate Crime*. For an example
of a National Action Plan that has been informed by the multiagency
approach, see UK Government, Home Office, *Action against Hate: The UK
Government's Plan for Tackling Hate Crime*, July 2016, https://assets
.publishing.service.gov.uk/media/5f8db94a8fa8f56ad07d1152/2016_Hate
_Crime_Action_Plan.pdf.

20 European Union Agency for Fundamental Rights, *EU LGBT Survey:
European Union Lesbian, Gay, Bisexual and Transgender Survey: Main Results*
(Vienna: EUAFR, 2020), https://fra.europa.eu/sites/default/files/fra-eu
-lgbt-survey-main-results_tk3113640enc_1.pdf.

21 See, for example, Caroline Erentzen and Regina Schuller, "Exploring the
Dark Figure of Hate: Experiences with Police Bias and the Under-Reporting
of Hate Crime," *Canadian Journal of Criminology and Criminal Justice* 62, no. 2
(2020): 64–97, https://doi.org/10.3138/cjccj.2019-0035; Sindy Joyce et al.,
Irish Travellers' Access to Justice (Limerick, Ireland: European Centre

for the Study of Hate, 2022), https://www.drugsandalcohol.ie/36509/1/ITAJ_Final.pdf.

22 See CT.Gov, Connecticut Hate Crimes Advisory Council, https://portal.ct.gov/hatecrimes/the-council?language=en_US.

23 Jennifer Schweppe, Amanda Haynes, and Emma Marie Macintosh, "What Is Measured Matters: The Value of Third Party Hate Crime Monitoring," *European Journal on Criminal Policy and Research* 26, no. 1 (2020): 39–59, https://doi.org/10.1007/s10610-018-9403-4.

24 Jennifer Schweppe, Amanda Haynes, and Mark A. Walters, *Lifecycle of a Hate Crime: Comparative Report* (Dublin: Irish Council for Civil Liberties, 2018), https://www.iccl.ie/wp-content/uploads/2018/04/Life-Cycle-of-a-Hate-Crime-Comparative-Report-FINAL.pdf.

25 Gail Mason et al., *Policing Hate Crime: Understanding Communities and Prejudice* (London: Routledge, 2017).

26 OSCE Office for Democratic Institutions and Human Rights (ODIHR), *Hate Crime Victims in the Criminal Justice System: A Practical Guide* (Warsaw: OSCE/ODIHR, 2020), https://www.osce.org/files/f/documents/c/5/447028.pdf.

27 Mason et al., *Policing Hate Crime*.

28 Mason et al., *Policing Hate Crime*.

29 UK National Police Chiefs' Council, "Report a Hate Crime," accessed January 23, 2025, https://www.report-it.org.uk/your_police_force.

30 It must be noted, however, that reporting incidents for LGBTQI+ people in Singapore will be complicated given the criminalization of same-sex intimacy and lack of LGBTQI+ rights protections.

31 See, for example, Singapore Police Force, *Police Report*, accessed March 20, 2025, https://eservices1.police.gov.sg/phub/eservices/landingpage/police-report.

32 OSCE/ODIHR, *Hate Crime Victims in the Criminal Justice System*.

33 OSCE/ODIHR, *Hate Crime Victims in the Criminal Justice System*.

34 For advice on setting up community support groups, see for example, Bard Center for the Study of Hate, Western States Center, and the Montana Human Rights Network, *A Community Guide for Opposing Hate*, accessed January 22, 2025, https://bcsh.bard.edu/files/2022/05/Opposing HateGuide-single-pages-8M-5-3.pdf.

35 Neil Chakraborti and Stevie-Jade Hardy, *LGB&T Hate Crime Reporting: Identifying Barriers and Solutions* (Manchester, UK: Equality and Human Rights Commission, 2015), https://www.equalityhumanrights.com/en/publication-download/lgbt-hate-crime-reporting-identifying-barriers-and-solutions.

36 Mason et al., *Policing Hate Crime*.

37 Schweppe, Haynes, and MacIntosh, "What Is Measured Matters."

38 Mason et al., *Policing Hate Crime.*
39 OSCE/ODIHR, *Hate Crime Laws: A Practical Guide*, 2nd ed. (Warsaw: OSCE, 2022), https://www.osce.org/odihr/523940.
40 European Commission against Racism and Intolerance, *ECRI General Policy Recommendation N° 11 on Combating Racism and Racial Discrimination in Policing* (Strasbourg: ECRI, 2007), 5, https://rm.coe.int/ecri-general -policy-recommendation-no-11-on-combating-racism-and-racia /16808b5adf.
41 *R. (on the application of Miller) v. College of Policing* [2021] EWCA Civ 1926.
42 Gov.UK, Home Office, "Non-Crime Hate Incidents: Code of Practice on the Recording and Retention of Personal Data (accessible)," June 20, 2023, https://www.gov.uk/government/publications/non-crime-hate-incidents -code-of-practice/non-crime-hate-incidents-code-of-practice-on-the -recording-and-retention-of-personal-data-accessible.
43 Mason et al., *Policing Hate Crime.*
44 Gov.UK, Home Office, "Hate Crime, England and Wales, 2022 to 2023, second edition," updated November 2, 2023, https://www.gov.uk /government/statistics/hate-crime-england-and-wales-2022-to-2023 /hate-crime-england-and-wales-2022-to-2023#:~:text=In%20the%20 year%20ending%20March%202023%2C%203%25%20of%20such%20 offences,what%20constitutes%20a%20hate%20crime.
45 OSCE/ODIHR, *Prosecuting Hate Crimes: A Practical Guide* (Warsaw: OSCE, 2014), https://www.osce.org/files/f/documents/0/0/124532.pdf.
46 Mark A. Walters, Susann Wiedlitzka, and Abenna Owusu-Bempah, *Hate Crime and the Legal Process: Options for Law Reform* (Brighton, UK: University of Sussex, 2017), https://www.iccl.ie/wp-content/uploads/2018/10/Hate -Crime-and-Legal-Process-%E2%80%93-Options-for-Law-Reform-England -and-Wales.pdf.
47 Human Dignity Trust, *Hate Crimes against the LGBT Community in the Commonwealth: A Situational Analysis* (London: Human Dignity Trust, 2020), https://www.humandignitytrust.org/wp-content/uploads /resources/2020-Hate-Crimes-against-the-LGBT-Community-in-the -Commonwealth_A-Situational-Analysis.pdf.
48 Adapted from Walters, Wiedlitzka, and Abenna Owusu-Bempah, *Hate Crime and the Legal Process*, 80. Further information on the use of indicators can also be found in Office for Democratic Institutions and Human Rights (ODIHR), *Prosecuting Hate Crimes: A Practical Guide* (Warsaw: OSCE/ODIHR, 2014), 47–8, https://www.osce.org/files/f/documents /0/0/124532.pdf.
49 Schweppe, Haynes, and Walters, *Lifecycle of a Hate Crime.*
50 Gov.UK, Crown Prosecution Service, "Homophobic, Biphobic and Transphobic Hate Crime – Prosecution Guidance," accessed January 23,

2025, https://www.cps.gov.uk/legal-guidance/homophobic-biphobic
-and-transphobic-hate-crime-prosecution-guidance.

51 European Parliament and the Council of the European Union, "Directive
2012/29/EU of the European Parliament and of the Council Establishing
Minimum Standards on the Rights, Support and Protection of Victims
of Crime, and Replacing Council Framework Decision 2001/220/JHA,"
Official Journal of the European Union, October 25, 2012, https://eur-lex
.europa.eu/legal-content/EN/TXT/HTML/?uri=CELEX:32012L0029.

52 Mason et al., *Policing Hate Crime*.

53 UK College of Policing, "Hate Crime," October 20, 2020, https://www
.app.college.police.uk/app-content/major-investigation-and-public
-protection/hate-crime/.

54 See, for example, Facing Facts, "About Facing Facts," accessed January 24,
2025, https://www.facingfacts.eu/.

55 Mark Austin Walters et al., "Hate Crimes against Trans People: Assessing
Emotions, Behaviors, and Attitudes toward Criminal Justice Agencies,"
Journal of Interpersonal Violence 35, no. 21–22 (2020), https://doi.org
/10.1177/0886260517715026.

56 Schweppe, Haynes, and Walters, *Lifecycle of a Hate Crime*.

57 Walters, Wiedlitzka, and Owusu-Bempah, *Hate Crime and the Legal Process*;
Schweppe, Haynes, and Walters, *Lifecycle of a Hate Crime*.

58 European Commission, "Report from the Commission to the European
Parliament and the Council on the Implementation of Council Framework
Decision 2008/913/JHA on Combating Certain Forms and Expressions of
Racism and Xenophobia by Means of Criminal Law," 2014, https://eur-lex
.europa.eu/legal-content/GA/TXT/?uri=CELEX:52014DC0027.

59 Samuel Walker and Charles Max Kanz, "Less Than Meets the Eye: Police
Department Bias Crime Units," *American Journal of Police* 14, no. 1 (1995):
29–48, https://doi.org/10.1108/07358549510799099.

60 Greg Moreau, "Police-Reported Hate Crime in Canada, 2018," *Juristat*,
Statistics Canada, Catalogue no. 85-002-X, February 25, 2020, https://
www150.statcan.gc.ca/n1/pub/85-002-x/2020001/article/00003-eng
.htm#r9.

61 European Commission against Racism and Intolerance, *ECRI General Policy
Recommendation N° 11*.

62 European Commission against Racism and Intolerance, *ECRI General Policy
Recommendation N° 11*.

63 See Mark Walters, Rupert Brown, and Susann Wiedlitzka, "Preventing
Hate Crime: Emerging Practices and Recommendations for the Effective
Management of Criminal Justice Interventions: Project Report," University
of Sussex, 2016, https://hdl.handle.net/10779/uos.23436158.v1.

64 California Legislative Information, Penal Code of California, section 422.86. (a), https://leginfo.legislature.ca.gov/faces/codes_displaySection .xhtml?lawCode=PEN&sectionNum=422.86.

65 See "2024 Colorado Revised Statutes, Section 18-9-121 – Bias-Motivated Crimes – Legislative Declaration," Justia U.S. Law, accessed March 20, 2025, https://law.justia.com/codes/colorado/title-18/article-9/part-1 /section-18-9-121/.

66 See Michael Kirby, *Connecticut Hate Crime Laws* (Hartford, CT: Office of Legislative Research, 2021), 9, https://www.cga.ct.gov/2021/rpt/pdf /2021-R-0104.pdf.

67 Aspen Institute, "Religion & Society Program Announces New Dismantling Hate & Extremism Cohort," press release, March 15, 2023, https://www.aspeninstitute.org/news/new-dismantling-hate-extremism -cohort/. See also Tyler Bishop et al., *Exploring Alternative Approaches to Hate Crimes* (Stanford: Stanford Law School and Policy Lab, and New York: Brennan Center for Justice, 2021), https://law.stanford.edu/wp-content /uploads/2021/06/Alternative-to-Hate-Crimes-Report_v09-final.pdf.

68 Mark Austin Walters, *Hate Crime and Restorative Justice: Exploring Causes, Repairing Harms* (Oxford: Oxford University Press, 2014).

69 Walters, *Hate Crime and Restorative Justice.*

70 Mark Austin Walters, Jenny L. Paterson, and Rupert Brown, "Enhancing Punishment or Repairing Harms? Perceptions of Sentencing Hate Crimes amongst Members of a Commonly Targeted Victim Group," *British Journal of Criminology* 61, no. 1 (2021): 61–84, https://doi.org/10.1093/bjc/azaa062.

71 Illinois General Assembly, "Illinois Compiled Statutes, Public Act 100-0197, Illinois," accessed March 20, 2025, https://www.ilga.gov/legislation/ilcs /fulltext.asp?DocName=072000050K12-7.1.

72 Walters, Brown, and Wiedlitzka, "Preventing Hate Crime."

73 Walters, Brown, and Wiedlitzka, "Preventing Hate Crime."

74 Schweppe, Haynes, and Walters, *Lifecycle of a Hate Crime.*

75 Chakraborti and Hardy, *LGB&T Hate Crime Reporting.*

76 Piotr Godzisz and Giacomo Viggiani, eds., *Awareness of Anti-LGBT Hate Crime in the European Union* (Warsaw: Lambda Warsaw Association, 2019), https://en.hatter.hu/sites/default/files/dokumentum/kiadvany/2019 -awareness-of-anti-lgbt-hate-crime-in-the-european-union.pdf.

77 Human Dignity Trust, *Hate Crimes against the LGBT Community.*

78 Kay Goodall and Mark Walters, *Legislating to Address Hate Crimes against the LGBT Community in the Commonwealth* (London: Human Dignity Trust, 2019), https://www.humandignitytrust.org/wp-content/uploads /resources/Legislating-to-Address-Hate-Crimes-against-the-LGBT -Community-in-the-Commonwealth-Final.pdf.

Editor's Introduction to Chapter 8

The January 6, 2021, insurrection rekindled interest in my book *A Force upon the Plain: The American Militia Movement and the Politics of Hate*, and I spoke with many radio and print journalists. One inevitable difference between the mid-1990s and today was that the anti-government conspiracy theories driving many of the militias years ago – among them that the numbers on the back of road signs were associated with the concentration camp the government will take you to; that Gurkha troops were being trained to come into every American's home without a warrant to search for evidence of gun ownership; that the government itself, and not Timothy McVeigh and Terry Nichols, was behind the April 19, 1995, Oklahoma City bombing – were largely relegated to the extremes. Back then, hardly any members of Congress were endorsing militia-think, for example. Now conspiracy theories reminiscent of what drove hate in the 1990s militias have a home in mainstream American politics, frequently around issues of vilifying an enemy, whether political or by immigrant status or color of skin or religion or sexual orientation or expression.

There were tools I and others advocated for combating this type of conspiratorial thinking when it was contained to followers of extreme movements. I was at a loss of what might work now when the challenges are so much broader, and asked for months about who in the academic world was thinking about these issues. Then a reporter from Spokane, Washington interviewed me about a neo-Nazi group, and I in turn asked him (because I was asking everyone) if he knew who was working on conspiracy theories. He sent me an article he had written looking at these theories, and said that without question the best person was Joe Uscinski. I was delighted when I spoke with Joe, after reading some of his work, including his book *Conspiracy Theories: A Primer*, and listening to some of his talks. I was particularly pleased that he, like me, didn't see easy answers to this problem. He said he'd think about it deeply, converse with the others, and at least be able to advise us all (and NGOs) what NOT to do about conspiratorial thinking.

Uscinski's chapter is a primer on how conspiracy theories function, who they are more likely to influence, some strategies to oppose them, and – importantly – the need for increased communication between scholars and NGOs about how conspiratorial thinking manifests as hate.

8 Hate and Conspiracy Theories

The 2022 shooting at a supermarket in Buffalo, New York, in which ten African Americans were murdered, the 2019 shooting at a mosque in Christchurch, New Zealand, in which fifty-one Muslims were murdered, and the 2018 shooting at the Tree of Life Congregation Synagogue in Pittsburgh, Pennsylvania, in which eleven Jewish people were murdered, were all committed by people claiming to act on the White Replacement conspiracy theory.[1] This conspiracy theory argues that powerful (Jewish) elites are systematically replacing white people with migrant people of color who provide cheaper labor and reproduce at higher rates than whites; this plot supposedly, while benefiting economic and political elites, will lead to the diminution of white culture and, eventually, to the extinction of the white race.[2] Such incidents therefore represent not only a hyper-defensive posture leading to a willingness to act – with deadly consequences – to protect one's ingroup from harm but also a complete lack of humility and a disdain for the lives of outgroup members. In other words, the perpetrators are so convinced of their righteousness that they are willing to bet other people's lives on it.

Similar incidents involving conspiracy theories have occurred across the world and over time. For example, in India, recent conspiracy theories about alleged kidnappings and harms coming to cows have sparked vigilante action, including the beating and murder of numerous innocent people.[3] In the United States, armed protests against drag shows,[4] bomb threats directed at children's hospitals,[5] and bombings occurred in 2022 in response to conspiracy theories alleging a widespread scheme to "groom" children.[6] Such incidents demonstrate the harms that can occur when vigilante *individuals* and *small groups* act on conspiracy theories.

Such harms are multiplied when it is *government* rather than vigilantes – individuals or small groups – acting on those conspiracy theories.[7]

This is because governments have a monopoly on the use of authoritative force that can allow them to inflict harms upon millions. Consider, for example, Hitler's antisemitic conspiracy theories that inspired the Holocaust,[8] or Stalin's conspiracy theories that led to mass starvations and murders.[9] On a smaller scale, theories about witches conspiring with Satan inspired numerous witch hunts backed by government force; these led to the drowning, crushing, and burning of numerous supposed "witches" in both medieval Europe[10] and colonial America.[11] Less deadly, but certainly violative of basic rights, were the US government's involvement in two Red Scares in the twentieth century that were motivated by fears of communist influence.[12]

Despite the numerous examples of conspiracy theories being intertwined with numerous acts of horrific and unnecessary violence, the widespread violations of rights, and negative outcomes, they are, and seem to have always been, rather ubiquitous in both ancient and modern societies.[13] Conspiracy theories are easily encountered online, on social media, in libraries, on television, in mainstream news, and in political speeches.[14] Conspiracy theories are also prominent in personal conversations between coworkers and loved ones.[15] Unsurprisingly then, public opinion polls suggest that most, if not all, people believe one, if not several, conspiracy theories.[16]

On the one hand, conspiracy theories can influence actions and motivate harms such as discrimination, harassment, crime, and violence.[17] Numerous high-profile instances of bad action, such as murders and political violence, suggest as much.[18] On the other hand, if conspiracy theories always caused harmful actions, then the streets would run red with blood given the sheer number of believers. Luckily, they do not. As such, the ubiquity of conspiracy theories and the widespread belief in those theories suggest that grave harms are not always, or even often, *caused* by conspiracy theories or by belief in those theories [19] This leaves practitioners who work with (1) populations who are vulnerable to harms that are potentially driven by conspiracy theories or (2) populations who are prone to believing or potentially acting on conspiracy theories with a series of important questions. Which conspiracy theories should be addressed due to their potential harmfulness? When, and under what conditions, might such conspiracy theories potentially be most harmful? Which populations need to be protected from the harms perpetrated by those motivated by hateful conspiracy theories? Which populations are most prone to believing and potentially acting on conspiracy theories in a harmful way? Given the seemingly infinite supply of conspiracy theories and the widespread belief in them,[20] knowing how and when to expend resources to prevent or address conspiracy theories is crucial.

Human behavior is, of course, hard to predict even when we know what a person believes. Unfortunately, violent behaviors are even more difficult to predict with any accuracy. However, there is some evidence from the growing literature on conspiracy theories that can potentially provide some guidance to practitioners working in relevant areas. In this chapter, I will attempt to distill what scholars have learned about conspiracy theories and their associated harms in the last decade in hopes of providing both some nuance to practitioners' understanding of conspiracy theories and their potential harms and some recommendations for how to best allocate scarce resources in the face of widespread conspiracy theories and their potential harms.

I begin by discussing what conspiracy theories are and then by discussing the numerous forms they may take. I seek to focus attention on conspiracy theories that target racial, ethnic, religious, and political outgroups, particularly those that accuse vulnerable groups of being part of the plot. I then move to discuss the sources of conspiracy theories and the factors that drive belief in those theories. Then, I will address various models for considering the effects of conspiracy theories in an attempt to drill down on (1) which conspiracy theories mostly likely need addressing, (2) which people may be most likely to be harmed by conspiracy theories, and (3) which people may be most likely to inflict harm on others due to their belief in conspiracy theories. My argument is that while most conspiracy theories, as well as beliefs in them, are relatively harmless, harms are most likely to come when certain conspiracy theories are believed by followers who prepossess a willingness to act in nonnormative ways against relatively soft, unprotected targets. I follow this with a discussion of potential interventions to prevent such harms. I conclude by discussing ways that practitioners can help inform the study of conspiracy theories so that their goals, methods, and experiences can be better integrated into the academic research agenda, creating synergies that are fruitful for both academics and practitioners.

What Is a Conspiracy Theory?

A *conspiracy theory* is an idea that attempts to explain past, present, or future events and circumstances by appealing to a conspiracy. A *conspiracy*, then, refers to the (assumed to be true) actions of a small group of usually powerful people working in secret for their own benefit, against the common good, and in a way that undermines bedrock ground rules against the use of force and fraud.[21] Because conspiracy theories involve the intentions and actions of powerful people, the mass violation of accepted norms, and widespread harms, they are inherently political ideas. They are also inherently Manichean (i.e., seeing the world as a battle between good and evil) and group-oriented in that they pit outgroups, who are portrayed as evil, against ingroups, who are portrayed as the good and innocent victims of the alleged conspiracy. This group element sets conspiracy theories apart from paranoid delusions in that conspiracy theories present *"us" vs. "them"* narratives, while paranoia is typically characterized by "they are out to get *me*" narratives.[22] Conspiracy theories are therefore often not the product of paranoid thinking as they are often portrayed, but conspiracy theory beliefs and paranoia can of course be found within the same people.

People define the term conspiracy theory in different ways, with some people using the term to denote irrational, false, or bizarre ideas[23] and other people using it more neutrally to denote an accusation of conspiracy that has yet to meet a particular epistemological bar.[24] Both for epistemological reasons (i.e., we may never know the truth about an alleged secretive plot) and for practical reasons (i.e., it might be better to treat beliefs and ideas as such rather than take on the burden of proving a potentially unfalsifiable idea to be false), practitioners might want to consider conspiracy theories as accusatory assertions that could be either true or false, but for which the relevant experts have not sided in favor of.[25] For example, theories asserting that Barack Obama faked his citizenship to illegally usurp the presidency in 2008 run counter to the declarations of numerous agencies and the available documents;[26] therefore, such "birther" theories are appropriately labeled "conspiracy theories" rather than "conspiracies."

When a person believes a conspiracy theory, they tend not to consider it a conspiracy *theory* at all, but rather a conspiracy, or a fact. While tautological, it bears repeating that when people believe an idea, they think that that idea is true; conversely, when people reject an idea, they think that that idea is false. Truth is not self-evident; therefore, numerous factors drive beliefs about what is true; these include people's own biased psychologies and their chosen biased sources of information that help make sense of their world.[27] In some ways then, questions of trueness and falseness should be bracketed away from questions of why people believe an idea.[28] Consider, for example, that both the believers and non-believers of a conspiracy theory claim that their beliefs are justified due to the "evidence," sometimes the same evidence. Thus, the underlying truth of an idea as well as the available evidence are not determinative of beliefs because people cannot see "Truth" and because evidence is interpreted through very thick and biased lenses. Thus, arguments between believers and non-believers about evidence are not really about evidence; they are instead about their personal and subjective ways of interpreting the evidence.[29] These ways of interpretation are driven by the same factors that determine what people believe to be true; this means, essentially, that truth or evidence are not as determinative of beliefs as are psychological, personal, and subjective factors.[30] Thus, arguing about evidence and truth may not change minds.[31]

Individuals set for themselves the standards by which they judge evidence, and those standards often shift radically, depending on who is being accused in the conspiracy theory.[32] People require more evidence to believe that their ingroup has conspired against others than they do to believe that an outgroup has conspired against others. For example, a study of attitudes toward the act of stealing political campaign yard signs showed that people were more concerned when the other side stole yard signs, but much less concerned when the sign-stealing was by their own side.[33] Consider also when New England Patriots' quarterback Tom Brady was accused of deflating game balls (i.e., the "Deflategate" scandal) to gain an advantage. The same evidence, both for and against the accusations, was publicly available to all; however, New Englanders – the people most likely to be fans of the Patriots – were the least likely to believe the accusations while people from other parts of the United States – the people least likely to be fans of the Patriots – were the most likely to believe in Brady's guilt.[34] The evidence, it seems, was not as persuasive as people's subjective interpretations of that evidence, which were largely based on their worldviews, group allegiances, predispositions, and ideologies. Even when there is clear evidence of a violation by one's ingroup that violates a person's moral values, they may still be unwilling to blame their ingroup for it.[35] Thus, people are more inclined to believe that they are the victims of others' bad behaviors rather than that they (or their ingroup) have harmed others through their own bad behavior.[36] On this point, people often believe that they are "victims" regardless of whether they have actually been harmed by others or not.[37]

In general, people find it easier to agree with conspiracy theories that coincide with how they already view the world and to disagree with conspiracy theories that do not; in this sense, conspiracy theories are no different than any other type of proposition. When arguments challenge their worldviews, people find ways to ignore or explain away the contradictory evidence through psychological processes such as selective exposure (i.e., selectively ignoring information that challenges existing worldviews, or selectively opting into information flows that flatter one's worldviews)[38] and motivated reasoning (i.e., giving less weight to counter attitudinal information).[39]

This is not to say that "Truth" itself is subjective, or that it does not exist, but rather that people view it through their own subjective lenses and, therefore, come to very different conclusions about it. People do occasionally lie about what they believe,[40] perhaps to denigrate an outgroup by claiming to believe something bad about the outgroup that they do not actually think is true.[41] But, when people are being sincere in claiming that they hold a belief, they really do believe it.[42] People cannot seek out ideas they believe are wrong and believe them anyway just so they can annoy or offend others. While it is often tempting to view the conspiracy theories that we personally disagree with as *obviously* false, the ideas are not *obviously false to all* given that some people believe them.[43] The believers are not consciously attempting to overlook reality; instead, they are trying to find it just like everyone else.[44] But, just like everyone else (ourselves included!), their personal biases lead them to their beliefs, which may be true or not.

The Diversity of Conspiracy Theories

Given that conspiracy theories are ideas that, just like other types of ideas, people make up, there are an infinite number of these theories.[45] To this point, there are no "official" versions of conspiracy theories. While an event might have one official version (e.g., the Warren Commission Report or the 9/11 Commission Report), there can be an infinite number of explanations for the same event that posit a conspiracy as the cause. This makes conspiracy theories similar to fan fiction in that everyone is free to speculate that a conspiracy has or is occurring if they wish. But, while they vary in numerous ways, all conspiracy theories allege that some group is working in secret for their own benefit and against the common good in a way that threatens the bedrock ground rules that are intended to protect against the widespread use of force and fraud.[46]

The conspirators, that is, those doing the conspiring, in various conspiracy theories range from powerful institutions to minority ethnic, religious, and racial groups, from groups on the political left to those on the political right, and from well-known and real groups, like the Freemasons and the World Health Organization, to groups that are lesser known (e.g., the Interstate Commerce Commission) and probably not real (e.g., the Illuminati). In short, anyone can accuse anyone of anything. A perusal through history shows that any group can be accused of conspiring and, over time, most groups are accused by someone of conspiring against others.[47] This being said, groups that are well known and actually powerful tend to attract more accusations than groups that are lesser known, universally liked, and powerless. Thus, many of the conspiracy theories that become salient in society accuse high-profile politicians (e.g., Donald Trump, Barack Obama) and other well-known institutions and organizations (e.g., the CIA, the "media"). Powerless groups – migrants, minorities, the poor – are not immune from accusations, but are less likely to be accused of orchestrating conspiracy theories themselves because it takes a greater leap of imagination to believe that marginalized and relatively powerless groups are powerful enough to pull off a far-reaching high-stakes scheme.[48] For example, conspiracy theories about an alleged plot to insert Sharia law into US courts accuses Muslims of orchestrating the plot, but such accusations usually assert that the plot involves the help of powerful actors, such as President Obama.[49]

This being said, less powerful groups, like racial, religious, and ethnic minorities, are often featured in conspiracy theories as the pawns of more powerful string pullers. For example, and as mentioned above, white genocide conspiracy theories allege that powerful elites in business, politics, and government are engineering the destruction of the white race;[50] non-white immigrants as well as the white women who have abortions and the gay people who do not propagate the white race are unwitting pawns in the scheme.[51]

Jewish conspiracy theories provide a unique case study on these points. Jews, while in most populations a statistical minority and a historically victimized group, have often been accused of orchestrating worldwide conspiracies to control events and circumstances at the expense of all others,[52] regardless of their actual power. This is often due to widespread antisemitism that is itself often intertwined with the belief that Jews as a group are uniquely powerful in society.[53] Jewish conspiracy theories remain widely believed across the world likely not just because of widespread antisemitism but also because Jews are overrepresented in high-level positions of power, which makes it easier to accuse them of abusing power in a conspiratorial way than it is to accuse other groups, like African Americans or immigrants, who are often underrepresented in the halls of power, of the same.[54] For example, white genocide conspiracy theories often allege that the shadowy elite string-pullers seeking to destroy the white race and culture are Jewish.[55]

Beyond *who* is alleged to be conspiring, conspiracy theories also vary in *when* the alleged plot took, or will take, place. For example, perhaps one of the most widely believed (to this day) conspiracy theories in the United States is that the 1963 assassination of President Kennedy was orchestrated by a broader conspiracy rather than by a lone gunman.[56]

Other conspiracy theories examine events that are more contemporary, such as the last election[57] or the melee at the local shopping mall.[58] Other conspiracy theories allege that the conspiracy will soon come to pass and be revealed (e.g., *the Illuminati will soon take over the planet!*). Some conspiracy theories seek to explain circumstances, such as income inequality or political polarization, as opposed to discrete events. The methods and goals of the supposed conspirators also vary. Across conspiracy theories, methods range from rather simple (e.g., stuffing ballot boxes) to quite elaborate (e.g., large coordinated schemes and cover-ups involving thousands of actors), and the conspirators' goals can range from committing election fraud, to orchestrating a genocide, to world domination.

While I have thus far attempted to define and provide the scope of the term conspiracy theory (*at least how I use it*), I note that other people use the term to refer to a wide variety of claims that would not fit my above definition (e.g., to refer to claims about the existence of Bigfoot). Further, people also use the term in a biased manner, such that the conspiracy theories that one believes will not be conspiracy theories to them, but rather facts,[59] and the allegations of conspiracy that one does *not* believe will be labeled conspiracy theories.[60] Thus, the application of "conspiracy theory" is rarely evenhanded or tied to a clear definition. As such, it is often a term of degradation.[61] Further, many people will take offense if you were to label their cherished ideas as conspiracy theories;[62] at the same time, many people will label your accusations of conspiracy as conspiracy theories if you were to accuse them or their group of being behind the alleged conspiracy.[63]

The same subjective forces that lead people to use the term conspiracy theory in a biased and self-serving way are the same subjective forces that lead different people to adopt beliefs in different conspiracy theories in the first place. People from different sociodemographic groups, political parties, countries, and regions tend to adopt different conspiracy theories when compared to other people.[64] These beliefs come about for reasons having to do with personal, subjective biases, for example, antipathy toward the accused outgroup,[65] a view of society in which undetected conspiracies are frequent,[66] or a willingness to claim victimhood when one may not be a victim.[67] In short, beliefs are partially due to exposures to the ideas, but also are largely due to who the believer is and where they are contextually situated. For example, a person in the United States who currently believes conspiracy theories in which the Holocaust was faked likely has a set of traits and experiences that make them prone to such beliefs despite their social unacceptability; these might include dark personality traits (e.g., psychopathy) and other anti-social characteristics.[68] But a believer who is situated in contexts in which such antisemitic beliefs are widely held and celebrated might believe the Holocaust was faked more due to cultural exposure and reinforcement.[69] Such beliefs might be strategic as well, being less about historical fact but rather about opposition to Jews (and Israel). Some denial in Eastern Europe right after the collapse of the USSR was helped along by anti-communist thinking, because the last great national heroes opposing the USSR were the Nazi-aligned governments in World War II. Some Palestinians are sucked into denial because if the Holocaust didn't happen, that's another weight to put on the scales of justice for Palestinians. In the latter case, the unreliable social epistemic norms are likely more to blame than personality traits.[70]

Why Do People Believe Conspiracy Theories?

Despite a widespread assumption that beliefs in conspiracy theories are held by those with psychopathologies, conservative viewpoints, or by anyone who goes online, the factors that seem to drive such beliefs are little different than the political, psychological, and social factors that drive beliefs in any other sort of idea.[71] These factors, again, involve some combination of exposure to the theory,[72] which sources of information the person frequents and trusts,[73] personal predispositions (i.e., worldviews, ideologies),[74] personality traits,[75] the groups they belong to and the status of those groups,[76] and contextual circumstances.[77] In short, rarely does exposure to a conspiracy theory *on its own* cause belief;[78] instead, the ideas that people already believe or are inclined toward play a large role in determining what ideas they will and will not accept. As such, two people exposed to the same conspiracy theory may come to very different conclusions about it given that they are different people. Even then, exposure may not always be necessary for someone to believe a conspiracy theory: people can simply make up conspiracy theories to explain events and circumstances without exposure.

A brief discussion of the political, psychological, and social factors known to undergird conspiracy theory beliefs is in order.[79] Beginning with the political factors, one the one hand, conspiracy theories are inherently political in that they address power: who has it and what are they doing with it when no one is looking. Thus, beliefs in conspiracy theories can, for some believers, be a rebuke to sources of institutional power such that they feel they have seen the light of a suppressed truth and are therefore an important part of a community that knows the hidden "truth." On the other hand, politicians have large megaphones through which to spread conspiracy theories to trusting and like-minded audiences.[80] Allegiances to political groups, like parties, drive which conspiracy theories members will believe in (i.e., members tend to accuse opposing parties).[81] Members of losing and minority parties tend to believe in and share conspiracy theories, given that they are being ruled by outsiders whom they do not trust.[82]

Psychological factors are those that arise from within an individual's mind, and include cognitive processes, personality traits, and emotional states. Cognitive processes are those that help people reason and make sense of information. Such processes, when biased, can lead people toward adopting conspiracy theories. For example, having a psychological need to understand why an event occurred (even when such answers may not be available) or being prone to reasoning fallacies may lead to beliefs in conspiracy theories.[83] This being said, the effect of cognitive factors on belief in conspiracy theories tends to be outweighed by other factors.[84] Personality traits, stable modes of thinking and behavior, are often found to be correlated with conspiracy theory beliefs. For example, dark personality traits (e.g., sadism, psychopathy), dogmatism, and conflictual personality styles are often found to be strongly predictive of (certain) conspiracy theory beliefs;[85] this signals that conspiracy theory beliefs will often be hard to reverse given that believers will often have personality traits and a sense of personal or group identity that make them impervious to attempts at correction. Finally, emotional states, such as anxiety, have been found to drive or exacerbate beliefs in conspiracy theories.[86] This being said, conspiracy theory beliefs tend to be longstanding and stable, at both the mass[87] and individual levels,[88] while emotional states tend to fluctuate.

Sociological factors include those having to do with group membership, group competition, and group placement within society. Such factors can drive conspiracy theorizing in at least two ways: (1) groups who have faced a history of maltreatment and exclusion may be more likely to believe conspiracy theories, likely because such theories mesh with historical experience,[89] and (2) groups will tend to accuse out-groups of conspiring rather than their own group.[90] The implication is that individuals will point fingers at opposing groups, but rarely at their own.[91]

What Is the Link between Conspiracy Theories and Hate?

Like the term "conspiracy theory," the term "hate" is used in a variety of ways. Here, I discuss hate as referring to animus toward an out-group comprised of people who are different in some way from those engaged in the hate. Given this definition, the conspiracy theories most likely to be intertwined with hate are those that involve religious, ethnic, political, or racial outgroups. Examples are numerous and include those accusing Jews of faking the Holocaust for political purposes,[92] Jews controlling the world's banks and markets,[93] migrants being the pawns of powerful sinister forces bent on remaking society,[94] and gay people being involved in a conspiracy to "groom" children.[95]

Such conspiracy theories that accuse or involve religious, ethnic, or racial outgroups can be particularly harmful for several reasons. First, they scapegoat groups of innocent people, blaming them for what ails society. Such scapegoating can lead to, or embolden, racism and other forms of discrimination.[96] Second, the groups scapegoated are often vulnerable and relatively powerless in society making them soft targets for racism, abuse, violence, and targeting by governments.[97] Third, they can incite people to action because they accuse the outgroup of having violated social and political norms in a grave way.[98] Thus, conspiracy theories that accuse or involve religious, ethnic, or racial outgroups are potentially more harmful than conspiracy theories that involve well-protected or nonexistent actors such as presidents and aliens.

Where the conspiracy theory fits in a causal chain involving hatred and hate-based behaviors is unknown. It could be that conspiracy theories influence people to hate others and then to act against those others in order to thwart what they see as a conspiracy against themselves. It could also be that people hate an outgroup and then attempt to rationalize their hatred by adopting conspiracy theories that blame that outgroup for their troubles.[99] It could also be that a person's underlying personality traits lead them to simultaneously adopt both hatred for and conspiracy theories about an outgroup.[100] Given this, simply cutting off the supply of conspiracy theories may not do much to stop hatred, as the conspiracy theories may only be rationalizations of pre-existing hatred.

As such, practitioners should not be concerned with all conspiracy theories. Instead, practitioners might focus their efforts toward conspiracy theories that are (1) markers of potential hatred toward vulnerable groups and (2) a willingness to act. For example, conspiracy theories about the Holocaust, a supposed gay "agenda," and those claiming that a white genocide is coming (i.e., those that target outgroups) scapegoat vulnerable groups and are often (at least in the United States) correlated with a set of anti-social traits that should concern practitioners. These include:

- dark personality traits (narcissism, psychopathy, Machiavellianism, and sadism)[101]

- conflictual personalities such that disagreement quickly escalates[102]
- support for political violence[103]
- a history of having committed violence (interpersonal or political) or participated in crimes[104]
- feelings of victimhood[105]

Thus, a conspiracy theory belief alleging harms from an outgroup in combination with the above-listed personality traits could easily lead to a situation in which a believer takes violent action with the intention of doing harm to others. We have witnessed numerous examples of this in recent years.[106] Unfortunately, many of these attitudes and traits also make it difficult for people to change their minds or be open to countervailing evidence. For example, people with high levels of narcissism and a conflictual personality will be likely to reject attempts at correction.

Strategies for Addressing Conspiracy Theories

What can be done? Researchers have attempted to dissuade people from their conspiracy theory beliefs in numerous ways, and with varying levels of success. An important consideration is that if conspiracy theories are a rationalization for, or outgrowth of, other underlying traits and worldviews, then reversing a specific belief about a conspiracy theory will do little to eliminate the hatred or behaviors that practitioners are concerned about.[107] Here are several methods that researchers have tried.

Prebunking

Scholars have found significant success in warning people in advance that they will be exposed to conspiracy theories. Such efforts are said to provide mental "immunity" prior to exposure to conspiracy theories in the same way a vaccine provides protection in advance of exposure to a virus. Numerous studies show positive benefits of this strategy.[108] However, it is not clear how effective it is against preexisting beliefs or how well it would work specifically on the conspiracy theories most linked to hate.

To provide some examples of how this might work, consider a situation in which a country was about to experience a large influx of migrants. A prebunking message such as "Beware of sensational, out-of-context, and fake news about migrants coming from politically motivated sources. To get the facts, click here" might be shared across mainstream or social media. Or, consider a situation in which a hotly contested election was approaching. A prebunking message might say, "Politically motivated groups will likely share fake news during the coming weeks in order to affect how you vote. Be aware of where information is coming from before you believe it." Such prebunking strategies could be deployed broadly to the masses.

Debunking

Debunking, or attempting to change someone's mind about a conspiracy theory with evidence and argument has a mixed track record.[109] Like prebunking, this strategy could be deployed at the mass level, and at the individual level as well. While some minds can be changed, particularly when the evidence and argument come from trusted sources,[110] there is a small possibility of a "backfire" effect in which a believer "doubles down" on their belief.[111] I therefore recommend that NGOs build trust with the communities they seek to persuade before attempting to change entrenched beliefs because trusted sources are more likely to affect attitude change than untrusted or unknown ones.

Ridicule

Believers in conspiracy theories often see a social cost in their beliefs, and, as such, may want to hide those beliefs for fear of ridicule.[112] Given this, researchers have found some success using ridicule to change conspiratorial beliefs.[113] That said, such a strategy has not been widely tested, and, as such, there may be serious side effects to such a strategy. For example, it could cut off the potential for further dialogue, making the strategy self-defeating. Examples might include messages attacking the logic of the conspiracy theory believers, comparing their theories to fringe ideas (like those about lizard people), or otherwise suggesting the believers are intellectually impaired.[114]

Deprogramming

In the wake of the COVID-19 pandemic and the January 6 US Capitol attack, many people began to liken conspiracy theory beliefs to cult membership. This led to subsequent calls for cult deprogramming techniques to be used on conspiracy theory believers.[115] Such a strategy is likely not cost effective and may be unethical. Further, it is not clear if such a strategy works: while there have been some clinics offering such services, it is unclear how much it has been used and with what rate of success.

Mental Health Therapy

Most conspiracy theory beliefs are not, themselves, the product of psychopathologies. And, most conspiracy theory beliefs do not present harms. However, when combined with psychopathologies, they could become problematic. For example, an unwell person may feel the need to act on their conspiracy theory beliefs in deleterious ways.[116] Thus, mental health counseling or therapy may be appropriate for people who are experiencing signs of mental disorder. With this said, the problem to be addressed is more the psychopathology than the conspiracy theory belief.

Conclusion

Conspiracy theories can be troublesome in that the evidence in their favor is often thin, if it is available at all. Nonetheless, some people do occasionally act on conspiracy theories with deadly consequences for themselves[117] as well as for others.[118] At the same time, conspiracy theory beliefs are not always or even often harmful, conspiracy theories could be true, and limiting the discussion of conspiracy theories in the public sphere is likely impossible.

For practitioners who work with (1) populations who are vulnerable to harms that are potentially driven by conspiracy theories or (2) populations who are prone to believing or potentially acting on conspiracy theories, there are several important things to consider when confronted with conspiracy theories. First, conspiracy theories are ubiquitous and given finite resources, attention is best spent on the conspiracy theories most likely to be involved with serious harms. These include conspiracy theories that accuse or involve groups in society that are vulnerable to harassment and violence. While the factors driving beliefs in such conspiracy theories will vary across contexts, it is likely that such conspiracy theories will be adopted by people who already possess a set of traits that may make them prone to acting on their beliefs.

It is important to consider that there is no one factor that explains conspiracy theory beliefs. Instead, there are likely a combination of factors that bring a person to adopt a particular belief. For a person to adopt an idea as a belief, it usually needs to mesh with their preexisting beliefs and worldviews. Thus, solutions such as limiting exposure to or debunking individual conspiracy theories may not do much to change minds on their own because the believer likely has a whole bunch of other similar and copasetic beliefs. Further, the same factors that drive beliefs in conspiracy theories that target vulnerable groups also appear to make the believers difficult to correct or negotiate with.[119]

When addressing those who believe conspiracy theories, practitioners should attempt to display high levels of intellectual humility and sympathy. First, there is nothing about a conspiracy theory that allows one to objectively judge its truth value. Second, the believer is likely just that: someone who believes that the conspiracy theories are true. Third, some people's minds may not be open to change, and unfortunately, those may be the minds most in need of change. Fourth, conspiracy theories beliefs are typically not psychopathological in themselves, but they could be accompanied by various psychopathologies. Some studies are beginning to suggest that the link between conspiracy theory belief and nonnormative behaviors lies in depression or other conditions.[120] Anecdotally at least, several of the high-profile acts of violence associated with conspiracy theories have been committed by people with schizophrenia or other similar disorders.[121]

Context matters as well. Many conspiracy theories may be widely believed, but due to a lack of cultural salience they will not motivate behaviors. However, when high-profile elites make a conspiracy theory salient, it could then encourage people who are already believers to act out. For example, leaders who scapegoat migrant or minority communities with demeaning or dehumanizing language may encourage vigilante action against those communities. Such has been the case with politicians' use of white genocide conspiracy theories (which have encouraged numerous mass shootings in the United States and elsewhere) and conspiracy theories about child "grooming" (which have encouraged the targeting of gay and trans people with violence and threats). Practitioners should understand that high-profile politicians and media personalities wield large megaphones, and have some semblance of authority given their positions. Thus, attempts at undercutting such messages may be needed – perhaps by prebunking politicians' conspiracy theories (e.g., "many politicians are going to make claims about immigration in the coming weeks, but many of these claims may not be based on fact") or by debunking them (e.g., President Smith said that immigrants are the cause of many of our problems, but the available evidence shows the exact opposite") – particularly to audiences in which the NGO has built trust.

I conclude by discussing the ways that practitioners can help inform the study of conspiracy theories so that their goals, methods, and experiences can be better integrated into the academic research agenda and create the synergies needed for fruitful collaboration. First, I encourage practitioners to document for scholars the conditions on the ground. Scholars are often locked in ivory towers working with sanitized data; as such, more accounts of the conspiracy theory beliefs and believers would be helpful to scholars. Second, I encourage practitioners to test the efficacy of their programs. Study the effects of what you do and keep records of both successes and failures. If practitioners are not experienced at doing such testing, seeking out scholars to collaborate with may be valuable. Third, practitioners should help scholars prioritize which conspiracy theories to study. For example, if particular conspiracy theories are becoming troublesome in certain communities, then that should be communicated to scholars so that they can focus their research efforts there. Conspiracy theories have been, and will continue to be, part of the human experience. Therefore, limiting any harms that spring from them should continue to be a priority.

NOTES

1 Jason Stanley, "Buffalo Shooting: How White Replacement Theory Keeps Inspiring Mass Murder," *The Guardian*, update May 16 and May 23, 2022, https://www.theguardian.com/commentisfree/2022/may/15/buffalo-shooting-white-replacement-theory-inspires-mass.
2 Mattias Ekman, "The Great Replacement: Strategic Mainstreaming of Far-Right Conspiracy Claims," *Convergence* 28, no. 4 (2022): 1127–43, https://doi.org/10.1177/13548565221091983.
3 Nadim Asrar, "In India, WhatsApp Stirs Up Deadly Rumours," *Al Jazeera*, July 17, 2018, https://www.aljazeera.com/features/2018/7/17/in-india-whatsapp-stirs-up-deadly-rumours.
4 Jay Ulfelder, "The Hate Drags On," *Counting Crowds* (blog), Crowd Counting Consortium, May 15, 2023, https://countingcrowds.org/2023/05/15/the-hate-drags-on/.
5 Brandy Zadrozny, Ben Collins, and Tom Winter, "FBI Charges Massachusetts Woman with Boston Children's Hospital Bomb Threat," *NBC News*, September 15, 2022, https://www.nbcnews.com/tech/internet/fbi-charges-massachusetts-woman-boston-childrens-hospital-bomb-threat-rcna47973.
6 Donald Padgett, "Ohio Man Pleads Guilty to Firebombing Church over Drag Queen Events," *Advocate*, October 25, 2023, https://www.advocate.com/law/firebombing-drag-queen-church.

7 Joseph Uscinski and Joseph M. Parent, *American Conspiracy Theories* (New York: Oxford University Press, 2014).

8 Sarah Ann Gordon, *Hitler, Germans, and the "Jewish Question"* (Princeton, NJ: Princeton University Press, 1984).

9 Chaim Shinar, "Conspiracy Narratives in Russian Politics: From Stalin to Putin," *European Review* 26, no. 4 (2018): 648–60, https://doi.org/10.1017/S1062798718000376.

10 Peter T. Leeson and Jacob W. Russ, "Witch Trials," *The Economic Journal* 128, no. 613 (2018): 2066–105, https://doi.org/10.1111/ecoj.12498.

11 Richard Latner, "'Here Are No Newters': Witchcraft and Religious Discord in Salem Village and Andover," *New England Quarterly* 79, no. 1 (2006): 92–122, https://www.jstor.org/stable/20474413.

12 Kathryn S. Olmsted, "Conspiracy Theories in U.S. History," in Joseph E. Uscinski, ed., *Conspiracy Theories and the People Who Believe Them* (New York: Oxford University Press, 2018).

13 Victoria E. Pagán, "Toward a Model of Conspiracy Theory for Ancient Rome," *New German Critique* 35, no. 1 (2008): 27–49, https://www.jstor.org/stable/27669218.

14 Max Ehrenfreund, "Donald Trump Apparently Has a Brand-New Conspiracy Theory," *Washington Post*, January 15, 2016, https://www.washingtonpost.com/news/wonk/wp/2016/01/15/donald-trump-has-a-brand-new-conspiracy-theory/.

15 For example, Nicholas Difonzo, "Conspiracy Rumor Psychology," in Joseph E. Uscinski, ed., *Conspiracy Theories and the People Who Believe Them* (New York: Oxford University Press, 2018).

16 Jennifer M. Connolly et al., "Communicating to the Public in the Era of Conspiracy Theory," *Public Integrity* 21, no. 5 (2019): 469–76, https://doi.org/10.1080/10999922.2019.1603045.

17 Daniel Jolley, Silvia Mari, and Karen M. Douglas, "Consequences of Conspiracy Theories," in Michael Butter and Peter Knight, eds., *Routledge Handbook of Conspiracy Theories* (London: Routledge, 2020).

18 Doha Madani, Andrew Blankstein, and Ben Collins, "California Dad Killed His Kids over QAnon and 'Serpent DNA' Conspiracy Theories, Feds Claim," *NBC News*, August 11, 2021, https://www.nbcnews.com/news/us-news/california-dad-killed-his-kids-over-qanon-serpent-dna-conspiracy-n1276611.

19 Joseph Uscinski et al., "Cause and Effect: On the Antecedents and Consequences of Conspiracy Theory Beliefs," *Current Opinion in Psychology* 47 (2022): 101364, https://doi.org/10.1016/j.copsyc.2022.101364.

20 Joseph Uscinski and Adam Enders, *Conspiracy Theories: A Primer*, 2nd ed. (New York: Rowman & Littlefield, 2023).

21 Joseph Uscinski and Adam Enders, "What Is a Conspiracy Theory and Why Does It Matter?," *Critical Review* 35, no. 1–2 (2022): 148–69, https://doi.org/10.1080/08913811.2022.2115668.

22 Roland Imhoff and Pia Lamberty, "How Paranoid Are Conspiracy Believers? Toward a More Fine-Grained Understanding of the Connect and Disconnect between Paranoia and Belief in Conspiracy Theories," *European Journal of Social Psychology* 48, no. 7 (2018): 909–26, https://doi.org/10.1002/ejsp.2494.

23 M R. X. Dentith, "Conspiracy Theories and Philosophy: Bringing the Epistemology of a Freighted Term into the Social Sciences," in Joseph E. Uscinski, ed., *Conspiracy Theories and the People Who Believe Them* (New York: Oxford University Press, 2018).

24 Uscinski and Enders, *Conspiracy Theories.*

25 Neil Levy, "Radically Socialized Knowledge and Conspiracy Theories," *Episteme* 4, no. 2 (2007): 181–92, https://doi.org/10.3366/epi.2007.4.2.181.

26 Devan Ray Donaldson and Colin Bradley LeFevre, "Records, Trust, and Misinformation: Using Birtherism to Understand the Influence of Conspiracy Theories on Human Information Interactions," *Journal of the Association for Information Science and Technology* 73, no. 11 (2022): 1579–93, https://doi.org/10.1002/asi.24697.

27 Uscinski and Enders, "What Is a Conspiracy Theory and Why Does It Matter?"

28 Jeffrey Friedman, "False Beliefs, the Myth of 'Post-Truth,' and the Need for a Capacious Political Epistemology," *Political Epistemology* 1 (2021): 21–34.

29 Uscinski et al., "Cause and Effect."

30 Joseph Uscinski et al., "The Psychological and Political Correlates of Conspiracy Theory Beliefs," *Scientific Reports* 12, no. 1 (2022): 21672, https://doi.org/10.1038/s41598-022-25617-0.

31 Joseph Uscinski et al., "Why Do People Believe in Conspiracy Theories? The Role of Informational Cues and Predispositions," *Political Research Quarterly* 69, no. 1 (2016): 57–71, https://doi.org/10.1177/1065912915621621.

32 Adam Enders and Joseph Uscinski, "What's the Harm? An Interrogation of the Societal Impact of Conspiracy Theories and Potential Remedies," paper presented at Lies, Free Speech, and the Law Symposium, Knight First Amendment Institute at Columbia University, April 18, 2022, https://knightcolumbia.org/content/whats-the-harm.

33 Ryan L. Claassen and Michael J. Ensley, "Motivated Reasoning and Yard-Sign-Stealing Partisans: Mine Is a Likable Rogue, Yours Is a Degenerate Criminal," *Political Behavior* 38, no. 2 (2016): 317–35, https://psycnet.apa.org/doi/10.1007/s11109-015-9313-9.

34 John M. Carey, Brendan Nyhan, and Mingnan Liu, "An Inflated View of the Facts? How Preferences and Predispositions Shape Conspiracy Beliefs about the Deflategate Scandal," *Research & Politics* 3, no. 3 (2016), https://doi.org/10.1177/2053168016668671.

35 Kyle Hull, Clarisse Warren, and Kevin Smith, "Politics Makes Bastards of Us All: Why Moral Judgment Is Politically Situational," *Political Psychology* 45, no. 6 (2024): 1013–29, https://doi.org/10.1111/pops.12954.

36 Adam Enders et al., "Are Republicans and Conservatives More Likely to Believe Conspiracy Theories?," *Political Behavior* 45 (2023): 2001–24, https://doi.org/10.1007/s11109-022-09812-3.

37 Miles T. Armaly and Adam M. Enders, "'Why Me?' The Role of Perceived Victimhood in American Politics," *Political Behavior* 44 (2022): 1583–609, https://doi.org/10.1007/s11109-020-09662-x.

38 Andrew Guess, Brendan Nyhan, and Jason Reifler, "Selective Exposure to Misinformation: Evidence from the Consumption of Fake News during the 2016 US Presidential Campaign," Center for the Study of Democratic Politics, 2018, https://about.fb.com/wp-content/uploads/2018/01/fake-news-2016.pdf/.

39 Milton Lodge and Charles S. Taber, *The Rationalizing Voter* (New York: Cambridge University Press, 2013).

40 Shane Littrell et al., "Who Knowingly Shares False Political Information Online?," *Misinformation Review*, August 25, 2003, https://misinforeview.hks.harvard.edu/article/who-knowingly-shares-false-political-information-online/.

41 Brian F. Schaffner and Samantha Luks, "Misinformation or Expressive Responding? What an Inauguration Crowd Can Tell Us about the Source of Political Misinformation in Surveys," *Public Opinion Quarterly* 82, no. 1 (2018): 135–47, https://psycnet.apa.org/doi/10.1093/poq/nfx042.

42 James J. Fahey, "The Big Lie: Expressive Responding and Conspiratorial Beliefs in the United States," *Journal of Experimental Political Science* 10, no. 2 (2022): 1–12, https://doi.org/10.1017/XPS.2022.33.

43 Uscinski and Enders, "What Is a Conspiracy Theory and Why Does It Matter?"

44 Uscinski and Enders, *Conspiracy Theories.*

45 Peter Knight, ed., *Conspiracy Theories in American History*, 2 vols. (Santa Barbara, CA: ABC-CLIO, 2023).

46 Uscinski and Parent, *American Conspiracy Theories.*

47 Uscinski and Enders, *Conspiracy Theories.*

48 Kenzo Nera, Paul Bertin, and Olivier Klein, "Conspiracy Theories as Opportunistic Attributions of Power," *Current Opinion in Psychology* 47 (2022): 101381, https://doi.org/10.1016/j.copsyc.2022.101381; Kenzo Nera et al., "A Power-Challenging Theory of Society, or a Conservative Mindset?

Upward and Downward Conspiracy Theories as Ideologically Distinct Beliefs," *European Journal of Social Psychology* 51, no. 4–5 (2021): 740–57, https://doi.org/10.1002/ejsp.2769; Kenzo Nera, Iustina Procop, and Olivier Klen, "Comparing the Ideological Correlates of Anti-Government and Anti-Roma Conspiracy Beliefs in Romania," *Journal of Pacific Rim Psychology* 17 (2023), https://doi.org/10.1177/18344909231162276.

49 See Southern Poverty Law Centre, "Frank Gaffney, Jr.," accessed March 18, 2024, https://www.splcenter.org/resources/extremist-files/frank -gaffney-jr/.

50 Ekman, "The Great Replacement."

51 Yotam Ophir et al., "Weaponizing Reproductive Rights: A Mixed-Method Analysis of White Nationalists' Discussion of Abortions Online," *Information, Communication & Society* 26, no. 11 (2022): 2186–211, https://doi.org/10.1080/1369118X.2022.2077654.

52 Richard Landes and Steven T. Katz, eds., *The Paranoid Apocalypse* (New York: New York University Press, 2011).

53 Michal Bilewicz and Ireneusz Krzeminski, "Anti-Semitism in Poland and Ukraine: The Belief in Jewish Control as a Mechanism of Scapegoating," *International Journal of Conflict and Violence* 4, no. 2 (2010): 234–43, https://doi.org/10.4119/ijcv-2828.

54 David A. Hollinger, "Rich, Powerful, and Smart: Jewish Overrepresentation Should Be Explained Instead of Avoided or Mystified," *Jewish Quarterly Review* 94, no. 4 (2004): 595–602, https://archive.org /details/richpowerfulsmart.

55 Andrew S. Winston, "'Jews will not replace us!': Antisemitism, Interbreeding and Immigration in Historical Context," *American Jewish History* 105, no. 1 (2021): 1–24, https://dx.doi.org/10.1353/ajh.2021.0001.

56 Art Swift, "Majority in U.S. Still Believe JFK Killed in a Conspiracy," *Gallup News*, November 15, 2013, https://news.gallup.com/poll/165893 /majority-believe-jfk-killed-conspiracy.aspx.

57 Kevin Arceneaux and Rory Truex, "Donald Trump and the Lie," *Perspectives on Politics* 21, no. 3 (2022): 863–79, https://doi.org/10.1017 /S1537592722000901.

58 Hunter Geisel, "Rumors of 'Shadow Aliens' at Bayside Marketplace Go Viral after Large Fight among Teens Creates Chaos," *CBS News*, January 25, 2024, https://www.cbsnews.com/miami/news/rumors-of-shadow -aliens-at-bayside-marketplace-go-viral-after-large-fight-among-teens -creates-chaos/.

59 Karen Douglas, Jan-Willem van Prooijen, and Robbie M. Sutton, "Is the Label 'Conspiracy Theory' a Cause or a Consequence of Disbelief in Alternative Narratives?," *British Journal of Psychology* 113, no. 3 (2022): 575–90, https://doi.org/10.1111/bjop.12548.

60 Uscinski and Enders, "What Is a Conspiracy Theory and Why Does It Matter?"

61 Katharina Thalmann, *The Stigmatization of Conspiracy Theory since the 1950s: "A Plot to Make Us Look Foolish"* (New York: Routledge, 2019).

62 Jaron Harambam and Stef Aupers, "'I Am Not a Conspiracy Theorist': Relational Identifications in the Dutch Conspiracy Milieu," *Cultural Sociology* 11, no. 1 (2017): 113–29, https://doi.org/10.1177 /1749975516661959.

63 Michael Wood, "Some Dare Call It Conspiracy: Labeling Something a Conspiracy Theory Does Not Reduce Belief in It," *Political Psychology* 37, no. 5 (2016): 695–705, https://www.jstor.org/stable/44132919/.

64 Joseph Uscinski et al., "Have Beliefs in Conspiracy Theories Increased over Time?," *PLoS One* 17, no. 7 (2022): e0270429, https://doi.org/10.1371 /journal.pone.0270429.

65 M. Steven Smallpage, Adam Enders, and Joseph E. Uscinski, "The Partisan Contours of Conspiracy Theory Beliefs," *Research & Politics* 4, no. 4 (2017), https://doi.org/10.1177/2053168017746554.

66 Adam M. Enders et al., "On Modeling the Correlates of Conspiracy Thinking," *Scientific Reports* 13, no. 1 (2023): 8325, https://doi.org/10.1038 /s41598-023-34391-6.

67 Armaly and Enders, "'Why Me?'"

68 John Pollard, "Skinhead Culture: The Ideologies, Mythologies, Religions and Conspiracy Theories of Racist Skinheads," *Patterns of Prejudice* 50, no. 4–5 (2016): 398–419, https://doi.org/10.1080/0031322X.2016.1243349; Daniel Allington, David Hirsh, and Louise Katz, "Antisemitism Is Predicted by Anti-Hierarchical Aggression, Totalitarianism, and Belief in Malevolent Global Conspiracies," *Humanities and Social Sciences Communications* 10, no. 1 (2023): 155, https://doi.org/10.1057/s41599 -023-01624-y.

69 Brendan Nyhan and Thomas Zeitzoff, "Conspiracy and Misperception Belief in the Middle East and North Africa," *The Journal of Politics* 80, no. 4 (2018): 1400–4, https://doi.org/10.1086/698663.

70 Basil Müller, "Bad Social Norms Rather Than Bad Believers – Examining the Role of Social Norms in Bad Beliefs," *Synthese* 203, no. 2 (2024), https://doi.org/10.1007/s11229-024-04483-5.

71 Matthew J. Hornsey et al., "Individual, Intergroup and Nation-Level Influences on Belief in Conspiracy Theories," *Nature Reviews Psychology* 2, no. 2 (2023): 85–97, https://doi.org/10.1038/s44159-022-00133-0.

72 Joseph E. Uscinski, Casey Klofstad, and Matthew D. Atkinson, "What Drives Conspiratorial Beliefs? The Role of Informational Cues and Predispositions," *Political Research Quarterly* 69, no. 1 (2016): 57–71, https://doi.org/10.1177/1065912915621621.

73 Dominik Stecula, Ozan Kuru, and Kathleen Hall Jamieson, "How Trust in Experts and Media Use Affect Acceptance of Common Anti-Vaccination Claims," *Misinformation Review* 1, no. 1 (2020), https://misinforeview.hks.harvard.edu/article/users-of-social-media-more-likely-to-be-misinformed-about-vaccines/.

74 Uscinski et al., "The Psychological and Political Correlates."

75 Shauna M. Bowes, Thomas H. Costello, and Arber Tasimi, "The Conspiratorial Mind: A Meta-Analytic Review of Motivational and Personological Correlates," *Psychological Bulletin* 149, no. 5–6 (2023): 259–93, https://doi.org/10.1037/bul0000392.

76 Uscinski and Parent, *American Conspiracy Theories*.

77 Hugo Drochon, "Who Believes in Conspiracy Theories in Great Britain and Europe?," in Joseph E. Uscinski, ed., *Conspiracy Theories and the People Who Believe Them* (New York: Oxford University Press, 2018).

78 Uscinski, Klofstad, and Atkinson, "What Drives Conspiratorial Beliefs?"

79 Karen M. Douglas et al., "Understanding Conspiracy Theories," *Advances in Political Psychology* 40, no. 1 (2019): 3–35, https://doi.org/10.1111/pops.12568

80 Joseph Uscinski et al., "Why Do People Believe COVID-19 Conspiracy Theories?," *Misinformation Review* 1 (2020): 1–12, https://misinforeview.hks.harvard.edu/article/why-do-people-believe-covid-19-conspiracy-theories/.

81 Smallpage, Enders, and Uscinski, "The Partisan Contours of Conspiracy Theory Beliefs."

82 Uscinski and Parent, *American Conspiracy Theories*.

83 Patrick J. Leman and Marco Cinnirella, "Beliefs in Conspiracy Theories and the Need for Cognitive Closure," *Frontiers in Psychology* 4 (2013): Article 378, https://doi.org/10.3389/fpsyg.2013.00378; Jakub Šrol, "Individual Differences in Epistemically Suspect Beliefs: The Role of Analytic Thinking and Susceptibility to Cognitive Biases," *Thinking & Reasoning* 28, no. 1 (2022): 125–62, https://doi.org/10.1080/13546783.2021.1938220.

84 Adam Enders and Steven M. Smallpage, "Who Are Conspiracy Theorists? A Comprehensive Approach to Explaining Conspiracy Beliefs," *Social Science Quarterly* 100, no. 6 (2019): 2017–32, https://doi.org/10.1111/ssqu.12711.

85 Uscinski et al., "The Psychological and Political Correlates"; Michael V. Bronstein et al., "Belief in Fake News Is Associated with Delusionality, Dogmatism, Religious Fundamentalism, and Reduced Analytic Thinking," *Journal of Applied Research in Memory and Cognition* 8, no. 1 (2018): 108–17, https://doi.org/10.1016/j.jarmac.2018.09.005.

86 Talia Leibovitz et al., "COVID-19 Conspiracy Beliefs: Relations with Anxiety, Quality of Life, and Schemas," *Personality and Individual Differences* 175 (2021): 110704, https://doi.org/10.1016/j.paid.2021.110704.

87   Uscinski et al., "Have Beliefs in Conspiracy Theories Increased Over Time?"

88   Moreno Mancosu and Salvatore Vassallo, "The Life Cycle of Conspiracy Theories: Evidence from a Long-Term Panel Survey on Conspiracy Beliefs in Italy," *Italian Political Science Review/Rivista Italiana di Scienza Politica* 52, no. 1 (2022): 1–17, https://doi.org/10.1017/ipo.2021.57.

89   Stephen B. Thomas and Sandra C. Quinn, "The Tuskegee Syphilis Study, 1932 to 1972: Implications for HIV Education and AIDS Risk Education Programs in the Black Community," *American Journal of Public Health* 81, no. 11 (1991): 1498–1505, https://doi.org/10.2105/AJPH.81.11.1498.

90   Daniel Jolley, Rose Meleady, and Karen M. Douglas, "Exposure to Intergroup Conspiracy Theories Promotes Prejudice Which Spreads across Groups," *British Journal of Psychology* 111, no. 1 (2020): 17–35, https://doi.org/10.1111/bjop.12385.

91   Enders et al., "Are Republicans and Conservatives More Likely to Believe Conspiracy Theories?"

92   Tom W. Smith, "A Review: The Holocaust Denial Controversy," *The Public Opinion Quarterly* 59, no. 2 (1995): 269–95, https://doi.org/10.1086/269473.

93   Jonathan Judaken, "Jewish Capitalists, Jewish Bolsheviks: Conspiracy Thinking and Modern Judeophobia," *Modern Intellectual History* 18, no. 3 (2021): 877–87, https://doi.org/10.1017/S1479244320000098.

94   Milan Obaidi et al., "The 'Great Replacement' Conspiracy: How the Perceived Ousting of Whites Can Evoke Violent Extremism and Islamophobia," *Group Processes & Intergroup Relations* 25, no. 7 (2022): 1675–95, https://doi.org/10.1177/13684302211028293.

95   James Kirchick, "The Long, Sordid History of the Gay Conspiracy Theory: Today's Right-Wing Campaign against 'Groomers' Is America's Latest Moral Panic," *Intelligencer*, May 21, 2022, https://nymag.com/intelligencer/2022/05/the-long-sordid-history-of-the-gay-conspiracy-theory.html.

96   Jolley, Meleady, and Douglas, "Exposure to Intergroup Conspiracy Theories."

97   Stanley, "Buffalo Shooting."

98   Casey Ryan Kelly, "COVID-19 Conspiracy Rhetoric and Other Primal Fantasies," *Quarterly Journal of Speech* 109, no. 2 (2022): 132–53, https://doi.org/10.1080/00335630.2022.2142654.

99   Daniel Williams, "The Marketplace of Rationalizations," *Economics and Philosophy* 39, no. 1 (2023): 99–123, https://doi.org/10.1017/S0266267121000389.

100   Uscinski et al., "Cause and Effect."

101   Uscinski et al., "The Psychological and Political Correlates."

102   Adam Enders et al., "How Anti-Social Personality Traits and Anti-Establishment Views Promote Beliefs in Election Fraud, QAnon,

and COVID-19 Conspiracy Theories and Misinformation," *American Politics Research* 51, no. 2 (2022): 247–59, https://doi.org/10.1177/1532673X221139434.

103 Enders et al., "On Modeling the Correlates."

104 Daniel Jolley et al., "Belief in Conspiracy Theories and Intentions to Engage in Everyday Crime," *British Journal of Social Psychology* 58, no. 3 (2019): 534–49, https://doi.org/10.1111/bjso.12311; Daniel Jolley and Jenny L. Paterson, "Pylons Ablaze: Examining the Role of 5G COVID-19 Conspiracy Beliefs and Support for Violence," *British Journal of Social Psychology* 59, no. 3 (2020): 628–40, https://psycnet.apa.org/doi/10.1111/bjso.12394.

105 Armaly and Enders, "'Why Me?'"

106 Zadrozny, Collins, and Winter, "FBI Charges Massachusetts Woman"; Matt Lavietes, "Gay California Legislator Gets 2nd Bomb Threat This Year," *NBC News*, December 7, 2022, https://www.nbcnews.com/nbc-out/out-politics-and-policy/gay-california-lawmaker-receives-2nd-bomb-threat-year-rcna60530.

107 Adam M. Enders et al., "On the Relationship between Conspiracy Theory Beliefs, Misinformation, and Vaccine Hesitancy," *PLoS ONE* 17, no. 10 (2022): e0276082, https://journals.plos.org/plosone/.

108 Cecilie Traberg, Jon Roozenbeek, and Sander fan der Linden, "Psychological Inoculation against Misinformation: Current Evidence and Future Directions," *The ANNALS of the American Academy of Political and Social Science* 700, no. 1 (2022): 136–51, https://doi.org/10.1177/00027162221087936.

109 Anna Helfers and Mirjam Ebersbach, "The Differential Effects of a Governmental Debunking Campaign concerning COVID-19 Vaccination Misinformation," *Journal of Communication in Healthcare* 16, no. 1 (2023): 113–21, https://doi.org/10.1080/17538068.2022.2047497.

110 Adam J. Berinsky, "Rumors and Health Care Reform: Experiments in Political Misinformation," *British Journal of Political Science* 47, no. 2 (2015): 241–62, https://doi.org/10.1017/S0007123415000186.

111 Brendan Nyhan and Jason Reifler, "When Corrections Fail: The Persistence of Political Misperceptions," *Political Behavior* 32, no. 2 (2010): 303–30, https://psycnet.apa.org/doi/10.1007/s11109-010-9112-2; Brendan Nyhan, Jason Reifler, and Peter Ubel, "The Hazards of Correcting Myths about Health Care Reform," *Medical Care* 51, no. 2 (2013): 127–32, https://doi.org/10.1097/MLR.0b013e318279486b.

112 Anthony Lantian et al., "Stigmatized Beliefs: Conspiracy Theories, Anticipated Negative Evaluation of the Self, and Fear of Social Exclusion," *European Journal of Social Psychology* 48, no. 7 (2018): 939–54, https://doi.org/10.1002/ejsp.2498.

113 Gábor Orosz et al., "Changing Conspiracy Beliefs through Rationality and Ridiculing," *Frontiers in Psychology* 7 (2016): Article 1525, https:// doi.org/10.3389/fpsyg.2016.01525.

114 Orosz et al., "Changing Conspiracy Beliefs."

115 Tovia Smith, "Experts in Cult Deprogramming Step In to Help Believers in Conspiracy Theories," NPR, March 2, 2021, https://www.npr .org/2021/03/02/972970805/experts-in-cult-deprogramming-step-in -to-help-believers-in-conspiracy-theories.

116 Matthew A. Baum et al., "The Political Consequences of Depression: How Conspiracy Beliefs, Participatory Inclinations, and Depression Affect Support for Political Violence," *American Journal of Political Science* 68, no. 22 (2024): 575–94, https://doi.org/10.1111/ajps.12827.

117 Daniel Wood and Geoff Brumfiel, "Pro-Trump Counties Now Have Far Higher COVID Death Rates," NPR, May 19, 2022, https://www.npr .org/2022/05/19/1098543849/pro-trump-counties-continue-to-suffer -far-higher-covid-death-tolls.

118 Madani, Blankstein, and Collins, "California Dad Killed His Kids."

119 Enders et al., "How Anti-Social Personality Traits."

120 Baum et al., "The Political Consequences of Depression."

121 Ben Collins, "How QAnon Rode the Pandemic to New Heights – and Fueled the Viral Anti-Mask Phenomenon," *NBC News*, August 14, 2020, https://www.nbcnews.com/tech/tech-news/how-qanon-rode -pandemic-new-heights-fueled-viral-anti-mask-n1236695; Madani, Blankstein, and Collins, "California Dad Killed His Kids."

Editor's Introduction to Chapter 9

Debates about how to handle hateful speech aren't new. Hateful expressions can cause anguish – famously, for example, the 1970s rally by American Nazis in a community of Holocaust survivors in Skokie, Illinois.

Some Americans want to use law to prohibit such expressions. They point to various European models that outlaw certain types of speech (Holocaust denial, for example) and suggest that America should do the same. Free speech advocates (myself among them) point out that it isn't as if Europe has less hateful speech and hateful political challenges because of their laws. In fact, during my years at AJC, it was frustrating to challenge certain European officials to speak out more about hateful acts, pointing out that if an antisemitic attack happened in a US city, mayors and other politicians would be lining up to condemn it. The Europeans sometimes hid behind the "hate speech" laws, saying they couldn't speak out because it would be seen as interfering with a legal process.

Further, having lived during the 1960s and 1970s, and witnessing the use of law against the civil rights movement and the anti–Vietnam War movement, I worry about giving government the ability to declare certain ideas out of bounds, since government will go after speech *it* doesn't like, not speech you or I might not like. In addition to the First Amendment problems of this approach, it reduces the paradigm to a false one: either outlaw the speech or ignore it. For example, on December 5, 2023, the US House of Representative's committee hearing with university presidents about antisemitism confused the matter further. Presidents were condemned for refusing to say that calling for the genocide of Jews would lead to discipline. Lost in this binary were two things: First, the fundamental difference between pure expression of an idea (no matter how ugly), on one hand, and true threats, harassment, intimidation, bullying, and discrimination, on the other. Second, think about neo-Nazi and former Ku Klux Klan leader David Duke. When he was a student at Louisiana State University in the late 1960s and early 1970s, he was an advocate of sending all Black people back to Africa and of exterminating Jews. On one occasion he wore a Nazi uniform. He was widely and correctly condemned for his speech. He likely would have loved to have been disciplined – it would have made him a free speech "martyr."

So if outlawing speech is legally impermissible and would likely backfire, how do you reduce the impact and volume of hateful speech? I've always encouraged counterspeech because it makes sense – hateful ideas are being promoted, and one way to oppose hateful ideas is to shine a light on them, expose them, debunk them, and explain why, despite perhaps having some level of attraction, they are based on faulty premises and are destructive to ideals many people hold dear. One of the earliest examples I know of this approach was when Teddy Roosevelt was New York City Police Commissioner in the late 1800s, and a preacher from Berlin was coming to the city to, in Roosevelt's words, "preach a crusade against the Jews." The Jewish community asked Roosevelt to "prevent him from speaking and not to give him police protection." Roosevelt told them that this "was impossible; and if possible would have been undesirable because it would make him a martyr. The proper thing was to make him ridiculous. Accordingly I detailed for his protection a Jew sergeant and a score or two of Jew policemen."[1]

I serve on the US Holocaust Memorial Council's Committee on Holocaust Denial and State-Sponsored Antisemitism. Years ago, Susan Benesch, a professor at American University, spoke to the committee about her work founding and running the Dangerous Speech Project. Her focus was on the relationship between speech and violence. Unlike some others who focused on "hate speech," her key points were (1) that not all speech leading to violence was hateful (although much was), (2) that the default answer of censorship was counterproductive, (3) that paying attention to "dangerous speech" could be a predictor of future genocides, and (4) that speech could be used to reduce the chance of violence. When I established the Center for the Study of Hate at Bard in 2018, I wanted Bard faculty and students to hear about the Dangerous Speech Project, and brought Susan's colleague, anthropologist Cathy Buerger, to campus. In 2022, Cathy wrote a first-of-its-kind report about the effectiveness of counterspeech. As I said, there are philosophical and tactical reasons to oppose censorship as the answer to hateful speech – focusing on what word one wants to censor, for example, at a university, blinds us to remedies that are more likely to work (like innovative courses, surveys, training, and so forth). But is the old quip that the answer to bad speech is good speech actually correct? I invited Cathy to expand upon her findings. Counterspeech sometimes is defined in a narrow way – x says this, y says that in reply. I also asked her to think about counterspeech more broadly, focusing on systemic ways to make hateful speech less likely to be used, promoted, and effective.

She asks us to look at what we want counterspeech to do. Is it effective in changing the attitudes or behavior of hateful speakers? Does counterspeech have an impact on the larger audience that might have heard the hateful speaker? What are the variables that might make counterspeech more effective? Does it matter who the counter-speaker is? Their race? Their stature (and thus "level of influence")? Does "bystander intervention" (such as people seeing hateful things on social media and commenting) work? Are there differences between counterspeech's effectiveness depending on the venue or media (person-to-person, on the internet, etc.)? Are there things NGOs and the rest of us can do to create a climate in which hateful speech is less effective and counterspeech more so? Are there ways to use new and emerging technologies in this effort, and what are the upsides and downsides of doing so? Given Uscinski's observations of how conspiracy theories work, and how to counter them, what are the implications for how we use counterspeech? All of these considerations obviously matter when NGOs (and the rest of us) think about how and when to use their voices against hate.

NOTE

1 Theodore Roosevelt, *The Autobiography of Theodore Roosevelt* (Overland Park, KS: Digireads.com Publishing, 2019), 136.

9 Counterspeech: NGO Strategies for Responding to Online Hateful Speech

CATHY BUERGER

Hateful speech can inflict harm on individuals and society in various ways. It can have a profound psychological impact on those targeted and can contribute to social divisions by fueling animosity between different groups and reinforcing stereotypes, prejudice, and discrimination. The normalization of discriminatory attitudes is another consequence, making it challenging to combat intolerance. Beyond verbal abuse, some speech has the potential to move its audience toward condoning or committing violence against members of another group (i.e., dangerous speech).

By eroding trust and cooperation, hateful speech undermines social cohesion, hindering efforts to build bridges between diverse communities. Although there is no consensus definition for hateful speech, there are two features shared by all definitions: a reference to hatred and the idea that the content expresses or engenders hatred for a person or people because they are part of some kind of human group. The United Nations, in its "Strategy and Plan of Action on Hate Speech," offered this broad definition: "any kind of communication in speech, writing or behaviour, that attacks or uses pejorative or discriminatory language with reference to a person or a group on the basis of who they are, in other words, based on their religion, ethnicity, nationality, race, colour, descent, gender or other identity factor."[1] Hateful speech can intensify existing inequalities and reinforce systemic discrimination, impeding progress toward the social justice that so many anti-hatred NGOs seek. It is therefore crucial to address hateful speech in order to undermine its harmful consequences, but care must also be taken to protect freedom of expression, a fundamental right.

One method of responding to hatred while upholding freedom of expression is counterspeech. The Dangerous Speech Project defines counterspeech as "any direct response to hateful or harmful speech which seeks to undermine it." The belief that it is better to reply to bad, and especially false, speech instead of banning it is often traced back to US Supreme Court Justice Louis D. Brandeis in a 1927 lawsuit called *Whitney v. California*. In a decision upholding the conviction of a California woman who had worked to establish the Communist Labor Party of America, Brandeis declared: "If there be time to expose through discussion the falsehood and fallacies, to avert the evil by the processes of education, the remedy to be applied is more speech, not enforced silence."[2]

For NGOs working to combat hatred, this understanding of the "marketplace of ideas" may seem daunting – especially considering the speed and scale at which hateful speech spreads online. What types of counterspeech responses are effective and practical for NGOs? In this chapter, I argue for a broad understanding of what it means for counterspeech to be "effective." When one speaks online, there are many people who may see it (the "troll" who inspired the response being only one such audience member). This provides an opportunity for NGOs to use strategic responses to hatred as part of larger public education campaigns.

Methodology

This chapter draws on over five years of empirical study of responses to hatred online. At the Dangerous Speech Project, we have documented many individuals and groups from around the world responding to online content that they believe is hateful, and I have interviewed over fifty people who participated in these responses. We located them in many ways – through online observation, mentions in the press, and word of mouth. The semi-structured interviews were generally done over Zoom, using a base list of questions that was adapted and expanded to capture the particularities of each effort.

The counterspeech examples included in this chapter embody a range of communicative and rhetorical techniques, including showing empathy, using humor, and providing support to those targeted by hateful speech. Some of the counterspeech efforts were planned in advance, while others emerged spontaneously, usually in response to a surge of hateful content online. In my conversations with them, interviewees described their motivations and strategies, their challenges, and their definitions of "success." I sought to understand the goals of the counterspeakers, asking them whom they were trying to reach and why. This rich qualitative data are useful in understanding the variety of reasons why NGOs may wish to engage in counterspeech as well as the methods through which they could do so.

How Counterspeech Works

People who engage in counterspeech (i.e., "counterspeakers") do so for a variety of reasons. Some believe that their response may be able to change the minds of those who are promoting hatred online. This can be extremely difficult to do, and researchers are split on whether engaging this way is an effective method of fighting hatred online. Some argue that counterspeech *can* change the behavior of those posting hateful content, convincing them to post, or seek out, less of such content.[3]

Other researchers suggest that counterspeech can change behavior if the specific circumstances are correct, for example, when there are more counterspeakers than hateful speakers and the opinions held by the hateful speakers are relatively moderate.[4] Still others found no evidence that counterspeech was an effective method of changing behavior among those posting hatred[5] or that it can even potentially make things worse, giving attention to "trolls" who seek it and amplifying the harmful content.

For some, these findings suggest that the best course of action is to ignore hateful speech online, following the common maxim that one should not "feed the trolls." But years of research with counterspeakers suggests that there are other pathways through which counterspeech may be more effective at challenging hatred. Interviews with counterspeakers revealed that most do not engage in the practice of responding to hatred with the goal of changing the mind or behavior of those posting such content. Instead, many described trying to reach the "silent readers" (or "byscrollers," as one called them).

Counterspeakers described multiple reasons for trying to reach this audience instead of the original speaker. Many said that they simply did not think it was a good use of time to engage with those posting hateful comments online, agreeing with researchers that the chances of changing their behavior were low and they risked emboldening those posting hatred online by engaging with them directly. As one counterspeaker explained, "The trolls will not be affected. They get energy from being debated with. It's other people that you try to stop from joining in on the hateful speech."

The decision to address an alternative audience is not solely driven by skepticism regarding the conversion of trolls, however. Counterspeakers also posit that those reading comments, but not writing their own, are an audience more able to be persuaded – either to change their mind or behavior. Some of those people, group members posit, will not have made up their mind yet about the topic being discussed, and therefore could be potentially swayed in different directions by the ideas in the comments. Those working to shift policy or public opinion on social issues such as abortion,[6] migration,[7] or LGBTQI + issues[8] often call this audience the "moveable middle," people who do not currently hold strong opinions about a particular topic and are therefore able to be swayed toward one side or the other. Activists generally see those in the moveable middle as the ideal target of messaging as they are more willing to listen sincerely to an argument than those who openly oppose it. There is support for this strategy in the literature. For example, researchers have found that even a small group of counterspeakers can influence the discourse within an online space if the audience that they are speaking to holds relatively moderate views.[9]

Counterspeech may also be able to have an impact on overall online discourse by encouraging others who already agree with the counterspeakers to speak up and add their own thoughts to comment threads. Researchers have found that once there is one counterspeech comment in a thread containing hatred, others often follow.[10] While this may not impact the presence of hateful comments, it can change the proportion of hateful to non-hateful comments, which, in turn, can change the overall effect of such speech.

Many scholars have also documented a so-called "contagion effect" online, noting that internet users take cues from others as to how they engage. Soo-Hye Han and LeAnn Brazeal found that people exposed to civil comments were more likely to write a civil comment themselves, but they did not find that exposure to incivility increased uncivil expressions (overall expressions of incivility were low in their study).[11] Conversely, other studies did find that exposure to anti-social or negative comments make a person more likely to post an anti-social comment.[12] Counterspeech can therefore have a positive impact on discourse in a space by modeling constructive conversation.

Lastly, counterspeech may positively impact those being targeted by hatred online. It can provide a sense of solidarity or a reminder that not everyone believes the generally false claims being made by those spreading hatred. For example, Magdalena Obermaier and colleagues showed Muslim study participants an Islamophobic statement, either by itself or accompanied by a counterspeech response, finding that when participants saw both the hatred and the counterspeech, they were less likely to respond hatefully themselves than when they saw just the Islamophobic comment.[13] As discussed in more detail below, some counterspeech efforts also attempt to provide support to those targeted by hateful speech by connecting them with services or by taking on the labor of responding so that it does not fall on those being targeted by the hatred.

How NGOs Can Engage

There are many reasons why an NGO may want to engage in counterspeech. In the sections below, I outline several ways through which organizations could do so.

1. Engaging as Subject Matter Experts

Dangerous and hateful speech is often false, which is not surprising, as it describes whole groups of human beings in appalling terms. Unfortunately, people can be quite easily persuaded of misinformation (false assertions) or disinformation (false assertions that are spread knowingly or intentionally). And when falsehoods are frightening, people may be even more likely to spread them quickly. A prime example of this occurred during the COVID-19 pandemic. During this period, misinformation and disinformation about the disease, its causes, and its cures were rampant. False remedies, misleading statistics, and baseless rumors about the origins of the virus spread quickly and widely, hindering efforts to combat the spread of the virus and adhere to effective public health measures. The World Health Organization along with others deemed the situation an "infodemic," a time in which there is too much information – much of it false – spreading quickly and making it difficult to discern what is true.

Founded in March of 2020, IMPACT (Illinois Medical Professional Action Collaborative Team) was created with the goal of amplifying accurate information being posted by doctors on social media. They created a private group messaging thread, connecting the Twitter (now X) accounts of thirty-nine medical practitioners from various specialties and racial and ethnic backgrounds. When combined, the accounts had 320,000 followers.[14] During the chaotic early days of the COVID-19 pandemic, the associated health professionals could communicate with each other privately through the messaging thread, and then IMPACT's organizational account would post accurate guidance and share posts from the associated medical professionals in order to counter health misinformation. This model allowed the content created by health professionals to reach a much larger audience than if they were each just posting on their own, helping to cut through the sea of information that existed during the infodemic.

Anti-hatred organizations and other affinity-based groups can, and often do, similarly use their expertise to counter hateful misinformation related to their work. For example, in 2023, amid a fierce disinformation campaign making false claims about the "harms" of gender-affirming care,[15] GLAAD posted on X (formerly Twitter), "Good morning! A reminder that healthcare for transgender people is settled science. Every major medical association supports this critical life-saving care," linking to a list on their website of each medical association's formal statement.[16] This post does not directly engage with the people posting misinformation, but instead addresses the audience, leveraging GLAAD's large platform to provide easy-to-access, factual information.

NGOs can also engage in this type of response by supporting, resharing, and, in general, amplifying the counterspeech of others who are working to counter hateful misinformation and disinformation related to the NGOs' missions. This method of doing counterspeech may be particularly attractive for small organizations or others that do not have the funding or capacity available to develop a new counterspeech project.

2. Fundraising as Counterspeech

Occasionally, organizations create campaigns that uphold norms against hatred while also raising funds for their (or another) organization. In fact, the fundraising is often done in the names of those posting hatred in an effort to get them to stop. The idea is to respond to online content with a real-world consequence that would appall its author, such as responding to a white supremacist by donating money to an organization that supports refugees. These Project Lemonade campaigns, as they are called in a report co-published by the Bard Center for the Study of Hate, Western States Center, and the Montana Human Rights Network, have been used since the 1990s in the United States.[17]

One example of this is Germany's Donate the Hate campaign, created by an organization called Rechts gegen Rechts (now called Hass Hilft or "Hate Helps" in English). In 2014, the organization sponsored an "involuntary walkathon" to accompany an annual neo-Nazi march in the town of Wunsiedel in Bavaria. Unbeknownst to those participating in the march, townspeople and activists "sponsored" each of the march's 250 participants, pledging that for each meter that one of the neo-Nazis walked, they would donate a particular amount of money to EXIT Deutschland, a group that helps people leave extremist groups in Germany. By the end of the march, the campaign had raised 10,000 euros.

The walkathon made international news.[18] After the success of the walkathon, Hass Hilft decided to move its efforts online, using a similar strategy. They called the program Donate the Hate. When people saw a hateful comment on Facebook, they could send the URL to Hass Hilft directly, sometimes along with a donation of one euro. The organization would then check the comment and the context in which it was posted to make sure that it conformed to its definition of hate comments: those that "humiliate, denigrate or belittle human dignity, or incite or threaten violence, based on [people's] actual or presumed affiliation to a social group, political views, social status or simply because of external characteristics."[19] If the comment met their definition, it sent a direct reply to its author.

The replies were generally humorous, such as "Right, extremely generous. Thanks Dirk W., you have automatically donated 1€ to a refugee project and EXIT Germany with your hate comment!" They were posted as images, all brightly colored with polka dots, adding to the lighthearted, sardonic feel. The campaign then also took a screenshot of the reply and posted it on its own Facebook page, making sure to remove the profile picture and the author's last name before doing so.

For Fabian Wichmann, creator of the Donate the Hate project, the point of the effort was always to "troll the haters" while also supporting communities targeted by hatred and helping to educate the audience reading the exchanges. As he said, "The comments that we are replying to are very hard comments. Some haters say things like, 'Let's open the doors of Auschwitz.' The guy who comments in that way knows what he writes. So I don't think I interact for changes. I want to act to irritate – to make the hate visible. To say 'I recognize the hate and I laugh at it.'"

Other organizations have also tried similar strategies. In 2016, a UK-based immigrant assistance NGO called Calais Action created a project called TrollAid. As the organization grew, it began receiving numerous hateful comments on its social media pages, primarily directed at the immigrants seeking to cross between France and Britain through the city of Calais.[20] The organization decided to start responding to the comments posted on its Twitter (now X) and Facebook pages with information about their organization, a link to a fundraising page, and an invitation for individuals to use the link to donate in the troll's name. It also encouraged others to use the link and strategy on other anti-immigrant comments that they saw on social media. Calais Action then tracked how much money was raised in a particular troll's name, and, if the comment was made on their own pages, later returned to let the troll know how much was raised in their name. The founder of the project stated that the goal was "to raise money, but also to annoy the trolls and put them off posting. Hopefully make them think about what they're doing and change their opinion."

In both cases, the NGOs involved leveraged their platforms and their followers' desires to fight hatred into a campaign that raised funds while creating unfavorable consequences for those posting hatred.

3. Change the Conversation through Counternarrative

Sometimes, people and organizations do not just want to reply to whatever hateful narratives are already circulating; they want to promote an entirely different story. Counternarratives, stories that challenge or oppose another view of a particular topic, issue, or event, can help advance those goals. They present an alternative interpretation, analysis, or understanding of historical events, social issues, cultural norms, or political ideologies.

Counternarrative campaigns are generally developed to challenge prevailing ideas or beliefs that support stereotypes, oppression, or exclusion. They aim to provide a voice to those who are often unheard or misrepresented in mainstream narratives. Counternarrative campaigns are also frequently used to challenge extremism. Short videos, ads, or even video games designed to go viral with a target audience are a common form for counternarrative campaigns.

One example is the project Average Mohamed, a series of animated videos about a Somali immigrant living in the United States, created by an NGO with the same name. The videos were designed to "create messages using Islamic principles that promote peace and encourage democracy" and "empower young Muslims through counter ideology messages and discourage them from joining Islamist-extremist groups."[21] For example, one video titled "A Muslim in the West" focuses on the identity crisis that young Muslims living in the West may experience – feeling that they must choose between the "old" ways and the "new." The video tells them to reject the false claims made by extremists that they must choose only one. Instead, they should see themselves as ambassadors, able to experience the best of both worlds.

Another such campaign was released by the International Rescue Committee (IRC) along with YouTube Creators for Change in 2017. They created a series of nine YouTube videos called #MoreThanARefugee, in which refugees interacted with YouTube creators and discussed their lives. The primary goal of the videos' creators was to show refugees – in Greece, Jordan, Serbia, Uganda, and the United States – as full people with interests, experiences, and goals that extend beyond their identities as refugees, something that challenged the often hateful and false anti-refugee narratives that often spread during times of rapid migration.

In both of these counternarrative campaigns, the NGOs involved decided on specific counter messages and then created sharable content that could reach a large audience. In other cases, however, counternarrative efforts grow through grassroot participation, often on social media around a common hashtag. One example of this type of response is the #MyFriend campaign, launched in 2015 by Burmese activist and former political prisoner Wai Wai Nu. Dangerous speech targeting Muslims in Myanmar – especially on social media – has received attention from scholars and human rights practitioners, and in 2018, United Nations investigators said that social media played a "determining role" in the campaign of crimes against humanity and genocide in which the Myanmar military killed more than 10,000 Rohingya Muslims.[22]

The #MyFriend campaign encouraged Burmese people to post selfies with friends of different religions and ethnicities along with the hashtags #MyFriend and #Friendshiphasnoboundaries with the goal of reducing "all forms of discrimination, hatred, hate speech, and extreme racism based on religion, ethnicity, nationality, color and gender" in Myanmar and encouraging "love and friendship" between groups. In Myanmar during this time, directly speaking out against the government meant risking prison or worse. The #MyFriend campaign was a subtle but clear rejection of messages teaching that Rohingya Muslims were a threat to Myanmar and its Buddhist majority.

4. Providing Support to Those Targeted by Hatred

Most NGOs that do counterspeech tend to focus on challenging the harmful speech – either by providing clarifying and authoritative information to the audience, condemning the hateful speech, or by promoting counternarratives that challenge the false assumptions underlying hateful comments. Some, however, take a different approach and place their primary focus on supporting those who have been harmed by the speech. At the Dangerous Speech Project, we consider these responses to be counterspeech because they seek to undermine the capacity of the hateful speech to cause harm. As the examples below demonstrate, providing support for the targets of hatred can come in many forms. Some seek to provide emotional support, while others help connect those harmed by hate and harassment with services.

One well-known effort is HeartMob, a tool launched in 2016 by an NGO called Right to Be (formerly HollaBack) to provide those experiencing online harassment with support. After experiencing harassment, individuals could submit a help request, appealing for a variety of forms of support, including assistance formally reporting the harassment or having HeartMob volunteers (called "Heartmobbers") send supportive messages. These supportive messages are designed to drown out the negative messages in someone's social media feed.

A study of the program conducted by Lindsay Blackwell and colleagues found that as of February 2017, Heartmobbers had taken a total of 4,555 support actions, with supportive messages being the most common type of action. The study found that help requests received a median of 41.5 support messages and 46.5 "Got Backs" (similar to the Facebook "Like" button).[23] This "mob" of support helps to overpower the harassment received by the individual while bolstering a feeling of solidarity among the person and an online community of bystanders. Right to Be continues to offer space for users to share their stories of harassment and also provides a resource library of tools and training for those who want to learn how best to respond to harassment.

Another very different approach to providing support to those targeted by hatred is Bye Felipe, an Instagram account on which women share the hostile, vitriolic responses they get from men they have rejected or ignored on dating apps. Alexandra Tweten started the account in 2014 after a private Facebook group discussion made her realize that she was far from alone, as a woman who had received terrible messages on dating apps from men after turning them down. Dozens of women posted screenshots of vitriolic messages they had received. "I was like 'Wow! I thought I was the only one!'" said Tweten.

Her original goal was to make fun of men who became hostile after being rejected, and in doing so, empower the women who had received the awful messages. After the account was covered in *The Atlantic*, it went viral, gaining about 25,000 followers in three weeks. (By January 2024, it had 426,000 followers.) Once that happened, Tweten felt there was an opportunity for larger impact: "It was kind of like, 'Maybe I can use this to start a national conversation about online harassment against women. Maybe I could show other men what it's like to be a woman.' And also just giving women a voice to talk about the things that are difficult and make them feel like they aren't alone," she said. "I want to give women the upper hand. These guys are just trying to take women down, and I just wanted to flip the script. And at the same time make women feel better – turn the power around."

When deciding which submissions to post, Tweten says she tries to "have something that's kind of funny," even if it is just her picture caption. "I try not to make the Instagram too dark, because I don't want people to get too depressed and then stop following it. The original goal was to make fun of guys who are assholes, so there has to be that level of comedy."

Several counterspeech efforts combine one of the aforementioned theories of change with the goal of providing support to members of the audience who feel attacked by the speech. One example of this is White Nonsense Roundup (WNR). Started in 2015, WNR is a volunteer-run effort active on Facebook and Twitter (now X) that seeks to take some of the burden of countering racist comments from people of color. As described by one of the project's founders:

> If someone is tired of explaining yet again why a certain statement is racist or why it's problematic to say "all lives matter" or to be colorblind and claim that you don't see color, what a great thing that we can do some of that work ... It should be white people engaging in a lot of the labor and work of tackling our own skinfolks to figure this out.[24]

When people of color receive or see racist comments online, it is often left to them to respond. WNR seeks to remove at least some of that burden.

When someone tags them in a post, a volunteer reads through the thread and then figures out the best way to respond. Although volunteers at WNR sometimes seek to change the behavior of an author of racist speech with counterspeech, more frequently they attempt to reach the larger audience. As one of the WNR founders noted, "If no one says anything, and it's just this racist comment left sitting there, what are we supposed to think? That all white people agree with that? So it's important to counter that. Also, if there is someone else silently reading the conversation – they may learn something."

The counterspeakers from WNR and Bye Felipe respond to hatred by speaking to the larger audience, but they do so with the explicit understanding that some members of that audience experience the speech differently. In the example of Bye Felipe, women may want a space to vent about their own similar experiences and find solidarity with others posting in the comments. For those who haven't experienced an interaction like the ones Tweten posts, the screenshots show them that this type of behavior occurs and clearly communicate that men should not treat women that way.

A last example of NGOs providing support for targets of hateful speech is TrollBusters, an organization created to serve as digital first responders for women journalists who have experienced or witnessed harassment and online abuse. When someone reaches out to TrollBusters, the organization can provide counterharassment messaging, coaching about what to do next, documentation for potential legal claims, and assistance in repairing an online reputation.

The efforts described in this section demonstrate the many ways that NGOs can help mitigate the harm caused by hateful speech. Organizations can respond directly to those targeted by the speech, providing a sense of emotional support and solidarity. They can remove some of the burden and unpaid labor often left to minority groups who must defend themselves online against hatred and harassment. They can also be a first point of call, providing or directing users to services that can support them after experiencing online abuse.

Additional Considerations – Mitigating Risks

Before engaging in counterspeech, NGOs should take time to understand the potential risks involved. Counterspeakers are sometimes criticized and attacked for what they do. Organizational risk management plans should include steps to protect employees (and the organization itself) before they embark on an organized counterspeech campaign.

PEN America, an NGO that works to defend freedom of expression, writers, and literature, produced Guidelines for Safely Practicing Counterspeech as part of a "field manual" for dealing with online harassment. The guide recommends first assessing the threat, both in terms of physical and digital security. Safety risks depend on the context. Some factors to consider are one's location, to whom – and on what topic – a person is responding, and how much of the counterspeaker's personal information is available online.[25]

The strategies used in a response can also help mitigate risks. #Defyhatenow Cameroon was started in 2018 as a response to the hateful and dangerous speech circulating on social media related to the "Anglophone Crisis" in Cameroon – a conflict between French-speaking government forces and separatists from the English-speaking regions of the country fighting to form their own nation. According to one of #Defyhatenow's staff members, one strategy they use to lower safety risks is to encourage people to challenge hatred with speech that is "very objective and general in its character. The information responds to the issue at hand without responding to the individual."[26] As an example, he described how their organization encouraged people to post an image to their social media accounts with their picture framed by two blue doves and the words "I stand for peace and a #hatefree-Cameroon." Another strategy used by the organization is to respond to hatred as an organization, rather than as individuals, as a way to protect members from direct confrontation that counterspeakers sometimes receive.

Conclusion

Hateful speech can have a significant impact on individuals and communities. Online hateful speech not only perpetuates discrimination, stereotypes, and exclusion but also poses real-world threats to the safety and well-being of targeted individuals. Counterspeech is one piece of the puzzle of how to mitigate these harmful effects. Not every NGO will have the capacity or desire to engage in online counterspeech in the ways suggested in this chapter. For those who do not, other anti-hatred efforts (both offline and online) such as education campaigns and coalition building also contribute to the positive norm change that counterspeech seeks. For NGOs that do choose to engage in counterspeech, their work can play a crucial role in challenging and debunking false narratives, promoting accurate information, and fostering a more inclusive and tolerant online environment. Additionally, responding to hateful speech allows NGOs to provide emotional support to those who are targeted, empowering them to navigate through the challenges of online harassment. Moreover, countering hateful speech aligns with the mission of many NGOs to defend human rights, promote social justice, and create positive social change. By addressing online hate speech, NGOs contribute to building a digital space that values diversity, equality, and respect, ultimately working toward a more just and harmonious society.

NOTES

1 See United Nations, "Strategy and Plan of Action on Hate Speech," June 18, 2019, https://www.un.org/en/hate-speech/un-strategy-and-plan-of-action-on-hate-speech.

2 Louis D. Brandeis, concurring opinion, *Whitney v. California*, 274 U.S. 357 (1927).

3 Michał Bilewicz et al., "Artificial Intelligence against Hate: Intervention Reducing Verbal Aggression in the Social Network Environment," *Aggressive Behavior* 47, no. 3 (2021): 260–6, https://doi.org/10.1002/ab.21948; Dominik Hangartner et al., "Empathy-Based Counterspeech Can Reduce Racist Hate Speech in a Social Media Field Experiment," *Proceedings of the National Academy of Sciences* 118, no. 50 (2021): e2116310118, https://doi.org/10.1073/pnas.2116310118; Erin Saltman, Farshad Kooti, and Karly Vockery, "New Models for Deploying Counterspeech: Measuring Behavioral Change and Sentiment Analysis," *Studies in Conflict & Terrorism* 46, no. 9 (2021): 1547–74, https://doi.org/10.1080/1057610X.2021.1888404.

4 Carla Schieb and Mike Preuss, "Governing Hate Speech by Means of Counterspeech on Facebook," paper presented at the 66th ICA Annual Conference, Fukuoka, Japan, June 2016, https://www.researchgate .net/publication/303497937_Governing_hate_speech_by_means_of _counterspeech_on_Facebook.

5 Jozef Miškolci, Lucia Kováčová, and Edita Rigová, "Countering Hate Speech on Facebook: The Case of the Roma Minority in Slovakia," *Social Science Computer Review* 38, no. 2 (2020): 128–46, https://doi.org/10.1177 /0894439318791786.

6 Victoria Lane, "Reframing to Reach the 'Movable Middle,'" Slideshare, April 10, 2018, https://www.slideshare.net/fairsay/reframing-to-reach -the-movable-middle.

7 International Center for Policy Advocacy, "Step 1: Finding a Focus and Opening," accessed February 1, 2025, https://www.narrativechange.org /toolkit/step-1-finding-focus-and-opening.

8 GLAAD and Them, "Why Queer Activists Should Direct Their Message to the 'Movable Middle,'" Them, April 24, 2019, https://www.them.us/story /movable-middle-glaad.

9 Schieb and Preuss, "Governing Hate Speech."

10 Miškolci, Kováčová, and Rigová, "Countering Hate Speech on Facebook"; Rocío Galarza Molina and Freddie Jennings, "The Role of Civility and Metacommunication in Facebook Discussions," *Communication Studies* 69, no. 1 (2018): 42–66, https://doi.org/10.1080/10510974.2017.1397038; Soo-Hye Han, LeAnn M. Brazeal, and Natalie Pennington, "Is Civility Contagious? Examining the Impact of Modeling in Online Political Discussions," *Social Media + Society* 4, no. 3 (2018), https://doi.org /10.1177/2056305118793404.

11 Soo-Hye Han and LeAnn M. Brazeal, "Playing Nice: Modeling Civility in Online Political Discussions," *Communication Research Reports* 32, no. 1 (2015): 20–8, https://doi.org/10.1080/08824096.2014.989971.

12 See, for example, Justin Cheng et al., "Anyone Can Become a Troll: Causes of Trolling Behavior in Online Discussions," *Proceedings of the 2017 ACM Conference on Computer Supported Cooperative Work and Social Computing – CSCW 17* (2017): 1217–30, https://dl.acm.org/doi/10.1145/2998181 .2998213.

13 Magdalena Obermaier, Desirée Schmuck, and Muniba Saleem, "I'll Be There for You? Effects of Islamophobic Online Hate Speech and Counter Speech on Muslim In-Group Bystanders' Intention to Intervene," *New Media & Society* 25, no. 9 (2021): 2339–58, https://doi.org/10.1177 /14614448211017527.

14 Regina Royan et al., "Use of Twitter Amplifiers by Medical Professionals to Combat Misinformation during the COVID-19 Pandemic," *Journal of*

Medical Internet Research 24, no. 7 (2022): e38324, https://www.jmir
.org/2022/7/e38324.

15 Aryn Fields, "ICYMI: AP Debunks Extremist Claims about Gender
Affirming Care," press release, Human Rights Campaign, April 25, 2023,
https://www.hrc.org/press-releases/icymi-ap-debunks-extremist
-claims-about-gender-affirming-care.

16 Glaad (@glaad), "Goodmorning, a reminder that healthcare for
transgender people is settled science." Twitter, May 19, 2023, https://
twitter.com/glaad/status/1659552178720178179.

17 The Bard Center for the Study of Hate, Western States Center, and the
Montana Human Rights Network, *A Community Guide for Opposing Hate*,
accessed February 5, 2025, https://bcsh.bard.edu/files/2022/05
/OpposingHateGuide-single-pages-8M-5-3.pdf.

18 Ed Mazza, "How a German City Found an Absolutely Genius Way of
Handling Neo-Nazis," *HuffPost*, August 17, 2017, last updated August 19,
2019, https://www.huffpost.com/entry/neo-nazi-walkathon_n_59952cfbe
4b0acc593e51ae5.

19 See the English version of the German website Hass Hilft: Donate the
Hate: The Involuntary Donation Campaign, accessed February 14, 2025,
https://www.hasshilft.de/index_en.html.

20 Jessica Haworth, "Refugee Charity Calais Action Sets Up 'TrollAid'
Fundraising Website to Give Cash to Migrants Every Time They're
Trolled," *The Mirror*, January 26, 2016, https://www.mirror.co.uk/news
/uk-news/refugee-charity-calais-action-sets-7248820.

21 Tanya Silverman et al., *The Impact of Counter-Narratives* (London: Institute
for Strategic Dialogue, 2016), 18, https://www.isdglobal.org/wp-content
/uploads/2016/08/Impact-of-Counter-Narratives_ONLINE_1.pdf.

22 Catesby Holmes, "Myanmar Charged with Genocide of Rohingya
Muslims: 5 Essential Reads," *The Conversation*, December 11, 2019, https://
theconversation.com/myanmar-charged-with-genocide-of-rohingya
-muslims-5-essential-reads-128742.

23 Lindsay Blackwell et al., "Classification and Its Consequences for Online
Harassment: Design Insights from HeartMob," *Proceedings of the ACM on
Human-Computer Interaction* 1, no. CSCW (2017): 1–19, https://doi.org
/10.1145/3134659.

24 Interview with author, January 30, 2018.

25 See also the "Security" section of the Bard Center for the Study of Hate,
Western States Center, and the Montana Human Rights Network, *A
Community Guide for Opposing Hate*.

26 Interview with author, July 6, 2021.

Editor's Introduction to Chapter 10

I've worked in the antihate non-profit sector since 1989, and ran a small foundation between 2014 and 2018. The structure and messaging of non-profits have a lot to do with the ability to raise money, which, in turn, has a strong influence on what NGOs combating hate choose to do (or not do). I often wondered about the tradeoff between institutional fundraising goals and a critical analysis of what may, or may not, be achieved by programs and projects funded by that money – an ethical issue related to Brudholm and Johansen's contemplation of the ethics of "doing no harm" in chapter 1 and Lowe and Jimenez's admirable emphasis in chapter 5 on sharing data that might show what your NGO did that failed.

Which is the more harmful, reducing the amount of money you can raise by failing to tap into the anger and sometimes hate in response to hate that can open the faucets, or tamping down emotions (including your own anger at incidents of hate) to think through what you can accomplish strategically (for example, not further feeding the "us"/"them" binary)?

Without being able to articulate it, over the years I also had a sense that the structures of philanthropy had an impact on how NGOs focused on hate. For example, when I worked at AJC I saw, after the financial crisis of 2008, a shift in the agency's desire to go after the $500,000 and $1,000,000 gifts rather than keep pursuing those who gave $5,000, $10,000 or $20,000. That may have made fundraising sense for the overall budget, but the big givers were more likely to be conservative on Israel, on internal agency labor relations, and on the perceived value of investing in domestic intergroup relations, among other things. Each of these megafunders also had much more sway in overall policy. Furthermore, across most of the Jewish community, when questions of antisemitism on the left came up, particularly regarding university campuses, I saw eager funders plowing money into right-wing efforts to vilify the left. I argued, largely unsuccessfully, that their money would be better spent helping those in the left address these concerns, because this was, indeed, a battle inside the left. But I suspect it felt more emotionally satisfying for funders to support efforts that vilified the left rather than pondering how to influence it.

Lila Corwin Berman's landmark book, *The American Jewish Philanthropic Complex*, made me think about these issues in a new and deeper way. It was a smart history of Jewish philanthropy, in which she dealt with important issues like the relationship between the state and philanthropies, for example: (1) tax deductions and non-profit status make philanthropies an arm of the state, and (2) the legal structure of philanthropies (directing what they can and can't do, ways to raise and to hold and to spend money, etc.) affects how they choose to do their work.

In the chapter that follows, she builds upon her earlier work, and raises difficult ethical and practical questions that ought to be contemplated by NGOs. If NGOs want philanthropy to support them as generously as possible, what interest could they possibly have in reforming how philanthropy works that might risk reducing the NGOs' finances? But what if, as Berman postulates, some of the current structure of the philanthropic world actually helps promote hate? Does philanthropy based on identity fuel "us" vs. "them" thinking? Does it promote politics that some might define as hateful? And, assuming for the sake of argument that that is true, what are the implications if we try to limit philanthropic endeavors that some might see as hateful and others might view as promoting the public good?

10 Funding Divides: How Philanthropic Systems Can Link Public Dollars to Social Division and Political Extremism

LILA CORWIN BERMAN

From the word's Greek roots, "philanthropy" suggests love (*philos*) of humanity (*anthropos*). This chapter explores the inverse of philanthropy's etymological promise by asking how, instead of spreading love, philanthropy sometimes stokes animosity; and instead of embracing humanity, philanthropy sometimes sets groups of people against one another. I contend that this darker side of philanthropy is, in fact, inseparable from the policies governing modern-day philanthropy. Any attempt to expunge philanthropy of its socially destructive tendencies must reckon with the political and economic system that has produced it.

The political theorist Rob Reich explains, "Philanthropy is not an invention of the state but ought to be viewed as an artifact of the state."[1] To properly chronicle how and when philanthropy fosters inequality, social division, or hatred is to shine a light on the public policies that allow it to do so. In what follows, I have largely focused my attention on American philanthropy, the largest philanthropic sector in the world. In addition to regulating the domestic operations of the system, American philanthropic policy has projected itself across the globe as a template for systems in many other countries and as the basis for international development and humanitarian programs.[2]

This chapter begins by examining the political and economic policies that tethered philanthropy to American statecraft and its central question of resource distribution. It then draws attention to how these policies, even as they sought to advance pluralism and check the power of the majority, fostered forms of economic inequality and social division. Finally, the chapter turns toward the elements of philanthropic policy that have not only replicated but also accelerated inequality and social division by helping to materialize these forces into extremist, hateful, or violent political movements.

All of us (and this may very well include all of humanity) who live under the sway of philanthropic systems bear the obligation to scrutinize them. Media reports may fabricate the cult of a single philanthropist, as if philanthropy's fruits or its misdeeds rest exclusively with the individual. This obscures the web of policies in which individuals act. Notwithstanding a cottage industry devoted to producing philanthropic strategy, state policies delimit the realm of possibility. They also place the power with the people to understand and, if necessary, reform the system that has allowed philanthropy to act contrary to the interests of the public.[3]

One note: In the discussion that follows, I offer some case studies from American Jewish philanthropy. This reflects my expertise in the subject matter as well as the growth and heft of American Jewish philanthropic institutions in the twentieth century. American Jewish philanthropy illuminates the distinctive priorities of Jewish communities, but it also bears the imprint of state policies. Delusional attacks that target Jewish philanthropy as proof of a global Jewish conspiracy have sometimes discouraged scholarly study of the topic. In my view, this is to the detriment of knowledge about American Jewish life and the American political economy. Instead, as I hope to demonstrate, necessary understanding of both is only possible through scholarly inquiry undeterred by threats of antisemitism. Even more so, clear-eyed examination of American Jewish philanthropy as a product of American state policy exposes the lie at the heart of describing it in any other way.[4]

Policies of Inequality: The Public Good and Taxation

In 2015, Darren Walker, the president of the Ford Foundation, posted a blog titled "Toward a New Gospel of Wealth." Invoking Andrew Carnegie, the Scottish-born American steel magnate who evangelized his Gilded-Age peers to spread and not hoard their wealth, Walker acknowledged the irony of trying to solve wealth inequality with more wealth. His command of a private foundation with over $12 billion in assets made him acutely aware of "the tension inherent in a system that perpetuates vast differences in privilege and then tasks the privileged with improving the system." Nonetheless, drawing on the legacy of Henry Ford, a complicated man who expressed his populism through both the high wages he paid his workers and the xenophobia and antisemitism he propagated, Walker hoped to help create "an economic system *that works for more people.*"[5]

As stirring as Walker's vision was, it almost entirely overlooked state-based policies that hitched philanthropy's evolution to enduring forms of inequality. The heart of those policies was the system of federal taxation birthed in the wake of the Civil War. Good intentions could not overcome the inequality by policy that had produced philanthropy.

Reeling from the near collapse of the nation, political leaders after the Civil War entertained the idea of a national income tax. A growing class of experts persuaded them that an income tax could efficiently raise revenue for the federal government to stitch together a new ideal of a unified nation. By appropriating those funds for public projects, the government could produce public goods alongside a revitalized concept of the American public good. In 1894, the Supreme Court thwarted Congress's attempt to raise such a tax, declaring it unconstitutional. But two decades and a constitutional amendment (the Sixteenth) later, Congress succeeded in instituting the federal income tax.[6]

Modeled on a progressive formula, the federal income tax was measurably different from the consumption taxes on goods that hit all earners at the same rate. With its highest tax applied to the biggest earners, it could smooth out the massive economic inequality that was the target of public outcry during the Gilded Age and enable the government to fund infrastructure and social welfare benefits. Truly a "fiscal revolution," as one historian has described it, the federal income tax also remained relatively rarefied for its first few decades of existence, only levied on a small subset of high earners. This changed during World War II, when wartime expenses prodded Congress to expand the tax to extract payments from over forty-six million Americans.[7]

A vector of economic redistribution, the federal income tax nonetheless contained the opposing force of economic concentration in the form of its exemption clause. Unchanged from the 1894 legislation that had been struck down, the clause specified that "corporations, companies, or associations organized and conducted solely for charitable, religious, or educational purposes" had immunity from the income tax, and in 1917 Congress extended these privileges to individuals who could deduct contributions (up to a certain percentage) to these organizations from their taxable income. Immunity, however, did not translate into tax neutrality; whereas income taxation was progressive, exemption was regressive, affording the highest rewards to the highest earners.[8]

American philanthropy took its shape from the policies of tax exemption, later described by a Treasury Department official as "tax expenditures." In designating certain forms of income as already acting on behalf of the public good, the government encouraged behaviors, such as charitable giving, by releasing potential tax dollars to underwrite them. Yet as the Treasury official explained, these tax policies tended "to have decidedly adverse effects on equity" and "make high-income individuals still better off and result in the paradox that we achieve our social goals by increasing tax millionaires."[9]

As the highest marginal tax rate increased, the wealthiest Americans stood to benefit the most from the exemption system. Dollar for dollar, donations that high-income individuals made to a "charitable, religious, or educational" institution offset their taxable income at a far higher rate than it did for a lower-income earner. Even once tax rates fell from their peak (reached in 1945, when income in the highest tax bracket was assessed at a 94 per cent marginal tax), the regressive effects of philanthropic tax policy remained notable, reflecting and fueling the growth of the philanthropic system.[10]

In the mid- to late-twentieth century, pro-philanthropy and often pro-market experts in tax law sought to augment the benefits of tax policy for philanthropists. Nowhere is this more apparent than in the rise of tax-exempt endowments, enshrined with the classification of operating in the interest of the public good, yet structured by a regressive logic that favored wealth accumulation over wealth distribution. Hardly an advent of the twentieth century, an endowment is a savings account that tends to regulate its spending to preserve and grow its corpus, generally through investment returns. Throughout the nineteenth century, American state governments had been wary of allowing charitable endowments (usually held by religious institutions) to swell. These endowments were not subject to state property taxes, and the more wealth they contained, the greater threat they posed to government power and to democratic rule. For these reasons, in exchange for exempting them from property taxes, many states regulated the governance practices of bodies that held endowments and limited their property holdings.[11]

The suspicion that philanthropic endowments imperiled government and the democratic process continued well into the twentieth century and motivated Congress to hold a series of hearings about charitable foundations beginning in the 1950s. By the 1960s, the House had appointed a special committee led by a populist Democrat from Texas that primarily investigated one philanthropic entity: the Ford Foundation. To fix the philanthropic process, it seemed logical to focus attention on its largest actor. Ford had become just that in 1948, after it absorbed a massive bequest increasing its endowment to $3.3 billion.[12]

The House committee's stated goal was to protect the public from a philanthropic structure that could withhold distribution or allocate funds in ways that might harm the public good. But many of the legislators also were concerned about the diminution of their own power in the face of bloated charitable entities. Worried that Ford or similar foundations could enact state-like power, all the while enriched by state dollars with hardly any public process of oversight, legislators contemplated new regulations, including spending rules and limited lifespans.[13]

In 1969, Congress passed a long-awaited tax reform bill meant to include the results of its investigations into philanthropy. But, in the end, the most ambitious proposals to regulate and constrain charitable accumulation had been tabled, in part due to lobbying pressures from philanthropic entities. Under the terms of the new law, organizations like Ford that were classified as private foundations took on perfunctory reporting requirements and an annual spend-out rate of 5 per cent of their corpus. The new law also designated so-called "public charities," like churches, hospitals, universities, and broad-based charities, as exempt from even these modest regulations.[14]

The 1969 Tax Reform Act, alongside deregulatory financial policies in the 1970s, served as a great boon for philanthropy and, especially, philanthropic endowments. The forces of economic inequality and the threats to democracy that had raised Congress's concerns just a decade earlier appeared even more pronounced with larger than ever stores of capital warehoused in endowments and with rates of growth far outpacing new spending mandates. At the same time, accountants and wealth managers honed techniques to shelter their wealthiest clients from high tax burdens by, in part, using legally permissible philanthropic vehicles. Not a tax scheme or even a tax irregularity, these were simply the products of state policies.[15]

In many cases, endowments and other philanthropic instruments spun off funds to advance truly public goods, but philanthropy was inextricable from the policies that fostered economic inequality. In 1976, Henry Ford II aptly characterized philanthropy as "in essence a creature of capitalism," yet politicians and philanthropists alike sustained the conviction that this face of state-nourished capitalist policy could ameliorate "the scourge of inequality," in Darren Walker's words.[16] Unwilling to attack a system that had ballooned into such a large and powerful force in American life and that contributed directly and indirectly to the American political process, lawmakers tended to avoid drawing attention to philanthropy's embeddedness in structures of inequality.[17]

Beyond political leaders' self-interest, the justification for maintaining America's philanthropic system stemmed from a long-held belief that equated philanthropy with the exceptional promise of America. In the 1830s, when French statesman and political theorist Alexis de Tocqueville toured the United States, he recorded his admiration for the country's "associationalism." In *Democracy in America,* he enthused, "In no country in the world has the principle of association been more successfully used." Tocqueville claimed that associations embodied "the principle of [self]-interest rightly understood" by allowing a diversity of interests to flourish and strengthen American democracy.[18]

In the lore of American exceptionalism, philanthropy was just one of many freedoms that enabled Americans to thrive. By allowing groups of people to form their own societies and advocate their own causes, a tyranny of the majority could be held in check. Yet the underbelly of this pluralism justification for philanthropy was a system that drew unequal enrichment from public dollars and could amplify social cleavages.[19]

Social Division: A Case Study of Jewish Identity Philanthropy

In the spring of 2020, a group of Jewish funders initiated the Jewish Future Pledge (rebranded as the Jewish Future Promise four years later). Modeled on the Giving Pledge created by Warren Buffett, Bill Gates, and Melinda Gates in 2010, it required signatories to commit at least 50 per cent of their charitable estate to support "the Jewish people and/or the State of Israel." Mike Leven, a real estate developer, and Amy Holtz, the owner and operator of Party City stores, came up with the idea because they anticipated a tremendous transfer of generational wealth and because they were anxious about the future of Jewish life. As baby boomers passed away, their children stood to inherit fortunes, but would they use them to support the causes most dear to their parents? As if chastising her children, an early pledger explained, "We made the money. This is how you have to spend it. You don't have endless options. If you want to save the whales, save the Jewish whales."[20]

The Jewish Future Pledge's commitment to advancing a group's interests may have been exactly what Tocqueville had in mind when he praised American associationalism. A group motivated by its unique interests organized to carve out space for itself in the fabric of American life. As a sign of encouragement, the government counted the group's activities on the public-good side of its ledger and forgave a portion of its members' tax burdens.

Ideally, philanthropic pluralism fosters a robust civil society, but here I am interested in how it can challenge that goal. The combination of the policies I described in the first section with the rise of what I will term "identity philanthropy" can heighten us-versus-them divisions and challenge the public good. Although one can observe this dynamic from multiple vantage points, I believe that American Jewish philanthropy offers a particularly clear illustration of the tension between the pluralism justification of philanthropy and the ways in which philanthropic practice may harden lines of social division.[21]

Over the twentieth century, Jewish philanthropy in the United States largely transformed from addressing the material needs of American Jews to serving their identity needs. Beginning in the 1920s, when the United States severely curtailed immigration, the number of Jewish newcomers seeking material support diminished. This was followed by a series of decades in which many American Jews gained opportunities through education, professions, and residential patterns that gave them access to wealth and put them in closer proximity than before with non-Jews.[22]

Jewish organizations that had been preoccupied with assimilating Jewish immigrants into American life through anti-poverty and Americanization programs pivoted toward identity projects during the decades after World War II. In 1959, the authors of an article in the *Journal of Jewish Communal Service* observed that Jewish fundraising carried a "functional significance" beyond generating money for a cause. They explained that the act of giving money was "the means by which millions of Americans visibly identify themselves as Jewish, as belonging to an entity known as the 'Jewish community.'" In other words, the value of philanthropy was greater than simply meeting American Jews' material needs, which were largely (though not entirely) satisfied after World War II. Rather, the new identity philanthropy, expressed through educational and experiential initiatives to stimulate Jewish pride, relied on donor dollars to fund it and, also, itself constituted a form of identity production.[23]

Ideals of Jewish sexual and national separation were critical to Jewish identity philanthropy, even as policies that blurred the line between American public dollars and Jewish communal wealth were instrumental to enacting these visions. By the late 1960s and early 1970s, anxiety about intermarriage and Israel emerged as its two most significant animators. Revealing American Jews' post-Holocaust trauma, these two sources of concern served as wellsprings to compel philanthropic gifts for the sake of what Jewish leaders called Jewish "survival" or "continuity."[24]

A Jewish program called Birthright illustrates identity philanthropy's reliance on integrative state policies, legitimated in the name of the public good, to advance separatistic nationalist and bio-political priorities. Established in the late 1990s by several Jewish philanthropists and philanthropic organizations, Birthright's goal was to send every young Jewish person to Israel for free. In the past, religiously or ideologically

defined organizations had offered separate teen tours, which generally were not free. Birthright's innovation was to fully subsidize the
trips as a unified endeavor of the Jewish people, though crucially with
the enrichment of American state dollars. In 2001, the Birthright Israel
Foundation incorporated as a charitable organization that would take
in hundreds of millions of philanthropic dollars over the next two
decades, including a total of $30 million from casino developer Shel-
don Adelson.[25]

Birthright's core goal was to strengthen American Jews' attachment
to Israel, but its corollary was to shape American Jewish identity by
encouraging relationships – and marriages – among Jews. In 2005, one
of the early funders of Birthright, hedge-fund manager Michael Stein-
hardt, donated $12 million to Brandeis University to establish the Stein-
hardt Social Research Institute, which chiefly served as the data collector
for Birthright. Key to its efforts to plot the success of the program was
evidence showing that rates of intermarriage were significantly lower
for participants than nonparticipants, a data point influenced by the
self-selection of young people who decided to go on Birthright.[26]

Framed by nationalistic and separatistic goals, Birthright nonetheless
was as much a product of American state policy as any other philanthropic endeavor. Like the Jewish Future Pledge, it attracted funders
through its promise to strengthen Jewish group identity, in part by
drawing a more rigid line of division between "us" (Jews) and "them"
(other Americans and Jews who did not subscribe to the goals of the
programs). Yet embedded as they were in the American philanthropic
system, both programs used American state dollars reserved for the
public good to advance their visions. On one hand, this might have
undermined their goals, since they could not escape the American
regulatory apparatus that demanded a basic pronouncement of their
commitment to the public good. Yet, it is at least clear that this materi-
ally helped them achieve their goals, though by no stretch did these
organizations offer the singular vision of Jewish public-good ventures.

Jewish identity philanthropy's twinned separatistic yet state-reliant
structure is even more starkly revealed in the efforts of an early twenty-
first-century Jewish organization called JLens Investor Network.
Founded by a former Wall Street banker in 2012, JLens's mission was
to persuade Jewish philanthropic institutions to align their investment
practices with Jewish values. Jumping on a trend popularized in elite
business schools in the early 2000s, it suggested that capitalist practices,
such as managing stock portfolios, could achieve goals beyond profit
making. JLens's "Jewish Advocacy Strategy" introduced a screening
process for publicly traded companies to be ranked on a scale from

metzuyan (Hebrew for "excellent") to *treif* (a Yiddish word for "nonkosher"), according to their adherence to a set of values defined as Jewish. Companies that did not make the mark would be excised from JLens's curated portfolios. Over time, JLens's primary interest in defending Israel through its financial tools became apparent.[27]

In 2018, Airbnb had decided to scrub its listings of properties in the West Bank settlements, Israeli residential communities illegal under international law. As a result, JLens threatened to downgrade the short-term rental company to *treif*, which would result in its expulsion from JLens's portfolios. With only about $200 million dollars invested in its portfolios in 2022 (and likely less in 2018), JLens's power was its optical sway more than its pecuniary power. In concert with Israeli officials, JLens rebuked Airbnb for "acquiescing to BDS [the Boycott, Divestment, and Sanctions movement]." Under pressure from JLens, as well as other Jewish organizations that threatened to sue the company, Airbnb backpedaled and announced that it would donate profits from settlement listings to human rights organizations.[28]

Shortly after its tangle with Airbnb, JLens directed its pressure campaign against another company called Sustainalytics, an investment rating entity much like JLens that developed its own set of mission-aligned investing criteria. According to JLens, Sustainalytics's metrics betrayed an anti-Israel bias because they characterized companies in the Occupied Territories as operating in a region with known human rights violations. As a result, those companies received a low rating, which JLens feared could convince some of them to boycott the Occupied Territories for the sake of a higher rating. Furthermore, JLens objected to the United Nations' data source and the terminology that Sustainalytics employed in its approach to Israel.[29]

In 2020, alongside several other Jewish organizations, JLens began a publicity campaign against Morningstar, Sustainalytics's parent company, relegating it to *treif* and expunging it from its portfolio. An outside investigator hired by Morningstar found no evidence of "systemic bias against Israel." Even so, in November 2022, the company agreed to refrain from using the term "Occupied Territories" and to stop consulting the United Nations Human Rights Council. With those promises, Morningstar came off JLens's *treif* list.[30]

Identity philanthropy gained the power to advance its interests well beyond what Tocqueville may have imagined in his musings about associationalism and self-interest "properly understood." Because so much money resided in charitable endowments, accrued thanks to policies that allowed philanthropic capital to grow with only modest regulation, identity philanthropy could advance separatistic interests even beyond the dollars it commanded. In 2022, the Anti-Defamation League (ADL) acquired JLens to help it fulfill its mission of combating antisemitism. By defining that fight as, in part, a fight against anti-Zionism and by adopting JLens's financial practices, the ADL pushed the boundaries of identity philanthropy to use the separatistic ideals of "us" to enforce the behaviors of "them," all with the nourishment of American public policy.[31]

This section has focused on American Jewish identity philanthropy, but a similar investigation into Catholic or evangelical Christian philanthropy would offer similar findings about nonprofits' mobilization of finance and identity to sharpen social divisions. For example, domestic and transnational anti-abortion movements have gained substantial power from Catholic charitable entities, which generally place their endowments in Catholic investment portfolios. These portfolios refuse to invest in corporations unless they adhere to Catholic values, including opposition to abortion. Some evangelical churches have organized similar funds, making for a robust infrastructure of anti-abortion philanthropy that favors the identity claims of certain religious movements above others and exacerbates us-versus-them divisions, all while drawing significant state resources to enrich views that are not held by the majority of the American public. Similarly, studies of evangelical Christian philanthropy note that international relief and humanitarian aid is often driven by proselytizing aims that use a share of public dollars to sharply designate between Christians and others.[32]

Attention to how groups can calcify us-versus-them lines within the policies governing philanthropy illuminates the divisive potential of the philanthropic system. In itself, social division may disrupt civil society, though as Tocqueville and others since him have argued, it also safeguards it from majority rule and enhances it with plural viewpoints and interests. Far more concerning, philanthropic policies that foster inequality and sharpen social divisions sometimes turn toward extremist ends that terrorize the very state that designed philanthropy to advance the public good.

Philanthropy and Hate: From Policy Inequality to Social Division to Political Extremism

When Mike Leven cofounded the Jewish Future Pledge, he also served on the advisory council of Turning Point USA, an organization established in 2012 by right-wing activist and radio host Charlie Kirk. Tax returns showed that from 2019 through 2021, Leven's private family foundation granted Turning Point USA's "Campus Leadership Project" half a million dollars to train student activists in conservative ideals such as "Capitalism is the most moral and proven economic system ever discovered," and, "The U.S. Constitution is the most exceptional political document every written." Turning Point USA also funded some of the buses that transported rallygoers to Washington, DC, for the "March to Save America," which culminated in the invasion of the Capitol on January 6, 2021.[33]

Aside from a shared concern about transmitting values to the next generation, Turning Point USA and the Jewish Future Pledge occupy very different roles in American philanthropy. Yet both reveal how philanthropy can function as a political lever that may run contrary to the interests of the broad public from which it draws enrichment. In the case of Turning Point USA, it did not simply advance the interests of one group or a set of priorities above others – a pluralistic logic that may justify philanthropy in some people's minds. Rather, it converted the state-sanctioned system of philanthropy into a violent aggressor meant to directly dismantle the state. And in this, it was not alone. The Oath Keepers, a militia group whose leader was found guilty of seditious conspiracy (before President Trump commuted his sentence in January 2025) in the attack on the Capitol, likewise gained state support through the philanthropic system by creating ancillary government-approved charitable organizations, such as the Oath Keepers Educational Foundation. (The Oath Keepers has never held official charitable status, though several similar organizations have, including Identity Evropa and National Policy Institute, both of which helped organize the 2017 Unite the Right rally in Charlottesville, Virginia.)[34]

Across the twentieth century, architects of American civil society were aware of the dangers of allowing philanthropic organizations to exercise political power, but the regulatory system they created ironically expanded philanthropy's political possibilities. The earliest iterations of federal tax law stipulated that only organizations operating "solely" for charitable, religious, or educational purposes gained exemption from the income tax. In the 1930s, that clause fell under the scrutiny of a lawsuit about whether a contribution to the American Birth Control League qualified for a charitable deduction. In response, Congress expanded its exclusive purpose test ("solely") to define more precisely what constituted disqualifying political activity and mandated that "no substantial part of the activities" of an exempt organization could be directed toward the "carrying on of propaganda or otherwise attempting to influence legislation." Twenty years later, and again under pressure to clarify the line between charitable and political activities, Congress accepted an amendment from the floor introduced by then Senator Lyndon B. Johnson to prohibit exempt organizations from participating in electoral campaigns.[35]

Although intended to limit the political clout of philanthropy, the legal framework provided cover for incredibly political endeavors. By narrowing its vision to the kind of politics it believed it could see and regulate, Congress dodged its avowed responsibility to reckon with the political pull of philanthropic endeavors. Such a circumscribed notion of politics instead allowed philanthropic entities to posture as if they were nonpolitical while pursuing political ends with impunity and minimal regulation.

Since the mid-twentieth century, the Internal Revenue Service (IRS) has emerged as the most important governmental agency to screen philanthropic behavior. It alone determines whether an organization meets the standards outlined in section 501(c)(3) of its code. Yet its limited resources and a rising flood of applications has led to an extraordinarily lax process. A 2009 report that surveyed two decades of data found that only 2 per cent of all 501(c)(3) applications had been rejected over that period. With such low rates of rejection, the number of tax-exempt organizations steadily grew, reaching almost two million by 2020. The report's authors concluded, "Oversight of the creation of nonprofit organizations, and the conferral of tax privileges that accompany nonprofit status is weak, bordering on non-existent."[36]

The laws restricting philanthropic organizations' political activities may have been intended to foster a maximally pluralist civic sector, but in practice they opened the door for politically active and sometimes extremist movements to access state resources. Several recent studies offer clear evidence of American public dollars channeled to politically extremist organizations. One analysis performed by *Sludge*, an independent investigative reporting outlet, discovered that four of the largest American charitable institutions allocated almost $11 million between 2014 and 2017 to thirty-four hate groups, as designated by the Southern Poverty Law Center.[37] Research on specific forms of hate and political extremism has found similar patterns. For example, the Council on American-Islamic Relations (CAIR) tracked several major charitable funds from 2014 through 2016 that supported the thirty-nine largest anti-Muslim groups.[38] Likewise, a Southern Poverty Law Center study uncovered the largest tax-exempt donors who supported VDARE, a far-right-wing website that spews anti-immigration vitriol and other white nationalist beliefs.[39]

A philanthropic investment tool called the donor-advised fund (DAF) emerged as a common player across almost every investigation of philanthropy and political extremism. Developed in the wake of the 1969

Tax Reform Act, DAFs enable individuals to hold charitable accounts within the housing of public charities, with their stripped-down regulations and favorable tax benefits. In name, DAFs are controlled by a public charity. But donors almost always retain control over how and when to spend the funds because the largest holders of DAFs are now charitable arms of commercial investment houses, such as Fidelity or Vanguard, or reside in general purpose community foundations. As a result, the only serious requirement for recipient organizations is that they possess 501(c)(3) status, which as we saw is a relatively easy bar to clear. In sum, an individual who opens a DAF can capitalize it with a mix of philanthropic dollars, tax benefits, and investment income generated from the principal, and then make allocations akin to those of a private foundation, but without adhering to the spend-out and transparency regulations that Congress placed on private foundations.[40]

Most significant in understanding the close relationship between DAFs and hate groups is DAFs' protection of donors' identities. Because by law DAFs are a subset of a public charity, only the public charity, not the individual, must report a gift. This means that donors can quietly contribute to organizations of their choice. DAFs offer a shelter against public reporting requirements that might exercise a check on a donor's decision to fund a hate group or, really, any group with which a donor might not wish to be publicly affiliated.[41]

For their anonymity, their favorable tax benefits, and their agility, DAFs take center stage when it comes to the funding sources for hate groups. As of 2024, $251.52 billion were held in DAFs, all funds that could serve as "dark money," subsidized by public tax dollars yet effectively inscrutable to the public. CAIR's study of an "Islamophobia Network," for example, found that the charitable subsidiaries of commercial banks, including Fidelity, Schwab, and Vanguard alongside the National Christian Charitable Foundation and the Jewish Communal Fund, ranked in the list of top-ten funders. But this offered very little insight into who the actual funders were. The same commercial DAF aggregators appear on the lists of funders for groups like VDARE. And following the massacre in southern Israel on October 7, 2023, researchers attempting to follow the trails of money that supported Hamas likewise found their maps stopped at the doors of major banks.[42]

Complicating the project of tracing the funding of hate groups are increasingly polarized definitions of what actually constitutes a hate group. For example, CAIR, which has collected some of the most important data about the financing of Islamophobia, is itself classified as an extremist group that trades in antisemitism and anti-Zionism according to the ADL. The battles over what speech and actions cross the threshold into hate (whether designated as illegal or not) reached a fevered pitch after October 7 and during Israel's subsequent military campaign in Gaza. Donors used their command of philanthropic resources to try to push institutions, especially universities, to accept their terms and to draw starker lines than ever between politically acceptable versus hateful positions. It remains an open question whether this kind of "donor revolt" was ultimately a signal of philanthropy's power to protect the public good or represented donor overreach that undermined the public good. But it is significant to observe that many large and well-capitalized institutions found it difficult to withstand donors' coercion, despite competing perspectives about what was and was not hateful among other stakeholders (for example, faculty and students at universities).[43]

Policies that increase the power of the wealthiest donors through regressive tax benefits combined with modes of identity philanthropy that can sow social division and exacerbate us-versus-them divisions would themselves be reason for concern. But when paired with structures that block transparency and have proven records of supporting politically extremist and sometimes violent organizations, this arrangement begins to appear unsuitable for any decent conception of the public good.

Conclusion

In the mid-1950s, when Congress initiated the first of several investigations into philanthropy that culminated in the 1969 Tax Reform Act, many of its members worried that philanthropy acted as a cloak for attacks on American state interests. Indeed, just a day before Senator Johnson succeeded in amending the tax law to bar philanthropic organizations from engaging in electoral campaigns, one of his colleagues endorsed a McCarthyite plan to strip all "subversive" organizations of their tax-exempt status, and a congressional committee similarly recommended "the complete exclusion of political activity" from all tax-exempt organizations. Motivated by fear, these 1950s lawmakers sought unbridled power to regulate philanthropy.[44]

While McCarthyite proposals to control philanthropy did not prevail in the 1950s, they serve as a reminder that regulation may be wielded as a weapon against the public good even when it justifies itself as safeguarding that same public good. In the effort to diminish the power of hatred in society, one must acknowledge the downsides and limitations of regulating philanthropy. Myriad forces beyond the scope of philanthropy – many addressed in this volume – arguably play a more significant role in perpetuating the most pernicious forces in our world today. And overreach to tame philanthropy could have unintended consequences of harming salutary movements and initiatives.

Nonetheless, because philanthropy is a creature of the state, it is uniquely responsive to reform through policy change in ways that many other causes of hatred are not. Furthermore, the public and its elected officials are empowered – and obligated – to serve as checks on the system, ensuring that the values authorizing it are upheld. For these reasons, policy reform that can limit the forces of social division and hate (and other effects, such as inequality) through philanthropic regulation should be pursued even if prudently.

The heart of any reform effort must begin with clear recognition of philanthropy's relationship to state policies of resource distribution. Far from an exclusively private matter, philanthropy represents a state-based tax expenditure. The historical evolution of charitable taxation and exemption reveals that it was constructed as a feature of twentieth-century statecraft. Over time, new legislative and judicial acts changed its nature to achieve different goals. One of the key questions that state actors have pursued is the extent to which resource distribution should be in the hands of private or public bodies. The state gains the power to regulate behavior by offering benefits to private entities in return for their adherence to state priorities. A grasp on how the philanthropic system developed and its embeddedness in state policies of resource distribution is a prerequisite for any meaningful reform.

With an understanding of philanthropy as a state-based system, one will be better equipped to confront its troubling dimensions. The social division and hatred that may be advanced through philanthropy cannot be addressed merely by tweaking a rule or enforcing an existing policy. In each case, the goal of the system must be reassessed.

As the philanthropic system stands, the public is seriously impaired from seeing how and when it promotes hatred and divisiveness. This will remain the case unless the system is made more transparent. Tax documents that lead an investigator to the impenetrable doors of a large investment bank or communal foundation are not working effectively. They are making it incredibly difficult for the public to know whether the laws governing philanthropy are being upheld. Furthermore, the obfuscation presently allowed by law – including the policies governing DAFs – hinders the spirit of laws that were meant to give the public oversight of the expenditures made in its name.

A donor or nonprofit that accepts the government's tax expenditure should expect to pay the price of transparency. The drawbacks of transparency, including public pressure campaigns or doxxing that could harm an individual or organization, should not stand in the way of the public's entitlement to monitor the system. It may be acceptable to designate a small-donation ceiling – perhaps $100 – below which charitable gifts could go unreported to prevent frivolous and sometimes hate-driven campaigns against donors to controversial causes. But beyond this, an individual or organization may always decide to step outside of the philanthropic system by not claiming tax benefits and then is perfectly free to transact as they wish, within the limits of other relevant laws.

In addition to bolstering the rules of transparency and philanthropic reporting, policy reform should intentionally bend the will of philanthropy toward public priorities, which include at the very least minimizing violent political extremism. To achieve this, political leaders and policymakers will have to treat philanthropy with the same discernment that they do other forms of public expenditures. They regularly suggest what activities or behaviors are deserving of resources, making the case to the electorate that certain priorities are the best or at least better than others.

By expanding the structure of incentives (and disincentives), the philanthropic system could better promote public priorities and avoid advancing forces of inequality, social division, and hatred. For example, some policy researchers have suggested rewarding higher spend-out commitments with more public investment (via tax benefits) on the theory that resources distributed are better than ones held when it comes to achieving the goals of equality and opportunity. Other recommendations include providing carrots for philanthropic gifts directed toward clearly identified public priorities. Identity-based or special-interest projects could remain in the philanthropic universe, but they simply would not receive the level of benefits reserved for broader public good commitments. A different strategy might focus instead on the practices of allocation, for example, encouraging broad-based public participation in identifying philanthropic priorities.[45]

Policy reform concerned with transparency and the calibration of state rewards could steer the philanthropic system to advance the public good that underwrites it. Over the twentieth century, Congress repeatedly expressed its conviction that philanthropy must be visible and must be regulated. Occasionally detractors have claimed that too much reform will crack the philanthropic system, sending billionaires off to use their money to buy yachts instead of making charitable gifts. Because philanthropy is just one vehicle among others to achieve resource distribution, I suggest we can sideline that worry in favor of concerns about how to make the philanthropic system better achieve public priorities and values.[46]

For philanthropy to come even close to embodying its etymological roots, state policies must nurture the very best aspirations of civil society. A pluralistic vision, where subsets of the public can pursue their interests, should not overwhelm care and compassion for the whole of society. It is conceivable that policies could prioritize certain philanthropic actions over others while still lending meaningful support to the value of pluralism. At the more extreme, when organizations promote hateful visions and stoke violence, public policy should have the muscle to divest funding from them. A reinvigorated public-purpose test, with careful attention to the rate of distribution to causes that meet clear whole-of-society priorities, could qualify certain organizations for higher levels of public investment.

Of course, varying political ideologies may define what is hateful in different ways and, in some cases, may demonize an entire group in the process, effectively claiming to fight hatred with more hatred. One might regard the second Trump administration's efforts to remove exempt status from some pro-Palestinian organizations as a move in the direction of using antihate efforts as pretext for political repression. Similarly, his intention to freeze grants to nonprofits that do not "align" with his agenda smacks of political animus, not public interest. Should nonprofit status simply become a partisan weapon, the entire case for a civil society and its advancement of democratic principles will sustain a serious blow. Congress need not define a sharp line between political priorities and the public good to agree that using the tax exemption to punish political opponents who engage in constitutionally protected behavior is impermissible. At the same time, Congress could designate broad categories of civic activism – for example, providing shelter, health care, education, and clothing for underserved people – as deserving more public support than other categories of civic engagement.[47]

NGOs and other institutions that share a mission of fighting hate should welcome reforms that in the long run promise to strengthen democracy and to divert tax dollars away from hate-filled visions. For the love of humanity, philanthropy must be reformed.

NOTES

1 Rob Reich, *Just Giving: Why Philanthropy Is Failing Democracy and How It Can Do Better* (Princeton, NJ: Princeton University Press, 2018), 26.
2 For an excellent overview of the history of American philanthropy upon which I have relied, see Olivier Zunz, *Philanthropy in America: A History* (Princeton, NJ: Princeton University Press, 2012). On the global implications of American philanthropy, see Daniel Immerwahr,

Thinking Small: The United States and the Lure of Community Development (Cambridge, MA: Harvard University Press, 2015); Maribel Morey, *White Philanthropy: Carnegie Corporation's* An American Dilemma *and the Making of a White World Order* (Chapel Hill: University North Carolina Press, 2021); Joanne Meyerowitz, *A War on Global Poverty: The Lost Promise of Redistribution and the Rise of Microcredit* (Princeton, NJ: Princeton University Press, 2021); and Amy Offner, *Sorting Out the Mixed Economy: The Rise and Fall of Welfare and Development States in the Americas* (Princeton, NJ: Princeton University Press, 2019). Researchers who study philanthropic systems in other national contexts offer crucial insight into the difference that national policy can make while also highlighting the transnational nature of philanthropy. See Thomas Adam, "Transatlantic Trading: The Transfer of Philanthropic Models between European and North American Cities during the Nineteenth and Early Twentieth Centuries," *Journal of Urban History* 28, no. 3 (2002): 328–51, https://doi.org/10.1177/0096144202028003003; Jens Beckert, *Inherited Wealth*, trans. Thomas Dunlap (Princeton, NJ: Princeton University Press, 2008); Ritu Birla, "C=f(P): The Trust 'General Public Utility', and Charity as a Function of Profit in India," *Modern Asian Studies* 52, no. 1 (2018): 132–62, https://doi.org/10.1017/S0026749X17000087; Matthew Hilton, "Charity and the End of Empire: British Non-Governmental Organizations, Africa, and International Development in the 1960s," *American Historical Review* 123, no. 2 (2018): 493–517, https://doi.org/10.1093/ahr/123.2.493; and Karen Wright, "Generosity v. Altruism: Philanthropy and Charity in the US and UK," *Voluntas* 12, no. 4 (2001): 399–416, https://www.jstor.org/stable/27927747.

3 For example, the effective altruism movement seeks to identify a set of principles beyond scrutiny to govern maximally efficacious giving. See William MacAskill, *What We Owe the Future* (New York: Basic Books, 2023); and Peter Singer, *The Most Good You Can Do: How Effective Altruism Is Changing Ideas about Living Ethically* (New Haven, CT: Yale University Press, 2015). Before the effective altruism movement arose, business schools developed rubrics to gauge "strategic philanthropy" that similarly put faith in individual decision-making as the basis for good philanthropic governance. A core statement of this movement is Michael Porter and Mark Kramer, "Philanthropy's New Agenda: Creating Value," *Harvard Business Review* 77, no. 6 (1999): 121–30, https://hbr.org/1999/11/philanthropys-new-agenda-creating-value.

4 Lila Corwin Berman, *The American Jewish Philanthropic Complex: The History of a Multibillion-Dollar Institution* (Princeton, NJ: Princeton University Press, 2020).

5 Darren Walker, "Toward a New Gospel of Wealth," Ford Foundation, October 1, 2015, emphasis in the original, https://www.fordfoundation .org/news-and-stories/stories/posts/toward-a-new-gospel-of-wealth/. See also Darren Walker, *From Generosity to Justice: A New Gospel of Wealth* (New York: Disruption Books, 2023). On the Ford Foundation, see Inderjeet Parmar, *Foundations of the American Century: The Ford, Carnegie, and Rockefeller Foundations in the Rise of American Power* (New York: Columbia University Press, 2012); and Karen Ferguson, *Top Down: The Ford Foundation, Black Power, and the Reinvention of Racial Liberalism* (Philadelphia: University of Pennsylvania Press, 2013). On Henry Ford, see Neil Baldwin, *Henry Ford and the Jews: The Mass Production of Hate* (New York: Public Affairs, 2001); and Victoria Saker Woeste, *Henry Ford's War on Jews and the Legal Battle against Hate Speech* (Stanford: Stanford University Press, 2012).

6 Ajay Mehrotra, *Making the Modern American Fiscal State: Law, Politics, and the Rise of Progressive Taxation, 1877–1929* (New York: Cambridge University Press, 2013). On Congress's expansion of its power during the Reconstruction era, see William Novak, *New Democracy: The Creation of the Modern American State* (Cambridge, MA: Harvard University Press, 2022).

7 Mehrotra, *Making the Modern American Fiscal State*, 8. On the forces of inequality in the Gilded Age and populist responses, see Michael McGerr, *A Fierce Discontent: The Rise and Fall of the Progressive Movement in America* (New York: Free Press, 2003). For data on the scope of the income tax, see W. Elliot Brownlee, *Federal Taxation in America: A Short History* (New York: Cambridge University Press, 2004), 115–16.

8 The Revenue Act of 1894, ch. 349, § 32, 28 Stat. 509, 556. On the history of the charitable deduction, see Mehrotra, *Making the Modern American Fiscal State*, 298–307; and Vada Waters Lindsey, "The Charitable Contribution Deduction: A Historical Review and a Look to the Future," *Nebraska Law Review* 81, no. 3 (2002): 1056–96, https://digitalcommons.unl.edu/nlr /vol81/iss3/5.

9 Stanley Surrey, "Tax Incentives as a Device for Implementing Government Policy: A Comparison with Direct Government Expenditures," *Harvard Law Review* 83, no. 4 (1970): 706, 721, 723, https://doi.org/10.2307 /1339837.

10 Brownlee, *Federal Taxation in America*, 115–16.

11 See Sarah Barringer Gordon, "The First Disestablishment: Limits on Church Power and Property before the Civil War," *University of Pennsylvania Law Review* 162, no. 1 (2013): 307–72, https://www.jstor.org /stable/24247891; Stanley Katz and Benjamin Soskis, "A Brief History of Giving in Time," in Ray Madoff and Benjamin Soskis, eds., *Giving in Time: Temporal Considerations in Philanthropy* (Lanham, MD: Rowman and

Littlefield, 2023); and John Witte, Jr., "Tax Exemption of Church Property: Historical Anomaly or Valid Constitutional Practice?," *Southern California Law Review* 64, no. 2 (1991): 363–414, https://ssrn.com/abstract=1851105.

12 On congressional investigations in the 1950s, see Eleanor Brilliant, *Private Charity and Public Inquiry: A History of the Filer and Peterson Commission* (Bloomington: Indiana University Press, 2000), chap. 2; and Peter Dobkin Hall, *Inventing the Nonprofit Sector and Other Essays on Philanthropy, Voluntarism, and Nonprofit Organization* (Baltimore, MD: Johns Hopkins University Press, 1992), 66–71. On the investigations in the 1960s stewarded by Representative Wright Patman (D-TX) and directed especially toward the Ford Foundation, see Ferguson, *Top Down*, 5 (for Ford valuation) and chaps. 2 and 3; and Alice O'Connor, "Foundations: Social Movements, and the Contradictions of Liberal Philanthropy," in Helmut K. Anheier and David Hammack, eds., *American Foundations: Roles and Contributions* (Washington, DC: Brookings Institution Press, 2010).

13 Zunz, *Philanthropy in America*, 202–7.

14 Thomas Troyer, "The 1969 Private Foundation Law: Historical Perspective on Its Origins and Underpinnings," *The Exempt Organization Tax Review* 27, no. 1 (2000): 52–65, https://www.caplindrysdale.com/media/publication /150097_The%201969%20Private%20Foundation%20Law.pdf.

15 Lila Corwin Berman, "How Americans Give: The Financialization of American Jewish Philanthropy," *American Historical Review* 122, no. 5 (2017): 1459–89, https://doi.org/10.1093/ahr/122.5.1459.

16 Walker, "Toward a New Gospel of Wealth."

17 On the role of philanthropy in nourishing late-twentieth-century American politics, see Lila Corwin Berman, "How Philanthropy Made and Unmade American Liberalism," in Brent Cebul and Lily Geismer, eds., *Mastery and Drift: Professional-Class Liberals since the 1960s* (Chicago: University of Chicago Press, 2025); and Lily Geismer, *Left Behind: The Democrats' Failed Attempt to Solve Inequality* (New York: PublicAffairs, 2022). Scholars and investigative journalists have tracked the role of so-called "dark money" in the political process, another factor that may account for the relatively weak political energy to reform the philanthropic system and one whose influence has become more profound since the Supreme Court's decision in *Citizens United v. Federal Election Commission* (2010). See, for example, Nancy MacLean, *Democracy in Chains: The Deep History of the Radical Right's Stealth Plan for America* (New York: Viking, 2017); and Jane Mayer, *Dark Money: The Hidden History of the Billionaires behind the Rise of the Radical Right* (New York: Anchor, 2016).

18 See Alexis de Tocqueville, *Democracy in America, Volume 1*, trans. Henry Reeve (London: Saunders and Otley, 1835; Project Gutenberg, January 21, 2006, last updated June 11, 2024), chap. 12, www.gutenberg.org

/files/815/815-h/815-h.htm; and Alexis de Tocqueville, *Democracy in America, Volume 2*, trans. Henry Reeve (London: Saunders and Otley, 1840; Project Gutenberg, January 21, 2006, last updated February 7, 2013), sec. 2, chaps. 5 and 8, http://www.gutenberg.org/files/816/816-h/816-h.htm. See also Rogers M. Smith, "Beyond Tocqueville, Myrdal, and Hartz: The Multiple Traditions in America," *American Political Science Review* 87, no. 3 (1993): 549–66, https://doi.org/10.2307/2938735.

19 Ian Tyrrell, *American Exceptionalism: A New History of an Old Idea* (Chicago: University of Chicago Press, 2021). For a description of the pluralism justification, see Reich, *Just Giving*, 153–9, and for an advocacy statement about it, see Heather Templeton Dill et al., "We Disagree on Many Things, but We Speak with One Voice in Support of Philanthropic Pluralism," *Chronicle of Philanthropy*, April 13, 2023, https://www.philanthropy.com /article/we-disagree-on-many-things-but-we-speak-with-one-voice-in -support-of-philanthropic-pluralism.

20 See Lila Corwin Berman, "The 'Jewish Future Pledge' Is Not the Hanukkah Gift Philanthropy Needs," *Chronicle of Philanthropy*, December 14, 2020, https://www.philanthropy.com/article/the-jewish-future-pledge -is-not-the-hanukkah-gift-philanthropy-needs. For details about the establishment and terms of the Jewish Future Pledge, see its website at https://jewishfuturepledge.org/. For a discussion of the total dollars that could be accrued via the pledge, see Jewish Federations, "Together We Have the Power to Secure the Jewish Future," accessed February 3, 2025, https://www.jewishfederations.org/how-we-help/power-philanthropy /jewish-future-pledge. A recording of the session where this comment was made in the spring of 2020 can be seen at Jewish Funders Network, "Tzedakah We Can Believe In: A $600 Billion Opportunity to Secure the Jewish Future," YouTube, n.d., video 45:21, accessed February 3, 2025, https://www.youtube.com/watch?v=HLplCizind8. In 2024, when the Jewish Future Pledge rebranded as the Jewish Future Promise, it noted that signees would have to make a "moral commitment" to donate a proportion of their estate funds to Jewish causes. See "A Pledge Renewed for Generations: The Jewish Future Pledge Becomes the Jewish Future Promise," PR Newswire, February 6, 2024, https://www.prnewswire .com/news-releases/a-pledge-renewed-for-generations-the-jewish -future-pledge-becomes-the-jewish-future-promise-302054231.html. For an analysis of the Giving Pledge, see Hans Peter Schmitz, George Mitchell, and Elena McCollim, "How Billionaires Explain Their Philanthropy: A Mixed-Method Analysis of the Giving Pledge Letters," *Voluntas* 32, no. 2 (2021): 512–23, https://doi.org/10.1007/s11266-021-00338-6.

21 I explore "identity philanthropy" in depth in Berman, *American Jewish Philanthropic Complex*, chap. 6.

22 On these post–World War II trends in American Jewish life, see Lila Corwin Berman, "American Jews and the Ambivalence of Middle Classness," *American Jewish History* 93, no. 4 (2007): 409–34, https://www.jstor.org/stable/23887596; and Rachel Kranson, *Ambivalent Embrace: Jewish Upward Mobility in Postwar America* (Chapel Hill: University of North Carolina Press, 2017).

23 Robert Hiller and Meyer Schwartz, "Fund Raising as a Social Work Process," *Journal of Jewish Communal Service* 36, no. 1 (1959): 59.

24 On the shift toward Zionism and Israel as a central pillar of American Jewish philanthropy, which occurred in the 1970s, see Matthew Berkman, "Coercive Consensus: Jewish Federations, Ethnic Representation, and the Roots of American Jewish Politics" (PhD diss., University of Pennsylvania, 2018); and Eric Fleisch, *Checkbook Zionism: Philanthropy and Power in the Israel-Diaspora Relationship* (New Brunswick, NJ: Rutgers University Press). See also Derek Penslar, *Zionism: An Emotional State* (New Brunswick, NJ: Rutgers University Press, 2023), chap. 4. On the discourse of continuity, see Lila Corwin Berman, Kate Rosenblatt, and Ronit Stahl, "Continuity Crisis: The History and Sexual Politics of an American Jewish Communal Project," *American Jewish History* 104, nos. 2/3 (2020): 167–94, https://doi.org/10.1353/ajh.2020.0017.

25 See Shaul Kelner, *Tours That Bind: Diaspora, Pilgrimage, and Israeli Birthright Tourism* (New York: New York University Press, 2011), chap. 2.

26 Lila Corwin Berman, "With Huge Gifts to Birthright Israel, Wealthy Donors Influence American Jewish Identity," *Inside Philanthropy*, September 30, 2020, https://www.insidephilanthropy.com/home/2020/9/30/with-huge-gifts-to-birthright-israel-wealthy-donors-influence-american-jewish-identity. On data about intermarriage, see for example, Leonard Saxe et al., *Beyond 10 Days: Parents, Gender, Marriage, and the Long-Term Impact of Birthright Israel* (Waltham, MA: Brandeis University, Cohen Center for Modern Jewish Studies, 2017), https://www.brandeis.edu/cmjs/pdfs/jewish%20futures/Beyond10Days.pdf. On the broader trend of Jewish demography funded by philanthropic entities, see Michal Kravel-Tovi, "Introduction: Counting in Jewish," and "Wet Numbers: The Language of Continuity Crisis and the Work of Care among the Organized American Jewish Community," in Michal Kravel-Tovi and Deborah Dash Moore, eds., *Taking Stock: Cultures of Enumeration in Contemporary Jewish Life* (Bloomington: Indiana University Press, 2016).

27 On the basic tenets of JLens's advocacy strategy, see "Overview," https://www.jlensnetwork.org/overview/. On the evolution of activist and mission-aligned investing, see Archie B. Carroll, "A History of Corporate Social Responsibility: Concepts and Practices," in Andrew Crane et al., eds., *The Oxford Handbook of Corporate Social Responsibility* (Oxford: Oxford University Press, 2008).

28 See JLens, "Airbnb Abandons Corporate Social Responsibility Values by Acquiescing to BDS Campaign," updated on July 28, 2022, https://www .jlensnetwork.org/airbnb-abandons-corporate-social-responsibility-values -by-acquiescing-to-bds-campaign/; and JLens Investor Network, *2022 Impact Report*, https://www.jlensnetwork.org/impact-overview/reports/. See Julia Jacobs, "Airbnb Reverses Policy Banning Listings in Israeli Settlements in West Bank," *New York Times*, April 9, 2019, https://www .nytimes.com/2019/04/09/world/middleeast/airbnb-israel-west-bank .html.

29 For reporting and analysis of the case, see Mari Cohen, "How a Giant of Responsible Investing Agreed to an Israel Exception," *Jewish Currents*, January 25, 2023, https://jewishcurrents.org/how-a-giant-of-responsible -investing-agreed-to-an-israel-exception.

30 See JLens, "Summary: JLens' Campaign to Combat BDS at Morningstar," November 2, 2022, https://www.jlensnetwork.org/post/summary-jlens -campaign-to-combat-bds-at-morningstar. On Morningstar's internal investigation, see "A Letter from Joe Mansueto and Kunal Kapoor," June 2, 2022, Morningstar, https://www.morningstar.com/company/esg -research-integrity.

31 See ADL, "ADL Expands Capabilities to Combat BDS and Antisemitism in ESG," press release, November 10, 2022, https://www.adl.org/resources /press-release/adl-expands-capabilities-combat-bds-antisemitism-esg?gcli d=CjwKCAjw6IiiBhAOEiwALNqncXK5fwcsdXKUtUL3AAXvO2C5jiYcpi 4L90dquRJDvOkyVFIGXpKDHRoCVg8QAvD_BwE.

32 Mary Ann Castle, "Abortion in the United States' Bible Belt: Organizing for Power and Empowerment," *Reproductive Health* 8, no. 1 (2011), https:// doi.org/10.1186/1742-4755-8-1; and Heather Curtis, *Holy Humanitarians: American Evangelicals and Global Aid* (Cambridge, MA: Harvard University Press, 2018). On Catholic investment practices, see Committee on Budget and Finance of the United States Conference of Catholic Bishops, *Socially Responsible Investment Guidelines for the United States Conference of Catholic Bishops* (Washington, DC: United States Conference of Catholic Bishops, 2021), https://www.usccb.org/resources/Socially%20Responsible%20 Investment%20Guidelines%202021%20(003).pdf. On the views of the American public on abortion, see "Where Do Americans Stand on Abortion," Gallup, July 7, 2023, https://news.gallup.com/poll/321143 /americans-stand-abortion.aspx.

33 See Turning Point USA, "About TPUSA," accessed February 3, 2025, https://www.tpusa.com/about; and on Leven's advisory position, see Turning Point USA, "Mike Leven," accessed February 3, 2025, https:// www.tpusa.com/mikeleven. For details on the foundation's contributions for the years 2019, 2020, and 2021, see "990-PF, Return of Private Foundation for Michael and Andrea Leven Family Foundation (2019),"

accessed February 3, 2025, https://pdf.guidestar.org/PDF_Images
/2019/274/093/2019-274093841-17369911-F.pdf?_gl=1*1jftg91*_ga*MjEw
MTY2NDQ4Mi4xNjgxODQyNzU0*_ga_5W8PXYYGBX*MTY4MTg0Mjc1
My4xLjEuMTY4MTg0Mjc4Ni4yNy4wLjA.&_ga=2.35965027.2144504327
.1681842754–2101664482.1681842754&_gac=1.19757130.1681842754.Cj0KC
QiAsqOMBhDFARIsAFBTN3fNrAhRN5kUgeoYnsMQEAZtL3DkNlaxux
5AsuWBwfcN0aoiwVmqUOMaAgkzEALw_wcB; "990-PF, Return
of Private Foundation for Michael and Andrea Leven Family Foundation
(2020)," accessed February 3, 2025, https://pdf.guidestar.org/PDF
_Images/2020/274/093/2020-274093841-202143169349101724-F.pdf?
_gl=1*1l4lqur*_gcl_aw*R0NMLjE3MDQ3MjUwODEuQ2owS0NRaUFzc
U9NQmhERkFSSXNBRkJUTjNmTnJBaFJONWtVZ2VvWW5zTVFFQVp
0TDNEa05sYXh1eDVBc3VXQndmY04wYW9pd1ZtcVVPTWFBZ2t6RU
FMd193Y0I.*_gcl_au*MTc1Mjc5MDc4NS4xNzAxMTMzODY5*_ga*MTQw
MDA2MzYxOS4xNzAxMTMzODY5*_ga_5W8PXYYGBX*MTcwNDcyNT
A4MS44LjEuMTcwNDcyNTE1MC42MC4wLjA; "990-PF, Return of Private
Foundation for Michael and Andrea Leven Family Foundation (2021),"
accessed February 3, 2025, https://pdf.guidestar.org/PDF
_Images/2021/274/093/2021-274093841-202242869349101034-F
.pdf?_gl=1*use4tz*_gcl_aw*R0NMLjE3MDQ3MjUwODEuQ2owS0NRa
UFzcU9NQmhERkFSSXNBRkJUTjNmTnJBaFJONWtVZ2VvWW5zTVF
FQVp0TDNEa05sYXh1eDVBc3VXQndmY04wYW9pd1ZtcVVPTWFBZ2
t6RUFMd193Y0I.*_gcl_au*MTc1Mjc5MDc4NS4xNzAxMTMzODY5*_ga*
MTQwMDA2MzYxOS4xNzAxMTMzODY5*_ga_5W8PXYYGBX*MTc
wNDcyNTA4MS44LjEuMTcwNDcyNTExNC4yNy4wLjA. On Turning
Point USA's involvement in the Capitol riot, see Peter Stone, "Money and
Misinformation: How Turning Point USA Became a Formidable Pro-Trump
Force," *Guardian*, October 23, 2021, https://www.theguardian
.com/us-news/2021/oct/23/turning-point-rightwing-youth-group
-critics-tactics; and Sarah Al-Arshani, "A Former Firefighter Charged in
the Capital Riot Took a Bus Organized by Turning Point USA to DC, Filing
Says," *Business Insider*, March 3, 2021, https://www.businessinsider.com
/man-charged-capitol-riot-went-dc-bus-turning-point-usa-2021-3. On
Leven's advisory position, see https://www.tpusa.com/mikeleven.

34 Elizabeth Schmidt, "Why It Isn't Surprising That the IRS Grants Tax-
Exempt Status to Extremists, Including an Oath Keepers Foundation,"
Chronicle of Philanthropy, May 19, 2023, https://www.philanthropy.com
/article/why-it-isnt-surprising-that-the-irs-grants-tax-exempt-status-to
-extremists-including-an-oath-keepers-foundation?sra=true; and Elizabeth
Schmidt, "IRS Granted Tax-Exempt Status to Extremists, Including an Oath
Keepers Foundation – Here's Why That's Not as Surprising as It Sounds,"
The Conversation, May 18, 2023, https://theconversation.com

/irs-granted-tax-exempt-status-to-extremists-including-an-oath-keepers
-foundation-heres-why-thats-not-as-surprising-as-it-sounds-201145. On
Trump's commutation, see Alan Feuer, "Trump Commutes Sentence
of Stewart Rhodes, Founder of Oath Keepers Militia," *New York Times*,
January 20, 2025, https://www.nytimes.com/2025/01/20/us/politics
/stewart-rhodes-trump-jan-6-oath-keepers.html.

35 See "The Revenue Code and a Charity's Politics," *Yale Law Journal* 73, no. 4
(1964): 666–8, https://doi.org/10.2307/794605; and Patrick O'Daniel,
"More Honored in the Breach: A Historical Perspective of the Permeable
IRS Prohibition on Campaigning by Churches," *Boston College Law Review*
42 (2001): 733–69, https://bclawreview.bc.edu/articles/1187/files
/63bd6c46b2456.pdf. Helpful to understanding how these laws functioned
is Wendy Brown's writing on depoliticization. See Wendy Brown,
Regulating Aversion: Tolerance in the Age of Identity and Empire (Princeton,
NJ: Princeton University Press, 2006), 15.

36 Rob Reich, Lacey Dorn, and Stefanie Sutton, *Anything Goes: Approval of
Nonprofit Status by the IRS* (Stanford: Stanford Center on Philanthropy and
Civil Society, 2009), 3, https://pacscenter.stanford.edu/publication
/anything-goes-approval-of-nonprofit-status-by-the-irs/. See also
"Number of Nonprofits Nearing 2 Million," *NonProfit Times*, July 19,
2021, https://thenonprofittimes.com/regulation/number-of-nonprofits
-nearing-2-million/.

37 Alex Kotch, "America's Biggest Charities Are Funneling Millions to Hate
Groups from Anonymous Donors," *Sludge*, February 19, 2019, https://
readsludge.com/2019/02/19/americas-biggest-charities-are-funneling
-millions-to-hate-groups-from-anonymous-donors/. See also Abbas
Barzegar and Anna Fink, "Who Pays for Hate?," *Inside Philanthropy*,
January 21, 2021, https://www.insidephilanthropy.com/home/2021
/1/21/who-pays-for-hate.

38 Council on American-Islamic Relations, *Hijacked by Hate: American
Philanthropy and the Islamophobia Network* (Washington, DC: CAIR, 2019),
https://pa.cair.com/islamophobia/cair-report/.

39 Alex Kotch and Michael Edison Hayden, "Donors Pumped Millions into
White Nationalist Group," *Hatewatch*, June 17, 2021, https://www
.splcenter.org/hatewatch/2021/06/17/donors-pumped-millions
-white-nationalist-group.

40 Lila Corwin Berman, "Donor Advised Funds in Historical Perspective,"
Boston College Law Forum on Philanthropy and the Public Good 1 (October
2015): 5–27, https://lira.bc.edu/work/ns/8f73ede8-14af-451c-9e7e
-92d6570e7a0f.

41 For a critical overview of DAFs that notes this attribute, see Lewis B.
Cullman and Ray Madoff, "The Undermining of American Charity,"

New York Review of Books, July 14, 2016, https://www.nybooks.com
/articles/2016/07/14/the-undermining-of-american-charity/.

42 CAIR, *Hijacked by Hate*, 28; and Kotch and Hayden, "Donors Pumped
Millions into White Nationalist Group." The former president and CEO
of Inland Northwest Community Foundation has offered thoughtful
reflections on DAFs and funding for hate groups, especially VDARE. See
Mark Hurtubise, "Philanthropy Must Not Support Hate," *Stanford Social
Innovation Review* 19, no. 1 (2021): 55–6, https://ssir.org/articles
/entry/philanthropy_must_not_support_hate; and Mark Hurtubise,
"Philanthropy Funding Hate Groups," Bard Center for the Study of Hate,
YouTube, January 28, 2021, video, 1:02:01, https://www.youtube.com
/watch?v=NvLSMm5VZMM&t=167s. See National Philanthropic Trust,
"The 2024 DAF Report," accessed February 3, 2025, https://www.nptrust
.org/reports/daf-report/.

43 For the ADL's assessment of CAIR, see ADL Backgrounder, "The Council
on American Islamic Relations (CAIR)," August 21, 2015, last updated
December 23, 2024, https://www.adl.org/resources/backgrounder
/council-american-islamic-relations-cair. On the role of philanthropists
after October 7, 2023, see Lila Corwin Berman and Benjamin Soskis, "The
Dangers of Donor Revolt," *Chronicle of Higher Education*, November 13,
2023, https://www.chronicle.com/article/the-dangers-of-donor-revolt.

44 The exact language from the 1954 congressional hearings is described in
Judith Kindell and John Francis Reilly, "Election Year Issues," US Internal
Revenue Service, accessed February 3, 2025, https://www.irs.gov/pub
/irs-tege/eotopici02.pdf. See also Roger Colinvaux, "The Political Speech
of Charities in the Face of Citizens United: A Defense of Prohibition," *Case
Western Reserve Law Review* 62, no. 3 (2012): 694–7, https://scholarly
commons.law.case.edu/caselrev/vol62/iss3/12.

45 See, for example, Roger Colinvaux, "Defending Place-Based Philanthropy
by Defining the Community Foundation," *Brigham Young University Law
Review* 2018, no. 1 (Fall 2018): 1–56, https://digitalcommons.law.byu
.edu/lawreview/vol2018/iss1/4. On participatory grantmaking, see Lila
Corwin Berman and Matt Berkman, "Democratizing American Jewish
Philanthropy: New Models for Capital Circulation," NYU Applied
Research Collective for American Jewry, 2019, https://static1.squares
pace.com/static/60bf7eeb36252e1b53064736/t/615cc74476840504
140e19d2/1633470277641/LC-DemocratizingAJP_121219.pdf. For
more general critiques of philanthropy that focus in particular on its
anti-democratic means, see Anand Giridharadas, *Winners Take All:
The Elite Charade of Changing the World* (New York: Knopf, 2018); Gara
LaMarche, "Is Philanthropy Bad for Democracy?," *The Atlantic*, October
30, 2014, https://www.theatlantic.com/politics/archive/2014/10/is

-philanthropy-good-for-democracy/381996/; and Vanessa Williamson, "The Philanthropy Con," *Dissent* (Winter 2019), https://www .dissentmagazine.org/article/the-philanthropy-con/.

46 See, for example, Howard Husock, "Donor-Advised Critics Miss the Point about the Value of These Tools," *Chronicle of Philanthropy*, October 27, 2016, https://www.philanthropy.com/article/donor-advised-critics-miss -the-point-about-the-value-of-these-tools/; and Andres Spokoiny, "Actually, the Jewish Future Pledge Is a Great Hanukkah Gift," *Chronicle of Philanthropy*, December 18, 2020, https://www.philanthropy.com/article /in-defense-of-the-jewish-future-pledge.

47 See, for example, "White House Memorandum for the Heads of Executive Departments and Agencies," February 6, 2025, https://www.whitehouse .gov/presidential-actions/2025/02/memorandum-for-the-heads-of -executive-departments-and-agencies/; and Ted Siefer, "Nonprofits Prepare for a Fight over Tax Policies," *Nonprofit Quarterly*, February 6, 2025, https://nonprofitquarterly.org/nonprofits-prepare-for-a-fight-over-tax -policies/.

Editor's Introduction to Chapter 11

So imagine you're an NGO board member, funder, or staffer digesting the strategic thinking about hate outlined by the experts in this book. Or you, as an individual, want to do what you can to reduce hate in your day-to-day life. How do you translate that information into an analysis of how you spend your time and money? Money and time are finite items – spend them one way, you cannot reclaim them to spend another way. What are the wisest choices for us to make?

Years ago I was asked my opinion about taking an American-based anti-bias educational program and having educators use it in Germany, after a series of attacks on immigrants. The educational model was largely Holocaust-based, and I first wondered if it would work differently in the country where the Holocaust actually happened. But then I pondered another question: How do we know if the anti-bias curriculum actually worked?

The short answer was, we didn't. When I called people associated with anti-bias educational efforts and asked how they evaluated the effectiveness of their programs, they said they asked the teachers who used their material what they thought. I said that's fine, and I'm glad the teachers seem to like using your materials, but how do you know they actually reduce bias? Many replies were indignant – of course our program works! These were people who deeply believed in what they did, and had a passion for fighting bigotry. But they were operating more on faith than data.

I get it. Resources are finite. If you believe in your product, you will spend your funds on increasing the number of people who can use it. To put money into evaluation, especially to see if there are long-term benefits, means taking money away from day-to-day operations. When you pitch funders that your programs are in x number of schools, you might have to point to a somewhat less impressive score card if your money is also going into evaluation.

But there is data to show that some educational programs don't work as advertised. Over the long haul, people who went through anti-drug or anti-smoking programs in their school years are about as likely as those who didn't to smoke or do drugs.[1]

So how should NGOs who believe their programs work well make sure they do? As Lowe and Jimenez discussed in chapter 5, and as will be expanded upon in this final chapter, that's a matter of better evaluation, and one of the goals of this book is to provide useful tools for that purpose. In fact, one of the premises of this book is that not only will it be a useful read but it will also stand as a manual that NGO boards and others can rely on for training on how to think deeply about what they are doing, why, and how to measure success.[2]

One of the pleasures of putting this book together was asking as many people as I could who the best expert was on the various topics to be addressed. The best at program evaluation clearly was Irit Houvras, who for many years ran that portfolio at American Jewish World Service (AJWS). She has written about program evaluation more generally too. When I first approached her, she described the models and theories behind how AJWS funds human rights programs in comparison to the public health initiatives she had worked on earlier in her career. The latter are, logically, easier to evaluate. You can assess how many shots are put into arms, or how many people are using mosquito nets, and track incidence of disease. But how do you know if the money given to a group that opposed anti-LGBTQI+ efforts was well spent? Diseases have specific causes, and vaccines and other therapies clearly have measurable impact. But hate – as we have seen – has many things that can increase or decrease it: how our brains work, our cultures, how politicians and leaders speak, and so much more. How, in this complex minefield, can we evaluate what likely works and what doesn't? To revisit the early metaphor in this book, how do we get a decent-enough picture of the entire elephant?

As a fitting end to this book, Houvras weaves in the observations of the other co-creators of this volume, employing their theories as markers for evaluation of programs. Houvras's observations – recast as a bullet-point summary that can be printed out and used as an easy-to-reference set of principles and practices[3] – are a guidepost not only for NGOs but for all of us thinking about how best to confront hate.

NOTES

1 See Walter G. Stephan and W. Paul Vogt, *Education Programs for Improving Intergroup Relations: Theory, Research and Practice* (New York: Teacher's College Press, 2004), 14.
2 The Bard Center for the Study of Hate will facilitate this – see https://bcsh.bard.edu/training-program-for-ngos-and-others-based-on-simply-human-a-guide-to-understanding-and-combating-hate/.
3 The summary checklist appears at the end of chapter 11 and can be found online at https://bcsh.bard.edu/simply-human-a-guide-to-understanding-and-combating-hate/.

11 Considerations for Evaluation: Center Learning

IRIT HOUVRAS

If your mission is to confront hate, you know success is possible despite the challenges. As the authors in this volume have pointed out, achieving eradication of hate may be an impossible pursuit for idealists (Brudholm and Johansen, chapter 1), or a multi-generational endeavor (Li, chapter 3), but we know that progress is possible (Badgett, chapter 6; Buerger, chapter 9; Levin, chapter 4; Lowe and Jimenez, chapter 5; Schweppe and Walters, chapter 7).

These chapters have presented evidence, insights, and possibilities for understanding hate and for addressing hate. Together, these chapters demonstrate the complexity of understanding the root causes of hate and suggest that preventing, mitigating, and responding to hate will require a combination of strategies and tactics. Each of these chapters offers important learnings for programming. At the end of this chapter, you will find a consolidated list of key takeaways to reflect on and consider how you have already or might newly incorporate these into your work. But first, consider how you approach learning and evaluation. How do practitioners understand whether and how their efforts are contributing to a larger goal in combination with other interventions and societal shifts, while also recognizing and considering alternative possibilities and effects of opposing forces? How do practitioners learn how they can improve, respond, or do better?

The complexity of addressing hate has implications for learning and evaluation. Regardless of how you define hate or the type of change you are seeking, understanding your contributions and identifying ways in which you can improve your work are difficult. The types of change illustrated in the chapters of this book include individual attitudes, individual behaviors, intergroup solidarity, public narratives, societal norms, and societal structures such as laws and policies and their transparency, implementation, and enforcement. Change will likely require a combination of approaches led by a broad spectrum of individuals and organizations. Understanding whether and how change is happening will be challenging for many reasons:

- Results can be tenuous and difficult to ascertain in the short term.
- Change is not linear, and it is difficult to sustain. Regress is normal and should be anticipated.
- The ecosystem is dynamic: there are many other actors and factors at play. Attribution is difficult if not impossible. And the sum effect is often greater, for better or worse, than one specific action or intervention.
- Responses can be counterintuitive. Backlash is normal and should be anticipated.
- Opposing forces are often powerful and strategic.
- Contexts are volatile, and yet culture is entrenched and can be so very slow to shift.

We also face internal organizational challenges. Those working to address hate do not set out with an intent to contribute to or cause harm, or to incite or escalate hate; and yet, we cannot always anticipate the consequences of our actions. To bolster our hope and belief that change is possible, that our work matters, we often get caught up in focusing on our discernible successes over often less visible, unintended consequences.

So, how can we understand whether our investments in change are making, if only incrementally, any difference in the short-term, while keeping our eye on the long-term vision for success – a better world, a loving world, a kinder world where all people enjoy and experience dignity and basic universal human rights? What is our obligation to understand how we are having an impact, contributing to unintended harm, or exacerbating backlash, and how do we best fulfill this obligation? How can a deeper understanding of our values, our biases and assumptions, failures and setbacks, be leveraged as an asset to strengthen our work?

Opportunity for learning and evaluation exists. Actors engaged in preventing, mitigating, or responding to hate have important and real choices to make with regard to learning and evaluation. Meaningful opportunities will emerge if some basic principles are in place: a desire to achieve change, a belief that there is a pathway to do so, accountability to invest in learning and act on findings – whether positive or negative and even if it means a complete change of course –

and a commitment to share learning as well as build on the learning of others.

Key Definitions

Learning is defined here as an iterative, responsive, and flexible practice in which there is critical and systematic reflection using evidence to understand and challenge assumptions, biases, and progress or regress toward desired and expected change to inform strategic decisions and respond dynamically to unanticipated developments or consequences. One example of a learning practice would be to facilitate periodic and inclusive convenings to review relevant research findings, to discuss the implications for your work, and to decide on what you will do differently.

Evaluation is defined here as the systematic gathering and analysis of evidence that helps us understand whether, how, and why change (positive or negative, intended or unintended) is occurring to inform judgments about projects or programs and their effectiveness, and support decisions about future strategies and tactics.[1] Evaluation is one tool that supports learning. Evaluation often leverages evidence from other tools that support learning, including research and monitoring. While commonly thought of as limited to a "look back" on what has worked and what has not, there are useful evaluation approaches and methods for all stages of a project or program lifecycle. Evaluation is often the entry point to developing learning practice and culture.

Evidence is defined here as information, or data, qualitative or quantitative, from any source. It can be gathered by anyone – including communities themselves – through a variety of means and methods, and from a variety of sources. Evidence should be gathered and triangulated in such a way that allows for an understanding of depth and diversity of perspective. It is important to be explicit about the limitations of any evidence (is it partial, contested, ambiguous?). It is also important to recognize any inherent bias (who has decided what evidence is important or valid?).

The terms learning, evaluation, and evidence are understood as intrinsically related. Learning is dependent on evidence, systematically gathered and analyzed through reflection, monitoring, evaluation, and/or research. Evaluations require an intentional and resourced process to actively engage with and apply learning from the findings.[2]

In this chapter, I offer recommendations for a learning and evaluation strategy: value learning as transformative, nurture a learning culture, measure what matters, and leverage and contribute your learning.

With the challenges of complex social change where there is not one clear and predictable solution and the context is dynamic, a solid foundation for learning is indispensable. This requires a dialogical space and mindset open to questioning (what could be improved, what is not working, what needs to change?), seeking possibilities, and acting on findings. The more inclusive the dialogical space, the greater potential for actors to share and learn together and foster greater change.

Throughout this chapter, I layer in reflection and questions related to understanding how learning and evaluation can contribute to social change, as any other programmatic intervention. This reflection goes beyond acknowledging the ethical obligation to evaluate, or the ethics involved in the process of evaluation so that no harm is done (i.e., ethics in data collection, misuse of data, etc.). These issues are important but will not be covered here. The premise follows the adage "knowledge is power" – the more we know, and the more people engaged in this active *knowing* or *mutual learning*, the more we are empowered to support and contribute to change.

While the intent of this chapter is to support those confronting hate directly, my most recent role has been as an internal evaluator for an organization that is both funder and ally. My perspective is undoubtedly influenced by function and exposure to a specific discourse. My hope is that this chapter serves as a resource for both NGO practitioners and funder/ally audiences. This chapter is further informed by the current discourse in the field of social change and evaluation, review by evaluation colleagues, and conversations convened by Ken Stern with NGOs and authors of the other chapters (see Acknowledgments).

Finally, it is important to note that it is beyond the scope of this chapter to offer specific methodological recommendations. There may be a desire to leap to the "how to" and practical advice on evaluation methodologies. However, decisions on evaluation design and tools used are dependent on knowing the particulars of the programmatic strategy and tactics and the specific learning questions. One can find innumerable resources on evaluation,[3] specific resources for evaluation of various strategies and tactics,[4] and experienced evaluators to support design and implementation.[5] The premise of this chapter is that before there is articulation of actionable learning questions, or subsequent selection of most appropriate methodology for each question, there must be intentional reflection on how to understand, commit to, and cultivate the power of learning. Strategically building this culture in your organization will energize a demand for both learning and evaluation, which will more meaningfully serve your overall programmatic goals.

Recommendations

1. Value Learning as Transformative

Why do you evaluate? To whom do you feel obligated when you are evaluating, if anyone? To whom do you feel accountable when you are evaluating, if anyone?

Whether you systematically evaluate every project or program, or have never evaluated your work before, reflecting on and clarifying your values with regard to learning and evaluation will be instructive. Our values are directly affected by our obligations, accountabilities, and our partnerships. Subsequent questions that will be important include: Who is involved in learning and evaluation, and what does involvement look like? How do you engage in learning and evaluation? What is considered evidence? How are assumptions and biases named and understood? How are learnings taken up and applied? As you clarify your organization's value for learning and evaluation, you will be able to (re)align your accountabilities, partnerships, practices, structures, and systems to reflect and reinforce your values, rather than undermine them.

Understand learning and evaluation as an essential tool to advance social change. Leveraging the power of learning and evaluation starts with a recognition that there is something to learn – that there may be existing evidence, other perspectives, and other possibilities that would positively and significantly improve your approach, that remaining open and curious can lead to something better. It requires an understanding that learning is an integral component of the work itself.

A number of chapters in this volume discuss the value of learning, including chapter 5 by Lowe and Jimenez. As they describe, Define American uses a "feedback loop of research, practice, and evaluation" that actively engages all staff in the process. Their learning is not limited to evaluation, but inclusive of research, monitoring, and ongoing reflection, supported and informed by trusting partnerships with those who are affected by hate, media industry experts, and researchers. This organization-wide practice of learning leads to conceptual clarity of what the organization wants to achieve, and how to best go about it. It also gives staff the ability to assess progress on a routine basis, using real-time data to make informed adjustments to improve their work. Lowe and Jimenez share how Define American's commitment to continuous learning is understood as not only integral to developing and improving its programmatic efforts, but also to its positioning as an "active contributor" in the field and "promoting positive cultural change."

Many readers will not contest this, having experienced the benefits of learning and evaluation. However, there are tensions presented by typical obligations and accountabilities that should be confronted, and priorities should be intentionally affirmed. This is true even where the work itself is led by representatives of communities most affected who have obligations and accountabilities to their constituents.

Recognize and prioritize multiple obligations and accountabilities. These priorities are first, to the community being served; second, to one's own organizational mission; and third, to funders. This shift to centering your primary obligations and accountabilities to those who are affected by hate may be radical rethinking. Jim Coe and Rhonda Schlangen have likened it to "pulling up the floorboards" to rebuild the system.[6] The Equitable Evaluation Initiative has touched on this as related to a number of areas where evaluation "orthodoxies" persist.[7] While funders are actively engaged in considering whether and how best to facilitate a reprioritization, NGOs need to make and advocate for this radical shift as well. Recognize that by "re-centering" those who you hope to benefit from your actions, you will serve to strengthen your (and your donors') understanding of what success looks like, and your understanding of obstacles and conditions for success. It will reshape your learning and evaluation systems, structures, and approaches – how and who you engage, determining what questions are asked, and what is considered "valid" or "rigorous" evidence to support analysis and decision-making. Perhaps most importantly, this recentering will fortify existing principles and obligations to *do no harm*, to know when unintended harm happens, and to know how to address it and learn from it.

NGOs often prioritize their funder obligations and accountabilities, which includes evaluation. Despite the long-term nature of change being sought, the reality is that organizations request and receive funding from donors (often with their own "upward" accountabilities) with the obligation to implement specific projects and the accountability to deliver *Impact*, or a *Return on Investment*. There is the expectation that *Impact* will be demonstrated in a short time frame and through evaluation.[8] This "upward" obligation and accountability can distort and disrupt the potential power of learning and evaluation, which is to engage in meaningful and mutual learning with communities most affected, to strengthen programmatic strategy, and to share learning within the broader sector.

An NGO may not make course corrections or report failure for fear of losing funding. NGOs often prioritize a set course of promised action responding to donor demands, rather than a learning agenda with questions meaningful to those engaged in/by the work. Systems are then built to deliver evidence to attract new donors, and to report to existing donors, with a focus on performance and results of positive impact. Thoughtfully constructed results frameworks and logic models with clearly defined indicators provided by the donors will not necessarily measure what matters or lead to energized, actionable learning. As *form follows function*, what you value is reflected in who and what obligations you prioritize, whether explicitly or implicitly, which has a direct effect on how you action your principles and design structures to support learning and evaluation.

Other organizations may successfully self-direct their learning and evaluation, focusing their accountabilities and obligations inward. An organization may hold its staff accountable for results based on its own mission and strategy, but still may not be centering those most affected. This can result in prioritizing a biased understanding of the problem, the solutions, and the results, and lead to extractive learning and evaluation practices. This approach reinforces latent or active power dynamics that unintentionally amplify the problem.

If there is an obligation to do no harm, and one's mission is to improve the lives of specific peoples, prioritize your obligations and accountabilities to those peoples. The lives you center in a program strategy should be those you center in your learning and evaluation strategy. As you aim to prevent, mitigate, or respond to hatred of a specific community, your obligations and accountabilities for evaluation should center these very same people.

Facilitate learning partnerships. Establishing internal and external (critical thinking) thought partnerships is important. As you center those who are most affected, build trusting relationships and learning partnerships with these communities, even where you represent the community itself. This was demonstrated by Schweppe and Walters in chapter 7, where they indicated the importance of engaging with victims and victim communities to build trust, and how civil society organizations (CSOs) play an active and meaningful role in a multi-agency approach to develop and reform national/ state strategies, action plans, justice interventions, and education campaigns.

Evaluators functioning in a donor-centered model may engage with meaningful participatory processes, but they may still ultimately be extractive – taking "findings" to inform strategy rather than engaging in mutual learning, meaning-making, and strategy design in partnership with the community. In a community-centered model, where relationships and trust are cultivated, these inclusive partnerships will serve to enrich and advance change and potentially amplify it by allowing everyone engaged to act on collective strategy, either formally or informally.[9]

Consider the "Resonance Spectrum" from Justice Funders[10] and reflect on your ideal relationship with the community you aim to benefit. The "Resonance Spectrum" describes a range of relationships to community: from extractive, to less extractive, to less restorative, to restorative:[11]

- **Extractive**: based on *risk-aversion, scarcity and fear* with *power over* or *controlling* engagement
- **Less extractive**: with communities responsive to *requests for time and knowledge and other resources*
- **Less restorative**: where *knowledge, expertise and lived experiences are acknowledged and respected*
- **Restorative**: where authentic partnerships *support their right to design solutions for their lives rather than have approaches imposed on them.*[12]

To what extent are your relationships with community extractive versus restorative? What would be your ideal relationship and what are the obstacles? How do your actions reflect your ideal relationship? Does your existing language about your relationships match your ideal relationship or your actions? How do your strategy, learning, and evaluation practices reinforce an extractive relationship or support a restorative relationship?

Reflect on the range of relationship possibilities with regard to your learning and evaluation practices, and how these are aligned with your values: from no engagement at all, to full participation in mutual learning and shared decision-making, to being community driven. Participatory engagement in collective learning and reflection (through research, monitoring, and/or evaluation) can contribute to better-defined issues and challenges, foster more useful and authentic relationships, support stronger feedback loops, lead to a larger base of supporters who are sharing perspective and building trust, and support that larger base in advancing the desired social change. Inclusive engagement in learning and evaluation as well as programmatic implementation means recognizing community or "those most affected" as partners, as opposed to resources of information to inform work through extractive practices. So often we do not recognize that we are learning from each other, or appreciate the power created by joining forces through collective engagement in all processes.

Reflect on your internal learning partnerships as well. Some donors will expect or require evaluation of the grants that they fund (motivated by different learning priorities and values, such as performance), and so many NGOs will have dedicated staff and/or budget to support this function. The role of evaluators offers a unique skill set and expertise, including frameworks, methodologies, and facilitation. Evaluators can support, complement, and enhance definitional and conceptual clarity. They support understanding of how success is defined, with a clearly articulated pathway of change – ensuring terms, goals, and objectives are specific. They draw attention to and challenge underlying assumptions and biases that often would otherwise remain obscured.

As a practice, evaluators consider and bring in diversity of perspective. However, in NGOs where it is not possible to have dedicated evaluation staff or budget to support external evaluators, it is important to intentionally establish alternative and inclusive learning partnerships with the aim of challenging assumptions and biases, seeking alternative explanations for successes, and uncovering and analyzing setbacks and failures. Consider facilitating dialogues where some staff are intentionally requested to engage as "devil's advocate," or bringing in substantive experts who hold lived experience and/or understanding of relevant research.

2. Nurture a Learning Culture

A learning culture is one where across the organization reflection and learning are valued, integrated, and cultivated rather than siloed and accommodated as the function of one specific unit to respond to donor accountabilities. Your values hold the potential to shape and support your learning culture. Your learning culture will support learning habits and practices, including the use of research, monitoring, and evaluation as a programmatic tactic in itself to advance your mission (such as community-led research and the monitoring of hate crime, as discussed by Levin, chapter 4, and Schweppe and Walters, chapter 7).

Reflecting on existing evidence, including research and evaluation, is essential to analysis and to establishing hypotheses of what will make a difference – what to do or try out, how to do it, and/or how to improve. Research and evaluation supports learning that has been done before. The authors of each chapter indicate what works and what doesn't, what is risky, and what questions remain. But how do you ensure that learnings such as these are engaged with and taken up effectively? Reflecting on your system and your learning habits can help. The Center for Evaluation Innovation (CEI) has invested in supporting the philanthropic evaluation community to reflect on their systems and habits, which are applicable to all organizations engaged in learning, including NGOs.

Leverage the system. Internally, reflecting holistically on your organization as a system will help you identify where there may be areas for strengthening, and which system levers may yield better results.

The tool developed by the Center for Evaluation Innovation[13] and adapted from Donella Meadow's work[14] is a useful framework for analysis. Use it to locate where in your system you might best intervene for greater and more durable change in support of learning. The tool outlines the list of twelve leverage points in order of strength, with the strongest leverage points related to *Leadership*, followed by *Structure, Information Flows, Design,* and *Individual Capacity*. The framework reinforces the importance of articulating one's values and establishing learning partnerships, as described in the first recommendation, and provides greater depth and nuance in possible levers for change.

Most often there is a tendency to focus on *Individual Capacity* (training, funding, time or space for learning); however, while this may be necessary, it gives us the least leverage for change in the system compared to higher levers. In contrast, leveraging *Leadership* through attending to *Paradigm* and *Purpose* means, "Leaders know the value of learning, prioritize it, back it," and, "Leaders speak and act as if quality learning was already a fact." This means leadership understands and makes actionable the value of learning and evaluation, through intentional and explicit engagements with the board, program staff, and strategy.[15] This is the strongest leverage point for systems change in support of a learning culture. As you strengthen your learning culture, they prompt you to consider the level(s) at which you are working, and whether you could intervene at a higher level or levels.

Cultivate learning habits. The Center for Evaluation Innovation has also identified five habits to support the building of a strong learning culture:

1. **Make your thinking visible.** *Are you defining your terms with specificity? Have you explicated the pathway or theory of change you anticipate? Are you being explicit about what you know and what you don't know and need to learn?*
2. **Ask powerful questions.** *Are you (collectively) asking specific learning questions with clear hypotheses that energize and will inform decisions and actions by everyone engaged?*
3. **Combat your biases.** *Are you naming your assumptions? Are you systematically and rigorously seeking alternative perspectives?*

4. **Attend to causal inference.** *Are you investigating both progress and regress, intended and unintended results, and seeking alternative explanations for the change observed?*
5. **Answer the "now what" question.** *Beyond understanding what happened and reflecting on the implications, are you actively engaged in discussing and determining whether and how you will apply this learning?*[16]

CEI's premise is that small shifts can lead to big changes. Consider your organization's learning habits and how you might bring your teams together to improve; as Julia Coffman suggests,

> **Practiced in organizations, keystone habits create cultures where change is contagious.** They act like mini experiments that help us test theories about barriers and opportunities, revealing lessons that we can build on to create further change.[17]

3. "Measure" What Matters

Learning should ultimately lead to action, so it is important to prioritize what you "measure" to achieve that goal. In this context, measurement is understood as any means of systematic data collection, whether quantitative OR qualitative.

Consider the following criteria to support prioritization: The "measures" you use to understand your progress or regress should be as **meaningful** as possible, while also being **minimally burdensome** (to community members, partners, and staff) and **maximally actionable** or useful in informing improvements to your work. Conceptual clarity and specificity on what you are trying to achieve, the challenges to achieving change, and what decisions are necessary or possible will support your understanding of what is meaningful for you to "measure." We often underestimate the resources it requires (financial and human) to systematically collect data for learning and evaluation. Consider the level of effort required, and from whom, to build trusting relationships and engage in learning. And we often measure too much – gathering more data than we can meaningfully use. These three criteria will help you prioritize your selection of measures.

Develop conceptual clarity. Making thinking visible is one of the five learning habits detailed above. I've found that this habit is a hallmark benefit of learning and evaluation. In order to determine what is most meaningful to measure, there must be conceptual clarity. NGOs' recognition of the importance of collectively defining ones' terms is discussed by Brudholm and Johansen in chapter 1 (even when we assume everyone holds the same definition, one term can mean so many different things). It is also critical to define what success looks like, what are the root causes of the problem, what is the theory or pathway of change, what would indicate that there is incremental progress toward that vision of success, and the assumptions underpinning your thinking. As you center your accountabilities on communities affected by hate, and hold learning partnerships with them, there will be associated shifts in how you define your terms, how you define success, how you understand root causes, and how you articulate your pathway or theory of change. You might also consider reflecting on how you are set up and showing up as an ally, with an aim to strengthening your relationships.

To further support conceptual clarity, identify what learning questions you have and how they will support decision-making and action. Learning agendas can be helpful in structuring this thinking. Too often there is the impulse to jump to tools and methods first – *we'll do a survey*, or *we'll do interviews*. Your learning questions should clarify what you already know and don't know, help prioritize what you need to better understand, and dictate the most effective methods to use. How you prioritize what learning questions to answer should also reflect your values. Consider your values in deciding who to engage, how they will be engaged, and who will be making decisions about what to measure. Make this explicit to all those who are engaged in the learning partnership.

The tensions described with regard to obligations and accountabilities affect measurement as well. Many donors will require logic models. These models will have you detail the pathway of change for the work they are funding, and require indicators of the change you are seeking (what success looks like), and indicators of incremental progress toward that success, often indicators that they have pre-selected and/or defined. You may also then have many logic models – one for each donor or project – rather than a broader, mission- or program-focused theory of change.

In this funder-driven dynamic, as success is the desirable result, indicators that are within one's control and measurable within the short term are prioritized regardless of meaning. Depending on the programmatic strategy and tactics employed, often these types of indicators are much more labor intensive and much less meaningful. For example, if you are engaged in advocacy for legislative change, the basic count of number of people reached is not so meaningful compared to other data, such as the relationship you hold with those people who have the power to effect legislative change: who is being reached and who is not, what are their positions and how have they changed over time if at all, and how influential are they with others. For those leading the advocacy efforts, the basic count of number of people reached will be tedious and meaningless – it will take time away from their work to respond, rather than informing their thinking about what has been effective and what to do next. Establishing conceptual clarity, supported by your own meaningful measures, may inform funder strategy and be an opportunity for negotiating accountabilities.

Be intentional, but also flexible and open to improvement and experimentation. At the start of this chapter, specific challenges were outlined that affect learning and evaluation of programming to address hate (including difficulty ascertaining results in the short-term, non-linearity of change, and dynamic vs. reactive ecosystem). If you are valuing learning as transformative, and building learning partnerships to support a learning culture, these challenges will be surmountable.

The cycle of learning should be familiar to most NGOs. It is clearly described in a number of chapters in this volume (see Lowe and Jimenez, chapter 5; Schweppe and Walters, chapter 7). The cycle reflects the regular use of existing evidence from research to inform strategy, and the subsequent and iterative systematic learning from monitoring and evaluation to manage strategy in support of improvements throughout implementation. Routine reflection on both positive and negative change (or no change at all) should be supported with analysis of context, and analysis of the ecosystem of actors and factors contributing to and influencing change, including opposing forces.

Strategy requires being intentional, but also nimble and flexible in response to contextual changes or due to emergent learning. Cultivating this ability to learn and respond can support intentional experimentation to advance change. Context is a critical element informing strategy, but it is also incredibly dynamic. Staying a path does not yield the best possible results if there have been significant learnings or changes in context. Strategy can be managed to incorporate dynamic response to the learnings and contextual change, but requires equal flexibility and nimbleness to engage in and utilize learning in a timely way.

4. Leverage and Contribute Your Learning

The more you focus on learning about what is important to advance change, the more important it is to share these learnings. As illustrated through the other chapters in this volume, research is ever evolving. Authors of nearly all the other chapters indicated limitations of evidence and a need for more real-world evaluation. Ensure your learning partners take time to document and engage in field level dialogue so that others can build upon this learning. Establish routine and inclusive dialogical space (these can range from mini internal meetings using before and after action reviews[18] to larger convenings or workshops) where learnings are presented and discussed and future actions identified, as these can instigate new ideas for experimentation, new partnerships, and other synergies that accelerate change.

Conclusion

Readers may recognize the recommendations as tautological – values will drive both why and how we evaluate and learn, and what we choose to evaluate and learn indicates and reinforces our values.

Organizations that value learning above proving success should attend to building strong learning partnerships and learning cultures, and focus on measuring what matters. Even if you are an active learning organization, explicitly reflecting on your learning values, systems, and habits can result in meaningful shifts that will improve how and what you do.

Understanding the importance of learning and evaluation, here are considerations for NGOs to take into account based on the multidisciplinary research, summarizing key points as expressed by the authors of the chapters in this volume. These considerations, shared in a checklist on the following pages, include what NGOs might do, or not do, and possible risks and consequences. These are listed by author for ease of referencing. There are similar points made by multiple authors with nuance based on their discipline. You can use the checklist to guide your discussion.

As you review and discuss these takeaways, ideally through an inclusive and participatory process – such as a meaning-making workshop – consider how these findings might inform and strengthen your work. There may be some takeaways that you are already actively addressing. With your mission and goals in mind, reflect on takeaways that resonate, surprise you, or challenge your thinking, consider additional takeaways or insights from the reading, and explore how you might experiment or what you could do differently in the future. Identify those findings that you can act on, and prioritize whether they are short-, medium-, or long-term actions. Document your decisions and assign who would be responsible for these actions, with the expectation that there will be discussions about progress both as appropriate during the year and at the next annual "checklist check in."[19]

Checklist for Organizations Working against Hate, and Their Supporters

☐ Think about what you mean by "hate." Define how you are conceptualizing hate, including what it is and what it is not, and reflect on how you use the term. (Brudholm & Johansen)

☐ Think about what you choose to do, or not do, and be able to articulate why you believe an action, or inaction, will not make things worse. (Brudholm & Johansen)

☐ Engage in and nurture open and intentional deliberation about the moral and ethical implications of what you choose to do, or not do, and how those choices will affect how successful you may be in the short term and long term (e.g., maintaining credibility, accurately representing attitudes or actions/events). (Brudholm & Johansen)

☐ Create space for reflection and discussion. Support an openness to questioning, corrections or alternative possibilities, and a commitment to truthfulness and trustworthiness – honesty, transparency, accountability. (Brudholm & Johansen)

☐ Reflect on how your organization is embodying or exemplifying its values in its practices. Periodically consider whether your passionate commitment against hate might be transforming into a vice of "moral obsession," and if it does, the implications thereof. (Brudholm & Johansen)

☐ Support staff to prevent and mitigate harm: working against hate can be taxing, all consuming, and pose risk. Engage in open and intentional conversation on implications and limits for engaging in this work (which is not finite and will always be required) and how to manage emotions, avert burnout, and attend to safety, security, and well-being. (Brudholm & Johansen)

☐ Understand (and leverage) that "us" vs. "them" is deeply hard wired in our brains: While there is "a basic human aversion to physically harming others," hatred can be a shared and unifying experience. The need to belong is a fundamental human motivation, as is the need to contribute. (Galván)

☐ Remember that hateful behavior can be experienced as rewarding and may help build a sense of community, that people are contributing to, or defending, their own group – and this is also true for those who hate the hate they are opposing. (Galván)

☐ Provide opportunities for greater exposure and meaningful interaction with members of outgroups and facilitate rehumanization. (Galván)

☐ Think about the differences between anger and hate – anger can potentially motivate constructive intergroup behavior, whereas hate almost always leads to destructive behavior. (Li)

☐ Address (or at least take into account) the unique characteristics and multi-layered antecedents of hate in devising approaches to combat hate: hate-motivated actions are informed by a range of factors including intergroup context, history, narrative, norms, and so on. (Li)

☐ Recall that hate, in moral and cognitive terms, means that the target is incapable of change, and thus the motivation of hate is not merely to harm the outgroup, but to remove the outgroup's members from the ingroup's social and physical environment. (Li)

☐ Think about other negative intergroup emotions and sentiments. Consider limitations and therefore risks of traditional psychological interventions (e.g., prejudice-reduction interventions). (Li)

☐ Consider structural factors such as systemic injustices, oppression, and victimization when addressing group-based hate. While there is some evidence that promoting a common ingroup identity, facilitating positive intergroup contact, and fostering perspective-taking with an outgroup MAY reduce prejudice and negative intergroup emotions, it is ambiguous how effective these interventions are in mitigating hate. The interventions may be ineffective for a number of reasons, including the lack of consideration for structural factors. (Li)

☐ Recall that high levels of identification with an ingroup (including the NGO's ingroup) can lower the threshold for perceiving collective threats, and that identifying with your ingroup in a glorifying and exclusionary manner can have destructive consequences. (Li)

☐ Partner with researchers to test real-world effectiveness of psychological interventions: this empirical research on hate is lacking. Research should consider both macro- and micro-level processes in tandem. (Li)

☐ Prioritize targeting social norms, as this can be more effective than targeting individual beliefs: Understand that social norms and conflict narratives (e.g., shifting a narrative about an "outgroup") can directly influence behavior, independent of personal beliefs and attitudes.

Promoting inclusive identities can challenge the rigid categorization of groups as good versus bad or us versus them, resulting in important attitudinal changes necessary for reducing hate. (Li)

☐ Use multidirectional memory framework to support communities affected by hate to seek out points of connection with others, while simultaneously acknowledging differences. (Levin)

☐ Recall that hate is frequently associated with how a group's memory of the past functions; memory isn't static and is more a reflection of current communal and political needs. It also intersects with and is informed by other groups' memories. New events can change how those memories work. However, when groups can find a way to see a parallel between their memories, while recognizing that not all forms of hate are the same and cannot be compared or "competed," new possibilities open for solidarity and can lead to joint action against hate. (Levin)

☐ Where possible collaborate with the media industry to leverage parasocial interaction – one-way mediated relationships fostering connections akin to friendship – for behavior change, modeling healthy conflict, and offering a variety of alternative points of view: Cast a lead spokesperson/actor that creates a sense of commonality with the audience (think mothers, sports fans, foodies). Telling a good human-centered story that audiences will lean into and listen to can impart lessons without a clearly stated "call-to-action." (Lowe & Jimenez)

☐ It is important to inform any media through use of research of audiences' perspectives and ongoing evaluation of audience response with an activated feed-back loop, as it is more difficult than ever to understand different points of view and easy to make false assumptions. (Lowe & Jimenez)

☐ Establish trusting relationships with stakeholders and influencers within media industry through the common ground of storytelling rather than advocacy: Engage individuals from impacted communities who identify as and opt in as storytellers. Create spaces that foster open dialogue. (Lowe & Jimenez)

☐ Consider how parasocial interaction can be implemented to strengthen other NGO narrative interventions across media (e.g., social media, TV, radio/podcasting, etc.). (Lowe & Jimenez)

☐ Build a culture of continuous evaluation, and make that a task for the whole agency as a collective responsibility. (Lowe & Jimenez)

☐ Acknowledge and share information about mistakes and failures in order to move the field forward. (Lowe & Jimenez)

☐ Complement the moral case against hate with analysis of the cost of hate and discrimination for individuals and economies. While economic arguments cannot replace the moral case against hate, framing inclusion as profitable and exclusion or hatred as costly leverages financial motivations and can lead to change in attitudes, unanticipated allyship, and inform and support policy and legislative advocacy (pivoting from us-them to win-win). (Badgett)

☐ Work with economic research and economists to fully understand technical details of economic arguments and/or expand issues related to hate that have an economic angle. Consider new ways to quantify the effects of hatred. (Badgett)

☐ Help educate the public on definitions of hate, hate crime laws, and hate crime reporting: Effectiveness of hate crime laws hinges on public awareness and understanding of what hate crime is, the existence of laws, and the importance of reporting. (Schweppe & Walters)

☐ Ensure victims of hate have accessible and reliable means to report incidents to the police, and ensure criminal justice agencies are ready and receptive: Reporting can include anonymous online reporting and third-party reporting processes, typically run by expert CSOs/NGOs that monitor cases, support victims, and also support training of criminal justice agencies on the impacts of hate crime and identifying evidence to prove hate motivation. (Schweppe & Walters)

☐ Recognize and address prejudice within institutions, particularly criminal justice institutions, as a means of promoting access to justice for victims of hate. (Schweppe & Walters)

☐ Help establish multiagency partnerships and advisory groups that engage CSOs/NGOs with policy makers and legislators in the development (and continued reform) of national/state strategies, holistic and resourced action plans, justice interventions, and education campaigns. Multiagency advisory groups require mechanisms to hold policy makers to account for implementing agreed targets, approaches, and measures. States/locales will also require the necessary logistics or resourcing to facilitate multiagency partnerships. Recognize that there cannot be an overreliance on CSO partners to deliver services (e.g., monitoring cases and supporting victims) without adequate funding/resourcing. (Schweppe & Walters)

☐ Consider exploring the potential opportunity for alternative justice mechanisms in supporting needs of victims and reducing recidivism, although be aware of the possible difficulties. (Schweppe & Walters)

☐ Consider how conspiracy theories may contribute to hate and fuel an "us" vs. "them" narrative. Conspiracy theories are proposed explanations of events and circumstances that place blame on the secretive actions of a supposedly powerful and evil outgroup. The outgroup can take the form of government institutions, political parties, ideological factions, or racial, religious, and ethnic groups. (Uscinski)

☐ NGOs should focus on the conspiracy theories most likely to be intertwined with, and express, hatred of outgroups most vulnerable to harassment or violence. (Uscinski)

☐ Note that most conspiracy theories, as well as the beliefs in them, appear to be relatively harmless. However, when conspiracy theories scapegoat groups like racial, religious, and ethnic minorities, those conspiracy theories can form a perfect storm, combining (1) accusations that serve as a call to action, (2) potential believers prone to antisocial thought patterns and behaviors, and (3) marginalized and vulnerable targets. (Uscinski)

☐ Warn those who may be exposed to conspiracy theories that they will be exposed: Advance warning – which also informs the general public and is called "prebunking" – can lead people to resist persuasive influence upon exposure. (Uscinski)

☐ "Truth" of an idea and evidence are not determinative of beliefs. Using evidence or argument to change someone's mind about a conspiracy theory has had mixed results and can backfire: evidence and argument *from trusted sources* is more important. Ridicule to combat conspiratorial belief has not been tested widely and can also result in significant negative consequences. Cult deprogramming techniques are likely not cost effective and may be unethical, and there is no clear evidence that such strategies work. (Uscinski)

☐ People require more evidence to believe that their ingroup has conspired against others than they do to believe that an outgroup has conspired against others. High profile elites can make a conspiracy theory salient enough to motivate behaviors and these voices are difficult to compete with. (Uscinski)

☐ Focus on the use of "counterspeech" to influence audiences holding relatively moderate views and/or support those targeted by hateful speech with services, accurate messages, and solidarity; counterspeech can be used as both a reply to an instance of hateful speech and also as a way to create an overall less hateful cultural norm. (Buerger)

☐ Counterspeech avoids the temptation toward calls for censorship and the attendant problems of sacrificing free speech principles. (Buerger)

☐ Consider "Project Lemonade" approaches that turn the hater's agenda on its head. This is done by piggybacking on the hater's activities to rally opposition toward an alternate goal – creating visibility of the hate and having the hater in effect raise funds to support an initiative fighting hate. (Buerger)

☐ Humor can be an effective ingredient of counterspeech. (Buerger)

☐ Use counterspeech carefully: Use your organizational platform to amplify voices of experts and counterspeakers. Understand and prepare for the potential for backlash. Seek new models for evaluating the impact of these efforts. (Buerger)

☐ Consider the implications of how the philanthropic structure implicates how your group functions. (Berman)

☐ Support transparency of philanthropy, as lack of transparency allows funding of hate (although be aware of the dangers to rights of association and problems such as doxing). (Berman)

☐ Explore how policy reform, for example requiring DAF spendouts or placing stricter regulations on companies that hold charitable funds, could limit the possibilities for philanthropic dollars to flow toward organizations/agendas associated with hate groups. (Berman)

☐ Consider unintended consequences and limitations of any regulation, as regulation may be wielded as a weapon as much as a safeguard for public good. (Berman)

☐ Attend to organizational values, culture, and practices to support learning, including evaluation. (Houvras)

☐ Recognize that addressing hate is not linear and requires ongoing and iterative reflection, learning, and evaluation. Reflect on organizational values and reprioritize multiple evaluation-related obligations and accountabilities, centering those who are affected by hate. Establish inclusive learning partnerships, nurture learning culture, develop conceptual clarity for your theory while maintaining flexibility to experiment and adapt strategies, and collectively identify and advance learning questions that are meaningful and actionable. (Houvras)

☐ Challenge assumptions or biases by facilitating dialogues where some staff are intentionally requested to engage as the "devil's advocate," and/or bring in substantive experts who hold lived experience and/or understanding of relevant research. (Houvras)

☐ Document and contribute your learning externally on what has worked, what hasn't, and where risks lie: Nearly all of the chapters in this volume indicate limitations on evidence and a need for more real-world evaluation. While context and culture must inform design of strategy and use of any tactic, recognizing effects in other contexts may serve to inform and avoid unintended consequences. (Houvras)

Acknowledgments

I would like to thank my colleagues, Rhonda Schlangen and Jim Coe, for their thoughtful review and feedback; Erin Healy for her generous support with editing this chapter; Ken Stern for his invitation and continued support throughout the editing process; and my fellow authors, including Ken Stern, for their collaboration in summarizing the key points for consideration.

NOTES

1 These definitions are based on how my colleagues and I defined these terms for an evaluation policy at American Jewish World Service.

2 For more about evaluation, see American Evaluation Association, "What Is Evaluation," accessed February 4, 2025, https://www.eval.org/Portals /0/What%20is%20evaluation%20Document.pdf.

3 See Better Evaluation at https://www.betterevaluation.org/ for a broad range of evaluation resources.

4 Consider your strategy and tactics and seek relevant and specific evaluation resources for complex and dynamic contexts. For example, there are specific resources to support evaluation of advocacy: see Jim Coe and Rhonda Schlangen, *No Royal Road: Finding and Following the Natural Pathways in Advocacy Evaluation* (Washington, DC: Center for Evaluation Innovation, 2019), https://evaluationinnovation.org/publication /no-royal-road-finding-and-following-the-natural-pathways-in -advocacy-evaluation/; for measuring narrative change, see Nikki Kalra et al., *Measuring Narrative Change: Understanding Progress and Navigating Complexity* (Seattle: ORS Impact, 2021), https://orsimpact.com /directory/Measuring-Narrative-Change.htm?categories=&keywords =&pg=1_4.

5 Expanding the Bench, "Find an Evaluator," accessed February 4, 2025, https://expandingthebench.org/ace/evaluators/.

6 Jim Coe and Rhonda Schlangen, "Pulling Up the Floorboards: Reshaping Accountability and Evaluation in an Era of Core Costs Grantmaking," 2022, https://floorboards.report/.

7 See the Equitable Evaluation Initiative, www.equitableeval.org/.

8 Donors are increasingly reflecting on their own power, increasingly supporting core support or general operating grants, discussing trust-based philanthropy models, and challenging typical evaluation "orthodoxies." For more information, see the Equitable Evaluation Initiative, www.equitableeval.org/.

9 See Hanh Cao Yu, "Transforming Foundation Learning and Evaluation into a Power Building Strategy," *Stanford Social Innovation Review*, August 21, 2023, https://ssir.org/articles/entry/transforming_foundation _learning_and_evaluation_into_a_power_building_strategy.

10 Justice Funders, *RESONANCE: A Just Transition Guide for Philanthropic Transformation*, 2nd ed., accessed February 4, 2025, https://justicefunders .org/resonance-framework/?source=post_page.

11 While the framework was developed focusing on foundations, it is relevant to NGOs, both in examining relationship to community but also as a possible input for discussion with funders.

12 Adapted from Justice Funders, *RESONANCE*, 56.

13 Julia Coffman, Jane Reisman, and Tanya Beer, "A Tool for Systems Change That Supports Learning in Foundations," Center for Evaluation Innovation, June 2022, https://evaluationinnovation.org/wp-content /uploads/2022/07/A-Tool-for-Systems-Change-that-Supports-Learning -in-Foundations.pdf.

14 Donella H. Meadows, *Thinking in Systems: A Primer* (White River Junction, VT: Chelsea Green Publishing, 2008).

15 For examples, see Coffman, Reisman, and Beer, "A Tool for Systems Change."

16 Center for Evaluation Innovation, "5-A-Day: Learning by Force of Habit," June 2018, https://evaluationinnovation.org/insight/5-a-day-learning -by-force-of-habit/.

17 Julia Coffman, "5-A-Day: Learning by Force of Habit," Medium, June 20, 2018, https://medium.com/@jcoffman/5-a-day-learning-by-force -of-habit-6c890260acbf.

18 See more on before and after action reviews as a tactic for emergent learning at the Emergent Learning Community Project, https:// emergentlearning.org/practices/.

19 The checklist is also available online at https://bcsh.bard.edu /simply-human-a-guide-to-understanding-and-combating-hate/.

Conclusion

I once wondered if hate, which is clearly so often destructive, could be cured, or at least reduced, with a drug. Of course, that would be a terrible idea, even if possible. Hate – an outgrowth of how our brains and culture and politics prime us to see who is "us" and who is "them" – is part of who we are. Without hate, we wouldn't be human. (And in fact, while hate is frequently harmful, there are times where it can be positive; hate of Nazis helped the Allies win World War II, for example.)

But that doesn't mean we can't reduce hate's negative effects. Yet doing so requires hard and smart work by all of us, but particularly by the NGOs in this field.

As I wrote in the preface, I looked for a team with vast and diverse expertise to share their insights and wisdom. What I hope that NGOs draw from this volume is not so much a simple list of things to do or not do, but a set of principles to think through and to make part of how they approach hate.

That's why, although all the chapters are important, I hope NGOs will take the bullet points from Houvras's discussion in chapter 11, print them out (here is the link to the checklist: https://bcsh.bard.edu /simply-human-a-guide-to-understanding-and-combating-hate/), and spend at least one staff meeting and one board meeting a year thinking about these principles, asking these questions, recording the answers, and reviewing them in subsequent years. I hope supporters of the NGOs, including philanthropies, will ask recipients if they have gone through such a reflective process.

When I worked at AJC, and thought about a project or program against antisemitism, I first headed to the archives. AJC was founded in 1906, and the likelihood was that someone in the decades before had considered a similar situation or idea. Reading those old documents helped me clarify what might be done when I had the responsibility for the antisemitism desk.

No one reinvents the wheel, but we don't always notice when wheels from long ago fall off. Such errors also happen around positions that NGOs advocate.

When it was clear that the United States was getting ready to invade Iraq under President George W. Bush in 2002, senior AJC staff discussed the then-potential war. I was one of two people opposed to the war (mostly because I feared that the lesson of the breakup of Yugoslavia was ignored – about how deadly ethnic hatreds might be unleashed in a political vacuum), and advocated that AJC at least not take a position. My point in raising this now is not that I was right (I've also many times been very wrong), but that the pro-war position was never thought about again. Wouldn't an intellectual autopsy have been useful? A revisiting of the communal and political pressures? A questioning of the assumption that AJC staff knew enough without bringing in the "devil's advocate" (as Lowe and Jimenez and Houvras suggest) to sharpen thinking? The unintended consequences of the Iraq war were significant (Iraq's falling apart helped strengthen Iran, to Israel's detriment I might add). Wouldn't pondering the lessons from that decision help inform future ones?

The major policy decisions shouldn't be the only ones revisited. NGOs that raise money from assertions that they are fighting hate are frequently reactive to the news, and the news cycle is much faster today than ever before. There's fear that if one doesn't put out a statement, the organization will look ineffective at best; funders will be upset with silence, and the opportunity to be quoted in the news will be missed (and if there are competitor organizations in the space, they might be quoted instead). Even before the internet and social media, a colleague in AJC's PR office had a sign that said "Better never than late." But I always thought the principles in Brudholm and Johansen's opening chapter were critically important – consider the ethics, and your credibility. You might need to say something, but is it better to be wrong (such as labeling an incident a hate crime when it might not be) than to be late? Their chapter focused on the need to be accurate as an ethical consideration, but as Berman notes in chapter 10, funding is required for NGOs to do their work, and if an NGO is silent or puts out a weak statement in the midst of a hate incident, might their funding suffer? NGOs likely believe that they are always doing good, so might they sacrifice a bit of due diligence in order to be quick, because the money they'd raise will allow them to do their work? At least NGOs should consider this trade-off.

A look back at statements made (or not made) would be useful to underscore this lesson, because there's a real possibility of making things worse.

~

While there are no simple answers to the complicated questions of hate, I hope NGOs will seek out new approaches and programs that resonate with the principles that come through in this book.

One hopeful lesson I take from the authors in this volume is the possibility of helping people see the humanness in those with whom we fundamentally disagree. It's something I've seen in other contexts too.

When I was teaching a course on antisemitism at Bard in the fall of 2016, I grounded the class in what we know about hate. I suspect most of my students were Hillary Clinton supporters, but one was particularly zealous. She skipped classes despite my insisting she couldn't afford to miss any more; she felt she needed to attend campaign events. A week after the election she took me aside and complained about some of her fellow Bard students; it distressed her to see them being unkind to the Trump-supporting women who worked in the mailroom. She understood that everyone is human, and that there's a fundamental difference between deep-seated disagreement and personal hate.

When I've spoken on campuses about the Israeli/Palestinian conflict, I've used some of the lessons that emerge from this book as well. I tell students that it's fine for them to feel passionately about this issue, but to realize that while none of them is likely to solve the conflict, they do have control over how they treat each other in their shared community. I encourage them to have the emotional empathy and intellectual curiosity to wonder why that otherwise friendly student whose views you define as wrong at best, evil at worst, thinks as they do. That when they see complicated issues as simple matters of justice, when they seek the comfort of certainty and simplicity, when they feel a heightened sense of community and reward in a binary world, alarm bells should go off. In other words, the mere exercise of being aware of why and how we – as haters but also as those who oppose hate – get into these thought patterns and emotions may make us less likely to be prisoners of the seductive power of hate.

Let me take an editor's prerogative and encourage NGOs to consider one specific pet project that is worth testing out, since in my view it resonates with the lessons of so many chapters here, and may help break down some "us" vs. "them" thinking. It's one that groups can do together, perhaps. I highlighted the idea in testimony before the US

House Homeland Security Committee in 2022 and again before the US Senate Judiciary Committee in 2024:

> There's an old study in social psychology called the Robbers Cave experiment,[1] a study that involved sending two groups of boys from very similar backgrounds to a summer camp in Oklahoma. Each group didn't know the other existed, but once each bonded separately as a unit, and then were given evidence of the other group's existence in a competitive environment, they not only had animosity toward each other, but acted on it. At the end, they, however, had to cooperate to fix the camp's drinking water supply. That superordinate goal – or perhaps the creation of a larger group identity – helped reduce the hate.

That suggestion – an additional layer of connected identity – is one I observed from colleagues during my years at AJC involved with intergroup relations. The groups that seemed to have the most staying power – say a project bringing together Blacks and Jews – were the ones that had an additional layer of identity (Black and Jewish lawyers or accountants, for example).

Years ago I was inspired by Colin Powell and others who suggested the potential societal and personal benefits of a program of national service for young people. I've long wondered, what if we had a national program that would offer to take teenagers from different backgrounds, say as they were finishing high school, and send them on a common public service mission? How about a Latinx person from Texas and a Jewish person from New York and a Black person from Los Angeles, and send them, together, to work for an organization that builds homes for Native American people in South Dakota, for example? There are lots of ways to mix and match such groups, but the idea of bringing people together from different groups that they might not have met before, have them interact with each other and form a new group identity, have them *together* help someone else, and create new and negotiated collective memories drawn from their own communal memories might, and I stress might, make them less likely to be drawn into the "us" vs. "them" thinking that threatens our democracy, and thus reduce the potential for antisemitic and other types of hate crimes. If later evaluation of such a pilot project documents a reduction of hate over time, there might be consideration for building such a national service program. It might even pay for itself, if it reduces the cost of hate.[2]

As I wrote in the preface, this was a team-created volume. When we met in June 2023 to discuss each other's drafts and outlines, none of us could have imagined the horrendous Hamas attack of gleeful murder and kidnapping on October 7, and the unrelenting Israeli response that has resulted in many tens of thousands of deaths, too many orphans to contemplate, children missing limbs, "safe spaces" being bombed, massive hunger, and other horrible consequences. This was also one of those "before and after" moments that shook the world, and it's still not clear as I write (in February 2025) how the world will resettle, and that was before adding the additional element of a new paradigm: the second Trump administration.

The content of Adam Levin's chapter 4 was affected the most by October 7. To illustrate the idea of multidirectional memory he focused, as you saw, on the story of how the Black community and Jewish community had memories that resonated with each other's and helped them build tools for fighting hate crime in South Africa. That was torn apart, especially as South Africa accused Israel of genocide, and former Black allies sided with another historical memory, the suffering of Palestinians. In some ways the lesson of this chapter was underscored by this change after Adam had written his earlier draft. Memories can change, and thus the implications of how groups – and NGOs – see each other.

I've also seen American NGOs struggling here too. As Levin noted, there's a generational divide in the Japanese-American community about whether it sees its history more aligned with Jews (who were also imprisoned, and worse, during World War II), or with the destruction of Gaza, the rubble of which may invoke memories of Hiroshima. And there's a generational divide inside the Jewish community too. While most Jews are supportive of Israel (if not its policies), many younger ones in particular are in the anti-Israel, anti-Zionist camp; many can't justify what's happening to Palestinians with what their Jewish identity tells them about how to treat the stranger, or how to repair the world.

I wrote a book in 2020 that was largely ignored at the beginning of the COVID-19 pandemic. *The Conflict over the Conflict: The Israel/Palestine Campus Debate* drew new attention after October 7, and has given me the opportunity to talk about how binary thinking ("us" vs. "them") leads so many, on campus and elsewhere, to crave simple answers and certainty, seeing all right and all wrong depending on which "side" you're on.[3]

I began that book with a story about how the Jewish community and the "peace and justice" community in Spokane, Washington, hadn't spoken to each other in years because the peace and justice group had a pro-boycott position regarding Israel, and the Jewish community called them antisemites. Yet they all realized that while they couldn't solve Israel/Palestine they had better work together because their community had organized white supremacists who were threatening everyone. And they did – using a lot of the lessons that, not surprisingly, you found in this book: thinking about ethics, costs, why they got into the "us" or "them" boxes in the first place, evaluating where the community was and how they might move forward together, recalling joint memories of why and how they had worked together against hate in the past, and other things. October 7 didn't change that understanding.

However, I've heard from some Jewish and non-Jewish human rights officials in the United States and Canada that the schism over October 7 has been harming their ability to confront hate in a troubling way: in some communities, each side of the Jewish community (mainstream groups versus groups that are non-Zionist and/or anti-Zionist) are insisting they, and not the other group, should be the ones at the communal intergroup table. I raise this issue not to suggest how to settle it, but to note the problem as an example of how the insights from this book might point to a way forward, or at least not make the problem worse. I get it that each side of this Jewish communal debate believes the other side is "un-Jewish" in a significant way, and that empowering the other side may make antisemitism (or, for mainstream groups, anti-Zionism, which is sometimes correlated with antisemitism, but is not always antisemitic) worse. But the groups should think through what are the collateral consequences. Are there ways to work together on common problems and yet disagree about Israel? What are the ethics? What are the costs, both communally and financially? If mainstream groups tell young anti-Zionist Jews that they are outside the tent, they will likely lose them when it comes to working in a Jewish space on other issues, such as feeding the hungry, opposing hate crimes, climate change, and religious freedom. The Jewish communal groups might decide that having a pro-Israel position is a requirement, rather than encouraging people to work together on other issues while disagreeing on Israel. But at least they should think through these difficult issues, and contemplate not only what they mean for the future of the Jewish community, but also how they impact our ability to fight hate.

Like Berman, I'm discussing the Jewish community, but other communities, and NGOs that work with these different constituencies, face similar challenges. Introspection, evaluation, questioning, revisiting, contemplating whether your actions unintentionally feed a binary (which, as we saw in Li, chapter 3, and Uscinski, chapter 8, can lead to violence or conspiratorial thinking, which is a mainstay of antisemitism), emphasizing costs (Badgett, chapter 6), collective memories

(Levin, chapter 4), human stories (Lowe and Jimenez, chapter 5), counterspeech (Buerger, chapter 9), and better ways to combat hate crimes (Schweppe and Walters, chapter 7) should be on the "to-do" list of every NGO.

As Galván noted in chapter 2, we are all human and have human brains, and the types of thinking that lead people to express hate also manifest in those who oppose (or even hate) hate. Being aware of how we react as humans, as well as the ethical considerations of what we choose to do, or not do, should be the cornerstone of every NGO's principles and understandings in this space.

While this is a book created by academics for NGOs and others interested in combating hate, it was never designed as something just to read and then put on a shelf. As noted above, the checklist in Houvras's closing chapter provides a strong outline of what NGOs might consider as part of their evaluation process.

The Bard Center for the Study of Hate will also help NGOs that want a facilitator or trainer for boards and staff to work through the lessons of this book in greater detail, and to tailor the training to the particular needs of any NGO helping us all manage hate better.[4]

I hope others in different academic disciplines also tackle the question the experts in this volume addressed: Knowing what you know, if you were running an NGO focused on hate, what would you do, what wouldn't you do, and why? The answers, inevitably, will help NGOs and the rest of us reject simple and comforting answers (like censorship, or vilification of people with different points of view), and focus more on the hard work we need to do together to reduce hate, guided less by gut feeling and more by theories and thought-out principles.[5]

Finally, this book was drafted in 2023 and 2024, before the re-election of Donald Trump, and the stark divisions and challenges exposed during the election cycle and its aftermath. As I write, a few weeks into the new administration, it's clear that the lessons from this book – always important – are even more worthy of consideration now.

Kenneth S. Stern
February 2025

NOTES

1 Muzafer Sherif, *Experimental Study of Positive and Negative Intergroup Attitudes between Experimentally Produced Groups: Robbers Cave Study* (Norman, OK: University of Oklahoma, 1954).

2 See "Written Testimony of Kenneth S. Stern, Director, Bard Center for the
Study of Hate, before the United States House of Representatives Homeland
Security Committee," October 3, 2022, https://bcsh.bard.edu/files/2023/01
/Written-Testimony-House-Homeland-Security-100322.pdf; and "Written
Testimony of Kenneth S. Stern, Director, Bard Center for the Study of Hate,
before the United States Senate Judiciary Committee," September 17,
2024, https://www.judiciary.senate.gov/imo/media/doc/2024-09-17_-_
testimony_-_stern.pdf.
3 You can find chapter 1, "Thinking about Thinking," with lessons from hate
studies about the conflict, available for free here: https://kennethsstern
.com/wp-content/uploads/2020/05/thinking-about-thinking.pdf.
4 Email me at kstern@bard.edu if you are interested in learning more about
this training program.
5 It was an honor to work with, and learn from, so many fine scholars as this
book came together. I thank them all, as well as the current and former
NGO officials and others who helped us think through what would be most
useful. This book would also not have been possible without the generous
support of the GS Humane Corp.

Contributors

M.V. Lee Badgett, PhD, studies the global cost of homophobia and transphobia, economic empowerment of LGBTQI+ people, and LGBTQI+ economic inequality. She's the chief economist and co-founder of Koppa: The LGBTI+ Economic Power Lab. She is also Professor Emeritx of Economics and former director of the School of Public Policy at the University of Massachusetts Amherst. Her latest book is *The Economic Case for LGBT Equality: Why Fair and Equal Treatment Benefits Us All* (Beacon Press, 2020).

Lila Corwin Berman is the Paul & Sylvia Steinberg Professor of American Jewish History at New York University, where she directs the Goldstein-Goren Center for American Jewish History. Her most recent book, *The American Jewish Philanthropic Complex: The History of a Multibillion-Dollar Institution* (Princeton University Press, 2020), was awarded the 2021 Ellis W. Hawley Prize from the Organization of American Historians. In addition to her scholarly articles, Berman has also written guest columns for the *Washington Post*, the *Chronicle of Higher Education*, and the *Chronicle of Philanthropy*.

Thomas Brudholm holds a PhD in Philosophy and is Associate Professor at the Department for Cross-Cultural and Regional Studies at the University of Copenhagen. He is specialized in the ethics of responses to wrongdoing and has written on both resentment, forgiveness, and hatred. His research on hate is internationally recognized and appears in several volumes on the topic, including *Perspectives on Hate* (American Psychological Association, 2020), *The Globalization of Hate* (Oxford University Press, 2016), and *The Routledge Handbook on Dehumanization* (Routledge, 2021). With Birgitte S. Johansen, he co-edited *Hate, Politics, Law: Critical Perspectives on Combatting Hate* (Oxford University Press, 2018).

Dr. Cathy Buerger is the Director of Research at the Dangerous Speech Project where her work is dedicated to understanding and mitigating harmful speech and its role in inciting violence. Buerger's work focuses oh how communities mobilize to resist political violence, with a particular interest in understanding the impact of counterspeech in online settings. She is a Research Affiliate of the University of Connecticut's Economic and Social Rights Research Group and Managing Editor of the *Journal of Human Rights*. She holds a PhD in Anthropology from the University of Connecticut.

Dr. Adriana Galván is a Professor of Psychology and the Dean of Undergraduate Education at the University of California, Los Angeles, and is committed to improving the scientific understanding of the period of adolescence. She is also the Co-Executive Director of the UCLA Center for the Developing Adolescent.

Irit Houvras is an innovator in strategic learning for global social movements and human rights work. She is dedicated to advancing social justice. With expertise in qualitative and participatory methodologies, facilitation, research and evaluation, she has worked internationally at community, national, and multi-country levels. For nearly a decade, she led strategic learning, evaluation, and strategy development for the American Jewish World Service, a human rights social movement funder. Prior to joining AJWS, she worked in global health for over fifteen years.

Charlene Joy Jimenez is an award-winning cultural and narrative strategist working at the intersection of entertainment and social impact. For the past fifteen years, she has led creative projects and communications at innovative companies like Define American, Lionsgate, and Legendary's Nerdist.com and has been a speaker at SXSW, The Television Academy, and the ATX Television Festival. Currently, she is the Director of Strategic Partnerships at Cinereach, a board member of The Impact Guild, as well as an advisory council member of FilAm Arts and the Yes, And … Laughter Lab. A proud first-generation child of immigrants, Charlene is passionate about using the power of pop culture to foster social good.

Birgitte Schepelern Johansen holds a PhD in Sociology of Religion and is Associate Professor at the Department for Cross-Cultural and Regional Studies at the University of Copenhagen. Her work has focused on the societal consequences of and political responses to hate and hate crime, and has been published in journals like *Frontiers*,

International Journal of Politics, Culture, and Society, and *Journal of European Ethnology*. Johansen has also co-edited *Hate, Politics, Law* (Oxford University Press, 2018) with Thomas Brudholm.

Adam Levin is a postdoctoral research fellow in the Department of English at the University of the Witwatersrand in Johannesburg, South Africa. His research focuses on how the field of memory studies can be utilized in community engagement and education. His work has appeared in journal publications such as *Holocaust Studies: A Journal of Culture and History* and *Literature, Critique, and Empire Today*, and he is the co-editor of *Poetry Non-Scenes: New Performance Poems beyond the Struggle* (uHlanga Press, 2024). He currently serves on the executive board of the International Network of Genocide Scholars (INoGS).

Joseph J. Levin Jr. is Co-Founder and Emeritus Board Member of the Southern Poverty Law Center in Montgomery, Alabama. He has successfully argued cases involving sex and race discrimination before the US Supreme Court, testified before the US House of Representatives and Senate on various constitutional issues, and served as the director of the Justice Department transition for the Carter administration. Following the transition, he was appointed Chief Counsel of the National Highway Traffic Administration.

Dr. Mengyao Li is a Lecturer in the School of Psychology at Queen's University Belfast. Prior to joining QUB, she was a Senior Research Fellow at the Max Planck Institute for Research on Collective Goods and obtained her PhD from the Peace and Violence Program at the University of Massachusetts Amherst. Her research lies at the intersection of social, political, and peace psychology. It broadly addresses the psychological processes of intergroup conflicts and their resolution, national and ethnic identity, transitional justice, as well as resistance and social change.

Sarah E. Lowe is the Director of Narrative Research + Evaluation at Define American and holds a PhD in Community Health with over twenty-five years of experience in narrative strategy. Her work examines systems of oppression, even within social good constructs, and advocates for Radical Healing as a force for lasting change. Sarah spent the first ten years of her career in corporate storytelling for Disney, The Discovery Channel, PBS, and other networks. In the past fifteen plus years, she has focused on advocacy that heals storytellers and moves lay audiences to action, primarily around immigrant communities. Sarah is a former undocumented immigrant, wife of an immigrant, and mother to two plucky bicultural kids. She believes that stories are both science and magic, uniting people in powerful and transformative ways.

Jennifer Schweppe holds a PhD from Trinity College Dublin and is a Professor of Law at the University of Limerick. She is co-director of the European Centre for the Study of Hate at that institution and her research explores the relationship between minority communities and criminal justice institutions, particularly through the lens of hate crime and access to justice. She is co-editor of two major collections with Oxford University Press (with M. Walters) and Palgrave (with A. Haynes and S. Taylor), and she is Co-Principal Investigator on the ground-breaking cross-border all-Ireland Public Understandings of Hate Crime project. She was appointed as an independent expert to the Council of Europe Committee of Experts on Hate Crime and tasked with drafting the comprehensive recommendation on combating hate crime, which was adopted by the Council in 2024.

Kenneth S. Stern is the Director of the Bard Center for the Study of Hate. An attorney and award-winning author, he has argued before the United States Supreme Court, testified before both the United States House of Representatives and the United States Senate, was an invited presenter at the White House Conference on Hate Crimes, and served as a member of the US Delegation to the Stockholm Forum on Combating Intolerance. His most recent book is *The Conflict over the Conflict: The Israel/Palestine Campus Debate* (University of Toronto Press, 2020).

Joseph Uscinski is Professor of Political Science at the University of Miami, Coral Gables, Florida. Professor Uscinski studies and teaches about conspiracy theories and the people that believe them. His research has appeared in numerous academic journals and in several books, including *American Conspiracy Theories* (Oxford University Press, 2014) and *Conspiracy Theories: A Primer* (Rowman & Littlefield, 2023).

Mark Walters is a Professor of Criminal Law and Criminology at the University of Sussex (UK). He has published widely on criminal law theory in relation to hate crime, the use of alternative justice mechanisms, and the impacts of targeted victimization. His books include *Hate Crime and Restorative Justice: Exploring Causes, Repairing Harms* (Oxford University Press, 2014), *The Globalisation of Hate: Internationalising Hate Crime?* (co-edited with J. Schweppe; Oxford University Press, 2016), and most recently, *Criminalising Hate: Law as Social Justice Liberalism* (Palgrave, 2022). Walters was also the draftsperson of the new PENAL CODE (AMENDMENT) BILL, 2024 (Seychelles), which introduces the first hate crime offenses in Seychelles.

Acknowledgments

Although I've written books and contributed to anthologies, this is my first experience as an editor. I can't thank the contributors enough. It was a pleasure to work with scholars I've admired for years, and also to meet others, to co-create this book. You all made the process easy and the final result outstanding. Thank you!

This book could not have been written without the generous support of GS Humane Corp. Thank you for believing in this project, your willingness to reimagine it during the pandemic, and your patience.

Thanks to the wonderful team at the University of Toronto Press. Natalie Fingerhut saw value in this idea and supported it from the beginning. Janice Evans and freelance editor Beth McAuley improved it with their careful editing skills. This is my second book with them, and I hope it isn't my last. Thanks also to Lucille Miranda, Aditi Parikh, and everyone else at the Press for their work getting this book out into the world.

Finally, to my family. My wife, Margie Slome, is always my first and most important (and most honest) reader. And she puts up with the mess writing sometimes creates. Our children, Daniel and Emily, are thoughtful adults and critical thinkers, and their ideas and support mean the world to me too.

Index